1.
2.
3.

1. *dream it*
2. *hold it*
3. *go for it*

PETZL

www.petzl.com

David Atchison-Jones
Editor & Photographer

TRADE DISTRIBUTION
visit
www.jingowobbly.com
for our list of EUROPEAN &
WORLD distribution agents

AVIGNON SOLEIL
Jingo Wobbly – Topo Guides
First Published in April 2006
By Jingo Wobbly Euro Guides
(An imprint of Vision PC).
Holmwood House, 52 Roxborough Park,
Harrow-on-the-Hill, London. HA1 3AY, Great Britain

Copyright © David Atchison-Jones
Graphics by Botticelli
Image Scanning – Classic, London & The Grain Store
Printing – Fratelli Spada SPA, Roma.

A CIP catalogue record is available from the British Library

ISBN-10   1-873665 61-X   ISBN-13   978-1-873665 61-9

AVIGNON SOLEIL

 JINGO WOBBLY CLIMBING BOOKS – LONDON

I would like to dedicate this book to the Wizzard - Malc, for introducing me to Buis-les-Baronnies all those years ago.

I would like to thank all the climbers that I have climbed with during the very many climbing trips to this area over the past 15 years. Writing a book and collecting information over such a long time has been a superb way to enjoy the entire area, both in climbing and cycling. A large thank you to the areas people, towns, campsites, cafés etc. that have welcomed climbers for years, and have made it a long time favourite for many UK climbers. A big thankyou for all the climbers who have equipped routes, so that other climbers can easily enjoy themselves. A big thanks too

for previous topo artists, in providing inspiration; and enabling the route names to be known and passed from one generation to another.

I have to especially thank Jim Bacon for some fantastic help in climbing relentless routes to be checked, plus all the other climbers who have helped out in climbing routes and giving accurate feedback. Thanks to Carrie for her wonderful support, and looking after the team - by serving cranking hard gin and tonics, and showing us how to crank on crimps. A cheers to brothers Glennie for enjoying many of the slightly difficult routes in such fine photo style. A big thanks to Virginie Percival for translating the intros into French, and Christian Groh for the German Intro.

Quick view chart - 7
Introduction (F) - 8
Introduction (GB) - 12
Introduction (D) - 16
Travel info - 20

Crillon-le-Brave

Avignon

Today, no wind &			Mistral &		Walk	Climb style	Routes in this book (Total routes)	Enough for a short day visit											
HOT	Warm	Cool	HOT	Cool				1-3	4	5	6a	6b	6c	7a	7b	7c	8a	8b	8c
yes	ok	no	ok	no	X	747	Aiguillette Lagarde-Turc	25 - (88)		★	★	★	★	☆	★	★			
am	yes	ok	ok	no	12	Zzz	Archéo	25 - (25)		★	★	★	☆	★					
no	yes	ok	yes	no	4		Baume Rousse	87 - (87)	☆	★	★	★	★	☆	★	☆	★	★	
no	yes	yes	ok	yes	3		Cascade	0 - (39)	☆	★		★	☆	★	☆	★	☆	★	
no	ok	yes	yes	no	4	Fun	Cascade-en-haut	8 - (8)				☆	★	★	★				
no	ok	yes	ok	ok	12		Centre - St. Léger	43 - (43)			☆	★	☆	★	☆	★	★	☆	
yes	ok	no	yes	no	17		Clapis Face nord	0 - (12)							★	★			
no	ok	ok	ok	no	12		Clapis Face sud	143 - (204)	☆	★	★	★	★	☆	★	☆	★		
no	ok	yes	no	yes	10	Pump	Colombier	19 - (19)	☆							★	☆		
pm	ok	ok	yes	ok	15	747	Combe Obscure	64 - (65)		★	☆	★	★	★	☆				
am	ok	ok	yes	ok	2	Pump	Corneirette	67 - (67)				☆	★	☆	★	★			
no	yes	yes	yes	ok	3	Fun	Couloir de la Glisse	9 - (12)		★	★	★	☆						
pm	ok	no	ok	ok	10		Envol	6 - (6)				★		★	★	★	☆		
no	ok	yes	ok	ok	10	Pump	Face Sud - St. Léger	77 - (77)			☆	★	☆	★	★	★	☆		
no	ok	yes	yes	yes	14	Fun	Gigondas face sud	0 - (29)	☆	★	★	★							
yes	ok	no	no	no	13		Gigondas Pousterle	0 - (61)		★	★	☆	★	★					
no	yes	ok	ok	ok	25	Pump	Gorges Quest - St.L.	57 - (57)		★	☆	★	★	☆	★	☆			
yes	ok	no	no	no	19	A	Grand Montmirail	0 - (12)	☆	★		★		★					
no	ok	yes	yes	yes	2	Fun	Grand Travers	42 - (43)	☆	★	★	★							
no	yes	ok	ok	no	15		Grande Muraille	0 - (26)			★	★	★	☆	★				
ok	yes	no	no	no	7	Zzz	Le Belvédère	0 - (30)			☆	★	★	☆	★				
no	yes	yes	yes	ok	1	Fun	Les Bourdons	20 - (30)	☆	★	★	☆							
yes	yes	no	ok	no	14		Les Florets	0 - (14)	★	★	★	☆							
no	ok	yes	ok	yes	1	Fun Bloc	Les Traverses	1 - (1)	★	★	★	★							
pm	yes	no	ok	no	1		Lou Passo	58 - (58)	★	★	★	★	★	★	☆	★	☆		
ok	ok	no	no	no	8	Zzz	Malaval	0 - (25)		★									
yes	yes	ok	ok	no	6		Mania - St. Léger	10 - (10)							★	☆	★		
pm	yes	no	yes	no	18		Mévouillon-Est	24 - (24)	☆	★	★	★	★	☆					
yes	yes	no	ok	no	22		Mévouillon-Ouest	12 - (12)			☆	★	☆	★	☆	★			
am	yes	no	ok	no	5		Mieyes-Bodon	8 - (8)				★	☆	★	☆				
-	-	-	-	-	?	Zzz	Pelleret	0 - (10)			☆	★	☆	★	☆				
no	ok	no	no	no	1	△	Plaisians	0 - (15)	☆	★	★	★	★	☆	★				
no	ok	yes	ok	yes	3	Sloper	Quinsan	63 - (63)			☆	★	☆	★					
yes	ok	ok	yes	ok	7	Pump	Rive Gauche - St.L.	39 - (39)			☆	★		★	☆	★	☆		
am	yes	ok	ok	no	2-18		Rocher Aiguier	44 - (47)		☆	★	★	☆	★	☆	★	☆		
yes	ok	no	yes	no	4		Rocher Blanchard	8 - (8)				★	☆	★					
no	yes	yes	yes	yes	5	Fun	Rocher Brunots	28 - (28)	★	★	★	★	☆	★	☆				
no	yes	yes	yes	yes	8	Pump	Rocher du Cayron	0 - (27)			☆	★	★	★					
yes	yes	ok	yes	ok	10	Pump	Rocher du Groseau	65 - (65)	★	★	★	☆	★	☆	★	☆	★		
am	yes	ok	yes	no	1	Fun	Rocher du Portail St-Jean	14 - (14)	☆	★	★	★			☆	★			
-	-	-	-	-	1	⊘	Ecole-Montbrun	0 - (6)											
am	yes	yes	yes	ok	18		Rocher Quebec	19 - (30)	☆	★	☆								
no	yes	yes	yes	no	5	CRIMP	Saint Christophe	13 - (58)	☆	★				☆	★	☆	★	☆	
no	yes	yes	yes	no	11		Saint Julien	40 - (240)			★	★	★	☆	★				
no	yes	yes	yes	yes	4		Saint Pierre	71 - (71)			★	★	★	☆	★	☆	★	☆	★	★
yes	ok	yes	yes	no	6	Zzz	Trois Rivières	112 - (112)	★	★	★	★	☆	★	☆	★	☆		
no	yes	yes	yes	ok	3	Fun	Tyrolienne	27 - (27)		★	★	★	☆						
am	yes	ok	yes	no	4	Bloc	Ubrieux	93 - (106)	★	★	★	★	☆	★	★				
no	yes	yes	yes	ok	?	Fun	Vague d'Étrave	0 - (10)		★	★	★	☆						
no!	no!	no!	no!	no!	1	△	Vaulongue	0 - (14)				☆	★	☆	★				
no	ok	yes	yes	yes	1	Pump	Venasque	106 - (106)		★	★	★	☆	★	☆	★	★	☆	★
no	yes	yes	ok	ok	8	Zzz	Vic	26 - (26)	★	★	★	★	☆	★	☆	★	☆		

Lorsque vous créez un guide d'escalade, deux choix s'offrent à vous: soit vous écrivez un guide très simple avec une information de base destinée tout particulièrement aux grimpeurs locaux qui connaissent parfaitement les falaises, ou bien vous faites un guide avec une information très detaillée, des photos couleur et des renseignements touristiques destinés aux grimpeurs qui ne connaissent pas la région. Nous avons suivi cette dernière approche avec ce livre qui sera particulièrement utile à tous ceux qui grimpent en cotation moyenne. Si vous êtes du style à consulter une carte du sud de la France et décidez d'aller dans cette région en vacance pour profiter du soleil, de l'escalade, des sports de plein air, de la nourriture, du bon vin, alors continuez à lire cette introduction ou mieux encore achetez le guide immédiatement (s'il vous plait).

La zone que nous avons choisi autour du Mont Ventoux est grande et de toute beauté avec 52 falaises situées dans des lieux très calmes vous permettant de passer des vacances dans une magnifique région de France. Il y a de nombreux campings, des gites et même des hôtels avec piscine. Les vignes de Châteauneuf-du-Pape, ainsi que de nombreuses autres que je recommande dans ce livre, sont divines. L'atout majeur de cette zone d'escalade est avant tout son ensoleillement, d'où notre titre – Avignon Soleil. Le soleil vous permet de grimper 365 jours de l'année si vous choissisez votre falaise judicieusement. En juillet les températures peuvent atteindre 34°, il est donc impératif de se lever de bonheur et de grimper à l'ombre. Cela vous permet de vous baigner en piscine l'après-midi et de dîner en soirée sur les terraces des restaurants bien sympathiques. L'hiver vous pouvez skier sur les pentes nord du Mont Ventoux ou grimper sur les falaises exposées sud des Dentelles de Montmirail. Si vous planifiez votre séjour judicieusement et intelligemment le soleil sera toujours votre allié. Du fait de ce très fort ensoleillement, il est nécessaire d'avoir un bon aperçu des 52 falaises afin d'organiser au mieux ses vacances. Ce livre a été conçu pour vous permettre d'une part d'étudier chacune des 320 pages en détail, d'autre part de consulter les 200 photos couleur chez vous tranquillement et enfin de vous aider à organiser votre visite. Avec cette information, vous pourrez planifier votre séjour par avance puisque vous serez où trouver les voies correspondant le mieux à votre niveau, et apprendrez à respecter et à profiter pleinement de la zone d'escalade que vous visiterez. Consultez notre section voyage et tourisme page 20 pour gérer au mieux votre visite.

Paysage et Climat

Le sud de la France est separé d'est en ouest par le Rhône qui coule jusqu'à Marseille. A environ 50km du nord d'Avignon, la rivière s'elargie sur une grande zone inondable. La chaleur de la Méditerranée aspire l'air frais des Alpes vers la vallée du Rhône créant le fameux mistral. C'est un vent étonnamment froid qui peut souffler à 60-80km/heure, parfois pour une seule journée mais le plus souvent pendant 10 jours ou plus. C'est un vent dévastateur qui peut vous rendre fou, mais en été il fait chuter la température d'un 30 degrés accablant à un merveilleux 22-23 degrés au soleil. Cela donne des conditions parfaites pour grimper - les meilleures que j'ai experimenté. Ainsi, comme avec le soleil, le vent peut être utilisé à votre avantage. La région est dominée par le Mont Ventoux (1909m). Ce n'est pas une montagne pour les grimpeurs mais pour les cyclistes à qui elle offre un veritable challenge. Sa présence est mystérieuse car il domine la région par sa taille. Son sommet est souvent dans les nuages alors qu'en revanche le soleil brille partout ailleurs. Il reçoit les premières et les dernières neiges et semblent vous prévenir de l'arrivée du mauvais temps. Vous pouvez en effet observer les nuages qui s'accumulent sur la montagne pour vous indiquer l'arrivée de la pluie, en particulier si vous essayez de grimper une dernière voie le dernier jour de vos vacances. La région autour de Carpentras est une grande plaine à seulement 100m d'altitude offrant un excellent climat en hiver. Les villes de Malaucène (300m) et Buis-les-Baronnies (384m) restent fraîches et peuvent meme être froides au printemps et à l'automne lorsque les conditions d'escalade sont parfaites. Il y a également des régions plus montagneuses, Sault (700m) et Mévouillon (900m) par exemple sont des zones isolées qui sont très agréables à visiter durant les grandes chaleurs d'été. En général le temps est plus ensoleillé et plus sec le plus près vous êtes d'Avignon. Par contre lorsqu'il pleut, il peut tomber plusieurs millimètres en quelques heures et c'est la raison pour laquelle nous vous conseillons de bien choisir votre camping! Heureusement cela n'arrive environ que 2 fois par mois et pendant 1 jour et demi seulement. Mais il faut noter qu'il y a souvent des averses localisées. Nous vous conseillons donc de suivre votre instinct et de vérifier la direction du vent afin de savoir quelle zone restera sèche le plus longtemps. Lors de la préparation de ce guide par exemple, il plu une journée entière à Saint Léger mais de l'autre côté du site à environ 1km le temps resta sec jusqu'en soirée. Il est préférable de choisir la falaise qui restera sèche le plus longtemps plutôt que la falaise avec le plus grand dévers car lorsqu'il se met a pleuvoir même les falaises les plus abruptes deviennent très humides.

Falaises et Escalade

Les 200 photos de ce guide, décrivent mieux que des mots la diversité et la solidité de la roche prédominante – le calcaire. Il y a huit falaises dont géologiquement la roche est calcaire mais qui peut faire penser à du grès. Il vous faudra une bonne technique sur les aplats, peu d'humidité et de basses températures pour avoir les meilleurs résultats sur ces falaises. Il y a une grande diversité, depuis d'horribles dévers de 15 mètres jusqu'à des voies classiques de 90 mètres avec 3 longueures. Il est toujours possible de trouver des falaises à l'ombre ou au soleil selon votre préférence, et il est rare qu'il vous faille marcher plus de 10 minutes pour arriver aux voies. Comme toujours avec le calcaire il y a des rochers branlants. Certaines falaises ont des voies equipées sur des rochers très suspects et nous avons essayé de les indiquer du mieux possible sur les cartes. Sur des voies de plusieurs longueurs où les cordes trainent sur les saillies, il y a une forte chance que de petites pierres tombent – il est donc recommandé de porter un casque. Attention également s'il y a des grimpeurs au-dessus de vous, le port d'un casque sera peu utile si un gros rocher chute. La majorité des falaises ont des broche qui sont collés avec de la résine et qui paraissent d'excellente qualité. Cependant j'ai également vu des broche scellée placés dans des rochers creux, ou avec un mauvais angle de positionnement, ou sur des rochers fissurés et branlants et ou en cas de chute vous risquez de vous faire très mal! Ce n'est certainement pas une salle d'escalade et il est donc nécessaire que vous choisissiez vos voies en considérant la manière dont elles ont été équipées par rapport à votre niveau d'escalade. Parmi les voies les plus faciles certaines ont été équipées par des personnes à l'aise dans le 7, alors si vous grimpez seulement en cotation 5, nous vous conseillons de choisir vos voies très judicieusement. Une corde de 70m et 12 dégaines sont parfaits pour ceux qui voyagent par avion et dont le nombre de bagages est limité. Personnellement je préfère avoir 2 cordes, une de 50m (10.2) pour les voies courtes mais abruptes et

de haut niveau, et une plus légère de 80m (9.1) pour les voies de plusieurs longueures (et une descente en rappel de 40m). Etudiez les voies que vous souhaitez faire et choisissez la meilleure longueure de corde pour votre visite, cependant rappelez-vous que la majorité des meilleures voies font entre 33 et 40m. Nous avons essayé de donner les longueures exactes de chaque voie et n'avons pas ajouté de mètre de sécurité. Nous vous conseillons de toujours faire un double noeud en 8 au bout de votre corde et d'y attacher également un mousqueton car ils ne passeront jamais par le système d'assurage (grigri et autres)! Pour les voies presentées dans ce guide vous ne devriez pas avoir besoin de plus de 16 dégaines. A Saint Léger certaines voies ont des sections très longues et difficiles et un manche (clip stick) pour placer les dégaines peut être, exceptionellement, préférable. Beaucoup de voies classiques, plus faciles, ne sont pas très bien équipées et nous pensons que 6 sangles seraient utiles à avoir. Il y a des voies avec des équipements très anciens et qui peuvent être protégées avec des coinceurs, mais je souhaite indiquer que ces voies ne sont pas faciles et qu'elles n'offrent pas beaucoup de placements.

Vacances

Pour plus d'information, consultez les pages touristiques de ce guide. La région est très accueillante mais il est essentiel de respecter les habitants locaux. Vous êtes un invité et il est donc important soit de camper, soit de rester en gite ou en hôtel afin de supporter l'économie locale. N'apportez pas votre nourriture mais faites plutôt vos courses dans les petits magasins locaux. Si les grimpeurs apportent leur support à la communauté locale alors cette dernière apportera son soutien aux grimpeurs. Garez vous toujours avec respect et ne laissez jamais rien dans votre voiture. N'utilisez pas la nature comme toilette. De nombreux villages ont des toilettes publics alors utilisez les avant d'aller grimper ou allez boire un café afin d'utiliser les wc. Certaines piscines n'acceptent pas les caleçons il est donc préférable d'avoir un slip de bain. La seule chose qu'il est impossible d'acheter localement est l'équipement pour l'escalade. Il faut faire quelques kilomètres pour acheter chaussons et cordes et la sélection reste très limitée. Enfin consultez notre site internet avant votre voyage www.jingowobbly.com pour nos mises à jour et nouvelles informations.

Les guides Jingo Wobbly sont faciles à utiliser et "Avignon Soleil" suit l'agencement des guides que nous avons publié dans le passé. Nous avons cependant amélioré notre design suite aux commentaires reçus des grimpeurs qui utilisent nos guides. Nous avons également introduit, et pour la première fois, de nouvelles caractéristiques et de nouveaux icônes ainsi qu'un nouveau système de cotation qui a pour but d'aider les grimpeurs moins expérimentés. La lecture de ces 2 pages vous permettra d'utiliser au mieux ce guide.

Pour apprendre à connaitre la zone d'escalade, il y a deux cartes donnant des vues d'ensemble: une à l'arrière de la couverture avant pour illustrer toutes les differentes zones d'escalade et une à la fin du livre pour indiquer les terrains de camping et les lieux touristiques. Nous commençons par décrire les falaises situées au sud-est. Vous pouvez trouver les falaises en utilisant la nomenclature des pages qui couvre les 31 sections du guide et qui est codée par couleur: jaune pour indiquer que la falaise est au soleil le matin, rouge pour le soleil l'après-midi, vert pour l'ombre et bleu s'il n'y a pas de soleil. Il y a un sommaire en page 5 suivi par un diagramme soleil/vent en page 7. Celui-ci a été crée spécifiquement pour ceux qui ne connaissent pas très bien la région et comprend les 52 falaises. Le guide vous permet donc de choisir votre lieu d'escalade par rapport aux conditions météorologiques, au style d'escalade qui vous convient, mais également à la distance qu'il faut pour rejoindre le site. Enfin vous pourrez voir si les voies sur la falaise que vous avez selectionnée ont des cotations qui vous conviennent. Pour les falaises qui ne sont pas incluses dans le guide, vous trouverez quelques informations en page annexe 304.

Les introductions pour chaque site d'escalade sont en anglais et en français et donnent l'information que les 200 photos couleurs ne peuvent pas fournir. Nous avons inclu un P bleu en haut de chaque topo pour indiquer le numéro de page pour le parking et la carte d'accès. Même si vous savez comment aller à une falaise nous vous conseillons de consulter ces pages pour vous assurer qu'il n'y a pas de changements au niveau de l'accès. Pour chaque falaise il y a une barre de navigation en bas de chaque topo qui indique les secteurs inclus dans le guide. Nous n'avons pas mis tous les secteurs des falaises les plus importantes afin de pouvoir imprimer un guide de taille raisonnable avec 320 pages environ. (Le topo Français - page 21)

Topos & cotations: Afin d'illustrer les falaises, nous réalisons tous nos diagrammes par ordinateur. Nous indiquons les placements des goujons ce qui est une aide précieuse pour reconnaître les voies. Tous nos topos sont dessinés à la main depuis le départ de chaque voie, ainsi la vue que vous en avez est la même que celle que vous aurez lorsque vous vous trouverez au pied de la falaise. Nous avons adopté un nouveau système pour marquer les voies tout simplement par des tirets et des points. Les tirets représentent le chemin de la voie tandis que les points de couleur représentent le niveau général de la voie dans les sections les plus faciles. S'il y a des mouvements avec une cotation plus élevée, ils sont illustrés par un point avec une couleur différente qui représente la difficulté. C'est un système très maniable que nous trouvons très utile pour illustrer les voies avec des mouvements clés difficiles. Les couleurs changent selon la difficulté en suivant le modèle européen des pistes de ski - vert, bleu, rouge, noir et suivent les couleurs utilisées sur les circuits de Fontainebleau. Nous utilisons également les cotations de 1 a 8c. Nos cotations de 1 a 5 sont très similaires au système alpin UIAA de difficulté. Nous avons découvert que 90% des grimpeurs pratiquent en 6a-7a et nous pensons que 4 zones de cotation sont essentielles à ce niveau. Nos 6a,b,c,7a correspondent aux 5a,b,c,6a anglais. J'ai découvert durant les 30 dernières années que ces 4 niveaux sont ceux qui sont les mieux reconnus par la majorité des grimpeurs, et également les plus utiles pour qualifier la puissance et la technicité des mouvements d'escalade. A 7b et au-delà les cotations existantes sont parfaites et nos 7b-8c équivalent les 7b-8c actuels. La grande différence avec nos cotations c'est l'utilisation de plus et de moins pour indiquer la difficulté prolongée d'une voie. Un moins illustre un ou deux mouvements et un plus indique 10 à 15 mouvements soutenus. Par exemple, une voie pour laquelle nous donnons 7a- aura un mouvement de 6a (Fontainebleau 5c). Traditionnellement ce type de voie est cotée 6a+ ou au plus 6b, cependant j'ai rarement vu un grimpeur de moyen niveau capable de passer des mouvements d'une telle difficulté. En donnant une cotation pour le mouvement le plus difficile et une cotation pour l'effort soutenu, il est plus facile de qualifier les voies ce qui est une aide précieuse pour les grimpeurs moins costauds. Nous avons mis en place ce nouveau système car nous trouvions très difficile de donner des cotations aux voies de niveau moyen lors de la réalisation de ce guide. C'est pourquoi de nombreuses voies que nous avons grimpé avant la mise en place de ce système ont des cotations

Dentelles de Montmirail

traditionnelles. Nous espérons que d'autres ''niveleurs'' verront la flexibilité de ce système à deux niveaux et l'utiliseront de manière effective. Nous donnons un index qui indique les voies que nous avons utilisées comme référence (page 306). Nos topos donnent également des informations plus générales comme le temps de marche depuis la falaise jusqu'au parking, la distance pour rejoindre les secteurs avoisinants et la hauteur de la falaise ainsi que son exposition. Nous indiquons également à quels moments le soleil arrive et quitte la falaise.

Informations internationales: En-dessous de chaque topo, l'information donnée est en anglais. Il y a une introduction du secteur avec de nombreux détails humoristiques sur la majorité des voies. Nous avons essayé d'indiquer les dangers sans donner d'informations essentielles sur les voies. Si nous les connaissons, nous avons donné aux voies leurs noms ainsi que leurs cotations (carrés blancs). Pour éviter de donner trop d'information sur chaque voie, nous avons inclu la hauteur et le nombre de dégaines nécessaires seulement si nous savons que cette information est exacte et correcte. Nous avons essayé de donner la difficulté du mouvement le plus difficile et de l'effort soutenu pour autant de voies que possible. Nous avons grimpé toutes les voies de ce guide sur une période

de 15 ans et n'avons commencé à utiliser ce système que très récemment ainsi nous nous excusons pour ne pas donner cette nouvelle information à chaque voie. En divisant les voies en sections, il nous est possible d'illustrer la manière dont le mouvement le plus difficile est protégé et d'indiquer le style du mouvement. Nous avons crée de nombreuses figurines Jingo Woobly pour décrire le style d'escalade et les chutes possibles, ce qui est assez marrant. Il y a un index complet à la fin de ce guide et les plus communes sont listées à l'arrière de la couverture avant. Nous avons illustré les voies pour lesquelles nous n'avons pas d'information précise avec un oeil. Vous devriez bien vous amuser à essayer de les faire à vu. Jingo & Wobbly représentent respectivement force et technique, ils vous permettent donc d'identifier rapidement la nature d'une voie. Les voies avec un éclair devraient être faciles à faire à vu. Certaines falaises ont des voies de plusieurs longueures c'est pourquoi nous avons répété certains des topos à la fin du livre. Ceci vous permet de détacher la page arrière pour la prendre avec vous sur une voie. Rappelez-vous que tout guide d'escalade est une représentation de l'expèrience passée et non une prédiction des futures conditions d'une voie. Certaines zones d'escalade sont sur des terrains privés et ce guide ne donne à personne le droit de pénétrer sur ces terrains.

You have two choices when making a climbing guidebook. You either write a simple book especially for expert local climbers who know the area, and with basic information for 7a-8a on sight climbing; or write a highly detailed guidebook for climbers that don't know the area at all, and make it bulging with colour photos and tourist information. Our approach is obviously the latter with this large book, and is for the benefit of mid grade climbers who struggle on 7a-8c's. The intended user is someone who looks at a map of the South of France, spots the giant mountain of Mont Ventoux (1909m), and decides to go there on holiday for some sunshine, climbing, fresh air sports, good food, good wine, and maybe even some cycling. If this is for you, then please carry on reading, or just buy the book immediately – thank you.

The area around Mont Ventoux that we have chosen is large, and is without a big and busy climbing centre like Arco or Orpierre. Its beauty is that the 52 separate climbing cliffs are quiet and spread out, and you can have a holiday in a nice rural part of France, as opposed to a busy outdoor climbing gym. There is a great selection of campsites to stay at, gites to rent, or even hotels to luxuriate by the pool. The vineyards of Châteauneuf-du-Pape are to die for, as are many others that I recommend throughout the book. The one dominating factor above anything else, is simply the incredible amount of sunshine that this area gets, hence our title - Avignon Soleil. The sun allows you to climb here 365 days a year if you choose your cliff sensibly. In July summer days it gets to 34°, so getting up early to climb in the shade is the only option; however, then you can have a gorgeous afternoon swimming in the pool, and enjoy the hot balmy evenings, eating outside on the terraces of the lovely restaurants. In winter, you can ski on the north slopes of Mont Ventoux, or climb on the low south facing cliffs of the Dentelles de Montmirail. If you plan wisely and intelligently, the sunshine will always be your friend. Because of the strong sunshine, you therefore need a really good overview of the 52 different climbing venues before you even think of planning your holiday. The concept of this book is that you can study every one of the 320 pages in detail, look at over 200 colour photographs in the luxury of your own home, then plan perfectly how to visit the area. With this information, you can then plan your visit in advance, know where to find routes that suit your level of climbing, but also know how to respect and enjoy the area that you are visiting. See our travel & tourism page 20 for planning your trip.

Landscape and climate.

Southern France is divided east-west by the giant river Rhône that flows down to Marseille. Around 50km to the north of Avignon, the river widens out to a large flood plain. The rising heat of the Mediterranean sucks the cool alpine air down the valley of the Rhône, to produce the famous wind known as the Mistral. It is a startlingly cold wind and can blow some 60-80km, sometimes for only a day, but at other times constantly for 10 days or longer. It is a ravaging wind that can drive you insane, but it also lowers the temperature from a 30 degree sweltering, to a wonderful 22-23 degrees in the sun, but with a breeze – and gives the most perfect climbing conditions I have ever experienced. Just like the sun here, the wind too can be used for your advantage. The area is dominated by Mont Ventoux (1909m), an oversize flat loaf with a communications spire on top. It's not a climber's mountain, but definitely is a cyclist's mountain with several roads up it. It has an uncanny presence though, because it dominates the whole area with its bulbous size, and the summit is often cloaked with cloud when everywhere else sparkles in brilliant sunshine. However, rarely a day goes past when you don't see Mont Ventoux. It gets the first and last snows of winter, and seems to warn you when bad weather is coming. You can observe any cloud build up on Mont Ventoux to use as your rain warning gauge, as you try to squeeze one last route in on the last day of your holiday. The area around Carpentras at 100m altitude is very much the lowlands, and has an excellent winter climate. The towns of Malaucène (300m) and Buis-les-Baronnies (384m) make very good cooler venues to stay near, but can be pretty chilly in spring and Autumn, even though the climbing is perfect at these times of year. There are highland areas too, such as Sault (700m) and Mevouillon (900m), which are lovely isolated spots, and are nice to visit in the heat of summer. The weather on average, is sunnier and drier - the nearer to Avignon you are. When a rainy frontal system comes through, it can rain several inches in hours, so choose your camping spot wisely! Usually this happens about twice in 8 weeks, for about a day and a half of concentrated downpour. The other type of rain you get is cloudy weather with very local rain showers. I recommend that you follow your instinct, see where the wind is blowing and work out what areas are likely to stay dry the longest. During the photography for this book, it rained all day long at one end of Saint Léger, yet 1km along at the other end, it was dry until

6pm. It is best to choose the cliff that will stay dry the longest, rather than the one that is most overhanging – when it rains, it rains, and even the steeper cliffs become power showers with amazing run off.

Cliffs & Climbing

The 200 photographs in the book, describe better than any words, the variation in rock styles, angles and solidity of the predominant rock - limestone. At 8 of the cliffs, the rock is geologically limestone, but climbers would call it sandstone or gritstone; you need sloper strength, combined with very low humidity and temperature to really get results at these cliffs. There is everything here from nasty 15 metre overhanging horror shows, up to gentle classic 90m walls with 3 pitches. You can always find cliffs either in the shade or the sun, and rarely do you ever have to walk more than 10 mins to get to the climbs. As always with limestone, there is loose rock. Some cliffs do have routes bolted up on very suspect rock, and we try out best to indicate where this is. On multi pitch climbing where ropes drag across ledges, the chance of small stones falling is high – helmets advisable. Think carefully also if there are climbers above you, simply putting on a helmet is of little use if a big rock comes down. Most of the cliffs have bolts for protection which are glued in place with resin and look exceptionally good. However, I have still come across some bolts in hollow sounding rock, or where a quickdraw rests on a sharp edge, or the angle of the bolt is wrong, or the rock around is cracked and loose, or if you fall you will hurt yourself! It is certainly not an outdoor climbing gym and you really need to make good decisions on the equipment for your own level of climbing. Many of the easier climbs are only bolted for the safety of a grade 7 climber, so if you only climb grade 5, then make careful - but good decisions. A single 70m rope plus 12 quickdraws, is adequate for anyone using budget air travel with baggage restrictions. I prefer to have two ropes; a 50m 10.2 rope for short steep high grade climbs; plus an 80m lightweight 9.1 rope for long climbs and mulitipitches (40m abseil). Look at the routes you want to do, and work out the best length of ropes to take on your trip, but be warned, a lot of the best climbs in the area are 33-40m. We try to give exact route lengths, and do not add anything for safety – that is your decision. Ultimately, always keep a double figure of 8 knot with a screwgate karabiner on the end of the rope, it simply doesn't go through any normal belay device! All of the routes in this book are sport climbs and 16 quickdraws

should be all that you need. Some routes are multi-pitch and you will need a cows tail-sling, plus an abseil device. Many routes at Saint Léger have long run-out crux sections, so a big clip stick maybe exceptionally preferable. A lot of the big classic easier routes are not very well protected, and climbing guides usually extend many of the runners with slings for young leaders, bringing 6 long extra slings will be useful for groups of mixed abilities. There are many other routes in this region with ancient equipment and can be protected with trad style nuts, but I would express that these routes are neither easy or offer that many gear placements due to type of rock, these are consequently very serious undertakings.

On holiday

For holiday recommendations, see the tourist pages in the book. The area is generally welcoming to holiday makers, but it is essential to keep the relationship between visitor and local – respectable. You are a guest in the area, so you must only stay on campsites, gites or hotels, and therefore support the local economy. Don't bring your own food, but buy it in the local shops, again supporting local life. The more climbers support the local community, the more the local community will support climbers. Always think where you are parking, and park with respect. Car break in's are notorious in France – so never leave anything in your car. If you are up a cliff and your car window is broken, you can't get down, so leaving your car unlocked is not such a bad option. The landscape is not your own personal toilet. Many villages have public toilets so please use them before you go climbing, or have a coffee and use the café facilities. Some swimming pools do not allow baggy shorts, so have a speedo swimstyle slip with you, just in case. The one thing that does seem impossible to buy locally, is climbing equipment. You have to drive a long way for shoes-ropes etc, and even then, the selection is very restricted. Page 21 has a few sugesstions should you need something. Finally, check out our website before travelling www.jingowobbly.com or updates with any new information that we may have been given.

Using a Jingo Wobbly topo guide should be easy, and most climbers will be able to use this book without any further help. However, we constantly improve our design and change important features after getting feedback from users in other areas. We have also introduced many new features and icons in this book for the first time, along with a special new grading system, especially to help climbers in the lower grades. By reading these two pages, it should ensure that you get the most out of this book.

Getting to know the area: There are two large overview maps, one on the inside cover is to illustrate all the different climbing locations; and the other inside the back cover, to show campsites & tourist locations. The cliff order in the book starts in the SE, then vaguely works clockwise around Mont Ventoux. You can also find these cliffs directly by using the page markers that run down the side. These are in two layers to cover the 31 main sections, and are colour coded: yellow for morning sunshine, red - afternoon sunshine, green for shade, and blue for no sun. There is a general contents list on page 5, followed by a sunshine and wind selection chart on page 7. This chart has been designed specifically for those unfamiliar with the area and includes all 52 cliffs. First you observe the type of weather today, checking the local paper whilst sipping your yummy cappucino; then choose your preferred climbing style, walk in time, and if the cliff is covered in this guidebook etc. Finally, you can see if there is good climbing at the cliff in the grade that suits you and your friends. Details for cliffs not included in this book, can be found in the appendix on page 304.

All area introductions are provided in both English and French, and give information that our 200 colour photos cannot give. We have included a blue parking-P at the top of every topo, which gives the page number for the parking and access map. Even if you are familiar with getting to a cliff, please look at the parking page to check on any recent access difficulties. This blue P, makes finding the access easy, when you have chosen to climb at a cliff by looking at a photo first. Each cliff has a navigation bar at the bottom of every topo, and shows the sectors included in the book from left to right. We prefer to keep our guidebooks to a manageable size of 320 pages, and therefore have not included all the sectors on the very large cliffs. (local guidebooks are illustrated along with travel information on pages 20-21)

Topos & grades: Our publishing style is to make all of our own computer diagrams, and use these clearly to illustrate different parts of a cliff. Incorporated on these are the majority of bolt placements, which makes route recognition a lot easier and less confusing than using fuzzy photos. All of our topos are hand drawn from the base of each climb, so the view is also very much the same as that you get when standing at the bottom of a climb looking for a route (unlike a photo taken from across the valley). We have adopted a new system of marking routes on our topos, of simply dashes and dots. The dashes represent the path of the climb, with the colour of the dashes representing the general level of climbing in the easier sections. If there are individual moves of a higher grade, these are illustrated by a dot, with a different colour representing this higher difficulty. It is a highly adaptable system and we have found it really useful to illustrate routes with substantially hard crux's. The colours increase in difficulty with the same concept as European skiing - Green-Blue-Red-Black, and are very similar to colours used on the bouldering circuits at Fontainebleau. We also like to use the full expanse of grades from 1 up to 8c. Our grades 1-5 are very similar to UIAA alpine difficulty, and results in a comfortable increase of easy grade routes up to and including grade 5. We find that 90% of regular climbers operate in mid grade climbing 6a-7a, so we think that 4 separations of this area is essential, our 6a,b,c,7a directly correspond with UK 5a,b,c,6a (easy-6a). I have found over the past 30 years, that these 4 separate levels are the most distinguishable to the majority of climbers, and also the most useful for grading the power and technicality of general mid grade climbing moves. At 7b and above, the existing sport grades work very well and our 7b-8c are equal to modern sport 7b-8c. The big difference for our grades, is that we use plus and minus to indicate how sustained the climbing is. We use minus to illustrate only one or two moves, and a plus to indicate 10-15 sustained moves, with a straight grade being something in between. Most mid grade climbers are not very strong, and simply cannot do really hard moves, even if there is only one hard move! A route we give 7a-, will have a single move of UK 6a, (Font 5c). Traditionally, this sort of route would only be given 6a+ or at the most 6b, yet I've never seen an average sport 6a, 6b or even 6c climber ever getting up these sort of moves! By giving a climb a crux grade, and a sustained grade, you can separate out unbalanced climbs, and really help mid grade climbers who aren't gigantically strong. This new grading system has come about, as a direct response from finding mid grade routes, impossible to grade during the making of this guidebook. Hence many of the routes that we climbed pre this system are just given general old style - sport grades. Hopefully other graders will see the flexibility of this two grade style and use it to good effect. We provide an appendix of famous routes, so that climbers can see which 'bloc moves' we have used for 'benchmark' status (page 306). Our topos show general extra information such as; walking time back to the car, time to get to the next sector, and general height of the cliff. A sun plan view is included when looking at the cliff, this shows when the sun comes onto the rock, and when it leaves; plus the general direction of the cliff.

International info: Beneath each topo, the information is given in 'International English.' We try to fit in a general résumé of the sector, and give a lot of humorous information to as many climbs as possible. We make every effort to describe the horrors involved, but try not to give any vital secrets away. Names of routes are given where known, and we provide sport grades (white boxes), that should be consistent with the majority of indoor climbing walls in northern Europe. To complete such a gigantic task with every single route detail would take over 10 years, so we simply include information (height, quickdraws etc.) that we know is exact and correct. We try to give the difficulty grade of the crux move, and the general sustained level moves, for as many routes as possible. Our research has been over 15 years in climbing most of the routes in this book, and hence before this new two tier system was invented, so please accept our apologies for not giving this crux/endurance information for every route. You will see how often the sport grade is an average of these two grades. By splitting the climb into sections, we can also illustrate how well the crux is protected, and the style of climbing on the crux move – which may be completely different to the sustained nature for the rest of the climb. We have designed a vast army of Jingo Wobbly icons to describe climbing styles-fall potential; which often provide plenty of amusement. Our general index for these is at the back of the book, with the most common being listed inside the front flap. Most people freak out when they see the 747-transatlantic flying

Rocher de l'Aiguier

icon, and especially when it illustrates the crux move! There were some routes that we have no accurate information and didn't have time to climb, so we give these an eyeball grade – the grade it looks like – ho, ho! You should have plenty of fun trying to onsight one of these climbs! Jingo and Wobbly, these two little fun icons represent strength and technique respectively, enabling you to quickly identify the general nature of a page. Any climb with a flash next to the sport grade should be straightforward to onsight. A few of the cliffs have multi pitch routes on, so we repeat some of these topos at the back of the book. This is so you can tear out the rear page and take it on the route with you. With any climbing guidebook, please remember - that all climbing guidebooks are a representation of past experience, but certainly not a prediction of future condition that the routes may be in! Some climbing areas are on private land, and this book does not give anyone the right to enter onto any private land.

Wenn man einen Kletterführer schreibt, hat man zwei Möglichkeiten. Entweder man schreibt ein kompaktes Buch für Experten, die die Gegend vielleicht schon kennen und nur noch etwas Zusatzinformationen für ihre 8a-onsight-Versuche benötigen. Oder man schreibt einen sehr detaillierten Kletterführer für Genusskletterer, denen die Gegend gänzlich unbekannt ist und pflastert ihn mit Farbfotos und zahlreichen Informationen über Land und Leute. Wir haben den zweiten Weg gewählt. Wir richten uns an Genusskletterer, die so bis 6c klettern. Es sind die Kletterer, die auf die Karte Südfrankreichs starren, den Mont Ventoux (1909m) entdecken und sich für einen Kletterurlaub dort entscheiden: Sonne, Klettern, gutes Essen, guter Wein, vielleicht ein bisschen Radfahren. Wer zu dieser Gruppe gehört, sollte also weiterlesen - oder sich bitte sofort das Buch kaufen.

Rund um den Mont Ventoux gibt es sehr viele Klettergebiete, es gibt allerdings kein grosses und geschäftiges Kletterzentrum à la Arco oder à la Orpierre. Das Gebiet besticht eindeutig durch seine Ruhe: man verbringt ein paar relaxte Tage in einem wunderschönen, ländlichen Teil Frankreichs und fühlt sich nicht an eine Outdoor-Kletterhalle erinnert. Es gibt viele Zeltplätze, gites, Ferienwohnungen und natürlich auch Hotels mit dem obligatorischen Swimmingpool. Und dann die Weine: Für einen Châteuaneuf-du-Pape könnte man sterben, genauso wie für einen der vielen anderen Weine, die wir hier auch empfehlen. Was jedoch wirklich auffällt, ist die schier unglaubliche Zahl an Sonnenstunden. Diese Tatsache macht es möglich, hier 365 Tage im Jahr zu klettern. Daher auch unser Titel: Avignon Soleil.

Im Juli kann es bis zu 35° heiss werden, früh aufzustehen ist dann die einzig richtige Entscheidung. Dafür kann man sich ja mit einem Gammelnachmittag am Swimmingpool entschädigen und später eine angenehm warme Sommernächte geniessen, natürlich auf der Terrasse eines hübschen Restaurants. Im Winter kann man auf den Nordhängen des Mont Ventoux Skifahren oder an den südlich ausgerichteten Felsen der Dentelles de Montmirail klettern. Bei intelligenter Planung wird die Sonne also immer mit euch sein. Ihre Omnipräsenz verlangt jedoch nach einem wirklich guten Überblick über die 52 Klettergebiete. Und das ist das Konzept dieses Kletterführers: nehmt euch zu Hause etwas Zeit, blättert durch die 320 Seiten mit ihren über 200 Farbfotos und plant euren Trip. So wisst ihr, wo die Routen in euerm Schwierigkeitsgrad sind und

erfahrt auch einiges über Land und Leute. Auf Seite 20 haben wir zusätzliche Informationen zur Anreise und touristischen Highlights zusammengestellt.

Landschaft und Klima.

Die gewaltige Rhône teilt auf ihrem Weg nach Marseille Südfrankreich in einen Ost- und einen Westteil. Ungefähr 50 km nördlich von Avignon ist das Flussbett breiter und verläuft in einer grossen Ebene. Die mediterrane Hitze zieht die kalte, alpine Luft durch das Rhônetal in Richtung Süden – das ist der berühmt-berüchtigte Mistral. Ein kalter, unangenehmer Wind, der bis zu 80km/h erreichen kann, der manchmal nur einen Tag herrscht, manchmal aber auch zehn Tage und länger. Ein wirklich rauer Wind, der einen verrückt macht, aber auch Vorteile hat, da er für Kühlung sorgt: statt über 30° hat man angenehme 22-23° in der Sonne. Je nachdem, wo man sich befindet, bekommt man nur eine leichte Brise mit - für mich die besten Kletterbedingungen überhaupt. Der Mont Ventoux (1909m) dominiert die Umgebung, ein überdimensionierter Brotlaib mit einem Funkmasten am Gipfel. Kein Kletterberg, aber einer für Radfahrer, da mehrere Strassen auf ihn hinauf führen. Durch seine schiere Grösse scheint er jedenfalls allgegenwärtig zu sein, und sein Gipfel ist oft in Wolken verhüllt auch wenn überall sonst noch die Sonne scheint. An nur ganz wenigen Tagen bekommt man ihn gar nicht zu sehen. Man findet den ersten und letzten Schnee des Winters auf ihm, und er scheint geradezu vor schlechtem Wetter zu warnen. Jede Wolke, die sich um ihn bildet, ist ein Hinweis auf Wetterverschlechterung, besonders natürlich am letzten Urlaubstag, in der letzten Route…

Rund um Carpentras (100m) haben wir – durch die tiefe Lage - exzellentes Winterklima. In den Städtchen Malaucène (300m) und Buis-les-Baronnies (384m) ist es schon deutlich kühler, im Frühling oder Winter manchmal fast ein bisschen zu kühl. Genau dann ist aber die beste Kletterzeit! Es gibt auch noch höher gelegene Orte, z.B. Sault (700m) oder Mévouillon (900m), die sich gut für den heissen Sommer eignen. Nähert man sich Avignon, wird das Wetter üblicherweise immer sonniger und trockener. Wenn eine Regenfront durchzieht, kann in kurzer Zeit enorm viel Wasser vom Himmel fallen, überlegt euch also gut, wo ihr euer Zelt aufstellt. Richtig heftiger Regen fällt an ungefähr eineinhalb Tagen in zwei Monaten. Wenn ansonsten die Sonne gerade mal nicht scheint, ist es meist leicht bewölkt und es kommt zu lokalen Regenschauern. Ich empfehle, ganz dem ureigenen Instinkt zu folgen, die Windrichtung zu bestimmen und dann dorthin zu fahren, wo es wahrscheinlich am längsten trocken bleibt. Während der Arbeit an diesem Kletterführer hat es beispielsweise in Saint Lèger an einem Ende des Felsriegels den ganzen Tag sehr stark geregnet, während es am anderen Ende – 1km entfernt - bis sechs Uhr abends trocken blieb. Es zahlt sich also aus, den Felsen auszusuchen, der wahrscheinlich am längsten trocken bleibt und nicht unbedingt den, der am meisten überhängt. Wenn es regnet, regnet es nun mal und selbst die steilen Felsen bekommen eine Dusche ab oder das Wasser drückt von oben her durch.

Felsen & Klettern

200 Farbfotos sagen mehr als Worte über die verschiedenen Felsarten, Felsneigungen und Qualität der vorherrschenden Gesteinsart, dem Kalk. Dabei handelt es sich an acht Felsen geologisch gesehen zwar um Kalk, ein Kletterer allerdings würde das Gestein als Sandstein oder Grit bezeichnen. Hier braucht man Kraft an Auflegern, niedrige Temperaturen und niedrige Luftfeuchtigkeit, um was wirklich Schweres hochzukommen. Sonst gibt es wirklich alles: vom 15m Überhang à la Frankenjura bis zur grosszügigen Wandkletterei mit drei Seillängen. Es gibt Sonnenfelsen und Schattenfelsen und selten ist der Zustieg länger als 10 Minuten. Wie überall, so gibt es auch hier Felsen mit etwas schlechterer Felsqualität: es kann bröckeln. Bei Mehrseillängenrouten, die über grasige Bänder verlaufen, kommt es leicht zu Steinfall – ein Helm ist anzuraten. Vorsicht, wenn sich Kletterer über euch befinden, bei grossen Felsbrocken bringt auch ein Helm nicht mehr viel. Die Absicherung mit geklebten Bohrhaken ist meist vorbildlich. Dennoch haben wir immer wieder Haken angetroffen, die entweder in schlechtem Fels sitzen oder etwas unglücklich angebracht sind. Trotz der allgemein guten Absicherung handelt es sich nicht um eine Outdoor-Kletterhalle! Viele der leichteren Routen sollte man wirklich im Griff haben, da die Hakenabstände etwas weiter sind.

Ein 70m Einfachseil und 12 Expressschlingen sind ausreichend, beides bekommt man üblicherweise auch ohne Beanstandung durch die Gepäckkontrolle am Flughafen. Ich bevorzuge zwei Seile: ein 50m Seil (10.2mm) für kurze, steile Klettereien und ein leichtes 80m Seil (9.1mm) für längere Routen und Mehrseillängen. (40m Abseillänge.) Schaut euch die Längen der Routen auf den einzelnen Toposeiten an und entscheidet selbst, was für ein Seil ihr mitnehmen wollt.

Viele wirklich lohnenswerte Routen sind jedoch zwischen 33 und 40m lang. Und vergesst nicht, einen Knoten ins Seilende zu machen!!

Alle in diesem Kletterführer vorgestellten Routen sind Sportklettereien, 12 Expressschlingen sollten genügen, Vorsichtige nehmen 16 mit. Für die Mehrseillängentouren braucht ihr ein Abseilgerät und eine Schlinge zur Selbstsicherung am Standplatz. In Saint Léger gibt es häufig Run-outs um die Schlüsselstelle herum, ein langer clip-stick könnte nützlich sein. Viele der leichteren oder klassischen Routen sind nicht sehr gut abgesichert, hier können erfahrene Vorsteiger die Zahl der Sicherungspunkte durch eine angemessene Zahl von Bandschlingen erhöhen. Es gibt auch viele Routen, die mit Normalhaken abgesichert sind oder wo man die Absicherung mittels mobiler Sicherungsmittel nachbessern muss. Allerdings sind diese Routen weder einfach zu klettern, noch einfach abzusichern; es handelt sich also um eher ernsthafte Unternehmungen.

Ferien

Für Empfehlungen touristischer Art konsultiert ihr am besten die entsprechenden Seiten im Kletterführer. Die Leute sind sehr offen gegenüber Touristen, man sollte ihnen jedoch den gebührenden Respekt erweisen. Man sollte nur auf ausgewiesenen Zeltplätzen, in gites oder Hotels nächtigen. Bringt nicht zuviel Lebensmittel von zuhause mit, sondern unterstützt die Menschen vor Ort und kauft in ihren Läden ein. Je mehr wir Kletterer Land und Leute unterstützen, desto mehr Unterstützung werden wir auch zurückbekommen. Parkt bitte nur auf den angegeben Parkplätzen. Leider sind Autoeinbrüche an der Tagesordnung in Frankreich – lasst euer Fahrzeug am besten immer leer und gebt keinen Hinweis darauf, dass sich irgendetwas wichtiges darin befinden könnte. Autos werden selbst für gebrauchte, aber deutlich von aussen sichtbare Jeans aufgebrochen. Vielleicht ist es eine gute Idee, das Auto gar nicht erst abzuschliessen, so spart man sich das Geld für eine oder mehrere neue Scheiben. Klettergebiete sind keine öffentliche Toilette. Viele Ortschaften haben öffentliche Toiletten, benutzt also diese oder trinkt irgendwo einen Kaffee in einer Bar und macht dort euer Geschäft. Boxershorts sind in einigen französischen Schwimmbädern nicht erlaubt, bringt also am besten eine kurze Badehose mit. Was wir vermisst haben, ist ein guter Shop mit Kletterequipment...Und schliesslich könnt ihr immer unter www.jingowobbly.com schauen, ob es updates oder neue Informationen gibt.

Die meisten Kletterer werden diesen Kletterführer ohne weitere Hilfe benutzen können – Jingo Wobbly Kletterführer bürgen für Einfachheit. Allerdings arbeiten wir ständig an unserem Design und ändern dies oder das. Wir haben uns viele neue Details, neue Symbole und ein neues Bewertungssystems ausgedacht, welches speziell Kletterern, die in leichteren Graden unterwegs sind, helfen soll. Die Lektüre dieser Einleitung erleichtert euch die Arbeit mit unserem Kletterführer.

Der erste Überblick: Eine grosse Übersichtskarte auf der vorderen Umschlagseite zeigt die einzelnen Klettergebiete: 52 Felsen!! Die Toposeiten selbst beginnen im Südosten und wir bewegen uns im Uhrzeigersinn um den Mont Ventoux. Die farbigen Seitenmarkierungen der Toposeiten stehen für die Sonnenausrichtung der Felsen: gelb=Sonne am Morgen, rot=Sonne am Nachmittag, grün=Schatten, blau=keine Sonne. Auf der zweiten Übersichtskarte auf der hinteren Umschlagseite gibt es Zeltplätze und touristische Sehenswürdigkeiten.

Auf Seite 5 findet ihr das Inhaltsverzeichnis und auf Seite 7 eine Felswahlhilfe, die insbesondere den Sonnenstand und die Windverhältnisse berücksichtigt.

Diese Felswahlhilfe nützt natürlich besonders Kletterern, die die Gegend gar nicht kennen. Startet eure Felswahl also mittels dieser Felswahlhilfe und der Wettervorhersage aus der Zeitung – am besten bei einem leckeren Café au lait in südfranzösischer Morgensonne. Dann überlegt ihr euch noch, was ihr heute klettern wollt (Überhänge, Platten, Mehrseillängen), wie lange der Zustieg sein darf usw. Und schliesslich könnt ihr sehen, ob auch der Schwierigkeitsgrad passt. Informationen zu Felsen, die wir nicht beschrieben haben, gibt es im Anhang auf Seite 304.

Die Einführung zu jedem Gebiet ist in Englisch und Französisch und enthält viele Details, die wir nicht mit unseren 200 Farbfotos einfangen konnten. Das blaue P am Kopf einer Toposeite weist auf die Seitennummer mit der Parkplatz - und Zustiegsinformation hin. Ein kurzer Blick auf diese Seiten ist auch dann hilfreich, wenn ihr die Gegend schon kennt; vielleicht hat sich ja etwas geändert. Am Fuss jeder Toposeite gibt es eine Navigationsleiste: sie enthält die verschiedenen Sektoren von links nach rechts. Wir wollten keinen (noch dickeren) Roman schreiben und haben daher in den grösseren Klettergebieten nicht alle Sektoren aufgelistet.

Secteur Kojak, Saint Léger

Topos&Bewertungen: Wir haben alle Topos von Hand vom Wandfuss aus gezeichnet. Daher sehen sie genau so aus, als wenn ihr selbst am Wandfuss stündet - nicht wie bei einem Foto von der anderen Talseite aus. Unsere Aufzeichnungen verarbeiten wir zu präzisen Computerdiagrammen. Eingezeichnete Bohrhaken erleichtern die Routenfindung - im Gegensatz zu unscharfen Fotos. Wir verwenden farbige Striche und Punkte, um die Routen zu markieren – eines unserer neuen Details. Die Striche zeigen den Routenverlauf, ein Punkt eine deutlich schwierigere Einzelstelle. Die Schwierigkeiten steigen von Grün über Blau und Rot nach Schwarz an. Das geübte Kletterauge fühlt sich natürlich an die Farbgebung der Boulder-Parcours in Fontainebleau erinnert.

Zu den Bewertungen: wir haben einen Teil der Routen neu bewertet. Unsere Grade 1 bis 5 entsprechen den jeweiligen UIAA (alpinen) Graden. Ab 7b entsprechen unsere Grade den gängigen Sportklettergraden (=französische Bewertung). Allerdings sind 90% aller Kletterer in den Graden 6a bis 7a unterwegs. Meine 30jährige Erfahrung lehrt, dass diese vier Grade von Kletterern sehr gut zu unterscheiden sind und dass sie die Kraft- und Technikanforderungen mittelschwerer Klettereien am besten wiedergeben. Daher finden wir es wichtig, speziell in diesem Bereich genau zu sein. Wir vergeben deshalb zusätzlich Plus und Minus: ein Minus, wenn die Route nur ein oder zwei schwierige Züge hat und ein Plus, wenn die Route 10-15 ungefähr gleich schwierige Züge hat. Eine Route mit glatten Grad liegt irgendwo dazwischen. Eine Route, die wir mit 7a- bewerten, hat also einen einzigen 7a Zug. Traditionell würde man eine solche Route mit 6a+ oder höchstens mit 6b bewerten. Dennoch kenne ich keinen durchschnittlichen 6a- oder sogar 6c-Kletterer, der einen solchen Zug schafft. Die meisten Kletterer, die sich in mittleren Graden bewegen, sind nicht sehr stark und scheitern an richtig harten Boulderzügen, auch wenn es nur einen davon gibt. Indem wir sowohl Einzelstellen als auch die Route insgesamt bewerten, können wir auf inhomogene, einzelstellenlastige Routen hinweisen und Kletterern helfen, die nicht gerade megastark sind. Diese Vorgehensweise ist unsere Antwort auf viele Routen, die wir während der Arbeit für dieses Buch kletterten, aber einfach nicht mit einem Standard-Sportklettergrad bewerten konnten. Wir hoffen, dass andere Kletterer, die Routen bewerten, die Vorteile unseres Systems erkennen und es verwenden. Da es sich um eine relativ neue Vorgehensweise handelt, wir aber bereits seit 15 Jahren die Routen in diesem Kletterführer klettern, konnten wir nicht alle Routen so differenziert behandeln – sorry for that.

In einem Anhang haben wir einige Benchmarkrouten aufgelistet, damit klar ist, worauf sich unsere jeweiligen Grade beziehen (page 306). Die Toposeiten informieren ausserdem noch über die Rückmarschzeit zum Auto, die Zustiegszeit zum nächsten Sektor, die Felsenhöhe und -ausrichtung, sowie über die Sonnenzeiten an diesem Felsen.

Allgemeine Information: auf jeder Toposeite gibt es eine allgemeine Information in Englisch. Wir fassen den Sektor zusammen und berichten - nicht immer ganz ernst gemeint – über möglichst viele Routen. Wir bemühen uns, die Schrecken und Besonderheiten einer Route zu beschreiben, ohne aber jedes kleinste Geheimnis einer Route zu verraten. Wir geben Routennamen (soweit bekannt) und Schwierigkeitsgrade an. Ausserdem gibt es Informationen zur Länge der Route und der Zahl der benötigten Expressen. Da wir eine Route in leichte und schwere Abschnitte unterteilen, verteilen wir Symbole für die Absicherung der Schlüsselstellen und für die Art von Kletterei. Dafür haben wir eine Armee von Jingo-Wobbly Symbolen erfunden… 🕷 **747** ☺ ▩ … Sie werden alle am Ende des Kletterführers erklärt, die wichtigsten findet ihr auf der Umschlaginnenseite. Die Symbole Jingo und Wobbly selbst stehen für athletische bzw. technische Kletterei, ihre Verteilung auf einer Toposeite gibt euch einen schnellen Überblick über die vorherrschende Art der Kletterei. Jede Route mit einem Blitz-Symbol sollte einen erfolgreichen onsight-Versuch zulassen. Weitere Symbole markieren die Absicherung bzw. das Flugpotential einer Route. Über einige Routen haben wir keine genaue Information (der Tag hat nur 24 Stunden…), von diesen Routen haben unseren pi-mal-Auge-Eindruck wiedergegeben. Ein onsight-Versuch einer solchen Route ist sicher eine spannende Sache. Einige Gebiete warten mit Mehrseillängentouren auf, die Topos dieser Felsen findet ihr am Ende des Buchs ein zweites Mal: diese Seiten könnt ihr rausreissen und mitnehmen.

Bitte denkt daran: alle Informationen in Kletterführern beruhen auf Erfahrungen der Vergangenheit, Verhältnisse (Absicherung, Felsqualität, Zustiegsmöglichkeiten, Regelungen zu Felssperrungen) können sich jederzeit ändern. Einige Felsen stehen auf Privatgrundstücken, dieses Buch gibt niemandem das Recht, dort einzudringen.

This is the page that goes out of date the quickest, since travel information can easily change from year to year. AIR: Low cost airlines certainly fly to Nîmes (35km west of Avignon), where you can rent a car at the airport, and drive quickly and easily to the SW climbing areas in around an hour. Fairly quick main roads will take you through the centre of Avignon and onto the very fast dual carriageway to Carpentras (Due a ring road, but add 30mins for going through the town in traffic). Leaving this road before at Monteux for the small road to Aubignan is a very good and sneaky quick route. Returning to the airport however is always advisable via Jonquièrs, A7-A9 to miss any possible traffic nightmares in either Orange or Avignon. Flying to Marseille is only slightly further (60km to Avignon), and compensated by the fact that the airport at Marseille is well to the north of the city and next to the autoroute to Avignon; you also end up on the correct side of Avignon. (About 1 hour to Carpentras).

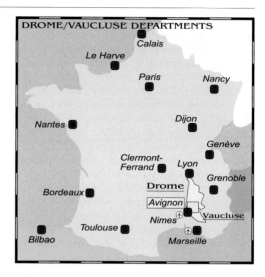

TRAIN: Taking the TGV-Eurostar is a very fast way to get to Avignon, and is an excellent and reliable service. For 4 people, it currently would be expensive, but it is an ideal way for a single friend to travel and join a group already in the area. There is a free bus from the TGV Avignon station into the town centre. From there, buses operate about 3 times daily to destinations of Carpentras-change-Beaumes de Venise & also Vaison-Nyons-Buis les Baronnies; not ideal journey lengths of 2 hours, but they do get you there. Travelling to the area in your own car is ideal, but be careful for speed cameras around the autoroute at Orange.

ACCOMODATION: This is an area keen on tourism, but without the seaside has remained sane, it is somewhat rurally delightful. There is no shortage of excellent campsites (page 71 & inside back cover), hotels, or gites to rent. This region is governed by two separate départments, The Drome (26) to the north, and the Vaulcuse (84) to the south. Neither départment will have any information on the other départment, so it can be highly frustrating in looking for information. Browsers beware! By going on the web and searching for anything to do with tourism, you do your head in pretty quickly with the zillions of cut price offers that bombard you with precisely what you don't want. Most worthwhile tourist

information can be picked up from local tourist information offices when you get here. These tourist offices are usually only open for a few hours in the morning, and a few hours in later afternoon, they often close at weekends, and can be closed during periods out of the main summer holiday season; so don't forget this book in other words. They do however publish two good magazines that are invaluable; one on 'rental holiday houses,' and the other on 'List of Campgrounds.' These are superb for planning you trip, have sumptuous information and photos, and are up to date, and are usually sent out by post on request.

HEALTH: There ia now a European travel card from 2006 available for reciprocal health arrangements, that is applicable for general medical health (www.dh.gov.uk). What this and most of a normal travel insurance does not cover, is the cost of a rescue from a cliff by helicopter. In France, rescue by helicopter is considered normal practice, so unless you are very wealthy, I recommend that you make sure you are covered for air rescue. Many national organisations run specific insurance policy's for climbers and can include multi-trips, specialist sport climbing, and skiing. (See advert for BMC travel and medical climbing insurance on page 122)

LOCAL CLIMBING GUIDES: If you like the photos of the climbing in this book, but feel that it is a bit scary and beyond your abilities, consider using a professional climbing guide that lives in the area. The local 'office de toursime' should be of help in finding local guides, but always please check that they have qualifications and find out insurance arrangements. (p-210, 216, 227)

LOCAL CLIMBING TOPO GUIDES: As most climbers know, visiting an area for the first time and finding climbing information is a nightmare. I have spent endless days often looking for an obscure topo, eventually finding that it is only sold in a remote shop, which displays the enticing front cover - however is closed for 2 weeks for annual holiday! Then finally when the shop opens, the advertisement on the door is just for show, and they sold out 3 months ago!!!! Our book will at least easily provide you enough climbing for your 2 week holiday – and a lot more. At present (2006), there are only locally published topos for 21 of the 52 cliffs in the entire region. These topos are usually only on sale, but only at the local Offices de tourisme closest to the cliff – and if it is in the same département. The advantage with these small and compact topos, is that they are basic and very cheap to produce and consequently get regularly updated - always worth looking for. Things change from year to year of course, but at present (2006), there is a topo to the Dentelles de Montmirail, 160 pages covering the 15 major cliffs. A good effort, but kept very minimalistic; black and white, just with route names and names of equippers and local grades. (Local grades here are bizarre/variable, and out of sync with many other European grades). At Buis-les-Baronnies, there are generally slim topo guides available. These have more information, and are with grades closer to the European norm, but with a few superb corker sandbags! In our book, we have tried to collect the maximum amount of information about areas not included in current published guidebooks, and hope where we have only given limited information, that you can buy the local topo guidebooks and explore fully what the area has to offer.

OTHER GUIDEBOOKS: Northern Provence is a difficult area to get information on, since the travel world seems to be obsessed by the coastline of the Mediterranean sea - and that area for the most part has been completely destroyed by over development. True, most bookshops will have no shortage of books on Provence, but if you get the chance, hunt out the INSIGHT guide, to Provence and the Côte d'azur. This book has a really good and comprehensive section to the area covered in this book, and will enhance your trip, plus give you some enticing reading on the trip down to Provence. Check out our website www.jingowobbly.com for any travel updates or latest information.

CLIMBING EQUIPMENT - BOUTIQUES:
Decathlon - Orange (SE), Avignon (NE)
Chaussures Regine - Buis-l-B. A few climbing shoes
Balade en Pvce. 20 Grand rue, Vaison; MgC03.
Le Pan d'Avignon, 82 R.de Montfavet, Avignon
Sport et Montagne, 50 rue Carnot, Avignon
Soescalade, 6 impasse du Rouvre, Les Angles

Lors de leurs jours de repos, de nombreux grimpeurs vont visiter les Gorges de la Nesque. En haut du belvédère vous pouvez pique-niquer et apprécier les jolies vues des alentours. Vous pouvez également voir les parois lisses qui sont situées de l'autre côté de la vallée. C'est l'endroit parfait pour profiter de l'air frais qui chemine à travers les gorges rendant une température de 30° supportable. Dans les gorges, les parois les plus importantes ne sont pas equipées. Elles paraissent très lisses et très abruptes. La zone entière est très impressionnante avec une hauteur de 330m, mais les gorges ne sont pas aussi imposantes que celles du Verdon. Les voies se situent sur la face nord sur des parois plus petites. Les 5 falaises qui ont été équipées offrent de bonnes voies courtes et faciles d'accès, à seulement une heure de route des Dentelles de Montmirail. Les voies sont variées dans leur style et leurs dévers et il y a suffisamment de voies différentes pour satisfaire tous les grimpeurs. C'est le lieu idéal pour ceux qui souhaitent grimper au calme et dans un cadre magnifique. Les gorges et la zone d'escalade ne sont pas adaptées pour y emmener des enfants. Il y a cependant un petit lac très proche avec des tables de pique-nique, parfait pour y passer la journée avec un bambin. Ne manquez pas de visiter la ville de Sault très proche et ses bars très sympas. Située à 800m d'altitude, il y fait un peu plus frais.

Rocher Malaval: 25 voies, 6c-7b+, 20-35m de hauteur, Alt 600m, exposé sud-est (pas de topo)
Rocher Blanchard: 9 voies, 6c-7b+, 19m de hauteur, Alt 750m, exposé est (1 topo)
Envol: 6 voies, 6c-8b, 20-25m de hauteur, Alt 550m, exposé sud-est (1 topo)
Archéo: 25 voies, 5-7b, 10-25m de hauteur, Alt 550, exposé sud (2 topos)
Belvédère: 30 voies, 5c-7a+, 25-45m de hauteur, Alt 650m exposé sud (pas de topo)

Most climbers take a leisurely drive up the Gorges de la Nesque to relieve throbbing fingertips on rest days. I can fully recommend having a picnic at the top belvédère, to enjoy the fabulous views on offer, and look in awe at the slender smooth walls on the opposite side of the valley. It is a perfect spot to enjoy the cool breeze funnelling up the ragged gorge, and making the 30° temperatures enjoyable. The major walls in the gorge are not developed, and look very smooth with giant overhangs. The whole area is very impressive with a 330m distance between the hill tops and gorge bottom, but is certainly not in the same league as the massive Gorges du Verdon. The climbing is to be found on the North side of the gorge on smaller cliffs, with simple access down from the road. Five cliffs that have been developed and offer very good short routes on relatively unclimbed rock. I have climbed here often over the past 10 years, but have never previously written down notes, and therefore can only offer limited information. This said, you might enjoy a more adventurous approach for once. It's always been a nice quiet hangout, since it takes just under an hour to drive to from the popular centre of the Dentelles de Montmirail. The cliffs are varied both in style, steepness and cliff direction, and there is generally something for anyone - somewhere here. It is an ideal venue for those who are looking for a nice peaceful place to climb in a very beautiful surrounding. The gorge itself and the climbing areas are highly unsuitable for kids and toddlers, but nearby there is a small lake with a lovely setting that has picnic tables, and serves as a perfect hangout for anyone on toddler duty for the day. Don't miss the local town of Sault, it is only a short distance away and has some nice relaxing bars, and enjoys some 'relative' coolness since it is situated at nearly 800m.

Rocher Malaval: 25 routes, 6c-7b+, 20-35m high, Alt 600m, SE facing (no topo)
Rocher Blanchard: 9 routes, 6c-7b+, 19m high, Alt 750m, E facing (1 topo)
Envol: 6 routes, 6c-8b, 20-25m high, Alt 550m, SE facing (1 topo)
Archéo: 25 routes, 5-7b, 10-25m high, Alt 550m, S facing (2 topo)
Belvédère:30 routes, 5c-7a+, 25-45m high, Alt 650m, S facing (no topo)

Gorges de la Nesque - Monieux

— 500m —

Sault

Monieux

D942

D96

Villes-sur-Auzon

Rocher Blanchard

Flaoussiers

GR 9

la Nesque

Malaval

Archéo

Envol

Chapelle St-Michel

Le Belvédère

Rocher Blanchard

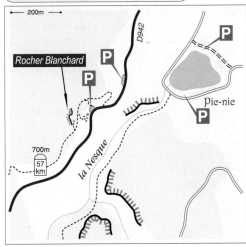

— 200m —

D942

Rocher Blanchard

P

P

Pic-nic

P

la Nesque

700m
57
km

Envol & Rocher Archéo

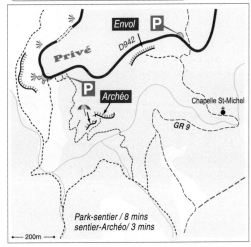

Envol   P

D942

Privé

P   Archéo

Chapelle St-Michel

GR 9

Park-sentier / 8 mins
sentier-Archéo/ 3 mins

— 200m —

Camping Municipal du Deffends*
Sault, 84390 Vaucluse (1.7km-NE par D950 rte. de St-Trinit)
Tel: 04 90 64 07 18
Notes: Town situated at 765 metres, and much cooler than the lower valleys. Site not visited.
Open: (Mai-Sept) - 100 places; about 9 hectares

Camping Les Verguettes
Villes-sur-Auzon, 84570 Vaucluse
Tel: 04 90 61 88 18   Fax: 04 90 61 97 87
Notes: Well advertised in the town with a banner across the road. Small town with nice restaurants and a quiet feel.
Open: (Mai-Sept) - 80 places; about 1 hectares

Bar: Sault, Villes-sur-Auzon
Shop: Sault, Villes-sur-Auzon
Petrol Station: Sault, Villes-sur-Auzon
Restaurant: Monieux, Sault
Supermarket: Sault
Tourist Bureau: Monieux, Sault

Access: There is certainly a long history of climbing in the Gorge, This area is very wild and has always been quiet, and an area much enjoyed by walkers, bird watchers and other wildlife enthusiasts. There is a long history of climbing, but only at a minimal level, so please try to blend in and keep this a quiet and tranquil spot.
Rocher Blanchard: You can't miss it.
Envol: Locate the parking near the GR9 footpath and signpost to Sainte Michel,downhill and back on yourself.
Archéo: Park just near the Belvédère (do not block the private drive or enter the land marked privé). A path runs parallel to the road for 50m before dropping straight down the hill. This path is marked with red and blue dashes. After 6 mins there is a vague path off to the left (do not take this because it takes you to to above the cliff and you cannot descend). At 8mins, the whole path turns left and you can clearly see two cliffs. The marked footpath descends into the gorge, whilst a small path leads past the big overhangs and up to the cliff. Total 13 mins.

Side tabs: BLANCHARD · ARCHÉO · CORNIRETTE · QUINSAN · VENASQUE · ST.PIERRE · COLOMBIER · CLAPIS · GLISSE · TYROLIENNE · CASCADE-HAUT · CHRISTOPHE · A.LA.GARDE · GRAND TRAV. · COMBE OBS. · GROSEAU

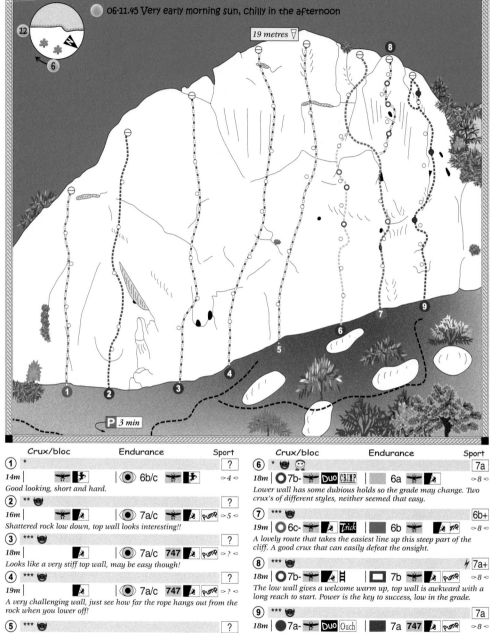

06-11.45 Very early morning sun, chilly in the afternoon

12

19 metres

N

6

8

7

9

5

6

4

3

2

1

P 3 min

	Crux/bloc	Endurance	Sport
(1) *			?
14m		● 6b/c	∘4∘

Good looking, short and hard.

	Crux/bloc	Endurance	Sport
(2) **			?
16m		● 7a/c Pump	∘5∘

Shattered rock low down, top wall looks interesting!!

	Crux/bloc	Endurance	Sport
(3) ***			?
18m		● 7a/c 747 Pump	∘?∘

Looks like a very stiff top wall, may be easy though!

	Crux/bloc	Endurance	Sport
(4) ***			?
19m		● 7a/c 747 Pump	∘?∘

A very challenging wall, just see how far the rope hangs out from the rock when you lower off!

	Crux/bloc	Endurance	Sport
(5) ***			?
19m		● 6b/c Pump	∘?∘

Maybe easier than it looks and with no hard moves, but you will need stamina though.

	Crux/bloc	Endurance	Sport
(6) *			7a
18m	○ 7b- Duo CRIMP	6a	∘8∘

Lower wall has some dubious holds so the grade may change. Two crux's of different styles, neither seemed that easy.

	Crux/bloc	Endurance	Sport
(7) ***			6b+
19m	○ 6c- Trick	6b mp	∘8∘

A lovely route that takes the easiest line up this steep part of the cliff. A good crux that can easily defeat the onsight.

	Crux/bloc	Endurance	Sport
(8) ***			⚡ 7a+
18m	○ 7b-	□ 7b Pump	∘8∘

The low wall gives a welcome warm up, top wall is awkward with a long reach to start. Power is the key to success, low in the grade.

	Crux/bloc	Endurance	Sport
(9) ***			7a
18m	● 7a- Duo Ouch	7a 747 Pump	∘8∘

Lower wall has some dubious holds so the grade may change. Two crux's of different style, neither seemed that easy.

Résumé. A lovely small crag in a very quiet setting above highland meadows with a small lake, plus excellent views of the area and across to Sault. At this altitude and facing east, a place to stay cool on hot days. Lower part of cliff is poor rock and will need a few sika holds in the future perhaps. Top half is superb limestone, but is still exceptionally sharp. Finger tape is helpful to protect 4th and 5th fingers. A lot steeper than it looks which makes onsighting a vicious affair! You could spend 2 days here, but your skin and fingertip pain threshold will be severely tested in only a single day.

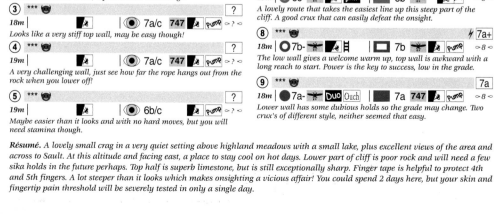

VOIE SIX (Facile 7b- bloc), Rocher Blanchard; Carrie Atchison-Jones

BLANCHARD

ARCHÉO

CORNIRETTE

QUINSAN

VENASQUE

ST-PIERRE

COLOMBIER

CLAPIS

GLISSE

TYROLIENNE

CASCADE-HAUT

CHRISTOPHE

A.LAGARDE

GRAND TRAV

COMBE OBS.

GROSEAU

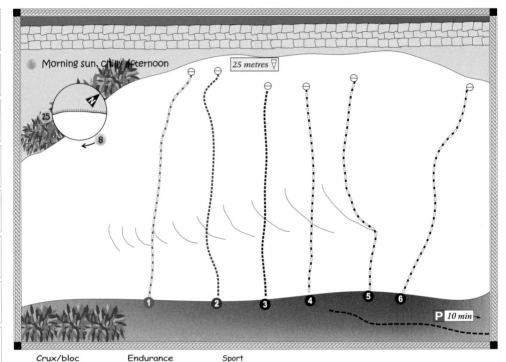

Morning sun, chilly afternoon

25 metres

	Crux/bloc	Endurance	Sport
1	Docteur from		6c
2	Mister Grany		7a+
3	Kohl chie dans les pres		7c
4	Titanesque		8a
5	Project		8 ?
6	Project		8a+ ?

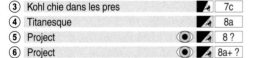

Résumé. *A small cliff that is a nice morning sun trap. A bit on the steep side for most people, and you have to get straight into pocket cranking with very little warm up. A couple of projects to go at for the strong climber.*

Access: *Take the GR9 footpath down towards the gorge and signposted Chapelle St. Michel. The cliff is soon seen to the right - just below the road. A path leads back to the base of the cliff. The right end overhangs by almost 10 metres!*

Envol

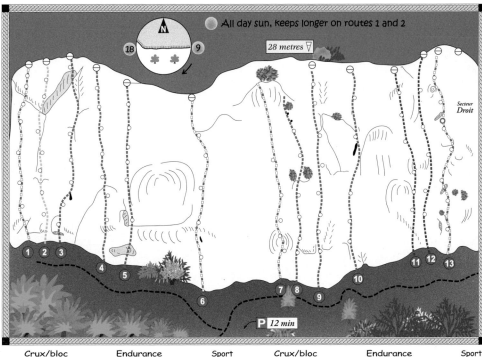

All day sun, keeps longer on routes 1 and 2

28 metres

Secteur Droit

P 12 min

	Crux/bloc	Endurance	Sport
1	?**		6b/c
	? m		
	Sharp rock, not climbed often.		
2	?**		6a
	? m		
	Sharp rock, not climbed often.		
3	?**		6a/b+
	? m		
	Sharp rock, not climbed often.		
4	?**		6a/b
	? m		
	Sharp rock, not climbed often.		
5	Ventougnol**		6a/b+
	? m		
	Sharp rock, not climbed often.		
6	?**		6b/c
	? m		
	Sharp rock, not climbed often.		

	Crux/bloc	Endurance	Sport
7	?**		6b/c
	? m		
	Sharp rock, not climbed often.		
8	?**		6a/b
	? m		
	Sharp rock, not climbed often.		
9	?**		6a/b
	26m		
	Sharp rock, not climbed often.		
10	?**		6a/b
	26m		
	Sharp rock, not climbed often.		
11	?**		6c/7a
	? m		
	Sharp rock, not climbed often.		
12	?**		7a/?
	? m		
	Sharp rock, not climbed often.		
13	?**		6b/c
	?m		
	Sharp rock, not climbed often.		

Résumé. *A very nice small crag that gives mainly vertical climbing. The limestone is classic Verdon style with water pockets (Gouttes d'eau), that demands strong fingers, but also good skill with the toes in trying to stand in such silly shaped holds. The rock is sharp and be prepared for edges to snap off as there has been little climbing here. This section does have some steep parts that offer some beefy moves. Nothing too difficult here. Quite sheltered from the wind at the base of a small hollow and with a bay to the left. Very quick drying and not much of a drainage problem. Great views without exposure, belaying can be dones either in sun, or the shade of the trees.*

Gauche　　　　　-　　　　　Droit

Side tabs: BLANCHARD, ARCHÉO, CORNEIRETTE, QUINSAN, VENASQUE, ST.PIERRE, COLOMBIER, CLAPIS, GLISSE, TYROLIENNE, CASCADE-HAUT, CHRISTOPHE, A.LAGARDE, GRAND TRAV, COMBE OBS., GROSEAU

Gorges de la Nesque - from the Belvédère

Archéo - centre left above overhanging section.

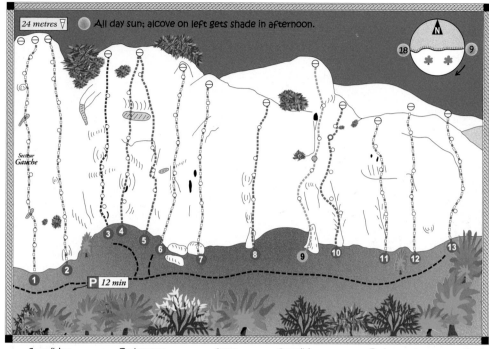

24 metres ▽   All day sun; alcove on left gets shade in afternoon.

Secteur
Gauche

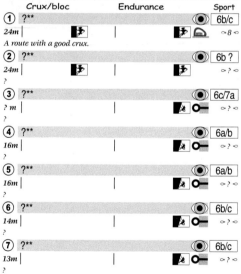
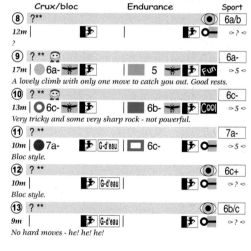

	Crux/bloc	Endurance	Sport
①	?**		6b/c
24m			∼8∼

A route with a good crux.

②	?**		6b ?
24m			∼?∼
?			

③	?**		6c/7a
? m			∼?∼
?			

④	?**		6a/b
16m			∼?∼
?			

⑤	?**		6a/b
16m			∼?∼
?			

⑥	?**		6b/c
14m			∼?∼
?			

⑦	?**		6b/c
13m			∼?∼
?			

	Crux/bloc	Endurance	Sport
⑧	?**		6a/b
12m			∼?∼
?			

⑨	?**		6a-
17m	6a-	5 Fun	∼5∼

A lovely climb with only one move to catch you out. Good rests.

⑩	?**		6c-
13m	6c-	6b- Cool	∼5∼

Very tricky and some very sharp rock - not powerful.

⑪	?**		7a-
10m	7a- G-d'eau	6c-	∼5∼

Bloc style.

⑫	?**		6c+
10m	G-d'eau		∼?∼

Bloc style.

⑬	?**		6b/c
9m	G-d'eau		∼?∼

No hard moves - he! he! he!

Résumé. This side is smaller and offers a good variety of routes. Routes on the far right are short, and require strong fingers to work in the gouttes d'eau (water pockets). Peaceful and still very sharp rock with excellent friction. Quite a sheltered sector and a sun trap to make a warm afternoon.

Gauche   -   Droit

BLANCHARD · ARCHÉO · CORNEIRETTE · QUINSAN · VENASQUE · ST.PIERRE · COLOMBIER · CLAPIS · GLISE · TYROLIENNE · CASCADE-HAUT · CHRISTOPHE · A.LAGARDE · GRAND TRAV · COMBE OBS. · GROSEAU

La route très populaire du sud de Venasque vous emmène au village de Murs en passant par Combe de Vaulounge (D4). Cette route a des emplacements de pique-nique très sympas et le paysage est superbe. Il y a même une falaise equipée sur cette route mais la roche est tellement friable que nous ne l'avons pas incluse dans ce topo. La meilleure zone d'escalade se trouve en quittant la D4 et en suivant la D177 vers Gourdes. Après environ 5 minutes, juste après un virage, vous découvrirez les falaises de Corneirette qui forment une gorge. Cette gorge a trois atouts majeurs: paix et tranquilité, un cadre idyllique et fraîcheur le matin (certains secteurs restent à l'ombre jusqu'à 15h). Certaines sections sont très abruptes et demandent beaucoup de force et d'endurance et si vous n'êtes pas à l'aise en 7a vous risquez de ne pas pouvoir beaucoup grimper sur ces falaises. La qualité de la roche varie entre excellente et très dangereuse. Les strates sont brisées et sur certains dévers il y a des blocs qui sont prêts à tomber. Certaines voies sont douteuses et c'est à vous de décider s'il vaut la peine de prendre le risque de les grimper. Cependant lorsque la roche est de bonne qualité les voies sont superbes et demandent un effort soutenu. C'est également une bonne alternative aux voies difficiles de Venasque et aux prises très rondes de Quinsan. Nous n'avons pas eu le temps de faire beaucoup de voies sur ces falaises mais celles que nous avons grimpées étaient aussi difficiles qu'elles le paraissaient. Bonne aventure!

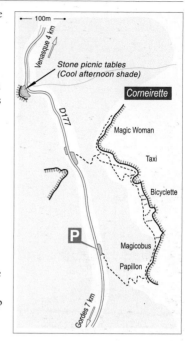

If you think that some of the rock at Venasque is dodgy!!! Well, head south to the gorges on the way to Buoux, and you can re-define the meaning of dodgy rock. The popular road south from Venasque takes the Combe de Vaulounge (D4) on the way to the village of Murs. This route has some great picnic spots and the scenery is fab. There is even an equipped cliff on this road, but the looseness of the rock eliminates it from topo inclusion in this book. The best climbing to be found in this area is when you turn off the main D4, and follow the D177 south towards Gourdes. Be warned, very soon after the turning up this road, the scenery changes into towers of tottering rock, held together by imaginary glue! After a 5 mins drive, you turn a bend and see a substantial section of cliffs that form a gorge fit for climbing. Welcome to the cliffs of Corneirette.

This gorge has three major attractions; peace and quiet, a lovely setting, and staying cool during the morning, (with some sectors staying in the shade up until 3pm). It also has some rather steep sections that demand considerable strength and stamina; so if you don't climb well – forget it. If you can't crank 7a happily, then you are unlikely to get much from a visit to this spot. It does however have a major detraction, in that the quality of rock varies from very good – to abominably awful and incredibly dangerous. The rock strata is shattered, and some overhangs have tottering loose blocks that makes walking below them – a very fearful experience! Some of the routes here are highly questionable, on whole sections of the cliff that could fall down. You really have to make a life and death issue if you want to climb on some of these routes. I am sure that you will see a few bolts on the ground in the years to come! This all said, when the rock is good, the routes are wonderfully sustained and give invigorating climbing of the highest standard. It also offers a really pleasant alternative to the ridiculous angle of the harder routes at Venasque, and the pumpy sweaty and rounded holds of Quinsan. We didn't have time to climb many routes here, so we can't give you precise info. Of the routes that we did climb, the historic grades that we had been given were usually complete sandbags in the lower grades, and the climbs were usually as hard as they looked. Enjoy your adventurous time here!

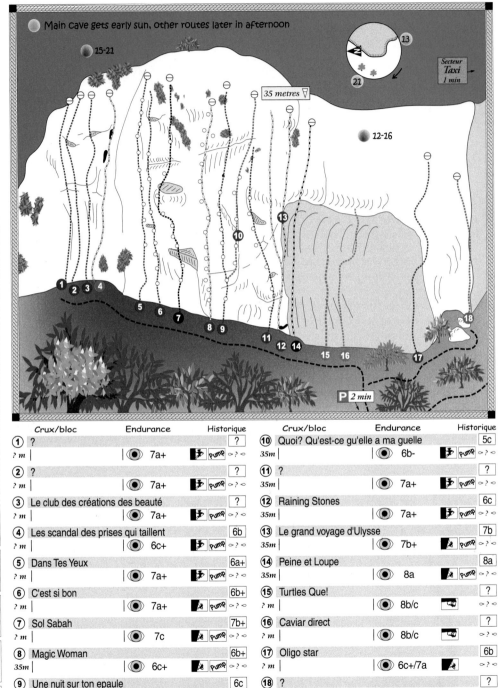

Main cave gets early sun, other routes later in afternoon

15-21

13

35 metres

Secteur Taxi 1 min

21

12-16

BLANCHARD | ARCHÉO | CORNEIRETTE | QUINSAN | VENASQUE | ST.PIERRE | COLOMBIER | CLAPIS | GLISE | TYROLIENNE | CASCADE-HAUT | CHRISTOPHE | A.LAGARDE | GRAND TRAV | COMBE OBS. | GROSEAU

	Crux/bloc	Endurance	Historique
①	?	7a+	?
②	?	7a+	?
③	Le club des créations des beauté	7a+	?
④	Les scandal des prises qui taillent	6c+	6b
⑤	Dans Tes Yeux	7a+	6a+
⑥	C'est si bon	7a+	6b+
⑦	Sol Sabah	7c	7b+
⑧	Magic Woman	6c+	6b+
⑨	Une nuit sur ton epaule	7a	6c
⑩	Quoi? Qu'est-ce gu'elle a ma guelle	6b-	5c
⑪	?	7a+	?
⑫	Raining Stones	7a+	6c
⑬	Le grand voyage d'Ulysse	7b+	7b
⑭	Peine et Loupe	8a	8a
⑮	Turtles Que!	8b/c	?
⑯	Caviar direct	8b/c	?
⑰	Oligo star	6c+/7a	6b
⑱	?	6a/b	?

Résumé. A very impressive sector that looks quite stiff. Some of the historic grades look a bit on the mean side in the lower grades, and from experience here - they are likely to be a lot harder than suggested. Worth checking out though.

| Magic Woman | - | Taxi | - | Bicyclette | - | Magicobus | - | Papillon |

Secteur Magic Woman, Corneirette

Secteurs Bicyclette-Papillon, Corneirette

View from Papillon secteur

Secteur Papillon

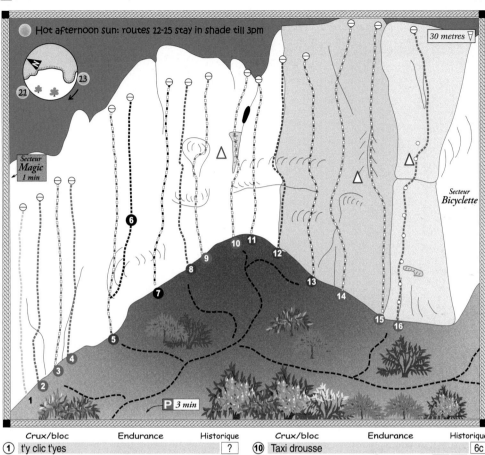

Hot afternoon sun: routes 12-15 stay in shade till 3pm

30 metres

Secteur *Magic* 1 min

Secteur *Bicyclette*

P 3 min

	Crux/bloc	Endurance	Historique
(1)	t'y clic t'yes		?
? m		6a+	∘?∘
(2)	Modeste et Geniale		?
? m		6b	∘?∘
(3)	Chamomile		6a
? m		6c	∘?∘
(4)	Réminiscence sompre aux couleurs d'améthyse		?
? m		6b	∘?∘
(5)	Ligne et Plasir		?
? m		7b+	Pump ∘?∘
(6)	?		?
? m		7c	Pump ∘?∘
(7)	Pignes et Desirs		?
? m		8a	∘?∘
(8)	Verdonerie △		6c
? m			Pump
(9)	Burque les briges aiment la Cornerette		6b+
? m		6c+	

	Crux/bloc	Endurance	Historique
(10)	Taxi drousse		6c
? m		6c+	DIEDRE ∘?∘
(11)	? Que		7b
? m		7b+	∘?∘
(12)	La Corne raide		7a
? m		7b	∘?∘
(13)	Mortilicou		7b
? m		7b+	∘?∘
(14)	?		6a
? m		6c+	∘?∘
(15)	Rio Grande		6b+
? m		6c+	
(16)	Pilier des Sages △		6a
? m		6b+	∘?∘

A well cleaned and excellent 6a first half. Dubious rock above may be lethal one day! Not recommended!

Résumé. This bay to the left of the big Pilier des Sages, has some horrific looking loose rock all over it. The climbing looks good in parts, but your belayer might need a helmet and body armour. Climbing here could be enjoyable, but a certain amount of caution would be prudent.

Magic Woman	-	Taxi	-	Bicyclette	-	Magicobus	-	Papillon

BLANCHARD · ARCHÉO · CORNEIRETTE · QUINSAN · VENASQUE · ST.PIERRE · COLOMBIER · CLAPIS · GLISSE · TYROLIENNE · CASCADE-HAUT · CHRISTOPHE · A.LAGARDE · GRAND TRAV · COMBE OBS. · GROSEAU

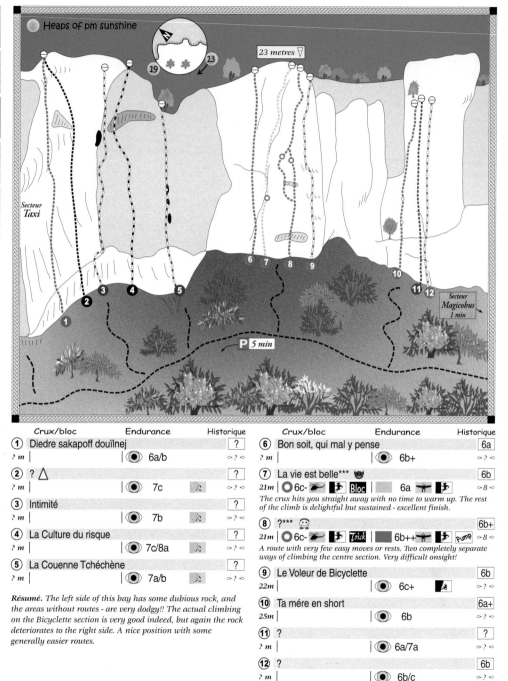

Heaps of pm sunshine

23 metres

Secteur Taxi

Secteur Magicobus 1 min

P 5 min

	Crux/bloc	Endurance	Historique
①	Diedre sakapoff douïlnej		?
? m		⊙ 6a/b	⌐?⌐
②	? △		?
? m		⊙ 7c	⌐?⌐
③	Intimité		?
? m		⊙ 7b	⌐?⌐
④	La Culture du risque		?
? m		⊙ 7c/8a	⌐?⌐
⑤	La Couenne Tchéchène		?
? m		⊙ 7a/b	⌐?⌐

Résumé. *The left side of this bay has some dubious rock, and the areas without routes - are very dodgy!! The actual climbing on the Bicyclette section is very good indeed, but again the rock deteriorates to the right side. A nice position with some generally easier routes.*

	Crux/bloc	Endurance	Historique
⑥	Bon soit, qui mal y pense		6a
? m		⊙ 6b+	⌐?⌐
⑦	La vie est belle*** 😎		6b
21m	◯ 6c- ✈ 🧗 Bloc	6a ☀ 🧗	⌐8⌐

The crux hits you straight away with no time to warm up. The rest of the climb is delightful but sustained - excellent finish.

⑧	?*** 😊		6b+
21m	◯ 6c- ✈ 🧗 Trick	6b++ ☀ 🧗 Pump	⌐8⌐

A route with very few easy moves or rests. Two completely separate ways of climbing the centre section. Very difficult onsight!

	Crux/bloc	Endurance	Historique
⑨	Le Voleur de Bicyclette		6b
22m		⊙ 6c+ 🧗	⌐?⌐
⑩	Ta mére en short		6a+
25m		⊙ 6b	⌐?⌐
⑪	?		?
? m		⊙ 6a/7a	⌐?⌐
⑫	?		6b
? m		⊙ 6b/c	⌐?⌐

BOREAL

LA VIE EST BELLE 6c-, Corneirette; Carrie Atchison-Jones

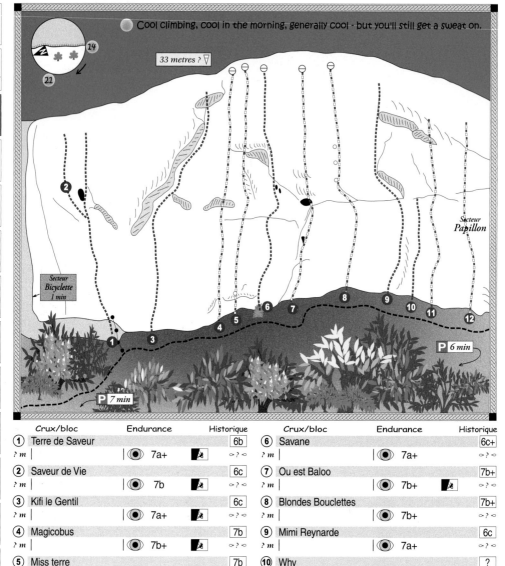

Cool climbing, cool in the morning, generally cool - but you'll still get a sweat on.

33 metres ?

Secteur Bicyclette 1 min

Secteur Papillon

P 6 min

P 7 min

	Crux/bloc	Endurance	Historique			Crux/bloc	Endurance	Historique
(1)	Terre de Saveur		6b		(6)	Savane		6c+
? m		7a+			? m		7a+	
(2)	Saveur de Vie		6c		(7)	Ou est Baloo		7b+
? m		7b			? m		7b+	
(3)	Kifi le Gentil		6c		(8)	Blondes Bouclettes		7b+
? m		7a+			? m		7b+	
(4)	Magicobus		7b		(9)	Mimi Reynarde		6c
? m		7b+			? m		7a+	
(5)	Miss terre		7b		(10)	Why		?
? m		7b+			? m		7a+/?	
					(11)	Tom regard Diamonds douces		?
					? m		7b+	
					(12)	Sous les jupes des filles		6c & 7a+
					? m		7b+	

Résumé. *This high sector is very impressive. Mostly stable rock but with a lot of small stones that are likely to come off, so be on your guard. A lot of the routes have been awarded grade 6 status; this could be a bit misleading since they look like easy grade sevens in reality. All of the routes are quite long and sustained, so you will need to be fit. It's most useful attribute is that it stays in cool shade until 2pm in summer, and with trees to belay in the shade. In winter it gets afternoon sunshine, but the belayer will need to wrap up. A lovely position and feels very airy.*

Side tabs: BLANCHARD · ARCHÉO · CORNEIRETTE · QUINSAN · VENASQUE · ST.PIERRE · COLOMBIER · CLAPIS · GLISSE · TYROLIENNE · CASCADE-HAUT · CHRISTOPHE · A.LAGARDE · GRAND TRAV' · COMBE OBS. · GROSEAU

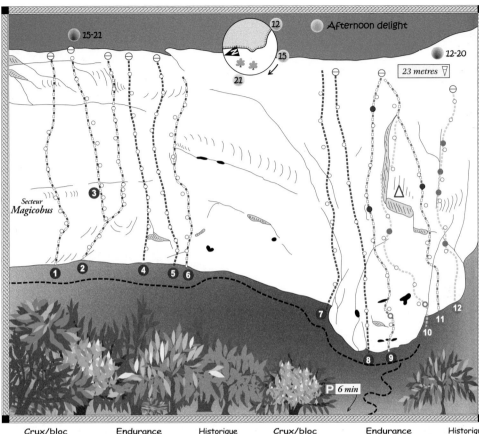

Secteur *Magicobus*

Afternoon delight

23 metres

P 6 min

Sidebar tabs: BLANCHARD · ARCHÉO · CORNEIRETTE · QUINSAN · VENASQUE · ST.PIERRE · COLOMBIER · CLAPIS · GLISSE · TYROLIENNE · CASCADE-HAUT · CHRISTOPHE · A.LAGARDE · GRAND TRAV · COMBE OBS. · GROSEAU

	Crux/bloc	Endurance	Historique
①	**Sous les jupes des filles**		6c & 7a+
? m		⊙ 7b	∽?∽
②	**Jeu de dupe**		7a+
? m		⊙ 7b	∽?∽
③	**Mistouflon**		7b
? m		⊙ 7b	∽?∽
④	**D'un Papillon a une etoile**	⚷	7a
? m		⊙ 7a+	∽?∽
⑤	**Planete fa**		7a+
? m		⊙ 7a+	∽?∽
⑥	**Lueur**		7a+
? m		⊙ 7b	Pump ∽?∽

Résumé. This top right sector gets the best views in the gorge and some lovely afternoon sunshine. Some of the rock is very poor, and large chunks will no doubt fall off at some point. Go carefully here because of this. Position is fantastic and the climbing moves are very good indeed, so most probably worth a check out.

Warning: Large pillar on the right is detached. There are bolts in it, but it could fall at any time!

	Crux/bloc	Endurance	Historique
⑦	**Bourinette**		7a
? m		⊙ 7a+	Pump ∽?∽
⑧	**Kiki le Honteux**		6c
23m		⊙ 7a	Bloc ∽8∽
⑨	**Le Chat dans le Vent**✶✶		6b+
21m	● 7a- Trick	☐ 6c Pump	∽8∽

Lower wall has some hard and powerful lock offs, much easier when you know how, top wall can prove quite tricky.

	Crux/bloc	Endurance	Historique
⑩	**Kokocelle** △		5c+
21m	○ 6c-	6a	∽8∽

A very powerful start is needed, footholds usually shatter off at this point. The wall above is climbed on good pockets, but is steep and tiring. Big flake will come away someday. A very dangerous area!!

	Crux/bloc	Endurance	Historique
⑪	**Cafe-chocolate** △		6a
? m		⊙ 6c-	CRIMP ∽?∽
⑫	**Vanille** △		5c
18m	● 6b	6a+ Pump	∽7∽

Poor rock and a dangerous top flake makes this an unsure outing. A few hard moves and without any rests either; the angle will spit off anyone not cruising 6c.

SIROCCO 7a+, Place de l'Ascle, Venasque; Vincent Maillocheau

Venasque est le village provençal par excellence, superbe et imposant sutout lorsque vous arrivez depuis le nord. Nous vous conseillons d'aller au café/restaurant "Les Ramparts" qui est très sympathique et idéal pour se relaxer avant d'aller grimper. Il est préférable de visiter le village à pied puisqu'il y est très difficile de s'y garer. Bien qu'assez petit vous y trouverez un bureau de poste, un office du tourisme et plusieurs galleries de peinture ainsi que des boutiques d'art mais rien d'aussi commercial que St Paul-de-Vence sur la Côte d'Azur. La vue sur Carpentras et le Mont Ventoux depuis la fontaine, à la sortie du village, est imprenable. S'il fait trop chaud pour grimper nous vous conseillons de visiter Le Beaucet, puis la Roque-sur-Pernes et enfin Saint-Didier. La falaise de Venasque est visible depuis le parking du haut du village. Il y a 10 falaises assez petites, certaines sur des terrains privés où l'escalade n'est pas autorisée. Il y a heureusement de nombreuses autres falaises où l'accès est autorisé et où les voies sont très bien equipées. Soyez respectueux lorsque vous grimpez dans cette zone, garez-vous convenablement et gardez les falaises propres. Enfin lisez les notices affichez et suivez les consignes. Il est apparent que la roche de Venasque est du même type que celle du calcaire des Molasses. Les grimpeurs anglais la compareait à du grès. Les prises sont rondes et elles vous fatigueront autant que si vous grimpiez sur les prises arrondies d'une salle d'escalade. Les goujons paraissent bien placés et ont été fixés avec de la colle à résine. Cependant attention à la roche qui est assez friable et qui peut se détacher par gros morceaux. Soyez en particulier très prudent après la pluie du fait des infiltrations d'eau. A Quinsan l'humidité est un élément crucial car de nombreuses prises primordiales sont des aplats très glissants. L'escalade y est pafaite un matin d'hiver ensoleillé. La partie centrale de Venasque a une sélection de voies qui testeront votre endurance. Le secteur Saint-Pierre a soit des dévers brutaux avec quelques prises fabriquées ou des voies très techniques. Les secteurs défilent les uns après les autres avec des voies excellentes mais qui sont essentiellement très difficiles. Leurs mouvements puissants ressemblent à ceux que l'on trouve en bloc.

Venasque, is one of the most quintessential Provencal hill top villages, looking both superb and commanding when you drive up towards it from a northerly direction. Take the right fork, which then allows you to wind up the hill to the right, and arriving at the top of the village. It is definitely worth seeking out the café restaurant, Les Ramparts, which has an excellent terrace and is an ideal spot to chill out before taking on some serious muscle stretching activities later. The village is best explored on foot since parking is at a premium. It's small, but does have a quaint shop, post office, tourist office, and several galleries and arty boutiquey booths; but fortunately nothing like the commercial transformation of St. Paul-de-Vence on the Côte d'Azur. The view from the fountain at the end of the village is superb towards the plain of Carpentras and beyond to Mont Ventoux. If the sun has gone into overdrive for the day, pick up some information from the tiny office de tourisme in the village, and take a leisurely tourist drive (past the main cliff of Venasque) to Le Beaucet, then La Roque-sur-Pernes, and eventually Saint-Didier. On the other hand, if it isn't too hot, from the parking at the top of the village you can look across to the cliffs opposite where the climbing is. There are about 10 small cliffs in the tiny valley west of Venasque. Some of these are on private land and there is no climbing allowed. Fortunately; there are delicate access agreements for many of the other cliffs, and these have well equipped routes. Please be very considerate and sensible about climbing in this whole area, park considerately, and keep the cliffs exceptionally clean and tidy, observe and follow any access signposts that are displayed. As soon as you see the cliffs beneath Venasque, the softness of the Molasses limestone becomes apparent. Any UK climber will call this sandstone or gritstone, and treat it as such. Rounded holds are the order of the day here, and you will get as pumped quite similar to an indoor climbing wall with large sloping holds. All the different sectors here have their own particular style, but it is very much a variation on a basic sandstone theme. The bolts in the rock look well placed and are resin glue placements. They are unlikely to break, but the rock in general is soft and can pull out in chunks, so beware. After wet weather with seepage the rock is substantially weaker. Qunisan is where most climbs have a series of holds – not too unusual, hmmm; but it's when these run out that it all goes pear shaped. The crux's tend to be slopers and slippery, so even though it faces north-east and is in shade on hot afternoons, low humidity is the most critical factor. Just like English gritstone, climbing here is perfect on a sunny winters morning with a soft breeze. Venasque centre section has an assortment of climbs with holds all the way! These simply test your stamina, and don't require too much brain power. Sector Saint-Pierre is either brutally overhanging with a few fabricated holds, or it's vertical and technical - just like Quinsan. Then the sectors just keep on coming with excellent climbing on variable rock, the routes are predominantly very hard, and have powerful boulder problem style crux's.

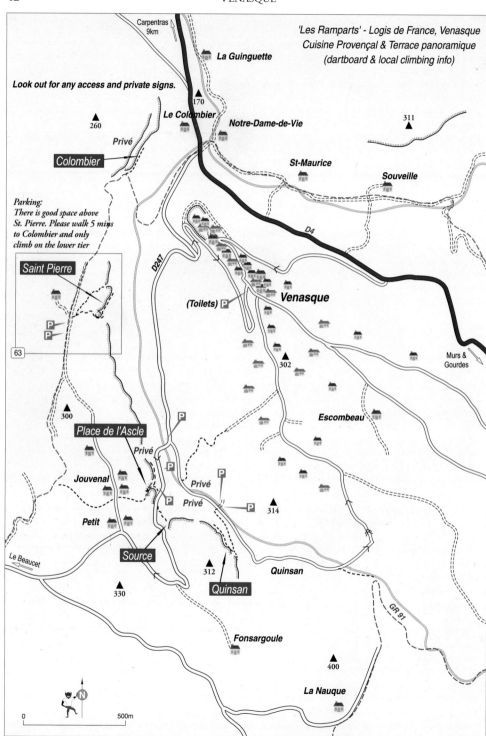

'Les Ramparts' - Logis de France, Venasque
Cuisine Provençal & Terrace panoramique
(dartboard & local climbing info)

Carpentras
9km

La Guinguette

Look out for any access and private signs.

170

Le Colombier

Notre-Dame-de-Vie

311

260

Privé

St-Maurice

Souveille

Colombier

D4

Parking:
There is good space above
St. Pierre. Please walk 5 mins
to Colombier and only
climb on the lower tier

D247

Saint Pierre

(Toilets) P

Venasque

63

302

Murs &
Gourdes

300

Escombeau

Place de l'Ascle

P

Privé

Jouvenal

Privé

P

Privé

P

314

Petit

Le Beaucet

Source

312

Quinsan

Quinsan

330

GR 91

Fonsargoule

400

N

La Nauque

0   500m

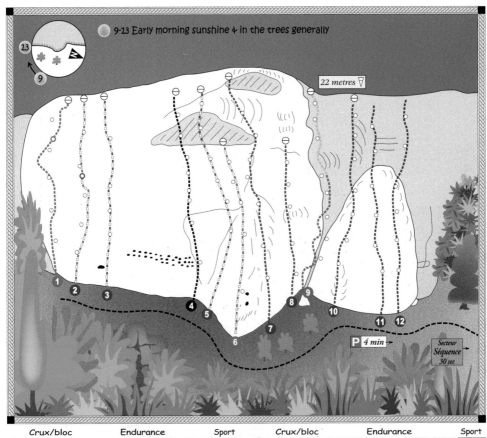

9-13 Early morning sunshine & in the trees generally

22 metres

P 4 min →

Secteur Séquence 30 sec

Right margin tabs: BLANCHARD · ARCHÉO · CORNEIRETTE · QUINSAN · VENASQUE · ST.PIERRE · COLOMBIER · CLAPIS · GLISSE · TYROLIENNE · CASCADE-HAUT · CHRISTOPHE · A.LAGARDE · GRAND TRAV · COMBE OBS. · GROSEAU

	Crux/bloc	Endurance	Sport
(1) Illustrator* 😊			6b
16m	6c- Sloper	6b 747	⊙ 5 ⊙

A very good wall climb and perfect for those with small fingers who like sustained climbing; not a very pleasant lead.

(2) Magazine			6c+
14m	7U- Sloper	0c	⊙ 6 ⊙

A really nasty section of wall on slopers - avoid in hot weather, and very difficult onsight.

(3) Profil			7a+
18m			⊙ ? ⊙

(4) Project			?
20m	Bloc	⊙ ?	⊙ 8 ⊙

(5) Ticket Repas 😊			7b+
21m	Bloc		⊙ ? ⊙

(6) L'etat de grace 😊			6b+
15m	Bloc		⊙ 5 ⊙

	Crux/bloc	Endurance	Sport
(7) Macintosh			7a
? m		Pump	⊙ 8 ⊙

(8) Gangster d'amour 😊			7a+
? m		Pump	⊙ 8 ⊙

(9) Hyper Brown* 😊			6b-
22m	6b- DIEDRE B///	6a	⊙ 9 ⊙

A really bizzare crack that is best climbed facing left, with a wide array of bridging techniques. Will crumple your best suit. Top is fun and still presents quite a challenge.

(10) Technofrite			7a+
? m			⊙ ? ⊙

(11) Biodynamique			7a
? m			⊙ ? ⊙

(12) 1992			7a
? m			⊙ ? ⊙

Résumé. *A nice sector of clean and very solid rock. Mostly wall climbing in the "just off vertical style." The classic diedre of Hyper brown is not to be missed. A nice tranquil sector and often very quiet.*

BLANCHARD | ARCHÉO | CORNERETTE | QUINSAN | VENASQUE | ST.PIERRE | COLOMBIER | CLAPIS | GLISSE | TYROLIENNE | CASCADE-HAUT | CHRISTOPHE | A.LAGARDE | GRAND TRAV | COMBE OBS. | GROSEAU

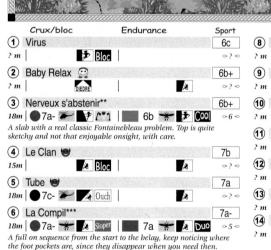

Mostly only morning sun and the bays getting shade 11am onwards.

22 metres

Secteur *Hyper*

Secteur *Feu* 15 sec

P 3 min

P 3 min

	Crux/bloc	Endurance	Sport
1 Virus	? m Bloc		6c ∞?
2 Baby Relax	? m DIEDRE		6b+ ∞?
3 Nerveux s'abstenir**	18m 7a 6b Cool		6b+ ∞6

A slab with a real classic Fontainebleau problem. Top is quite sketchy and not that enjoyable onsight, with care.

	Crux/bloc	Endurance	Sport
4 Le Clan	15m Bloc		7b ∞?
5 Tube	18m 7c- Ouch		7a ∞?
6 La Compil***	18m 7a Sloper 7a Duo		7a- ∞5

A full on sequence from the start to the belay, keep noticing where the foot pockets are, since they disappear when you need then.

	Crux/bloc	Endurance	Sport
7 Jour pour jour	22m Pump		6c ∞8

	Crux/bloc	Endurance	Sport
8 Action	? m		7a+ ∞8
9 Séquence Passion	? m		6b+ ∞8
10 Nicotine & Goudron	? m		6c ∞?
11 Microcosme	? m		6b ∞?
12 Le Pilier des aléas	? m		7a ∞?
13 Les arts ménagers	? m		6b ∞?
14 ?????	? m		6a ∞?

Résumé. *An impressive and substantial sector that offers some good routes. Rarely do you get offered good holds and you are guaranteed to get pumped. Some of the bolting seems a bit mean in the lower grade routes, simply because of the lack of good holds! Some of the routes look considerably hard for the grades and require a lot dogging practice to work out the moves. Beta lowers the grade massively.*

COMPIL 7a-, Quinsan; Jim Bacon

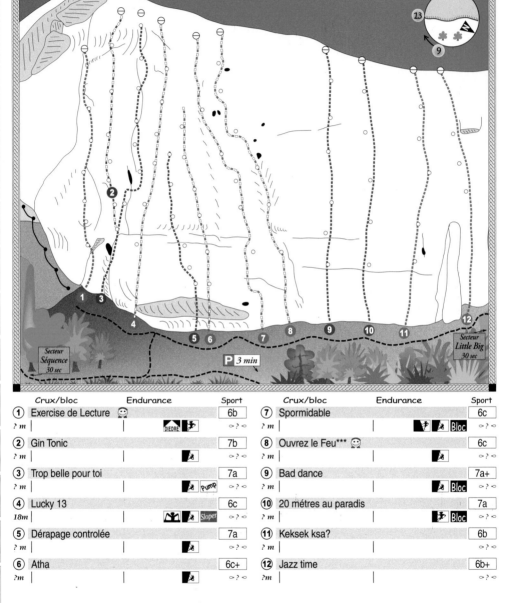

	Crux/bloc	Endurance	Sport		Crux/bloc	Endurance	Sport
①	Exercise de Lecture ☺	DIEDRE	6b	⑦	Spormidable	Bloc	6c
	? m		∽?∽		? m		∽?∽
②	Gin Tonic		7b	⑧	Ouvrez le Feu*** ☺		6c
	? m		∽?∽		? m		∽?∽
③	Trop belle pour toi	Pump	7a	⑨	Bad dance	Bloc	7a+
	? m		∽?∽		? m		∽?∽
④	Lucky 13	Sloper	6c	⑩	20 métres au paradis	Bloc	7a
	18m		∽?∽		? m		∽?∽
⑤	Dérapage controlée		7a	⑪	Keksek ksa?		6b
	? m		∽?∽		? m		∽?∽
⑥	Atha		6c+	⑫	Jazz time		6b+
	?m		∽?∽		?m		∽?∽

Résumé. *Some very good looking routes with plenty of sustained climbing on Quinsan slopers.*
Access: You can get to the next sector on the left, by taking the nice lower path - rather than the rope in the muddy gulley.

LUCKY 13   6c, Quinsan; Victor Lant

MAUVAIS COUP 7a+, Quinsan; Bill Launder

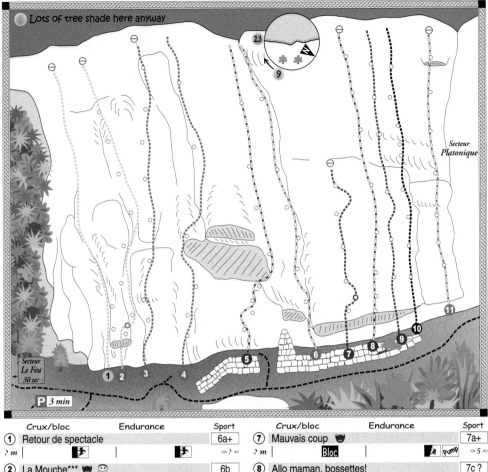

Lots of tree shade here anyway

Secteur
Platonique

Secteur
Le Feu
30 sec

P 3 min

	Crux/bloc	Endurance	Sport
(1)	Retour de spectacle		6a+
? m			○ ? ○

	Crux/bloc	Endurance	Sport
(2)	La Mouche***		6b
23m	○ 6c-	6a+ DIEDRE	○ 9 ○

*You are attacked by a thuggy small roof at the start, then the route
becomes a delightful bridging experience, coolness is required.*

	Crux/bloc	Endurance	Sport
(3)	Urban Jungle		6b+
? m			○ ? ○

	Crux/bloc	Endurance	Sport
(4)	Little Big Man		6b+
? m			○ ? ○

	Crux/bloc	Endurance	Sport
(5)	Sympathy for the Devil		7b
? m			○ ? ○

	Crux/bloc	Endurance	Sport
(6)	Envie de toi		6c
? m			○ ? ○

	Crux/bloc	Endurance	Sport
(7)	Mauvais coup		7a+
? m	Bloc	Pump	○ 5 ○

	Crux/bloc	Endurance	Sport
(8)	Allo maman, bossettes!		7c ?
24m			○ ? ○

	Crux/bloc	Endurance	Sport
(0)	Acromégalie		/à
? m			○ ? ○

	Crux/bloc	Endurance	Sport
(10)	Plat de résistance		7b
? m		◉ 7c	○ ? ○

	Crux/bloc	Endurance	Sport
(11)	On n'est pas des zéros		6c+
? m			○ ? ○

Résumé. *This is the central area of the cliff with a good area to picnic
and hang out, whilst watching everyone dogging up the heinous
excursions of slopers after slopers. Steeper routes in this section which
will appeal to the Jingo style climbers, but the softness of the rock can
mean that critical holds may break off, and therefore change the grade
of a route. Plenty of tree shade in summer, so it is not a recommended
venue after rain. Anti mosquito protection useful on calm and still
days, best when a breeze is blowing.*

Hyper Brown - Sequence Passion - Le Feu - Little Big Man - Platonique

BLANCHARD · ARCHÉO · CORNERETTE · QUINSAN · VENASQUE · ST.PIERRE · COLOMBIER · CLAPIS · GLISSE · TYROLIENNE · CASCADE-HAUT · CHRISTOPHE · ALAGARDE · GRAND TRAV · COMBE OBS. · GROSEAU

9-12 Early morning sun, but generally in the trees

20 ? metres

Secteur - Little Big Man

P 4 min

	Crux/bloc	Endurance	Sport
1	Amicalement vôtre		6b
? m			○ ? ○
2	Rockland		7a+
? m			○ ? ○
3	Silencers		7a+
? m			○ ? ○
4	La déchirure		7b
? m			○ ? ○
5	Jeu de paume		7a
? m		Pump	○ ? ○
6	Platine		7b
? m			○ ? ○
7	Platonique		6c
? m			○ 5 ○

	Crux/bloc	Endurance	Sport
8	Nulle part ailleurs		6c
? m			○ ? ○
9	Papy bosseur		6c
? m			○ ? ○
10	Déclaration de fin de chantier		?
? m		◉ 6c+	○ ? ○
11	Mamie brossa		7a
? m			○ ? ○
12	Faut pas en faire un plat		6c
? m			○ ? ○
13	L'astronaute ☺		6b
15m	○ 6c- Sloper	6b Pump	○ 6 ○

Climb to a hold at 7m, then find another at 12m, and then the top.
Any 6b leader will still get pumped solid, knowing the route is
essential.

14	Pleine lune ☺		6b
14m	● 6b- Sloper	6b Pump	○ 6 ○

It looks oh-so-easy; so enjoy a complete struggle on slopers,
uncomfortable for a low grade aspirant. A pleasant warm up if you
have a lot of stamina and crank in the higher grades.

Résumé. A good sector of slightly steep rock with hardly any
holds to be found on it. Super sloper territory and nasty on
sweaty days. A real nightmare for onsighting if the routes have
no chalk on.

Hyper Brown - Sequence Passion - Le Feu - Little Big Man - Platonique

LE SOURCE: Résumé. This sector is really a continuation of Quinsan, but you need to get access from the main parking at Place de l'Ascle.
Access: Walk south, slightly up the hill on the road for about 200 metres, before locating a small (80cms) wall on the left of the road. Take a vague descending track behind the wall, to arrive in five mins at a chaotic area of dams, wells and shelters for man and/or beasts. This is La Grotte.
The obvious overhanging lines of Libéré José Bové and Ressource Toi are now straight ahead, with 4 the last 4 other routes up a short slope to the right. Routes start from far left end and run left to right.

SECTOR COEUR DE LION

?	6a+	Au dédale des dalles	6b+
?	6c	Trouvailles ardéchoises	6b+
?	6b+	Paul et Mick	7a+
La Virtuose	7b	Lierre de rien	7a+
La chute enfantée	7a+	Jardine land	7a
Tibet libre	7a	Clean me up	7a
Tyro	7a+	Tête de mule	6c
Noir dez ...	6c+	T'as pas l'oeil	7a
Rasta plat	6c+	Manque de complicité	6c+
Clandestino	6b	Le bon plan	7b
Mi yamore	6b+	Ca va pas s'arranger	7a
Ras le front	6c	Chacun fait ce qui lui plaît	7a
Retour au source	6b	Coeur de lion	7a
Quatre metres à l'heure	6a	Massive attack	6b+
Surchauffe	6a	Soirée mousse	6b
L'été indien	6a	Entre deux chaises	6a
Plein les ... chaussettes	6a	Coupdebrosse	6a+
DJ mode	6a+	Tam Tam etc	6b
Ma petite puce	6a	Vue de face	5c
Le platypus	6b+	de profil	6b

SECTOR GROTTE

Le cri du Ché	7b+
Libéré José Bové	7b
Ressource toi	7c
?	7a
Attac	6c
?	6b
?	6a

LOCAL INFORMATION: The rock in this area is quite soft and routes constantly change grade. You can often buy a local topo to these cliffs with constantly updated grades from the tourist office in the village of Venasque. Usually, money from these sales will go directly back into equipping the cliffs; so if you do want to contribute to this, please make the extra effort to visit the village and either buy a local topo or give a donation to help the equipping of the Venasque cliffs.

BLANCHARD | ARCHÉO | CORNEIRETTE | QUINSAN | VENASQUE | ST.PIERRE | COLOMBIER | CLAPIS | GLISSE | TYROLIENNE | CASCADE-HAUT | CHRISTOPHE | ALAGARDE | GRAND TRAV | COMBE OBS. | GROSEAU

Left sidebar tabs: BLANCHARD · ARCHÉO · CORNIERETTE · QUINSAN · VENASQUE · ST.PIERRE · COLOMBIER · CLAPIS · GLISSE · TYROLIENNE · CASCADE-HAUT · CHRISTOPHE · A.LAGARDE · GRAND TRAV · COMBE OBS. · GROSEAU

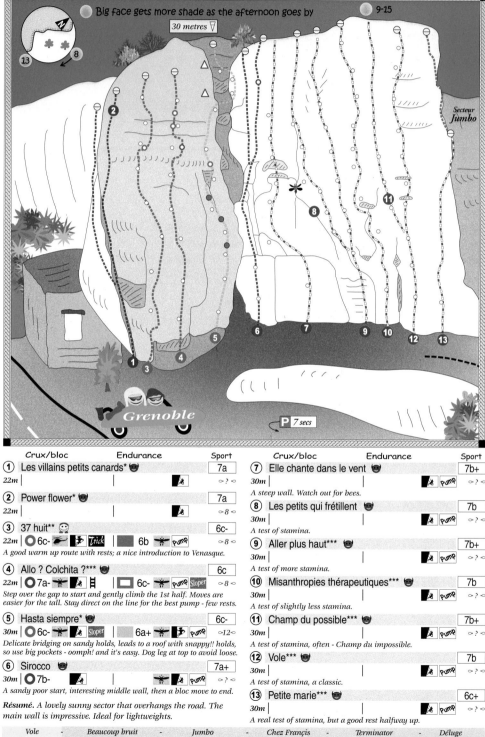

Big face gets more shade as the afternoon goes by   9-15

30 metres

Secteur Jumbo

Grenoble

P 7 secs

	Crux/bloc	Endurance	Sport
1	Les villains petits canards* 🌞		7a
22m		🧗	◦?◦

	Crux/bloc	Endurance	Sport
2	Power flower* 🌞		7a
22m		🧗	◦8◦

3 37 huit** 😊 — 6c-

22m ⭕ 6c- 🧍 Trick ▮ 6b ☀ Pump   ◦8◦

A good warm up route with rests; a nice introduction to Venasque.

4 Allo ? Colchita ?*** 🌞 — 6c

22m ⭕ 7a- ☀ 🧗 ▦ ▯ 6c- Pump Sloper ◦8◦

Step over the gap to start and gently climb the 1st half. Moves are easier for the tall. Stay direct on the line for the best pump - few rests.

5 Hasta siempre* 🌞 — 6c-

30m ⭕ 6c- ☀ 🧗 Sloper ▮ 6a+ ☀ 🧍 Pump ◦12◦

Delicate bridging on sandy holds, leads to a roof with snappy!! holds, so use big pockets - oomph! and it's easy. Dog leg at top to avoid loose.

6 Sirocco 🌞 — 7a+

30m ⭕ 7b- 🧗   ☀ 🧗 Pump ◦?◦

A sandy poor start, interesting middle wall, then a bloc move to end.

Résumé. *A lovely sunny sector that overhangs the road. The main wall is impressive. Ideal for lightweights.*

	Crux/bloc	Endurance	Sport
7	Elle chante dans le vent 🌞		7b+
30m		🧗 Pump	◦?◦

A steep wall. Watch out for bees.

	Crux/bloc	Endurance	Sport
8	Les petits qui frétillent 🌞		7b
30m		🧗 Pump	◦?◦

A test of stamina.

	Crux/bloc	Endurance	Sport
9	Aller plus haut*** 🌞		7b+
30m		🧗 Pump	◦?◦

A test of more stamina.

	Crux/bloc	Endurance	Sport
10	Misanthropies thérapeutiques*** 🌞		7b
30m		🧗 Pump	◦?◦

A test of slightly less stamina.

	Crux/bloc	Endurance	Sport
11	Champ du possible*** 🌞		7b+
30m		🧗 Pump	◦?◦

A test of stamina, often - Champ du impossible.

	Crux/bloc	Endurance	Sport
12	Vole*** 🌞		7b
30m		🧗 Pump	◦?◦

A test of stamina, a classic.

	Crux/bloc	Endurance	Sport
13	Petite marie*** 🌞		6c+
30m		🧗 Pump	◦?◦

A real test of stamina, but a good rest halfway up.

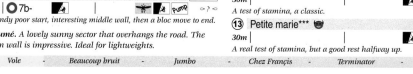

VOLE 7b, Place de l'Ascle, Venasque; Remy Martin

14-17 afternoon sun for a while

07-10.30

32 metres

Secteur Jumbo

P 2 secs

	Crux/bloc	Endurance	Sport
①	Petite marie*** 😊		6c+
32m			

	Crux/bloc	Endurance	Sport
②	Blacks Blancs Beurs***		7a-
32m	7a- Sloper	6b Pump	10

Awkward to read the slopers on the lower bulge. Top arete is superb and not too hard, having good power is useful on this route.

	Crux/bloc	Endurance	Sport
③	??		?
32m	Sloper	7b-	

	Crux/bloc	Endurance	Sport
④	Rêves brulés*** 😊		6a+
30m	6b- Sloper	6a+ Pump	12

A very good long pitch, but some very hollow sounding rock too! At least the bolts are in the best pieces of rock. Top overhang will catch out those without bags of stamina, going right has big holds & fun too.

	Crux/bloc	Endurance	Sport
⑤	Laissons les dire*** 😊		5+++
30m	6a-	5++ Pump	12

A fabulous climb with superb holds all the way, but also a few thoughtful moves thrown in. The angle and length make this a complete pump fest.

	Crux/bloc	Endurance	Sport
⑤	Beaucoup de bruit pour rien*** 😊		6a+
30m	6a- Trick	5++	11

A very good stamina fest, difficulty culminates in forearm anguish.

	Crux/bloc	Endurance	Sport
⑦	Jusqu'au bout*** 😊		6b-
31m	6b- Bloc	5++ 747 Cool Pump	11

Spaced bolts and a definite hard move, makes this quite an undertaking for leaders. Final roof has big holds, but can easily prove too much for big, fat, lardies who eat too many pies.

	Crux/bloc	Endurance	Sport
⑧	Le moldus au balcon		6a
? m			

	Crux/bloc	Endurance	Sport
⑨	Camino de piedra 😊		6a
? m	△ Bloc		

	Crux/bloc	Endurance	Sport
⑩	Con la luz 😊		6a
? m	△ Bloc		

	Crux/bloc	Endurance	Sport
⑪	Mieux vaut en rire		6a
? m	△		

	Crux/bloc	Endurance	Sport
⑫	A la fraîche		6a
? m	△		

Résumé. *This is the busiest section of the crag - just opposite the parking. The climbing is superb, but the rock is soft, so always be aware that stones may fall down. Routes in the back passage are cool, but the rock is like honeycomb - bee careful!*

PETITE MARIE (Arête) 6c+, Place de l'Ascle, Venasque; Camile Verdot

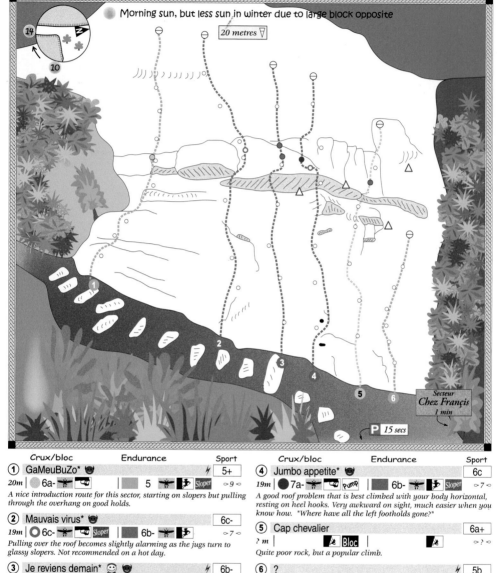

Morning sun, but less sun in winter due to large block opposite

20 metres

Secteur
Chez Françis
1 min

P 15 secs

	Crux/bloc	Endurance		Sport
1	GaMeuBuZo*			5+
20m	6a- Sloper	5		9

A nice introduction route for this sector, starting on slopers but pulling through the overhang on good holds.

	Crux/bloc	Endurance		Sport
2	Mauvais virus*			6c-
19m	6c- Sloper	6b-		7

Pulling over the roof becomes slightly alarming as the jugs turn to glassy slopers. Not recommended on a hot day.

	Crux/bloc	Endurance		Sport
3	Je reviens demain*			6b-
19m	6b-	6b- Sloper		7

A nice technical lower wall - leads to a large roof, with large holds, that are a large distance apart. Difficult for the onsight.

	Crux/bloc	Endurance		Sport
4	Jumbo appetite*			6c
19m	7a- Pump	6b- Sloper		7

A good roof problem that is best climbed with your body horizontal, resting on heel hooks. Very awkward on sight, much easier when you know how. "Where have all the left footholds gone?"

	Crux/bloc	Endurance		Sport
5	Cap chevalier			6a+
? m		Bloc		?

Quite poor rock, but a popular climb.

	Crux/bloc	Endurance		Sport
6	?			5b
10m			Pump	6

A very short but well protected route.

Résumé. *A popular sector that is just above the parking. A very nice and technical lower wall has some large overhangs at mid height. The rock at the overhang is poor and footholds come off with regularity, and someday the whole roof may collapse! It does provide some pretty good and substantial holds though, so when you find them, you can power up this short section.*

Sector gets the morning sun, but is then shaded by the big block of 'Beaucoup bruit,' which has a bigger shade effect in winter as the sun is lower.

JE REVIENS DEMAIN 6b-, Place de l'Ascle, Venasque; Rémy Escoffier

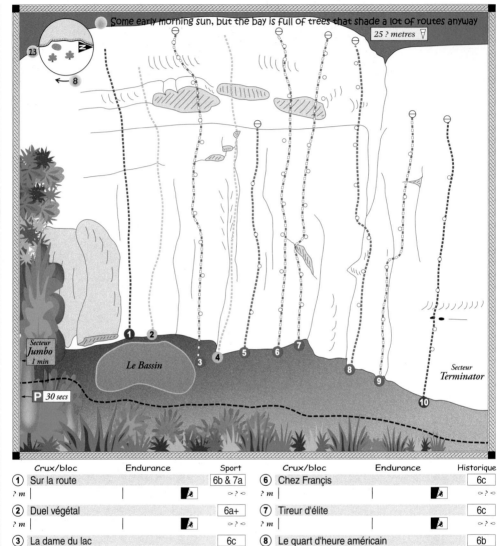

Some early morning sun, but the bay is full of trees that shade a lot of routes anyway

25 ? metres

13

8

Secteur
Jumbo
1 min

Le Bassin

P 30 secs

Secteur
Terminator

Sidebar (left margin, top to bottom): BLANCHARD · ARCHÉO · CORNERETTE · QUINSAN · **VENASQUE** · ST.PIERRE · COLOMBIER · CLAPIS · GLISSE · TYROLIENNE · CASCADE-HAUT · CHRISTOPHE · A.LAGARDE · GRAND TRAV · COMBE OBS. · GROSEAU

	Crux/bloc	Endurance	Sport		Crux/bloc	Endurance	Historique
1	Sur la route		6b & 7a	**6**	Chez Françis		6c
	? m		⚬ ? ⚬		? m		⚬ ? ⚬
2	Duel végétal		6a+	**7**	Tireur d'élite		6c
	? m		⚬ ? ⚬		? m		⚬ ? ⚬
3	La dame du lac		6c	**8**	Le quart d'heure américain		6b
	? m		⚬ ? ⚬		? m		⚬ ? ⚬
4	La partie continue		6a	**9**	Allô ?! La terre		6c+
	? m		⚬ ? ⚬		? m		⚬ ? ⚬
5	Play-list		6b+	**10**	Fête des pères		7a+
	? m		⚬ ? ⚬		? m		⚬ ? ⚬

Résumé. *A dark and sometimes damp sector, tucked in heavy shade from the trees. The pool at the bottom is very still water and attracts mosquito's, so come with repellent. It also can be a real pain when pulling ropes on routes 1 & 2. Mainly vertical pumpy climbing with steep and hard finishes.*
Access. *This sector is some 80 metres away from the large Vole block.*

VENASQUE, view towards Mont Ventoux

VENASQUE, road from Carpentras

EH TARDADO MUCHO 7a, Place de l'Ascle, Venasque; Camile Verdot

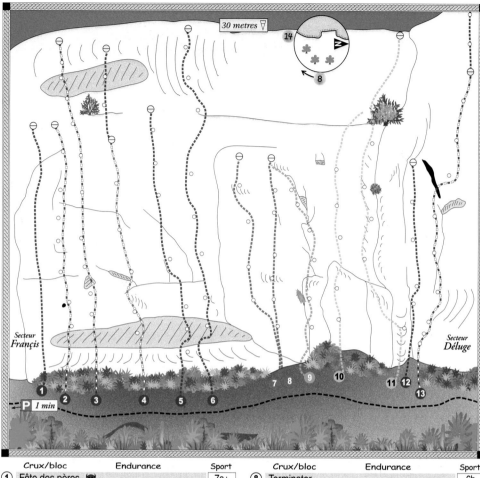

	Crux/bloc	Endurance	Sport
1	Fête des pères		7a+
2	Trésor caché		7b
3	Blédina carotte		7b
4	La restanque		6c &7a+
5	Boule de calin		7a
6	Eh tardado mucho	Flexi	7a
7	Mise au vert		6b+

	Crux/bloc	Endurance	Sport
8	Terminator		6b
9	Colère de lait		5c
10	Feu		6a+
11	Sortie ouest	DIEDRE	6a+
12	Bézingougne		7a+
13	L'intégrale de Peuterey	Pump	7b

Résumé. *A big undercut wall that has very hard starts to the first few routes. Mostly sustained climbing on reasonable holds.*

Vole   -   Beaucoup bruit   -   Jumbo   -   Chez Françis   -   Terminator   -   Déluge

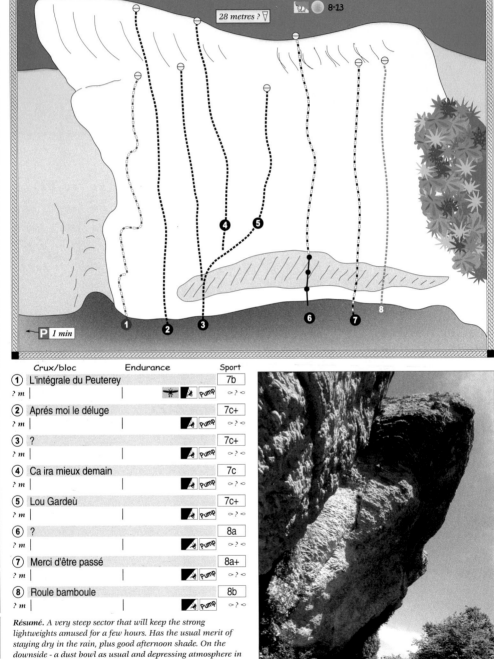

28 metres ?

8-13

P 1 min

	Crux/bloc	Endurance	Sport	
1	L'intégrale du Peuterey		7b	
	? m			
2	Aprés moi le déluge		7c+	
	? m			
3	?		7c+	
	? m			
4	Ca ira mieux demain		7c	
	? m			
5	Lou Gardeù		7c+	
	? m			
6	?		8a	
	? m			
7	Merci d'être passé		8a+	
	? m			
8	Roule bamboule		8b	
	? m			

Résumé. A very steep sector that will keep the strong lightweights amused for a few hours. Has the usual merit of staying dry in the rain, plus good afternoon shade. On the downside - a dust bowl as usual and depressing atmosphere in the trees. Best to enjoy on a crisp, sunny winters morning as the sun lights up this really golden rock.

Secteur DÉLUGE

Sidebar tabs: BLANCHARD · ARCHÉO · CORNIERETTE · QUINSAN · VENASQUE · ST.PIERRE · COLOMBIER · CLAPIS · GLISSE · TIROLIENNE · CASCADE-HAUT · CHRISTOPHE · A.LAGARDE · GRAND TRAV · COMBE OBS. · GROSEAU

| Vole | - | Beaucoup bruit | - | Jumbo | - | Chez François | - | Terminator | - | Déluge |

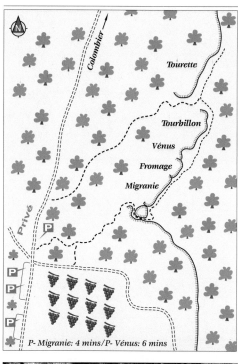

Tourette

Colombier

Tourbillon

Vénus

Fromage

Migranie

Privé

P

P

P

P

P- Migranie: 4 mins / P- Vénus: 6 mins

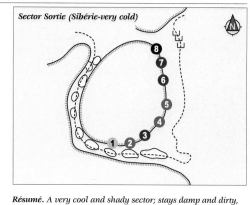

Sector Sortie (Sibérie-very cold)

Résumé. *A very cool and shady sector; stays damp and dirty, and damp rock is never that reliable. Not of major importance.*

	Crux/bloc	Endurance	Historique
1	Sortie de secours		6a
2	Move extrem		6b
3	Sortie médiatic		7a+
4	Le roi Charlemagne		6b+
5	Plat chaud		6c+
6	Comiques associés		7a
7	Grimpeur des magazines		7a+
8	Grand		7b+

BLANCHARD · ARCHÉO · CORNERRETTE · QUINSAN · VENASQUE · ST.PIERRE · COLOMBIER · CLAPIS · GLISSE · TYROLIENNE · CASCADE-HAUT · CHRISTOPHE · A.LAGARDE · GRAND TRAV · COMBE OBS. · GROSEAU

Secteur Migranie, Saint Pierre, Venasque

LA MIGRANIE 7b, Saint Pierre, Venasque; Beth Bennett

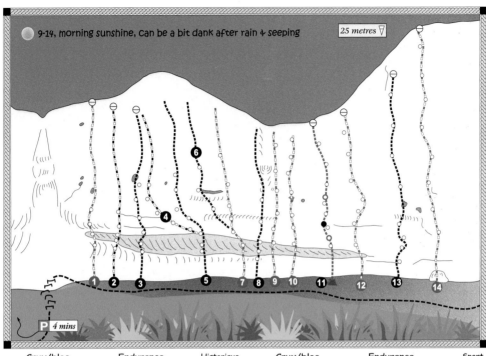

9-14, morning sunshine, can be a bit dank after rain & seeping

25 metres

P 4 mins

Crux/bloc	Endurance	Historique		Crux/bloc	Endurance	Sport
① Mange		7b+		⑧ Trompe couillons		7c+
? m				? m		
② O.K. ! Kéké ! !		8a		⑨ La brigade des stups		7b
? m				? m		
③ Mes meilleurs ennemis		7c+		⑩ La peste faune		7b
? m				? m		
④ Y'a pas d' os ! !		8a		⑪ La Migranie**		7b
? m				23m ● 7c- Sloper	7a+ Pump	

A handy cut down tree to start, then a mono move (nasty for the short) leads straight into the power crux on slopers, then sustained.

⑤ C'est bon le saucisson		7c+		⑫ G.D.R.		7b
? m				? m		
⑥ Faut pas rêver !		7c+		⑬ Un monde parfait !		7c
? m				? m		
⑦ Pierre Oppidum		7b+		⑭ Contrôle antidopage		7b
? m				? m		

Résumé. *A very impressive roof sector that makes routes a touch on the physical side. Power is the name of the game here. Getting up the routes will give you considerable difficulty. Many holds have been manufactured, but on the minimal side, so don't get your hopes up too much. Even the easiest route here has 7c bloc moves on it; so if you can't crank like a beaver - don't bother coming here.*

BOREAL

Sortie - Migranie - Fromage - Vénus - Tourbillon - Tourette

BLANCHARD ARCHÉO CORNEIRETTE QUINSAN VENASQUE ST.PIERRE COLOMBIER CLAPIS GLISSE TYROLIENNE CASCADE-HAUT CHRISTOPHE A.LAGARDE GRAND TRAV COMBE OBS. GROSEAU

LE PÈRE NÖEL EST PARMI NOUS 6c- Saint Pierre, Venasque; Jim Bacon

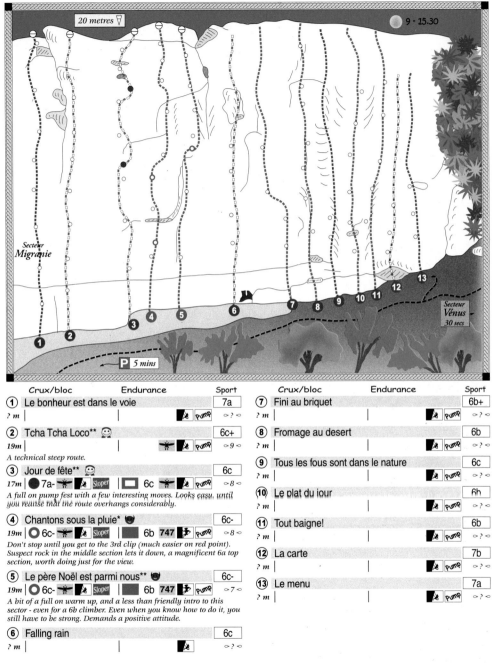

	Crux/bloc	Endurance	Sport
①	Le bonheur est dans le voie		7a
? m		🏃 Pump	∞?∞

	Crux/bloc	Endurance	Sport
②	Tcha Tcha Loco** 😊		6c+
19m		☀🏃 Pump	∞9∞

A technical steep route.

	Crux/bloc	Endurance	Sport
③	Jour de fête** 😊		6c
17m	● 7a- ✦ 🏃 Sloper	▢ 6c ☀🏃 Pump	∞8∞

A full on pump fest with a few interesting moves. Looks easy, until you realise that the route overhangs considerably.

	Crux/bloc	Endurance	Sport
④	Chantons sous la pluie* 👁		6c-
19m	○ 6c- ✦ 🏃 Sloper	■ 6b 747 🏃 Pump	∞8∞

Don't stop until you get to the 3rd clip (much easier on red point). Suspect rock in the middle section lets it down, a magnificent 6a top section, worth doing just for the view.

	Crux/bloc	Endurance	Sport
⑤	Le père Noël est parmi nous** 👁		6c-
19m	○ 6c- ✦ 🏃 Sloper	■ 6b 747 🏃 Pump	∞7∞

A bit of a full on warm up, and a less than friendly intro to this sector - even for a 6b climber. Even when you know how to do it, you still have to be strong. Demands a positive attitude.

	Crux/bloc	Endurance	Sport
⑥	Falling rain		6c
? m		🏃	∞?∞

	Crux/bloc	Endurance	Sport
⑦	Fini au briquet		6b+
? m		🏃 Pump	∞?∞

	Crux/bloc	Endurance	Sport
⑧	Fromage au desert		6b
? m		🏃 Pump	∞?∞

	Crux/bloc	Endurance	Sport
⑨	Tous les fous sont dans le nature		6c
? m		🏃 Pump	∞?∞

	Crux/bloc	Endurance	Sport
⑩	Le plat du jour		6b
? m		🏃 Pump	∞?∞

	Crux/bloc	Endurance	Sport
⑪	Tout baigne!		6b
? m		🏃 Pump	∞?∞

	Crux/bloc	Endurance	Sport
⑫	La carte		7b
? m		🏃 Pump	∞?∞

	Crux/bloc	Endurance	Sport
⑬	Le menu		7a
? m		🏃 Pump	∞?∞

Résumé. *This is the popular area for grade six climbers, but essentially you want to be climbing at the top end of the grade 6 scale, Be prepared to find most of the routes very tough: and onsight they all feel like 7a, just easier and harder versions. It's the steepness of the first half of the routes, along with the similarity of all the holds that blows up your forearms onsight. When you know how, it just becomes like an outdoor cranking gym. Anyone not used to steep rock will find themselves in trouble here.*

Sortie	-	Migranie	-	Fromage	-	Vénus	-	Tourbillon	-	Tourette

Side tabs: BLANCHARD, ARCHÉO, CORNEIRETTE, QUINSAN, VENASQUE, ST.PIERRE, COLOMBIER, CLAPIS, GLISSE, TYROLIENNE, 2SCADE-HAUT, CHRISTOPHE, A.LAGARDE, GRAND TRAV, COMBE OBS., GROSEAU

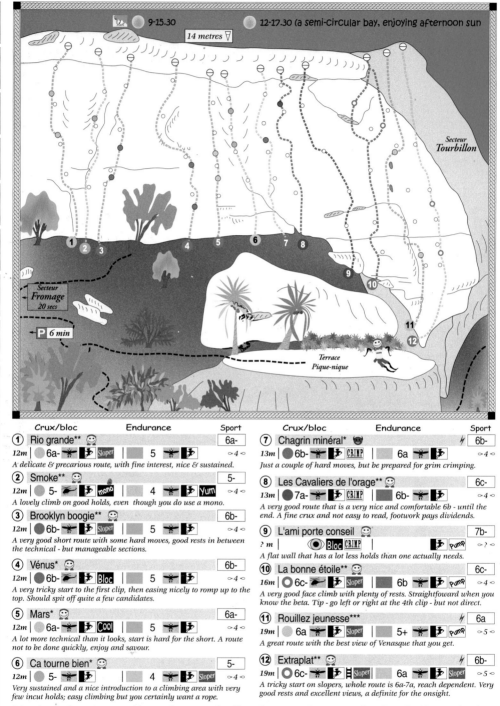

9-15.30   12-17.30 (a semi-circular bay, enjoying afternoon sun

14 metres

Secteur **Tourbillon**

Secteur **Fromage** 20 secs

P 6 min

Terrace Pique-nique

Side tabs (top to bottom): BLANCHARD · ARCHÉO · CORNIRETTE · QUINSAN · VENASQUE · ST.PIERRE · COLOMBIER · CLAPIS · GLISSE · TYROLIENNE · CASCADE-HAUT · CHRISTOPHE · ALAGARDE · GRAND TRAV' · COMBE OBS. · GROSEAU

	Crux/bloc	Endurance	Sport
①	Rio grande** 😊		6a-

12m | 6a- Sloper | 5 | ⌐4⌐

A delicate & precarious route, with fine interest, nice & sustained.

| **②** | Smoke** 😊 | | 5- |

12m | 5- mono | 4 Yum | ⌐4⌐

A lovely climb on good holds, even though you do use a mono.

| **③** | Brooklyn boogie** 😊 | | 6b- |

12m | 6b- Sloper | 5 | ⌐4⌐

A very good short route with some hard moves, good rests in between the technical - but manageable sections.

| **④** | Vénus* 😊 | | 6b- |

12m | 6b- Bloc | 5 | ⌐4⌐

A very tricky start to the first clip, then easing nicely to romp up to the top. Should spit off quite a few candidates.

| **⑤** | Mars* 😊 | | 6a- |

12m | 6a- Cool | 5 | ⌐4⌐

A lot more technical than it looks, start is hard for the short. A route not to be done quickly, enjoy and savour.

| **⑥** | Ca tourne bien* 😊 | | 5- |

12m | 5- | 4 Sloper | ⌐4⌐

Very sustained and a nice introduction to a climbing area with very few incut holds; easy climbing but you certainly want a rope.

	Crux/bloc	Endurance	Sport
⑦	Chagrin minéral* 😊		⚡ 6b-

13m | 6b- CRIMP | 6a | ⌐4⌐

Just a couple of hard moves, but be prepared for grim crimping.

| **⑧** | Les Cavaliers de l'orage** 😊 | | 6c- |

13m | 7a- CRIMP | 6b- | ⌐4⌐

A very good route that is a very nice and comfortable 6b - until the end. A fine crux and not easy to read, footwork pays dividends.

| **⑨** | L'ami porte conseil 😊 | | 7b- |

? m | Bloc CRIMP | Pump | ⌐?⌐

A flat wall that has a lot less holds than one actually needs.

| **⑩** | La bonne étoile** 😊 | | 6c- |

16m | 6c- Sloper | 6b Pump | ⌐4⌐

A very good face climb with plenty of rests. Straightfoward when you know the beta. Tip - go left or right at the 4th clip - but not direct.

| **⑪** | Rouillez jeunesse*** | | ⚡ 6a |

19m | 6a Sloper | 5+ Pump | ⌐5⌐

A great route with the best view of Venasque that you get.

| **⑫** | Extraplat** 😊 | | ⚡ 6b- |

19m | 6c- Sloper | 6a Sloper | ⌐5⌐

A tricky start on slopers, whole route is 6a-7a, reach dependent. Very good rests and excellent views, a definite for the onsight.

Résumé. *A lovely sunny sector with great views over to the village of Venasque. The routes are short, but still pack a punch and make a visit well worthwhile. Not too bad on hot days as the trees shade a lot of routes on the left side.*

LE CAVALIERS DE L'ORAGE 6c- Saint Pierre, Venasque; David Atchison-Jones

BLANCHARD

ARCHÉO

CORNERETTE

QUINSAN

VENASQUE

ST.PIERRE

COLOMBIER

CLAPIS

GLISSE

TYROLIENNE

CASCADE-HAUT

CHRISTOPHE

A.LAGARDE

GRAND TRAV

COMBE OBS.

GROSEAU

SECTOR TOURBILLON: Résumé. *A very impressive wall as seen from the other side of the valley, and just to the is the continuation of Vénus sector. Lower third though is very poor rock and some of the starts have collapsed. Not very popular, but still has some classic mollasses limestone climbs.*

	Crux/bloc	Endurance	Historique
(1)	Laisse lucie faire		6c+
(2)	variation gauche		6b+
(3)	Scéne de ménage		6c
(4)	Ca va aller		6b+
(5)	Poule		6c
(6)	?		7b+
(7)	...craint...		7c+
(8)	Le tourbillon de la vie		7a+

SECTOR TOURETTE GAUCHE: Résumé. *A small slabby sector with some fun routes for kids.*

	Crux/bloc	Endurance	Sport
(1)	Promenous nous 😊	⚡	2-

10m | 2- 🦅🧗 | 2 🦅🧗 Fun | ∽4∽
A very nice fun lead for kiddies.

| (2) | Le gros nounou 😊 | ⚡ | 3- |

13m | 3- 🕷️🧗 Sloper | 2 🦅🧗 | ∽5∽
A few delicate step ups on non positive holds, a kids climb.

| (3) | Allez-y-en famille 😊 | ⚡ | 4- |

12m | 4- 🦅🧗 Flexi | 2 🦅🧗 | ∽6∽
An interesting move by the 4th clip keeps you awake.

| (4) | Douce Catalogne 😊 | ⚡ | 3- |

13m | 3- 🕷️🧗 | 3 🦅🧗 Fun | ∽5∽
An interesting move by the 4th clip keeps you awake.

| (5) | Black scorpion* 🌑 | | 6c- |

13m | ⭕6c- 🕷️🪨 | 6b- 🕷️🧗 Fun | ∽5∽
A nasty sting at the 2nd clip on this one. A good effort for the onsight and stops a lot of 6c leaders. Steeper and more tiring than it looks: nipping right into the niche keeps it hard and up to 6c endurance.

SECTOR TOURETTE DROIT: Résumé. *A good climbing sector with some full on routes. The rock strata slopes the wrong way, which sends you sliding off the holds the whole time; a ghastly nightmare on hot days - even in the shade. Generally very hard.*

	Crux/bloc	Endurance	Historique
(1)	Petit d'homme		6c+
(2)	Les ronchons, dehors !!!		7a+
(3)	Sommeil paradoxal		7b
(4)	Les Huil		6c+
(5)	La comète		6b+
(6)	Ecran géant		6c+
(7)	E finito managaré		6c+
(8)	Résistance		7a
(9)	Desperado		7b+
(10)	Champagne		7a
(11)	Corona extra		7?
(12)	Ni flic, ni mâitre (Vincent Cottalorda)		7c
(13)	Mauvais limonade		8?
(14)	Plus loin que le ciel (Cyril Ollagnier)		8a+
(15)	Gros rectangle		8?

SECTOR BEAU PILIER - encore 150m

(1)	? (Serge Jaulin)		6c+
(2)	? (Serge Jaulin)		6c
(3)	? (Serge Jaulin)		6c
(4)	? (Serge Jaulin)		6b+

Sortie - Migranie - Fromage - Vénus - Tourbillon - Tourette

SECTOR COLOMBIER: Résumé. *A more recent development of high grade routes that overlook the village and are south east facing.*

Attention: Do not climb on the routes above this sector.

Attention: Il est interdit de dans le grimper le voies au dessus de ce secteur.

SECTOR COLOMBIER: Access. *Carry on down the track from the parking for St. Pierre. You reach the sector in 10 mins. Map at the start of the Venasque sector - page 42*

	Crux/bloc	Endurance	Historique
(1)	Papillon du jour		6a
(2)	Dubatif à cheval		6a
(3)	Un jardin en hiver**		6b+
(4)	Belle et Rebelle**** Pump		7b
(5)	Voleurs de poules** 747		7c
(6)	Viens Poupoule, viens****		7a
(7)	Assibounanga***		7a
(8)	Nationale****		7a
(9)	Papette et gouine qui couinent*** Bloc Bloc		7c
(10)	Lagune** Bloc		7c
(11)	Il écoutait pousser les fleurs*** 🌑		7a+
(12)	Huevos Papas Cincuentas Bloc 目		7c+
(13)	T'es toute nue***		6b
(14)	Jolie Môme***		6c
(15)	Petit Bout Immense Amour		6c+
(16)	Chli-pou-ni		6b
(17)	Dragon feu		5b
(18)	Pikachou		3a
(19)	Manuelita - traverse		4a

There must be almost a hundred campsites in the whole area that this guidbook covers. Many of the smaller campsites do not have websites of their own, but will often be referenced on the www of the local office de tourisme. (Many of the campsites are summer only.) This page includes the two well situated campsites that have good opening times for climbers. The mistral wind can blow for days, even testing a strong mountain tent. Camping chalets for hire come highly recommended, and between a group they offer very good value for money.

 ROQUEFIGUIER

Roquefiguier Camping (www)
Routes de Lafare
84190 Beaumes-de-Venise
Tel: 04 90 62 95 07
Open: 01-04 / 31-10

Some English spoken. A very good and tidy municipal site. Basic campsite in village, no shop - but you are only 3 mins walk from village centre where you can buy anything to eat or drink. Tree shade too. Local swim-pool, very close.

La Fontaine d'Annibal swimming pool, with cliff of Ubrieux in the background.

 FONTAINE D'ANNIBAL

Fontaine d'Annibal (www)
26170 Buis-les-Baronnies
Tel: 04 75 2 03 12
Open: Mostly all year

Some English spoken. A very good site with nice big emplacements, and a to die for lovely swimming pool. Has plenty of facilities - which generally open and operate on demand. Part of a family hostel so it remains open even when quiet. A good selection of nice chalets. Very close to town and the cliffs.

Useful campsite info

Blauvac - Aéria: Camping Municipal, 12 spaces and basic, quiet and away from it all. (South)
Bédoin - Camping in town with a pool, big site, no grass and barren. (South)
Bédoin/Obscure - 2 sites between town & cliff (Sth of road), quiet and family style . (South)
Aubignan - Big site, good facilities. (also small farm camping B-Venise-Sarrians road)
Villes-s-Auzon - Camping in town with swim pools, 70 spaces. (South)
Entrechaux - 2 basic sites near river - See Trois Rivières cliff for details (Central)
Vaison-I-R. - Lots of giant sites, long opening - C-Int-Carpe Diem has lots chalets (Central)
Eygaliers - Small campsite on in farmland, quiet (Area has other sites too).(Upper central)
Buis-I-B. - Good municipal site in town, opposite fab huge super pool.(Upper central)
Buis-I-B. - Nice site 1km to the south of village, pool, check web for chalets.(Upper central)
Sainte-Jalle - Les Cigales, quiet municipal site in lovely tiny village. (North)
St-Sauveur - Small farm campsite with 14 places - see Aiguier cliff - seasonal (North)

If you visit the area in the winter, you are likely to find a lot of campsites closed. However, there are a lot of gites available for rent in the winter months at good prices. Local tourist offices are usually very helpful. The main websites for these are www.gites-de-france.fr (page 216 also)

Pour la majorité des grimpeurs, l'idée d'écrire un guide d'escalade semble être un rêve devenu réalité – l'excuse parfaite pour aller grimper durant toute une saison. Non seulement vous reviendrez bien musclé d'avoir grimpé de 6a a 8c mais vous reviendrez aussi avec de magnifiques photos. La réalité est totalement différente. Pour écrire un guide Jingo Wobbly il faut en moyenne 3000 heures de travail. Lorsque vous considérez qu'une année de travail en France compte en moyenne 1700 heures, vous comprenez la raison pour laquelle il est nécessaire d'avoir 2 personnes à temps plein sur une année pour travailler sur un tel projet. Il faut en effet 3000 heures car nous prenons toutes les photos nous-mêmes, nous faisons tous les dessins et recherchons toutes les informations liées aux falaises et aux voies. Cela surprendra peut-être plus d'une personne mais lorsque vous écrivez un guide, grimper n'est pas une priorité majeure. En général on apprend plus d'une voie en regardant un autre grimpeur plutôt qu'en la grimpant soi-même. J'ai beaucoup d'expérience en 7 et 8 mais il est nécessaire de garder un bon niveau en 6 pour écrire un guide afin de déterminer au mieux les cotations pour les débutants et les grimpeurs avec peu d'expérience. Ces derniers ont en effet besoin de guides avec de bonnes descriptions et des cotations justes.

Lorsque vous écrivez un guide d'escalade il vous faut également prendre de sérieuses décisions. Publier un bestseller dont la vente est supérieure à 50,000 exemplaires est une garantie d'argent, mais financièrement les bénéfices n'apparaissent qu'à partir du moment où 10,000 copies sont vendues sur une année. Les guides d'escalade ne font même pas un dixième de ce chiffre "Dieu merci." L'environnement serait complètement detruit si un si grand nombre de grimpeurs visitaient les falaises, et ce n'est pas quelque chose que je souhaite. Par conséquent vous allez perdre de l'argent quelque soit la manière dont vous essayez d'arranger votre comptabilitée. Ma décision est de porter tous mes efforts sur la création du meilleur guide d'escalade possible sur une zone d'escalade précise. Certains éditeurs soustraient une partie de l'argent destinée à créer le guide pour aider à l'équipement des falaises. De ce fait la publication du guide en souffre car ni le photographe, ni l'écrivain, ni l'imprimeur ou ni le bailleur de licence de logiciel ne perçoivent d'indemnitées pour les services qu'ils ont rendu et en final le guide est de mediocre qualité. Je supporte et j'approuve la mobilisation de fonds pour l'équipement des voies soit par des donations ou par la vente d'autocollants dont 99.5% des bénéfices sont utilisés à l'équipement des falaises. Pour la publication d'un guide la majorité des fonds sont utilisés à la vente, la distribution, la photographie et l'impression et si vous utilisez une partie de cet argent pour autre chose, vous risquez de compromettre la qualité du livre. J'espère que cette explication vous permet de comprendre pourquoi nous utilisons 100% de notre argent à la production des meilleurs guides d'escalade possibles.

For the majority of climbers, the idea of writing a book sounds like a dream come true - a wonderful excuse to go off climbing for a giant season. You not only get fit and crank up everything from 6a to 8c, you also come home with superb photos of everyone doing one arm pull ups from overhangs. The reality is different, because to produce a high quality Jingo Wobbly climbing book, you have to spend an average of 3000 hours working on the project. Considering that a normal working year in France is 1700 hours, you can see why it needs 2 people to complete a book in a single year. It takes 3000 hours because we take all of our own photos, make all of our own drawings, and research as well as possible the climbs that we see. It will surprise many people, that in writing a guidebook, climbing itself is quite a low priority. An observant writer will learn far more about routes by watching others climb, than going on the route personally. I have a wealth of experience of grade 7 and 8 climbing of course, but you need to maintain a grade 6 level for good guidebook writing, otherwise you just don't feel how hard the climbs are for beginners and less experienced climbers. These are the people that really need books with accurate grades and good descriptions.

You also have to make some serious judgements when making books. Publishing a best seller that sells over 50,000 copies is simply a licence to print money of course, but it is financially impossible to make any profit until a book sells over 10,000 copies in a single year. Climbing books don't even sell a tenth of that **'thank goodness.'** The environment would be totally destroyed if that number of people were to go climbing at a local cliff, and it is something I certainly don't want. Consequently, you are going to loose money, no matter how you want to fiddle the accounts. The judgement I make, is to put all the effort I can into making the best possible published book on climbing in an area. Some climbing publishers take money out of this 'operation,' and give it to equipping cliffs. Consequently, the publication will definitely suffer, because the photographer or writer or printer or software licenser, gets no money for the services they have provided, and you usually end up with a sub-standard book. I support and approve of raising money for equipping climbs by direct donation - or buy selling stickers, where 99.5% of the money goes directly to the equipment fund. In publishing, so much money goes in sales, distribution, photography and printing, that if you take any money out of this, you really compromise the quality of the book. I hope this explains why we put 100% of our money back into book production to make the best climbing books possible.

Beaumes-de-Venise is an ideally sized small village with plenty of parking in a large area opposite the tourist office and petanque (boules) area. Across from here, you can stroll into the main drag next to this fountain & just down some steps from the large church. It is an ideal meeting area, and has a lively bar-restaurant opposite. There is another charismatic bar, higher up the main drag, & where there is a small but sensible market on Tuesday mornings. There is a good assortment of small shops that seem to stay open all hours, and a choice of two bakers, my favourite being the lovely rustic breads & cakes served up at J.-M.Vogelweid, by the church; yummy scrummie. Don't miss the butcher's just inside the old walled town, excellent meats.

There are many local winemakers that entice you in for wine tasting. Nearly all the wines are excellent, but the village is most famous for its sweet white - Muscat - wine. Not cheapo, but fabulous and serene. Ideal as an aperitif with a cube of ice to cool it; does go well with oysters, crayfish, or tiger prawns served as a canapé (doesn't mix so well with smoked fish or caviar - I would normally recommend champagne).

Beaumes-de-Venise is named after the caves (Baumes) that lie beneath the village, and was in the 17th century, a very powerful medieval fortress. The old town behind the ancient walls is very quiet, but does have a few very interesting boutiques - don't miss that one girlies.

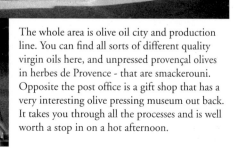

The whole area is olive oil city and production line. You can find all sorts of different quality virgin oils here, and unpressed provençal olives in herbes de Provence - that are smackerouni. Opposite the post office is a gift shop that has a very interesting olive pressing museum out back. It takes you through all the processes and is well worth a stop in on a hot afternoon.

BENEDETTI 6b-, Vistemboir, Clapis-Sud, Dentelles de Montmirail; Jim Bacon

Le nom Dentelles de Montmirail vient des falaises blanches situées au-dessus des vignes entre les villages de Beaumes de Venise et Gigondas. Ces magnifiques pics en dents de scie attireront votre attention depuis l'autoroute A7 Lyon-Marseille. Les falaises sont également magnifiques sous un coucher de soleil. C'est un endroit fabuleux que vous n'oublierez jamais. Nous vous conseillons de séjourner au village de Beaumes de Venise car il est proche des falaises et seulement à 30 minutes de Venasque et Combe Obscure, deux sites parfaits en hiver. Durant les mois chauds d'été, il est préférable de grimper sur les voies à l'ombre qui sont accessibles depuis Gigondas.

Les Dentelles de Montmirail représentent une vaste zone d'escalade et bien que les falaises paraissent assez rapprochées sur une carte, elles sont en fait très distancées les unes des autres. Il est donc préférable de conduire d'une falaise à l'autre plutôt que de marcher. Il y a 6 endroits différents pour se garer et vous pouvez choisir aisément le parking le plus proche de la falaise de votre choix. Les falaises géantes de 80-90 mètres ressemblent à une chaîne montagneuse. La chaîne du Gigondas est considérablement plus élevée en altitude mais n'est pas assez haute pour protéger la chaîne du Clapis lorsque le Mistral souffle. Il y a des falaises plus petites qui font face à la vallée mais les falaises principales sont exposées au nord ou au sud. A l'est il y a une zone composée de falaises très diverses formant le troisième secteur principal. Pour les grimpeurs les Dents est une description assez ironique: en effet les falaises sont d'un blanc étincelant, sont très lisses et les voies ont du mordant. Grimper sur ces grandes falaises peut-être terrifiant pour ceux qui ne sont pas très à l'aise dans les côtations élevées, en effet de nombreuses voies en-dessous de 7a ne sont pas très bien equipées. Cependant les vues et l'escalade sont exceptionnels. Toutes les falaises sont affectées par le Mistral et nous vous conseillons de consulter notre guide météorologique en page 7 pour vous aider à choisir la falaise la mieux adaptée aux conditions atmosphériques (consultez les guides locaux – page 21).

The name Dentelles de Montmirail (lace of the Montmirail), derives from the white cliffs set above the vineyards between the villages of Beaumes de Venise and Gigondas. These wonderful jagged peaks will immediately catch your attention when you approach the area from the main A7- Autoroute Lyon-Marseille, and are guaranteed to get you chomping at the bit. Alternatively, they look fabulous if you are returning at sunset over from the col south of Malaucène, when an amber red sun sinks slowly into there midst. It is an enchanting area, a large one, and one that you will never forget. Beaumes-de-Venise is an ideal village to stay in or nearby, especially when the weather is on the cooler side since it is at very low altitude. It also has the advantage of only being a 30 min drive to Venasque or Combe Obscure, where the entertainment is of a completely different style, but both practical winter venues. In the hot summer months, the ideal climbing in the shade is accessed from the Gigondas side.

The Dentelles de Montmirail is an extensive area, and even though the cliffs look close together on a big map, they are a considerable distance apart. Choosing to walk from one cliff to another, rather than driving, is usually a one-off bad decision. There are 6 different parking spots around these hills, and choose your ideal spot closest to the cliff of your choice. Understanding the geography of the area from the map can be confusing. From the north or the south, you can see the giant 80-90m cliffs that presumably form a mountain ridge. However, these actually form a saddle with a quiet valley between (vineyard). The northern Gigondas Chaîne is substantially higher in altitude, but not high enough to really protect the southern Chaîne du Clapis from the savage Mistral wind when it blows. There are minor cliffs overlooking the inner valley, but the main cliffs are either south or north facing. At the East end, there a whole area that is a real mixture of cliffs that face different directions and form the third main area. From a climbers point of view, Dents (teeth), would be a wry description, since the cliffs are gleaming white, very smooth, and offer climbing with a distinct bite – plus the occasionally loose, giant manky filling. On these large cliffs, the climbing can be terrifying to those operating in the lower grades; they obviously ran out of bolts when equipping the routes below 7a. The views and climbing however is exceptional, and is a must on any climber's agenda. All the cliffs here are affected by the Mistral wind and I suggest that you refer to our weather guide on page 7 before choosing a cliff for the day. (local guidebook also – see page 21)

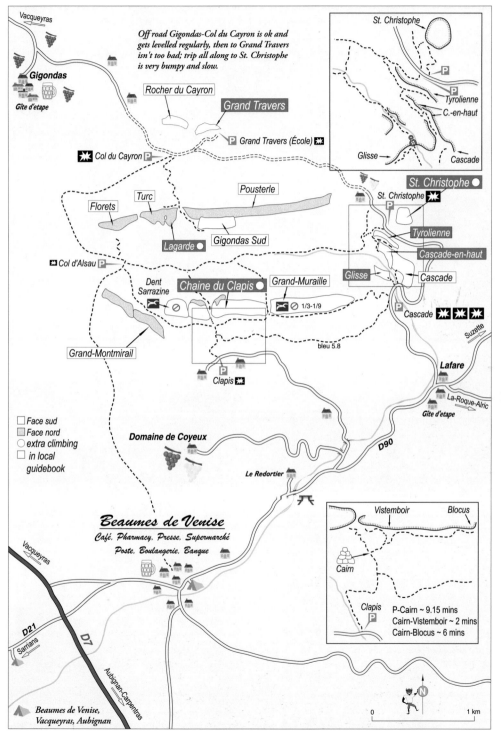

BLANCHARD | ARCHÉO | CORNEIRETTE | QUINSAN | VENASQUE | ST.PIERRE | COLOMBIER | CLAPIS | GLISSE | TROLIENNE | CASCADE·HAUT | CHRISTOPHE | A.LAGARDE | GRAND TRAV | COMBE OBS. | GROSEAU

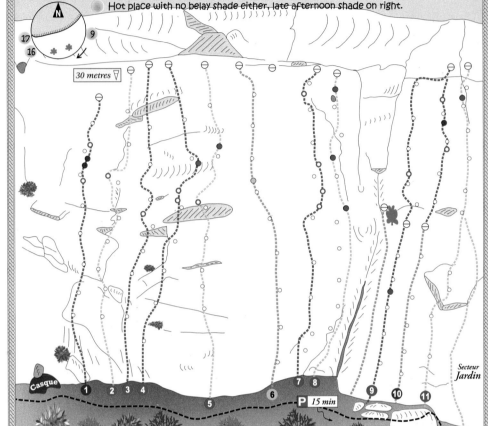

Hot place with no belay shade either, late afternoon shade on right.

30 metres

Casque

Secteur Jardin

P 15 min

	Crux/bloc	Endurance	Sport
① Electric soupçon ** 😊			7a-
29m	● 7a- 747 CRIMP	□ 6c- 747 COOl	⌐7⌐

A very good wall climb and perfect for those with small fingers who like sustained climbing; not a very pleasant lead.

② Pan bagnat ** 😊			6c-
31m	○ 6c-	6a+ 747 CRIMP	⌐9⌐

There are 9 bolts, but mostly where you don't want them or difficult to clip. Very lonely crux and not that enjoyable for grade 6 leaders.

③ Chagrin d'humeur ** 😊			6c-
31m	○ 6c- 747 Trick	6b 747 COOl	⌐6⌐

Mostly steady climbing on jugs. Difficult crux to onsight at the grade, but skilful use of a heel hook just keeps it at 6c-.

④ Brazil			6c-
31m	○ 6c- Bloc	6b	⌐7⌐

A superb route - on a top rope! Falling off whilst clipping the 6th clip would be nasty to say the least, stamina of grade 7 - recommended.

⑤ Silence ** 😊			6c-
30m	○ 6c- Sloper	6a+ 747	⌐7⌐

A route likely to cause considerable chuntering as you flail around the crux - too polished for comfort. Good incuts soon arrive though.

⑥ Cheeseburger *** 😊			⚡ 5++
30m	● 6a-	5++ 747	⌐9⌐

A great route, long run outs, but not when the moves are hard.

	Crux/bloc	Endurance	Sport
⑦ Nid d'écureuil * 😊			⚡ 6c-
27m	○ 6c- 747	6b 747	⌐9⌐

A wonderful 27m of climbing on a top rope. Not too bad to read, but slippery polish makes the moves very on-off.

⑧ Jeu d'artifice *** 😊			⚡ 6b-
27m	● 6b- COOl	6a+ 747	⌐8⌐

A lovely climb, spaced bolts - but where you want them. Good pockets and good rests, a classic of the area.

⑨ Des destes pour le faire *** 😊			⚡ 6c-
31m	○ 6c-	6b 747	⌐11⌐

Both the lower and upper wall provide fingertip entertainment.

⑩ Château de sable *** 😊			⚡ 6c
31m	● 7a- CRIMP	6b 747 COOl	⌐9⌐

A really good and technical slab climb; at least you can rest to work out the moves, but even good beta is not enough - footwork is the key.

⑪ Bayonnette *** 😊			⚡ 6b-
31m	● 6b-	6a 747	⌐10⌐

A superb classic & 2 starts. Polished footholds at the top make life awkward, but tiny pockets save the day in an incredible position.

Résumé. *These slabs on the left side offer great climbing, but the routes are definitely scary. There are multi-pitch routes above; but all look considerably harder and not very friendly.*

CHEESEBURGER 5++, Clapis-Sud, Dentelles de Montmirail; Jim Bacon

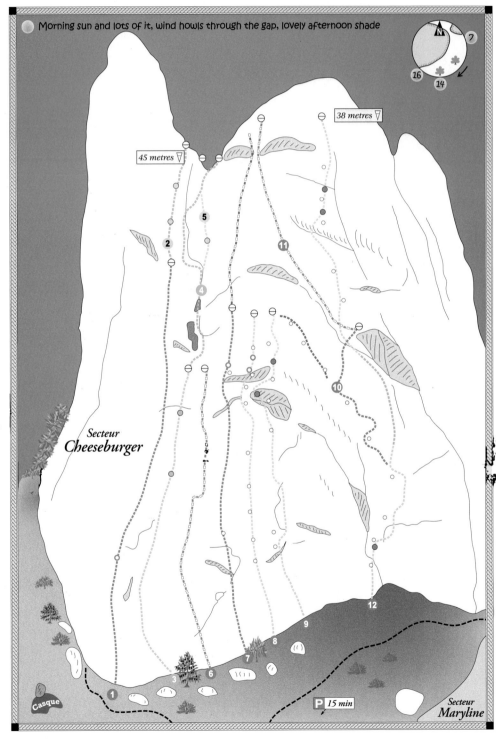

Morning sun and lots of it, wind howls through the gap, lovely afternoon shade

45 metres

38 metres

Secteur
Cheeseburger

Casque

P 15 min

Secteur
Maryline

CHEESEBURGER-JARDIN, Clapis-Sud, Dentelles de Montmirail (Chaîne du Gigondas to right)

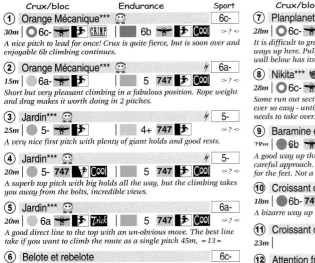

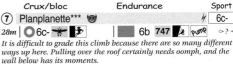

	Crux/bloc	Endurance	Sport
(1) Orange Mécanique* 😊			6c-
30m	6c- ☀️ 🧗 CRIMP	6b ☀️ 🧗 COOl	⊶?⊶

A nice pitch to lead for once! Crux is quite fierce, but is soon over and enjoyable 6b climbing continues.

(2) Orange Mécanique* 😊			6a-
15m	6a- ☀️ 🧗	5 747 🧗 COOl	⊶?⊶

Short but very pleasant climbing in a fabulous position. Rope weight and drag makes it worth doing in 2 pitches.

(3) Jardin* 😊			5-
25m	5- ☀️ 🧗	4+ 747 🧗	⊶?⊶

A very nice first pitch with plenty of giant holds and good rests.

(4) Jardin* 😊			5-
20m	5- 747 🧗 COOl	5 747 🧗	⊶?⊶

A superb top pitch with big holds all the way, but the climbing takes you away from the bolts, incredible views.

(5) Jardin* 😊			6a-
20m	6a ☀️ 🧗 Trick	5 747 🧗 COOl	⊶?⊶

A good direct line to the top with an un-obvious move. The best line take if you want to climb the route as a single pitch 45m, = 13 =

(6) Belote et rebelote			6c-
25m	6c ➡️ 🧗 CRIMP	6c+ ➡️ 🧗 Pump	⊶?⊶

An excellent space of rock to climb on. Bolts don't follow the natural and easiest line, and are almost impossible to clip. A lot of fun and variations can be enjoyed on a top rope.

	Crux/bloc	Endurance	Sport
(7) Planplanette* 😊			⚡ 6c-
28m	6c- ☀️ 🧗	6b 747 🏃 Pump	⊶?⊶

It is difficult to grade this climb because there are so many different ways up here. Pulling over the roof certainly needs oomph, and the wall below has its moments.

(8) Nikita* 😊			6c-
28m	6c- ☀️ 🏃 CRIMP	6a+ 747 🧗 Pump	⊶?⊶

Some run out sections low down but aren't too bad. Overhang seems ever so easy - until the lip where the holds run out and crimping needs to take over.

(9) Baramine et belles écailles* 😊			6b-
28m	6b ☀️ 🧗	6a 747 🧗 🐕	⊶?⊶

A good way up this section of the crag. Very run out and demands a careful approach. Good holds all the way but often relying on friction for the feet. Not a recommendation for novice or young leaders.

(10) Croissant chaud 😊			6b-
18m	6b- 747 🧗	6a 747 🧗 🐕	⊶?⊶

A bizarre way up the lower wall.

(11) Croissant chaud			6c
23m		DIEDRE	⊶?⊶

(12) Attention fragile* 😊			6b-
38m	6b- ☀️ 🧗	5 ➡️ 🧗 COOl	⊶8⊶

A superb way up this right side of the crag and a full length 38m pitch. Run out in the middle but not hard, great top wall. A few nuts for the middle section could help nerves.

Résumé. *A tremendous looking piece of rock that offers many different styles of climbing. When you get used to the friction footholds and flow calmly, the routes don't seem too hard. Route finding is often difficult, so you will often be climbing at a higher standard than you actually need. Great in the morning sunshine or afternoon shade. I call it the Jardin du Vent (garden of wind), since if there is any wind blowing at all, it comes straight through the col and blasts you literally off the rock. If the mistral wind is blowing strongly, then this is just about the windiest place on the Dentelles. On a hot, calm day, it feels like an incinerator. There are two trees at the bottom for a bit of belay shade, but they don't help that much. Picnic away from the rock - stonefall.*

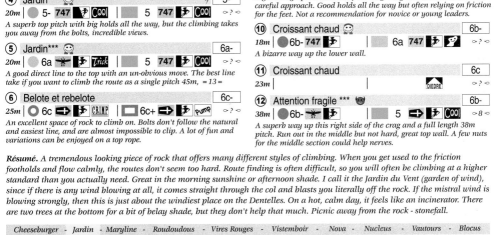

Side tabs (right margin): BLANCHARD | ARCHÉO | CORNEIRETTE | QUINSAN | VENASQUE | ST.PIERRE | COLOMBIER | CLAPIS | GLISSE | TYROLIENNE | CASCADE-HAUT | CHRISTOPHE | ALAGARDE | GRAND TRAV | COMBE OBS. | GROSEAU

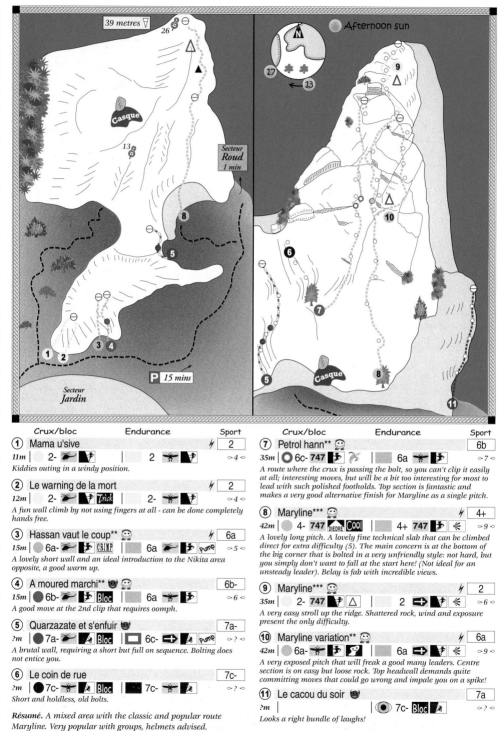

Crux/bloc	Endurance	Sport

① Mama u'sive   ⚡ 2

11m | 2- 🪨 | 2 | ∽4∽

Kiddies outing in a windy position.

② Le warning de la mort   ⚡ 2

12m | 2- 🪨 Trick | 2- | ∽4∽

A fun wall climb by not using fingers at all - can be done completely hands free.

③ Hassan vaut le coup★★ 😊   ⚡ 6a

15m | 6a- 🪨 CRIMP | 6a 🪨 Pump | ∽5∽

A lovely short wall and an ideal introduction to the Nikita area opposite, a good warm up.

④ A moured marchi★★ 😊😊   6b-

15m | 6b- 🪨 Bloc | 6a 🪨 | ∽6∽

A good move at the 2nd clip that requires oomph.

⑤ Quarzazate et s'enfuir 😊

?m | 7a- 🪨 Bloc | 6c ➡ Pump | ∽?∽

A brutal wall, requiring a short but full on sequence. Bolting does not entice you.

⑥ Le coin de rue   7c-

?m | 7c- 🪨 Bloc | 7c- | ∽?∽

Short and holdless, old bolts.

Résumé. *A mixed area with the classic and popular route Maryline. Very popular with groups, helmets advised.*

Crux/bloc	Endurance	Sport

⑦ Petrol hann★★ 😊   6b

35m | ⭕ 6c- 747 🪨 | 6a 🪨 | ∽7∽

A route where the crux is passing the bolt, so you can't clip it easily at all; interesting moves, but will be a bit too interesting for most to lead with such polished footholds. Top section is fantastic and makes a very good alternative finish for Maryline as a single pitch.

⑧ Maryline★★★ 😊   ⚡ 4+

42m | 4- 747 DIEDRE COOL | 4+ 747 🪨 | ∽9∽

A lovely long pitch. A lovely fine technical slab that can be climbed direct for extra difficulty (5). The main concern is at the bottom of the big corner that is bolted in a very unfriendly style: not hard, but you simply don't want to fall at the start here! (Not ideal for an unsteady leader). Belay is fab with incredible views.

⑨ Maryline★★★ 😊   ⚡ 2

35m | 2- 747 🪨 △ | 2 ➡ 🪨 | ∽6∽

A very easy stroll up the ridge. Shattered rock, wind and exposure present the only difficulty.

⑩ Maryline variation★★ 😊   ⚡ 6a

42m | 6a- 🪨 | 6a ➡ 🪨 | ∽9∽

A very exposed pitch that will freak a good many leaders. Centre section is on easy but loose rock. Top headwall demands quite committing moves that could go wrong and impale you on a spike!

⑪ Le cacou du soir 😊   7a

?m | | ⭕ 7c- Bloc | ∽?∽

Looks a right bundle of laughs!

Sector Maryland, Clapis-Sud, Dentelles de Montmirail

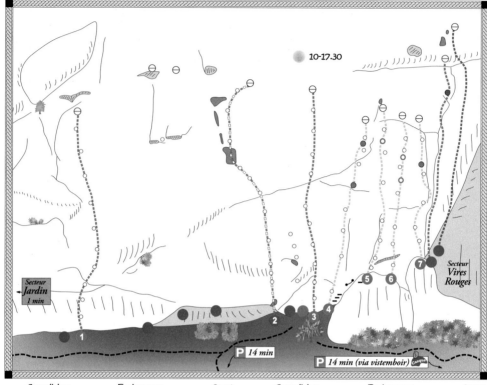

10-17.30

Secteur
Jardin
1 min

Secteur
Vires
Rouges

P 14 min

P 14 min (via vistemboir)

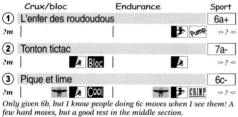

	Crux/bloc	Endurance	Sport
(1)	**L'enfer des roudoudous**		6a+
?m		Pump ∽?∽	
(2)	**Tonton tictac**		7a-
?m	Bloc	∽?∽	
(3)	**Pique et lime**		6c-
?m	Cool	CRIMP ∽?∽	

Only given 6b, but I know people doing 6c moves when I see them! A few hard moves, but a good rest in the middle section.

Résumé. A very impressive part of the cliff with some steep and hard routes, a lot of hang dogging takes place with most leaders. Vertical routes on the right are easier and very pleasant, before getting steeper and harder again. Section is often very sheltered when a big mistral wind is blowing. A furnace in a heat wave! We didn't have time to fully check out.

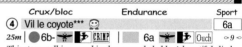

	Crux/bloc	Endurance	Sport
(4)	**Vil le coyote*** ☺		6a
25m	6b- CRIMP	6a Ouch ∽9∽	

This steep wall is covered in sharp crozzly holds. A beautiful climb with a couple of good and committing moves close to gear - in ideal warm up.

	Crux/bloc	Endurance	Sport
(5)	**Bouge de là** ☺		6b
23m	6c- CRIMP	6a Ouch ∽8∽	

A superb crimpy & abrasive wall gives incredible friction. Only one hard move that demands fingertip strength, bad footwork - expensive.

	Crux/bloc	Endurance	Sport
(6)	**Le pire ami du loup*** ☺		6b
24m	6c- CRIMP	6a Ouch ∽8∽	

A very good climb, low in the grade. A very pleasant wall leads to a slab of crimps, taken direct all the way on small holds.

	Crux/bloc	Endurance	Sport
(7)	**Les novis** ☺		6a+
15m	6b-	6a ∽6∽	

A lovely short climb up a good arête with positive holds all the way.

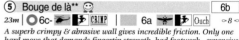

Roudoudou, Vires Rouges & Vistemboir sectors

PIQUE ET LIME 6c- Roudoudou, Clapis-Sud, Dentelles de Montmirail; Mireille Berthoud

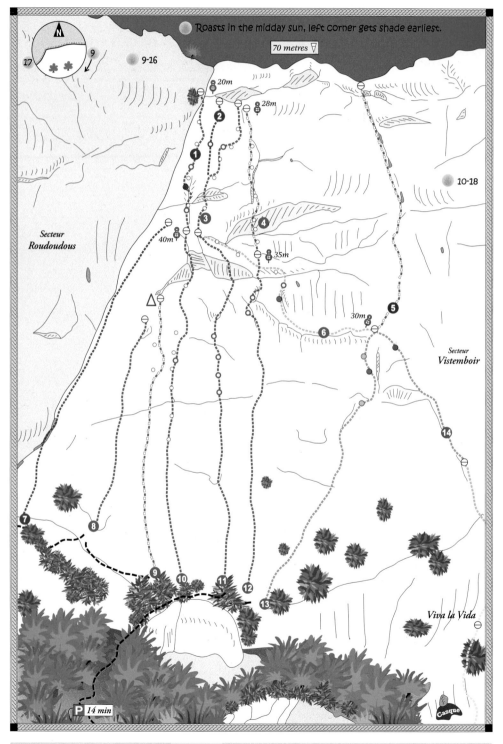

Roasts in the midday sun, left corner gets shade earliest.

70 metres

9-16

10-18

Secteur **Roudoudous**

Secteur **Vistemboir**

Viva la Vida

P 14 min

BLANCHARD | ARCHÉO | CORNIERETTE | QUINSAN | VENASQUE | ST.PIERRE | COLOMBIER | CLAPIS | GLISSE | TYROLIENNE | CASCADE-HAUT | CHRISTOPHE | A.LAGARDE | GRAND TRAV | COMBE OBS. | GROSEAU

Crux/bloc	Endurance	Sport

① Vires rouges** 😊 ⚡ 6c-

19m | ● 7a- 🦴 Bloc | 6b 🦴 | ○?○

All the difficulty is in the first half - we give no clues, except that the second half is on excellent pockets and a fun technical teaser.

② Rapt à la tronçonneuse* 😊 7a

20m | ◐ 7b- 747 CRIMP | 7a- 747 COOL | ○?○

You won't find people que-ing to lead this bundle of laughs! A nasty pitch onsight, but a very rewarding onsight. Moving left out of Le Ph. begins quite easily with tiny ripples and sharp edges providing inadequate support. Self levitation on imaginary holds is the key to success. Knowing where to grab the final ramp - is convenient!

③ Le philanthrope** 😊 6c-

18m | ● 6c- BIZ | 6b Pump | ○?○

A very difficult pitch to onsight. Challenging & steep moves lead up from the belay to the right. A silly long reach to a crimp, is the beginning of some moves that require flexibility and ingenuity. Highly sustained with poor rests.

Crux/bloc	Endurance	Sport

⑥ Vires rouges*** 😊 6c-

? m | ● 6c- Bloc | 6a COOL | ○?○

Not a pitch for incompetent wally's. A good traverse line is easy but still cock-up-able, with a second falling into space and unlowerable! The crux headwall is possible due to the giant flake glued on, enough to unsettle nerves; finding holds at the top is problematic!!!

Crux/bloc	Endurance	Sport

⑦ Le philanthrope 7a

? m | | DIEDRE | ○?○

A groove that looks a tremendous line, and doesn't look too easy either.

⑧ Andropète 6b

? m | | | ○?○

A climb that enjoys popularity, but not so many clean ascents.

⑨ Grotte a gateau 😊 0c-

30m | ◐ 6c- 747 CRIMP | 6b 747 | ○7○

Not an enjoyable lead at all. Very sustained crimping, and keep to the right of the last 3 bolts for the easiest way up. Calm nerves are essential, since a fall would be somewhat abrasively painful Agghh!

⑩ Rêve d'ô*** 😊 6c-

40m | ● 6c- CRIMP | 6b+ Fab | ○11○

A superb long pitch with 35 metres of solid climbing. A crimpy mid wall can catch you out, and is tiring onsight. The top overhang is a stroll, but short climbers have to maximise their technique. The final headwall on jugs proves exhilarating.

Crux/bloc	Endurance	Sport

④ New Baby*** 😊 ⚡ 6c

25m | ◐ 6c- CRIMP | 6c COOL | ○9○

Sufficient holds appear just when you need them. The steepness may appear daunting, but presents little difficulty. Stamina and crimping delicate brown cornflakes - requires coolness in the top part. Not a climb to take a struggling second on, as they will be faffing out in space and out of sight - drama or what!

⑤ Philippus*** 6c

? m | | Pump | ○?○

A superb line and up a very impressive headwall. Be alert for any birds nesting in the large pockets, maybe keep for autumn.

Crux/bloc	Endurance	Sport

⑪ Rapt à la tronçonneuse* 😊 6c-

39m | ● 6c 747 CRIMP | 6b+ 747 | ○14○

Plenty of bolts low down on the easy section, then it all goes wrong and the climbing gets hard and run out - sustained fingertip crimping. Top overhang is a jugfest - whoopee!

⑫ New Baby*** 😊 6b+

35m | ◐ 6c- CRIMP | 6b+ Pump | ○?○

A fabulous pitch. The first half warms you up, but as the angle increases, so does the difficulty. Everything tends to go very pear shaped at the top of the ramp. Stamina is essential, as is luck in unlocking the sequence first time. You can power through at 7a/b easily, but you avoid the challenge. Seems longer than 35m.

⑬ Vires rouges** 6a

? m | ● 6b- CRIMP | 6a- COOL | ○?○

A good intro pitch, but hardly a warm up. The slab steepens with increased attitude, then a combination of moves near dodgy rock lead to the hanging belay - bottleneck.

⑭ Philippus* 6a

? m | | | ○?○

Résumé. This is one of the great sectors in the Dentelles. A 70m rope is essential, and an 80m corde is even better (saves having to ab off New Baby all the time). A real mixed bag of equipping with some very challenging flat walls. When you know the routes and all the correct crimps are chalked up - it can seem a doddle. First time out it feels very lonely and you get very razzed fingertips. The top routes are very exposed and will test the nerves for those straight out of the climbing gym. Be very careful when lowering anyone down here, and have a spare rope if yours is not long enough.
There is a nice picnic terrace in front, and is clear of most stonefall, a lovely position.

Tear out topo - back of book

BLANCHARD · ARCHÉO · CORNEIRETTE · QUINSAN · VENASQUE · ST.PIERRE · COLOMBIER · CLAPIS · GLISSE · TYROLIENNE · CASCADE-HAUT · CHRISTOPHE · ALAGARDE · GRAND TRAV · COMBE OBS. · GROSEAU

NEW BABY 6b+ Vires Rouges, Clapis-Sud, Dentelles de Montmirail

PHILIPPUS 6c Vires Rouges, Clapis-Sud, Dentelles de Montmirail

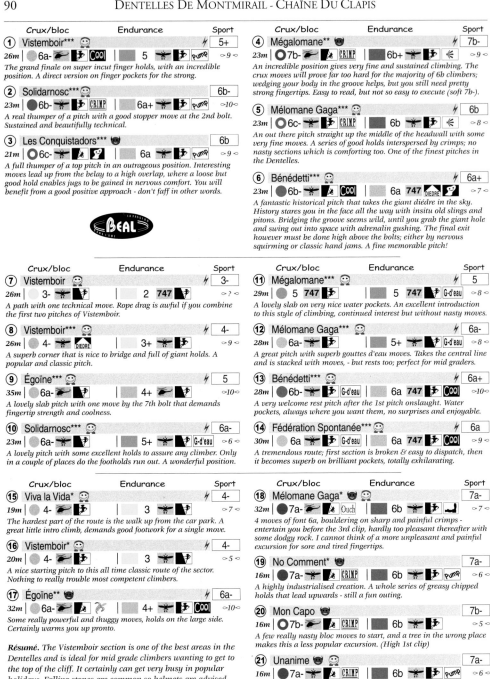

	Crux/bloc	Endurance	Sport

(1) Vistemboir* 😊
26m • 6a- 🔌 **Cool** | 5 ☀️ **pump** ∞9∞ | **5+**

The grand finale on super incut finger holds, with an incredible position. A direct version on finger pockets for the strong.

(2) Solidarnosc* 😊
23m ● 6b- ☀️ **CRIMP** | 6a+ ☀️ **pump** ∞10∞ | **6b-**

A real thumper of a pitch with a good stopper move at the 2nd bolt. Sustained and beautifully technical.

(3) Les Conquistadors* 🐾
21m ● 6c- ☀️ | 6a ☀️ ∞9∞ | **6b**

A full thumper of a top pitch in an outrageous position. Interesting moves lead up from the belay to a high overlap, where a loose but good hold enables jugs to be gained in nervous comfort. You will benefit from a good positive approach - don't faff in other words.

(4) Mégalomane 🐾
23m ○ 7b- 🔌 **CRIMP** | 6b+ ☀️ ≪ ∞9∞ | **7b-**

An incredible position gives very fine and sustained climbing. The crux moves will prove far too hard for the majority of 6b climbers; wedging your body in the groove helps, but you still need pretty strong fingertips. Easy to read, but not so easy to execute (soft 7b-).

(5) Mélomane Gaga* 😊
23m ● 6c- ☀️ **CRIMP** | 6b ☀️ ≪ ∞8∞ | **6b**

An out there pitch straight up the middle of the headwall with some very fine moves. A series of good holds interspersed by crimps; no nasty sections which is comforting too. One of the finest pitches in the Dentelles.

(6) Bénédetti* 😊
23m | 6b- 🔌 **Cool** | 6a 747 **DIEDRE** ∞7∞ | **6a+**

A fantastic historical pitch that takes the giant diédre in the sky. History stares you in the face all the way with insitu old slings and pitons. Bridging the groove seems wild, until you grab the giant hole and swing out into space with adrenalin gushing. The final exit however must be done high above the bolts; either by nervous squirming or classic hand jams. A fine memorable pitch!

	Crux/bloc	Endurance	Sport

(7) Vistemboir 😊
26m | 3- ☀️ | 2 747 | **3-**

A path with one technical move. Rope drag is awful if you combine the first two pitches of Vistemboir.

(8) Vistemboir* 😊
26m | 4- ☀️ **DIEDRE** | 3+ ☀️ ∞9∞ | **4-**

A superb corner that is nice to bridge and full of giant holds. A popular and classic pitch.

(9) Égoïne* 😊
35m | 6a- ☀️ | 4+ ☀️ ∞10∞ | **5**

A lovely slab pitch with one move by the 7th bolt that demands fingertip strength and coolness.

(10) Solidarnosc* 😊
23m | 6a- ☀️ | 5+ ☀️ G-d'eau ∞6∞ | **6a-**

A lovely pitch with some excellent holds to assure any climber. Only in a couple of places do the footholds run out. A wonderful position.

(11) Mégalomane* 😊
29m | 5 747 | 5 747 G-d'eau ∞8∞ | **5**

A lovely slab on very nice water pockets. An excellent introduction to this style of climbing, continued interest but without nasty moves.

(12) Mélomane Gaga* 😊
28m | 6a- ☀️ | 5+ ☀️ G-d'eau ∞8∞ | **6a-**

A great pitch with superb gouttes d'eau moves. Takes the central line and is stacked with moves, - but rests too; perfect for mid graders.

(13) Bénédetti* 😊
28m | 6b- ☀️ G-d'eau | 6a 747 **Cool** ∞10∞ | **6a+**

A very welcome rest pitch after the 1st pitch onslaught. Water pockets, always where you want them, no surprises and enjoyable.

(14) Fédération Spontanée* 😊
30m | 6a ☀️ G-d'eau | 6a 747 **Cool** ∞9∞ | **6a**

A tremendous route; first section is broken & easy to dispatch, then it becomes superb on brilliant pockets, totally exhilarating.

	Crux/bloc	Endurance	Sport

(15) Viva la Vida* 😊
19m | 4- 🔌 | 3 ☀️ ∞7∞ | **4-**

The hardest part of the route is the walk up from the car park. A great little intro climb, demands good footwork for a single move.

(16) Vistemboir* 😊
20m | 4- 🔌 | 3 ☀️ ∞5∞ | **4-**

A nice starting pitch to this all time classic route of the sector. Nothing to really trouble most competent climbers.

(17) Égoïne 🐾
32m | 6a- 🔌 ✂️ | 4+ ☀️ **Cool** ∞10∞ | **6a-**

Some really powerful and thuggy moves, holds on the large side. Certainly warms you up pronto.

(18) Mélomane Gaga* 🐾😊
32m | 7a- 🔌 **Ouch** | 6b ☀️ ∞7∞ | **7a-**

4 moves of font 6a, bouldering on sharp and painful crimps - entertain you before the 3rd clip, hardly too pleasant thereafter with some dodgy rock. I cannot think of a more unpleasant and painful excursion for sore and tired fingertips.

(19) No Comment* 🐾
16m | 7a- ☀️ **CRIMP** | 6b ☀️ **pump** ∞6∞ | **7a-**

A highly industrialised creation. A whole series of greasy chipped holds that lead upwards - still a fun outing.

(20) Mon Capo 🐾
16m | ○ 7b- 🔌 **CRIMP** | 6b ☀️ ∞5∞ | **7b-**

A few really nasty bloc moves to start, and a tree in the wrong place makes this a less popular excursion. (High 1st clip)

(21) Unanime 🐾😊
16m | 7a- 🔌 **CRIMP** | 6b ☀️ **pump** ∞6∞ | **7a-**

About five hard moves in a row, which are both technical and quite powerful, the wall after seems easy if you are fit and light.

(22) Bénédetti 🐾
35m | 6b- 🔌 **pump** | 6a+ 747 ☀️ ∞10∞ | **6b-**

The holds are generous; but route finding & hold finding at this angle will prove too tiring for many. Multiple crux's - no rests!

Résumé. The Vistemboir section is one of the best areas in the Dentelles and is ideal for mid grade climbers wanting to get to the top of the cliff. It certainly can get very busy in popular holidays. Falling stones are common so helmets are advised, especially on the left side, but the rock is generally superb and solid. Main descents are down Égoïne and Bénédetti. There are more top pitches than bottom ones (which get very busy anyway), so take some water and spend the day up high. The views from the top here are stunning.

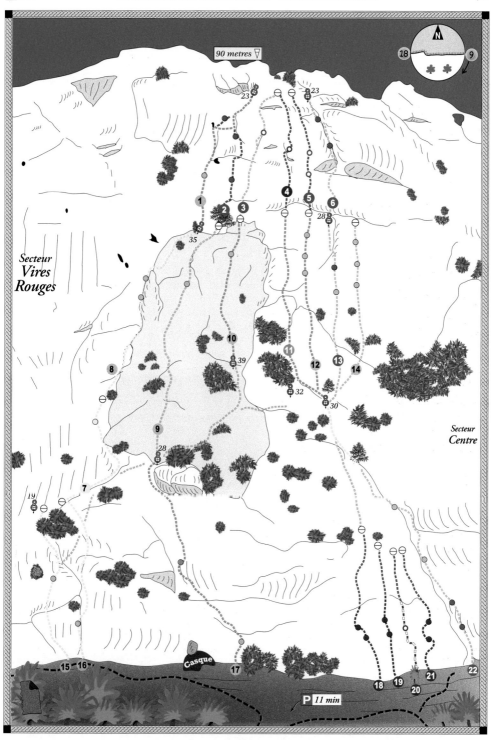

Secteur
*Vires
Rouges*

Secteur
Centre

90 metres

Casque

P *11 min*

The food in this area is very different from our other book to the Bourgogne, it literally has a Mediterranean feel. The fish, served both in the restaurants and sold in shops & markets is always worth hunting out. The intense heat of Provence gives rise to a lot of olives, apricots and cherries, and you will see these combined into many local dishes. There are simply stacks of excellent restaurants to hunt out, but I can recommend a few specials not to miss: **Monieux**, a lovely rustic joint in the quiet backstreets; **Venasque** – see area map; **Beaumes-de-Venise**, two lovely small restaraunts just down past the post office - offer a very relaxed & informal atmosphere with very good food. Look out for the sign of Gôut, which means a special tasting award; **Caromb**, just on the

Pic-nic Gorges de la Nesque - Jingo Wobbly style

right before the main street as you approach from B-de-V, nice exterior enclosed courtyard with very nice atmos; **Crillon-le-Brave**(2), expensive but fab; **Bédoin**, uppermost hotel-restaurant opposite boules area – best food in town; **Gigondas**, Le Oustalet – has a lovely outside terrace under big trees in village centre & with rustic charm – daily specials a must; **Vaison**, about 300m up the hill into the very

Auberge St. Roch; Beaumes-de-Venise

old town, superb pizza from open fire oven & lovely view over Vaison (ideal on a rainy day), also the top notch Moulin à Huile(7eve,1) £ ouch; **Entrechaux**, St. Hubert(2,3) comes by good recommendation; **Brantes**, a lovely auberge just NE of the village – cracking food; **La Roche-s-Buis**, very good bistro with a terrace, plus excellent evening sunshine & views (limited opening); **St.Auban-s-l'Ouveze**, don't miss this lovely rustic auberge, La Clavelière, and a nice lunchtime terrace with views. The final place you just have to experience!! is la Clue(1) at **Plaisians**. This is a rustic habitat, where if you are a veggie - you don't want to even think of going – a high protein feast of dark but succulent ex-living mammals – simply fantastic if you are a meaty rural chomper, a classic night out with excellent wines too - & don't miss out chatting with the chef. I could carry on but alas – this is a climbing book! (closed 1- mon)

Brantes

Centre secteur of Le Clapis (Local topo only) - superb high level climbing with a great view of Mont Ventoux.

View from Le Clapis over the plain of Comtat de Venaissin towards Carpentras, Venasque and the Luberon hills in the distance.

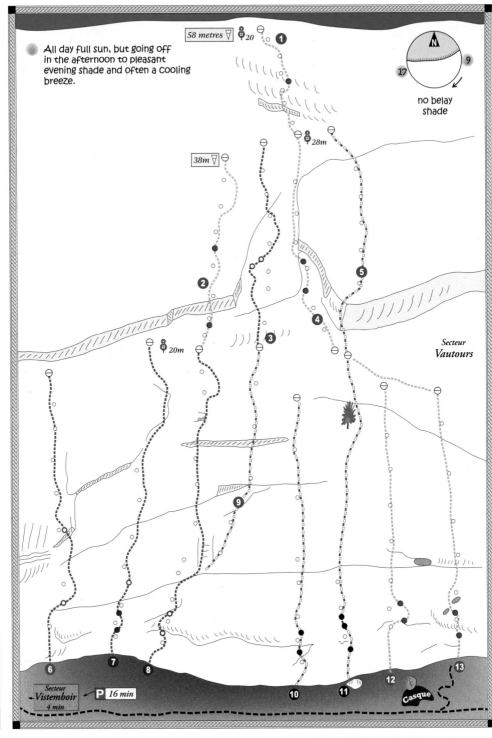

All day full sun, but going off in the afternoon to pleasant evening shade and often a cooling breeze.

58 metres   20

38m

28m

20m

no belay
shade

Secteur
Vautours

Secteur
Vistemboir
4 min   P 16 min

Casque

BLANCHARD
ARCHÉO
CORNEIRETTE
QUINSAN
VENASQUE
ST.PIERRE
COLOMBIER
CLAPIS
GLISSE
TYROLIENNE
CASCADE-HAUT
CHRISTOPHE
A.LAGARDE
GRAND TRAV
COMBE OBS.
GROSEAU

Crux/bloc	Endurance	Sport

(1) La Nova*  6b-

18m | 6b- | 6a+ pump ◦6◦

An out there pitch, smile - you're on camera. The rock looks disgustingly loose, but is actually very sound in most of the parts that you climb on. Good holds in the right places allow you to work out the climb as you go and make a perfect onsight possible; dig deep, hang on and commit yourself - you will be rewarded.

(2) Mandragore*  6b-

18m | 6b- | 6a G-d'eau ◦6◦

A superb pitch; getting to the overhang proves interesting. Then finding a jug is semi brilliant, only to find another jug as incredibly brilliant. A super fest of enjoyment, technical interest continues.

(3) Super nova*  6c-

18m | 6c- 747 | 6b 747 ◦6◦

A weird pitch and not over enjoyable to lead. The bolts are in a straight line, but a good climbing line goes in a different path, so this is one perhaps best enjoyed with the freedom of a top rope. The start is hard, so watch out on the belay.

(4) La Nova*  6b-

28m | 6b- DIEDRE | 6a COOL ◦10◦

A pitch that seems to flourish with plants and greenery. Most bolts are hidden by plants and it looks like an unprotected horror nightmare scenario. However, the rock is good and the route is well protected. Good technical climbing keeps the grade lower than it looks; nervous but not strenuous.

(5) Coup de boule  6b+

? m | | ◦?◦

NOVA 6b-, Le Clapis, Dentelles de Montmirail; Carrie Atchison-Jones

Crux/bloc	Endurance	Sport

(6) Lagagne 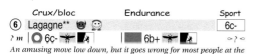 6c-

? m | 6c- | 6b+ ◦?◦

An amusing move low down, but it goes wrong for most people at the overlap, hanging around to find the holds, takes its toll on the flash.

(7) Sacrilège 7a-

? m | 7a- | 6c ◦?◦

A hard and complicated start, and with continued interest up to the flake with some undercuts that usually entertain a grimace.

(8) Mandragore*  7b-

? m | 7b- | 6b ◦9◦

The start is full on power from sloper to crimp; the rest will seem like a walk in the park - take your dog along.

(9) Supernova  7b-

? m | 7b- | 6c- ◦?◦

Not very good rock and often avoided, especially by moi.

(10) Pervers dévers  7c-

? m | 7c- | ◦?◦

This gets a visual high grade, by virtue of the number of people who fail on this brutal start.

Crux/bloc	Endurance	Sport

(11) Malpertuis  7c-

? m | 7c- | ◦?◦

Another comical move to leave the ground, a very popular swing around, strong climbers need only apply.

(12) Une idée en l'air* 6b-

18m | 6b- | 6a+ CRIMP ◦6◦

A very good route with a bit of everything. Taking a curving line to the right keeps the grade friendly on good holds (direct 7b-). Then it gets all nice and crimpy, a good outing.

(13) Nucleus*  6a

18m | 6b- | 6a CRIMP ◦6◦

Very easy 6b moves, but cranking of a one finger mono still counts as a 6b move, especially when the footholds are polished; fun thereafter.

Résumé. *The Nova section is just before the main promontory of the highly popular Vautours section, a very busy place on a holiday weekend and definitely helmet territory with loose rock on the second pitches of most routes. A pity that the starts are so hard because the top of this section is great climbing at a reasonable standard. Views from the top are stunning and belay positions are generally comfortable. Ideal on a sunny midweek day with a light wind blowing.*

BLANCHARD | ARCHÉO | CORNEIRETTE | QUINSAN | VENASQUE | ST.PIERRE | COLOMBIER | CLAPIS | GLISSE | TYROLIENNE | CASCADE-HAUT | CHRISTOPHE | A.LAGARDE | GRAND TRAV | COMBE OBS. | GROSEAU

LES VAUTOURS 6a, Le Clapis, Dentelles de Montmirail; Elisabeth Maret

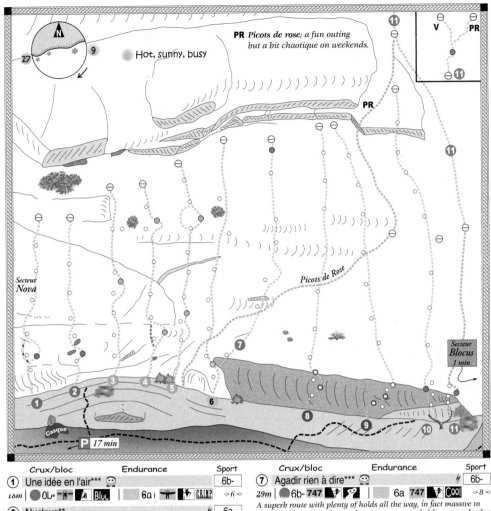

PR *Picots de rose; a fun outing but a bit chaotique on weekends.*

Hot, sunny, busy

Secteur Nova

Picots de Rose

Secteur Blocus 1 min

Casque

P 17 min

Side tabs: BLANCHARD · ARCHÉO · CORNEIRETTE · QUINSAN · VENASQUE · ST.PIERRE · COLOMBIER · CLAPIS · GLISSE · TYROLIENNE · CASCADE-HAUT · CHRISTOPHE · A.LAGARDE · GRAND TRAV · COMBE OBS. · GROSEAU

Crux/bloc	Endurance	Sport

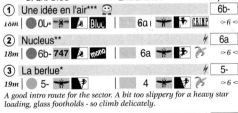

① Une idée en l'air* ☺ — 6b-
18m | 6b- | 6a | ○6○
A good intro route for the sector. A bit too slippery for a heavy star loading, glass footholds - so climb delicately.

② Nucleus — 6a
18m | 6b- 747 mono | 6a | ○6○

③ La berlue* — 5-
19m | 5- | 4 | ○6○

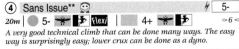

④ Sans Issue ☺ — 5-
20m | 5- Flexi | 4+ | ○6○
A very good technical climb that can be done many ways. The easy way is surprisingly easy; lower crux can be done as a dyno.

⑤ Soupçons* ☺ — 5-
26m | 5- | 4+ | ○7○
A steep initial section can be climbed technically, almost without strength.

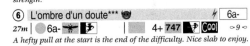

⑥ L'ombre d'un doute* — 6a-
27m | 6a- | 4+ 747 COOL | ○9○
A hefty pull at the start is the end of the difficulty. Nice slab to enjoy.

Résumé. *Popular sector; sticks out attracting a cooling breeze.*

Crux/bloc	Endurance	Sport

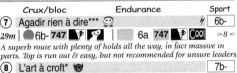

⑦ Agadir rien à dire* ☺ — 6b-
29m | 6b- 747 | 6a 747 COOL | ○8○
A superb route with plenty of holds all the way, in fact massive in parts. Top is run out & easy, but not recommended for unsure leaders.

⑧ L'art à croft* — 7b-
32m | 7b- CRIMP | 6a | ○9○
An obvious 4 metre section of impending rock, tends to impend progress for many, not hard to work out - just to do!

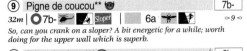

⑨ Pigne de coucou* — 7b-
32m | 7b- Sloper | 6a | ○9○
So, can you crank on a sloper? A bit energetic for a while; worth doing for the upper wall which is superb.

⑩ Rêve de singe* ☺ — 6b-
37m | 6b- | 6a++ | ○12○
A stupendous pitch, don't hang about at the 1st overhang because you will fade quickly. Ideal as a long single pitch.

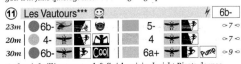

⑪ Les Vautours* — 6b-
23m | 6b- | 5- | ○7○
20m | 4- | 4 | ○7○
30m | 6b- COOL | 6a+ Pump | ○9○
A classic brilliant route - left finish original, right Picots de rose.

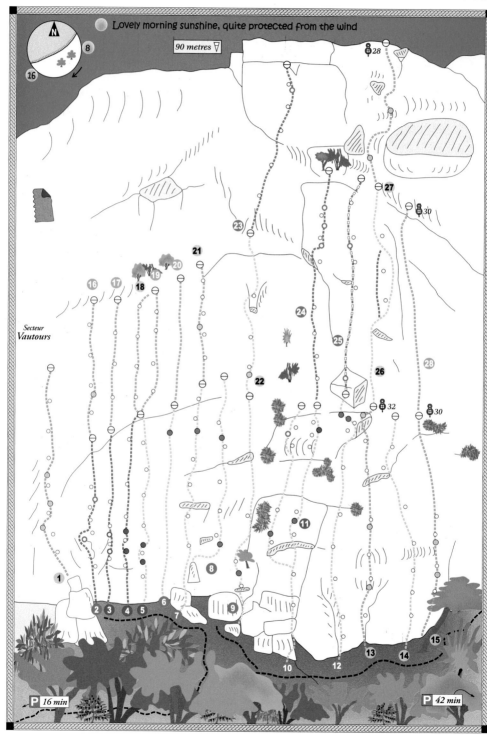

Lovely morning sunshine, quite protected from the wind

90 metres

Secteur **Vautours**

BLANCHARD

ARCHÉO

CORNEIRETTE

QUINSAN

VENASQUE

ST.PIERRE

COLOMBIER

CLAPIS

GLISE

TYROLIENNE

CASCADE-HAUT

CHRISTOPHE

A.LAGARDE

GRAND TRAV.

COMBE OBS.

GROSEAU

P 16 min   P 42 min

Crux/bloc	Endurance	Sport

① Guelle de loup* — 6a-
30m | 6a- | 5+ 747 | ○7○
Start from the top of the pinnacle on very hollow sounding flakes, go carefully. Top 20 metres is wonderful on lovely water pockets - bold.

② Italian shoes* — 6c-
22m | 6c- 747 | 6b 747 Cool | ○5○
A butch start to a hollow flake, taken well on the left. Mid section is very fingery & run out - needs confidence & ability to enjoy.

③ Turbostyle — 7b-
22m | 7b- | 6b | ○?○
A rather difficult start on sharp holds, high in the bloc grade.

④ Pinpin et yéyé** — 7a-
22m | 7a- Ouch | 6b Cool | ○?○
A leaning wall that is blind & crimpy; just keep going on the tiny flakes until you reach the gouttes d'eau.

⑤ Garogolot* — 7a-
? m | 7a- BVZZ | 6a G-d'eau | ○?○
A very weird start ending up with an awkward hand change, then a long reach right; easy thereafter.

⑥ Scorpigouille** — 6a+
25m | 6b- Cool | 6a+ G-d'eau | ○7○
A very good route that is continued superb climbing ending with a good hard crux at the end, a positive approach is required.

⑦ Douce romance** — 6a
24m | 6a- 747 CRIMP | 6a 747 | ○?○
Climb to the 1st bolt at 8m, then enjoy a lovely wall on good holds; this is followed by a terror slab where the bolts seem suicidally apart. Not too hard, but certainly not enjoyable.

⑧ Histoire d'aulx*** — 6b-
24m | 6b- CRIMP | 6a 747 G-d'eau | ○8○
A very good technical pitch, so long as you are not likely to come off at all; an ideal fun pitch for a 7a climber.

⑨ Pilier central direct*** — 6b-
25m | 6b- | 6a G-d'eau | ○7○
Some very nice gouttes d'eau. A hefty warm up with the crux thumping in early on.

⑩ Dernier tango au clapis*** — 6c-
28m | 6c- Bloc | 6a | ○7○
A very good pitch with some powerful moves and sharp gouttes d'eau. Take the steep upper wall to the left of the bolts.

⑪ Tango direct* — 7a-
28m | 7a- Ouch | 6a | ○8○
An unbalanced climb, mostly 6a with interesting moves. Crux is bloc style cranking and rather painful.

⑫ Mad Max*** — 6a+
32m | 6b- | 6a+ G-d'eau | ○?○
A very nice and sustained groove to a headwall, 7b crimps to the left and scary; climb via the right which is lovely & fun.

⑬ Blocus*** — 6a-
32m | 6a- 747 Cool | 5+ 747 | ○?○
A run out pitch needing a steady head, delicate.

⑭ Roc d'azur — 6a
31m | 6a- 747 CRIMP | 6a 747 Ouch | ○7○
A bewildering start, not ideal for the 1st route of the day (not if you have a serious hangover!) Fingertip crozzlers, well run out & sustained, a climb for experienced climbers only.

⑮ Extrême droite** — 6a-
31m | 6a- | 5+ | ○?○
A well protected nice wall with good balance moves. Nothing too hard or complicated. (Pitches 1 & 2 together, rope drag is terrible)

⑯ Italian shoes** — 6a-
23m | 6a- CRIMP | 5 Cool | ○?○
A butch start to a hollow flake, taken well on the left. Mid section is very fingery & run out - needs confidence & ability to enjoy.

⑰ Turbostyle** — 5
?m | 5- | 5 G-d'eau | ○?○
Very nice climbing, and worth doing for grade 5 climbers.

⑱ Pinpin et yéyé** — 5
?m | 5- | 5 G-d'eau | ○5○
A very nice top pitch on excellent gouttes d'eau. Delicate moves and keep you concentrated.

⑲ Garogolot** — 6a-
? m | 6a- | 747 G-d'eau | ○3○
Lots of very nice climbing on good incuts, with one very thoughtful move - can't remember where though. Spaced bolts!

⑳ Scorpigouille** — 6a-
21m | 6a- | 5 747 G-d'eau | ○5○
Lots of good letterbox holds, and with one move to catch you out.

㉑ Douce romance*** — 6a-
21m | 6a- 747 CRIMP | 5 747 | ○5○
An interesting move by the 2nd bolt provides the entertainment for the pitch, an enjoyable outing.

㉒ Pilier central direct*** — 6a-
24m | 6a- 747 | 6a 747 | ○5○
A nice powerful pitch on good holds all the way

㉓ Pilier central direct*** — 6c-
29m | 6c- CRIMP | 6b Cool | ○8○
A classic pitch with its fair share of uncomfortable moments. Getting to the first clip proves awkward! then big run out sections lead to clipping a bolt, where the art of crimping is tested.

㉔ Dernier tango au clapis*** — 6c
28m | 6c Pump | 6b | ○7○
A superb top pitch that is highly exposed. Good footwork and cool nerves are very useful when the holds disappear, just sustained.

㉕ Mad Max*** — 6c+
32m | 6c | 6c+ G-d'eau | ○?○
A mantle from hell to start! The groove is climbed direct on stunning gouttes d'eau and is tough on the forearms & calves.

㉖ Blocus*** — 6a+
32m | 6a- CRIMP | 6a+ | ○?○
A very fine wall pitch. Keep left if you want a sustained 6b version, nice 6a on the right side.

㉗ Blocus*** — 6a-
28m | 6a- | 5 | ○?○
A long reach for the 1st clip, a giant jug fest in the sky, whollops of exposure, a fantastic finale to complete this classic.

㉘ Extrême droite** — 5+
28m | 5 | 5+ | ○?○
A pitch that looks very easy, but still has a few tricky moves to certainly keep you awake.

Résumé. This is the final sector before the col-Breche de deux heures. A deservedly popular area for the easier climbs here. Worth window cleaning the top left of the cliff for lower grade climbers. Good belay shade.

BLANCHARD · ARCHÉO · CORNEIRETTE · QUINSAN · VENASQUE · ST.PIERRE · COLOMBIER · CLAPIS · GLISSE · TYROLIENNE · CASCADE-HAUT · CHRISTOPHE · A.LAGARDE · GRAND TRAV · COMBE OBS. · GROSEAU

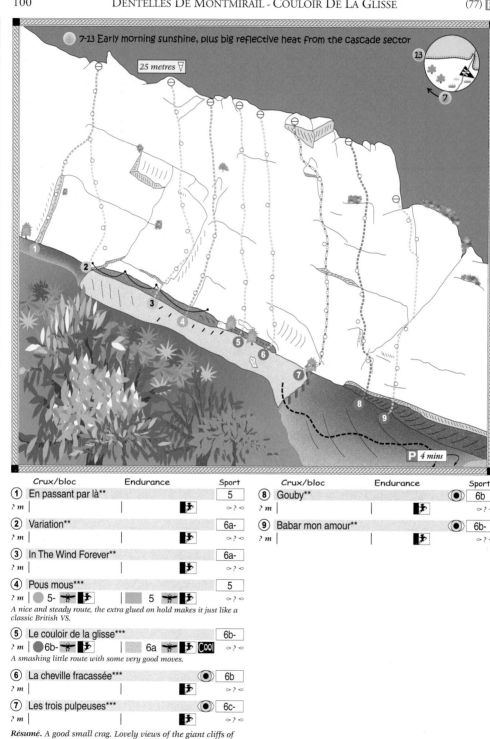

7-13 Early morning sunshine, plus big reflective heat from the cascade sector

25 metres

P 4 mins

	Crux/bloc	Endurance	Sport
1	En passant par là**		5
	? m		⌐? ◁
2	Variation**		6a-
	? m		⌐? ◁
3	In The Wind Forever**		6a-
	? m		⌐? ◁
4	Pous mous***		5
	? m	5- ☀	5 ☀	⌐? ◁

A nice and steady route, the extra glued on hold makes it just like a classic British VS.

5	Le couloir de la glisse***		6b-
	? m	6b- ☀	6a ☀ Cool	⌐? ◁

A smashing little route with some very good moves.

6	La cheville fracassée***	●	6b
	? m		⌐? ◁
7	Les trois pulpeuses***	●	6c-
	? m		⌐? ◁

	Crux/bloc	Endurance	Sport
8	Gouby**	●	6b
	? m		⌐? ◁
9	Babar mon amour**	●	6b-
	? m		⌐? ◁

Résumé. A good small crag. Lovely views of the giant cliffs of the Cascade opposite, cool in the afternoon, belays awkward.

Glisse	Tyrolienne/Giani	-	Tyrolienne/Salino	-	Cascade-en haut/Ratas	St. Christophe/Gilky

Cascade secteur, opposite Glisse; Gorge has plenty of water in spring - but dries out completely during the summer. Lots more climbing too.

LA CHEVILLE FRACASSÉE 6b-, Couloir de la Glisse, Dentelles de Montmirail; Jim Bacon

LES BLAIREAUX 6a-, Secteur La Tyrolienne, Dentelles de Montmirail; Vicky Hardy

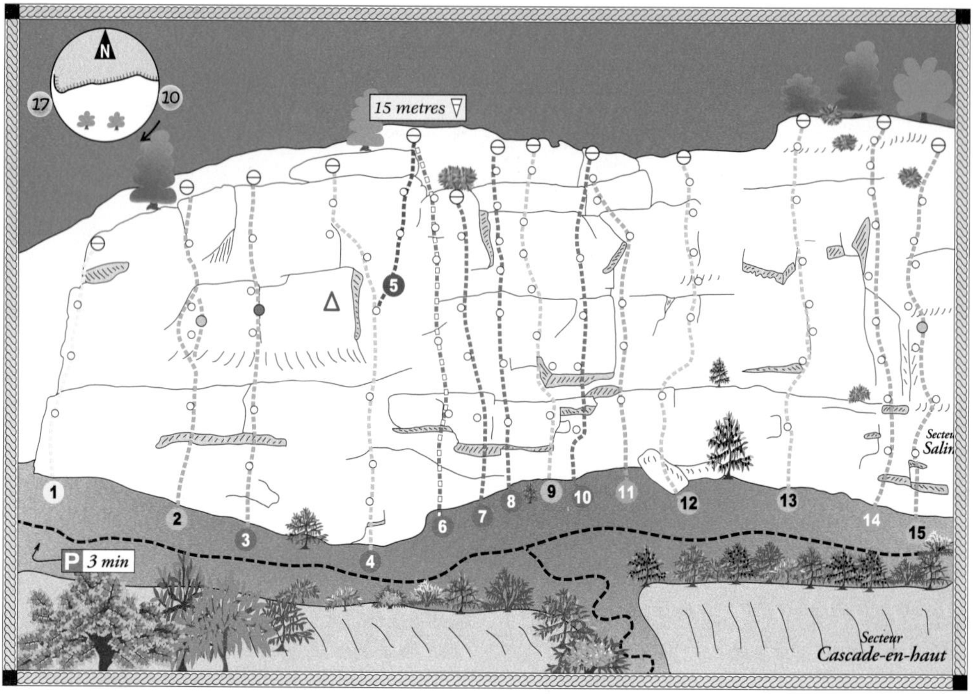

15 metres

Secteur Salino

Secteur Cascade-en-haut

P 3 min

	Crux/bloc	Endurance	Sport
1	La ragoût tonton		2
7m	2-	2	○ 4 ○

A very small climb, ideal for very young kids, massive holds.

	Crux/bloc	Endurance	Sport
2	L'escagasse		5-
11m	5-	5-	○ 5 ○

Two variations here, keep left for grade 5, or right for grade 6a-.

	Crux/bloc	Endurance	Sport
3	Les Filochons		6b-
13m	6b-	5-	○ 5 ○

A more entertaining outing with very good moves before the 4th clip.

	Crux/bloc	Endurance	Sport
4	La mémée de là-haut		6a-
? m			○ ? ○

	Crux/bloc	Endurance	Sport
5	À fleur de roc		7a-
? m			○ ? ○

	Crux/bloc	Endurance	Sport
6	Giani		6c-
? m			○ ? ○

	Crux/bloc	Endurance	Sport
7	Désolé si j'imisse		6b-
? m			○ ? ○

	Crux/bloc	Endurance	Sport
8	Parpinasse à gogo		6b-
? m			○ ? ○

	Crux/bloc	Endurance	Sport
9	Vendage en délire		6a-
? m			○ ? ○

	Crux/bloc	Endurance	Sport
10	Le marc à pinard		6b-
? m			○ ? ○

	Crux/bloc	Endurance	Sport
11	La piquette		5-
? m			○ ? ○

	Crux/bloc	Endurance	Sport
12	Le muscat d'ici		6a-
? m			○ ? ○

	Crux/bloc	Endurance	Sport
13	La fougasse		6a-
? m			○ ? ○

	Crux/bloc	Endurance	Sport
14	Mulot intrépide		5-
? m			○ ? ○

	Crux/bloc	Endurance	Sport
15	Les blaireaux** ☺		6a-
14m	6a-	5	○ 7 ○

Not too hard a few years ago, but now is really polished so you get spat out of the groove - easier for the tall.

Résumé. *A very good introductory sector that is only seconds from the car and easy to set up top ropes (please use your own screwgate karabiner to prevent wear on the fixed gear, a screwgate quickdraw is handy at the top since you can reach most routes from each other.) It is a popular spot and invariably the critical holds are polished, but the climbing is good and most of the routes are very achievable. Routes tend to be a lot harder than the historic grades with all the difficulty concentrated in the crux section. Good belay shade.*

Sidebar tabs (left margin): BLANCHARD · ARCHÉO · CORNIERETTE · QUINSAN · VENASQUE · ST.PIERRE · COLOMBIER · CLAPIS · GLISSE · TYROLIENNE · CASCADE-HAUT · CHRISTOPHE · A.LAGARDE · GRAND TRAV · COMBE OBS. · GROSEAU

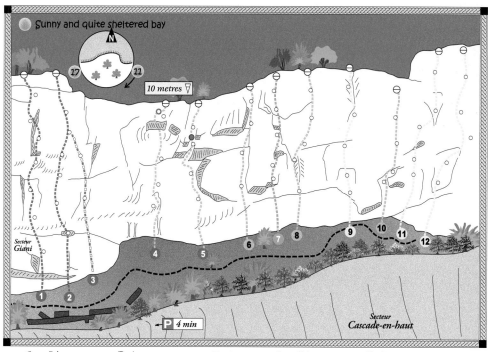

Sunny and quite sheltered bay

N

17   11

10 metres

Secteur
Giani

Secteur
Cascade-en-haut

P 4 min

	Crux/bloc	Endurance	Sport
(1)	Gaston		6b
? m			
(2)	Salino		6b
? m			
(3)	Les escoubilles		6c
? m			
(4)	Les coucougnettes à monsieur Bean*		6b
10m	6c- Bloc	6a-	∘4∘

The difficulty is exactly where you imagine it will be, if you know where the holds are, all you need is strength.

	Crux/bloc	Endurance	Sport
(5)	Les mollets de Daniel*		6a
10m	6b- Bloc	6a-	∘4∘

A few chunky moves around the roof, nice and easy for the grade.

Résumé. *The right hand side of the sector offers a lot easier climbs that keep the sun till late afternoon. The routes on the far right being ideal for novices.*

Cascade-en-haut sector:
This is directly below this area, and is all part of the Cascade sector - however, it is quickest to access via this approach rather than parking at the bottom of the casacde. Be very careful not to dislodge anything over the edge since it will take out any climbers below. To access the sector you return to the Giani sector and take a very steep path down, 2 mins. Take your sacs with you, because you would be unaware if anyone took them in er-error!

	Crux/bloc	Endurance	Sport
(6)	Morgan aussi		4
? m			
(7)	Gratte-cul		5
? m			
(8)	Chibrette		4+
? m			
(9)	Figue molle		2
? m			
(10)	?		4- ?
? m			
(11)	?		3- ?
? m			
(12)	?		2- ?
? m			

BLANCHARD · ARCHÉO · CORNEIRETTE · QUINSAN · VENASQUE · ST.PIERRE · COLOMBIER · CLAPIS · GLISSE · TYROLIENNE · CASCADE-HAUT · CHRISTOPHE · A.LAGARDE · GRAND TRAV · COMBE OBS. · GROSEAU

Vertical tabs (left margin): BLANCHARD | ARCHÉO | CORNIERETTE | QUINSAN | VENASQUE | ST.PIERRE | COLOMBIER | CLAPIS | GLISSE | TYROLIENNE | CASCADE-HAUT | CHRISTOPHE | A.LAGARDE | GRAND TRAV | COMBE OBS. | GROSEAU

Secteur Tyrolienne

30 metres

P 4 min

Casque

18 — 10

P 6 min →

Casque

	Crux/bloc	Endurance	Sport
① Nada			**6c-**
14m			⌐5⌐

A reasonable looking wall, but a top overhang with a stopper move; short, but not sweet & maybe very tough for the grade!

	Crux/bloc	Endurance	Sport
② Croupionite **			**5+**
16m			⌐6⌐

A nice excursion with a fabulous view, a bit slippery but not too bad.

	Crux/bloc	Endurance	Sport
③ Rapetous **	6c-	6a	**6a+**
16m			⌐6⌐

A nice vertical wall with steady climbing. Now the crux is polished you have to concentrate, easy bloc move for the grade.

	Crux/bloc	Endurance	Sport
④ Les Ratas ***	6b- Cool	6b Pump	**6b**

A classic climb with holds. An intimidating wall, and moves away from the bolts, climb the rock at its easiest - and not direct.

	Crux/bloc	Endurance	Sport
⑤ Les Éclopés			**6b**
22m			⌐8⌐

	Crux/bloc	Endurance	Sport
⑥ Papy flingueur		Pump	**6b+**
? m			⌐?⌐

	Crux/bloc	Endurance	Sport
⑦ Les canards de cholon		Pump Pump	**6c+**
? m			⌐?⌐

	Crux/bloc	Endurance	Sport
⑧ Clopin Clopan		Pump Pump	**7a+**
? m			⌐?⌐

Résumé. An excellent sector but sometimes confusing. Best approached from the parking above if you are doing the easier routes at the top; if you are only interested in the hard routes at the bottom, then park at the cascade low down and walk up. The cliff is situated in a very steep gully that gives total belay shade. The cliff is actually quite high up the gorge and usually gets a breeze. The climbing is very exposed and superb in quality. It is sometimes called the Bizarroide sector, but this name is for a route that is beneath the sector and opposite the Glisse sector - and best approached from below.

RAPETOUS 6a+, Cascade-en-haut, Dentelles de Montmirail; Vicky Hardy

ÉLEUSIS 6c, Saint Christophe, Dentelles de Montmirail; Jim Bacon (photo of Saint Christophe also page 305)

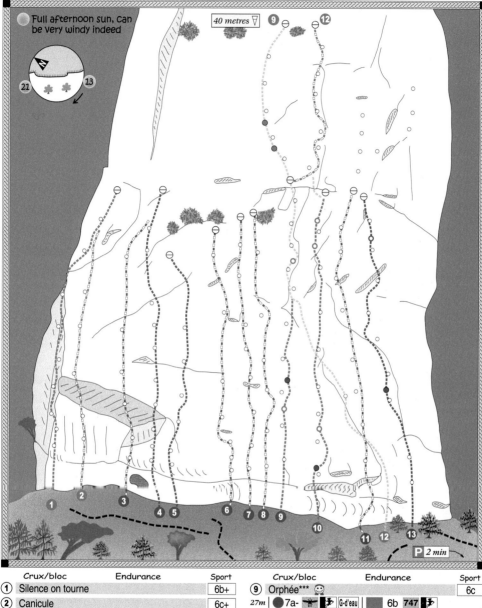

Full afternoon sun, can be very windy indeed

40 metres

	Crux/bloc	Endurance	Sport
1	Silence on tourne		6b+
2	Canicule		6c+
3	É té ouf toa		7b
4	La démisson du pachyderme		7a
5	Oxygène		7a+
6	Le phaléne		7b
7	Photographie tendresse		7b+
8	Télé-ragot		7b
11	Le grand méchant look		7b
13	Citron pressé		7a

	Crux/bloc		Endurance		Sport
9	Orphée*** 😊				6c
27m	7a- ☀️ 🦶 G-d'eau		6b 747 🦶		
15m	6b- ☀️ 🦶 G-d'eau		6a ☀️ 🦶		∽5∽
10	Éleusis*** 😊				6c
29m	7a- ☀️ 🪨		6b+ 747 🦶 Pump		∽8∽

Superb, but you need to be crusing 6c-7a to enjoy this one

12	Gilky***				6c
29m	6c- ☀️ 🦶 😊		6a+ ➡️ 🦶 🦶		∽9∽
15m	6c- ☀️ 🦶 COOL		6c ☀️ 🦶 Pump		∽6∽

The low crux is a bugger, even when you know how to do it. Top pitch is far better as a continuation of Éleusis, but technically harder.

BLANCHARD | ARCHÉO | CORNEIRETTE | QUINSAN | VENASQUE | ST.PIERRE | COLOMBIER | CLAPIS | GLISSE | TYROLIENNE | CASCADE-HAUT | CHRISTOPHE | A.LAGARDE | GRAND TRAV | COMBE OBS. | GROSEAU

When it comes to marketing, Châteauneuf-du-Pape is one of the big success stories in French wine. In visiting the village and local area, you will observe a few scrawny vines struggling up through the desperately pebbly ground, and be either roasted to a cinder by the intense sun, or blown off the face of the earth by the mighty Mistral wind gushing down the Rhône valley. I am sure you will agree, that to turn this desert into one of the worlds leading wine growing regions, is a stroke of pure genius. The old defunkt castle being centrepoint to the marketing strategy, enabling the bottles to be granted a wonderful embossed glass pattern of chivalrous esteem, and to slap on a

label so grand that even Louis XIV would have raised an eyebrow. The contents idea - to allow any blend of 14 grapes was even more genius, since many people don't like some particular grape varieties like gamay etc. and in this melange, a single flavour can never be distinguished. Allow up to 400 different wine makers to operate independently, so any iffy year for a winemaker is not really noticed amongst the giant wave of wine – which at a healthily high 14%, is going to blast the socks of any lightweight Barolo or Bardolino. Yes, all the perfect ingredients are in place here to protect the whole concept of C-d-P. What the appellation (governing authority) has done however thankfully, is to also deliver the goods alongside to razzmatazz. I would say at the lower end, you pay more for the label - than the wine; but at the higher end, you get an absolute bargain. It really is one of those wine areas, where tasting is essential before a substantial purchase. Unfortunately, the success of C-d-P comes at a price and many of the wine tasting venues in town are over commercial, running a sales pitch towards those from across the Atlantic. A lot of top growers have more demand than supply, and hence avoid the whole tasting bash. What I can recommend (you will need an alcohol free driver), is to hunt out a large tasting venue on rue Maréchal Foch in the centre of town - Maison des Vins (shown below). Here the representation of a large amount of growers is excellent, and the sheer variety in depth of tasting is exceptional; as was the amusing discussions we had with the owner about the flavours of all the different wines – and of course their inferiority to those of Bourgogne.

There is simply no excuse for apathy in this area on a rest day. You must be completely charged up and ready to regenerate your body, caressing the lightness of a delicate glass with your blown out arms, and allowing the redness of your sore fingertips to match that of the vibrant glowing of the magical red liquid. Swill the wine lightly at first to allow the aroma to circulate in the top of the glass; sniff well – for it is essential to start up the quizzical tendencies of the brain as to what this amazing red wine is going to taste like - then enjoy the flavours of complexity that the different wines in this area have to offer. You are in an amazing area for diversity of wine, along with quiet and picturesque villages, and small restaurants and bistros to die for. A visit to the local office de toursime is a top tip, and pick up a few pamphlets that are coloured intinéaire - Route de Vins. These show you all the places to visit along the wine trails, opening hours, and give you essential direction and zestful purpose in your day out – not for the lighthearted (then neither is climbing). Wine is essentially priced by demand - and lack of supply; rather than actual quality, or to your own personal taste. So by actually going out there and trying wines from less famous areas, you are highly likely to find both excellent results and substantial savings. Gigondas at the foot of the Dentelles is famous and worth sampling of course, but the hidden secrets lie in the villages of Sablet, Séguret, Rasteau and beyond – seek and ye shall find.

View from Gigondas towards Sablet and Rasteau

BLANCHARD

ARCHÉO

CORNIERETTE

QUINSAN

VENASQUE

ST.PIERRE

COLOMBIER

CLAPIS

GLISSE

TYROLIENNE

CASCADE-HAUT

CHRISTOPHE

A.LAGARDE

GRAND TRAV

COMBE OBS.

GROSEAU

North west facing, very cool on hot days, somber and quite unhealthy on cold winter days

No sun

9   17

N

85 metres

P 11 min

Casque

Casque

	Crux/bloc	Endurance	Sport

① Crack en stock* 😊 — **6a**
28m | 6a- DIEDRE | 6a Pump | ∘ ? ∘
A groove that gives a lot of leaders a hard time, technique please!

② Tout Crapato* 😊 — **4**
30m | 4- 747 △ | 4 747 | ∘ ? ∘
The climbing is quite straightforward, but there are a lot of loose stones and you are almost definitely going to knock something down.

③ Week-end à Vichy* 😊 — **6c**
30m | 6c- | 6b+ 747 Pump | ∘ ? ∘
Lovely technical climbing on fingertip holds.

④ Spartacus* 😊 — **6b**
30m | 6c- | 6b 747 | ∘ ? ∘
Excellent climbing with a single hard move low down. A fragile block at the top could be dangerous!

⑤ Boule et bill* 😊 — **6a**
33m | 5- 747 | 4 747 | ∘12∘
22m | 6a- 747 | 6a 747 | ∘7∘

⑥ Petite Émeline* 😊 — **5+**
70m | 6a- △ | 4 747 | ∘ ? ∘
A very popular outing up to the smaller of the holes. Loose rock in abundance, helmets obligatory.

⑦ Arête est de l'Aiguillette Lagarde* 😊 — **6a+**
32m | 6b- ← | 6a+ 747 Pump | ∘ ? ∘
A wonderful climb up the arete, steep and very sustained for a 6a climber.

	Sport

⑧ Kébra le loub* 😊 — **6b+**
28m | 6c- | 6b+ Pump | ∘ ? ∘
Plenty to keep you occupied, technical and a bit slippery!

⑨ Garganta* — **6a**
28m | 6a
27m | 6a | ∘ ? ∘
Another highly popular excursion to a giant hole!

⑩ Vibration* 😊 — **6c+**
32m | 6b+ | ∘ ? ∘
25m | 6c+ | ∘ ? ∘
25m | 6c DIEDRE | ∘ ? ∘

⑪ Hamburger* 😊 — **6c+**
25m | 6c | 6c+ Pump | ∘ ? ∘
20m | 6a- | 5 | ∘ ? ∘

⑫ Référentiel bondissant* 😊 — **7b**
30m | 7b- | 7a+ Pump | ∘ ? ∘

⑬ Terre Étrangère* 😊 — **7a+**
30m | 7a- | 7a+ Pump | ∘ ? ∘

⑭ Morizot parot* — **6a**
42m | 5 | ∘ ? ∘
27m | 6a | ∘ ? ∘

Résumé. *A selection from the 50 routes in this sector to keep you busy for a day - buy the local topo for more information.*

ARÊTE EST DE L'AIGUILLETTE LAGARDE 6a+, Chaîne de Gigondas, Dentelles de Montmirail; Carrie Atchison-Jones

LE TOUT 3-, Grand Travers, Dentelles de Montmirail; Catherine Duperrier

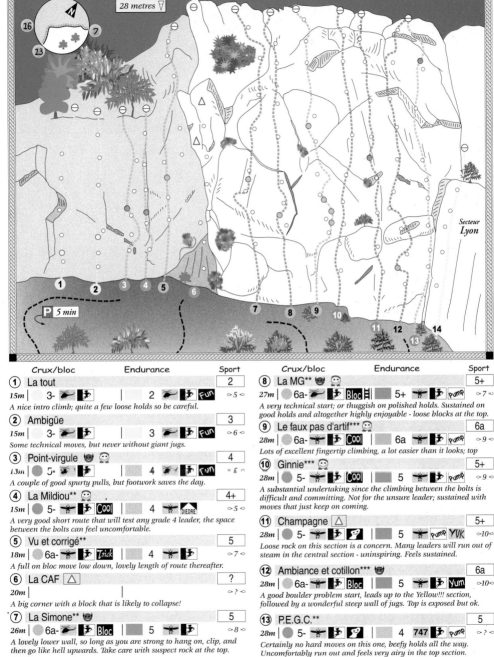

28 metres

Secteur Lyon

P 5 min

	Crux/bloc	Endurance	Sport

① La tout — 2
15m | 3- | 2 Fun | ⚬5⚬
A nice intro climb; quite a few loose holds so be careful.

② Ambigüe — 3
15m | 3- | 3 Fun | ⚬6⚬
Some technical moves, but never without giant jugs.

③ Point-virgule 😊😊 — 4
13m | 5- | 4 | ⚬5⚬
A couple of good spurty pulls, but footwork saves the day.

④ La Mildiou** 😊 — 4+
15m | 5- Cool | 4 DIEDRE | ⚬5⚬
A very good short route that will test any grade 4 leader, the space between the bolts can feel uncomfortable.

⑤ Vu et corrigé** — 5
18m | 6a- Trick | 4 | ⚬7⚬
A full on bloc move low down, lovely length of route thereafter.

⑥ La CAF △ — ?
20m | | | ⚬?⚬
A big corner with a block that is likely to collapse!

⑦ La Simone** 😊 — 5
26m | 6a- Bloc | 5 | ⚬8⚬
A lovely lower wall, so long as you are strong to hang on, clip, and then go like hell upwards. Take care with suspect rock at the top.

Résumé. A nice and sunny bay at the top of this small cliff. A good selection of climbs in the lower grades, and with great views. Rock is suspect in parts and a few bits have come away. Climbs are quite steep for their grade, people overweight and unfit - will struggle, sweat and toil.

	Crux/bloc	Endurance	Sport

⑧ La MG** 😎😊 — 5+
27m | 6a- Bloc ▤ | 5+ Pump | ⚬7⚬
A very technical start; or thuggish on polished holds. Sustained on good holds and altogether highly enjoyable - loose blocks at the top.

⑨ Le faux pas d'artif** 😊 — 6a
28m | 6a- Cool | 6a Pump | ⚬9⚬
Lots of excellent fingertip climbing, a lot easier than it looks; top

⑩ Ginnie** 😊 — 5+
28m | 5- Cool | 5 Pump | ⚬9⚬
A substantial undertaking since the climbing between the bolts is difficult and committing. Not for the unsure leader; sustained with moves that just keep on coming.

⑪ Champagne △ — 5+
28m | 5- | 5 Pump YUK | ⚬10⚬
Loose rock on this section is a concern. Many leaders will run out of steam in the central section - uninspiring. Feels sustained.

⑫ Ambiance et cotillon** 😎 — 6a
28m | 6a- Bloc | 5 Yum | ⚬10⚬
A good boulder problem start, leads up to the Yellow!!! section, followed by a wonderful steep wall of jugs. Top is exposed but ok.

⑬ P.E.G.C.** — 5
28m | 5- | 4 747 Pump | ⚬?⚬
Certainly no hard moves on this one, beefy holds all the way. Uncomfortably run out and feels very airy in the top section.

⑭ La Petpluoktoncul ⚡ — 4
18m | 3- | 3 | ⚬5⚬
Perhaps the safest route in Provence.

M.G. - Lyon - Vivier

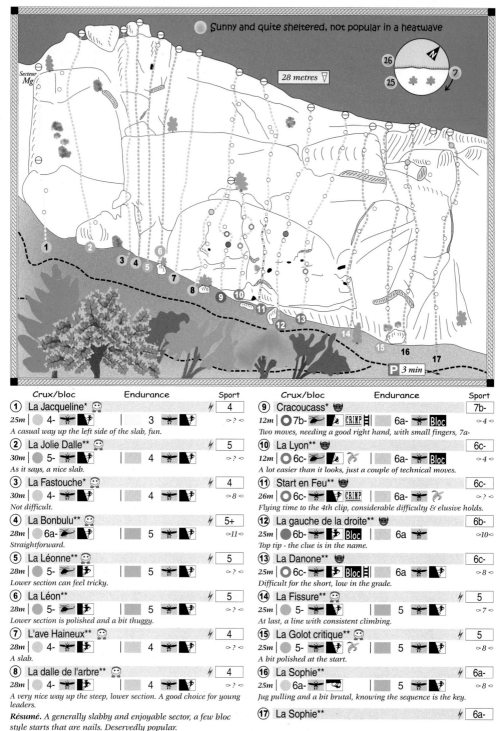

Sunny and quite sheltered, not popular in a heatwave

Secteur Mg

28 metres

	Crux/bloc	Endurance	Sport
1	La Jacqueline* 😊		4

25m | 4- | 3 | ○?○

A casual way up the left side of the slab, fun.

2	La Jolie Dalle** 😊		5

30m | 5- | 4 | ○?○

As it says, a nice slab.

3	La Fastouche* 😊		4

30m | 4- | 4 | ○8○

Not difficult.

4	La Bonbulu** 😊		5+

28m | 6a- | 5 | ○11○

Straightforward.

5	La Léonne** 😊		5

28m | 5- | 5 | ○?○

Lower section can feel tricky.

6	La Léon**		5

Lower section is polished and a bit thuggy.   ○?○

7	L'ave Haineux** 😊		4

28m | 4- | 4 | ○?○

A slab.

8	La dalle de l'arbre** 😊		4

28m | 4- | 4 | ○?○

A very nice way up the steep, lower section. A good choice for young leaders.

Résumé. *A generally slabby and enjoyable sector, a few bloc style starts that are nails. Deservedly popular.*

	Crux/bloc	Endurance	Sport
9	Cracoucass*		7b-

12m | 7b- | CRIMP | 6a- Bloc | ○4○

Two moves, needing a good right hand, with small fingers, 7a-

10	La Lyon**		6c-

12m | 6c- | | 6a- Bloc | ○4○

A lot easier than it looks, just a couple of technical moves.

11	Start en Feu**		6c-

26m | 6c- CRIMP | 6a- | ○?○

Flying time to the 4th clip, considerable difficulty & elusive holds.

12	La gauche de la droite**		6b-

25m | 6b- Bloc | 6a | ○10○

Top tip - the clue is in the name.

13	La Danone**		6c-

25m | 6c- Bloc | 6a | ○8○

Difficult for the short, low in the grade.

14	La Fissure** 😊		5

25m | 5- | 5 | ○7○

At last, a line with consistent climbing.

15	La Golot critique** 😊		5

25m | 5- | 5 | ○8○

A bit polished at the start.

16	La Sophie**		6a-

25m | 6a- | 5 | ○8○

Jug pulling and a bit brutal, knowing the sequence is the key.

17	La Sophie**		6a-

P 3 min

Side tabs: BLANCHARD | ARCHÉO | CORNIERETTE | QUINSAN | VENASQUE | ST.PIERRE | COLOMBIER | CLAPIS | GLISSE | TYROLIENNE | CASCADE-HAUT | CHRISTOPHE | A.LAGARDE | GRAND TRAV | COMBE OBS | GROSEAU

CRACOUCASS 7b- bloc, Grand Travers, Dentelles de Montmirail; Jim Bacon

LA LÉON 5, Grand Travers, Dentelles de Montmirail; Bruno Beccaro

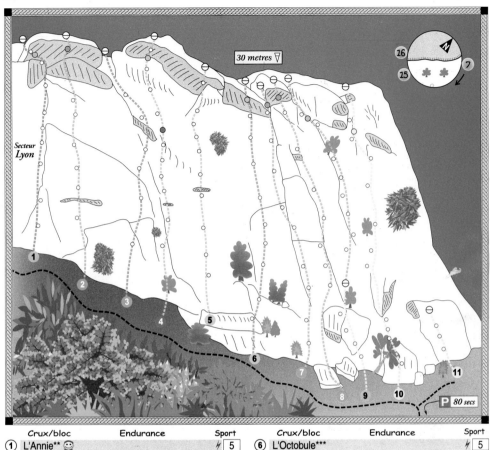

Secteur **Lyon**

30 metres ▽

16
15   7

P   80 secs

Side tabs: BLANCHARD · ARCHÉO · CORNIERETTE · QUINSAN · VENASQUE · ST.PIERRE · COLOMBIER · CLAPIS · GLISSE · TYROLIENNE · CASCADE-HAUT · CHRISTOPHE · ALAGARDE · GRAND TRAV · COMBE OBS. · GROSEAU

	Crux/bloc	Endurance	Sport
①	**L'Annie**** 😊		⚡ 5

26m | 6a- | 5 | ○9○

A quizzical top overhang to keep you amused.

| **②** | **D7**** | | ⚡ 5- |

27m | 5- | 4 | ○9○

The final overhang may look difficult but be prepared to find some good holds.

| **③** | **La G.G.***** | Yum | ⚡ 5- |

26m | 5- | 5 | 747 | ○10○

A very good route that is sustained at the grade, and nice to enjoy onsight. Polish on the rock makes little difference.

| **④** | **L'Enface de l'Art***** 😊 | | 6a |

27m | 6b- | 6a- | ○10○

Not an easy lead, and far more pleasant with the quick draws in place. A great position, requires good reading of moves on slippery holds. An all time classic.

| **⑤** | **L'Ivaldi*** | | ⚡ 5- |

27m | 6a- | 6a | ○10○

Enjoy the top overhang.

Résumé. *This is the first sector that you arrive at, and is very popular as a teaching venue for belaying etc. Often busy when the rest of the cliff is empty. A good selection of easier climbs, of very nice length, and most are well bolted.*

	Crux/bloc	Endurance	Sport
⑥	**L'Octobule*****		⚡ 5

30m | 6a- | 5 | ○10○

Steady jug pulling leads to brilliant moves over the final overhang.

| **⑦** | **La Niquedouille***** | DIEDRE | ⚡ 5- |

30m | 5- | 4 | ○10○

The top groove is the fun.

| **⑧** | **La Garce***** | | ⚡ 4 |

30m | 5- | 4- | ○10○

A slightly easier outing and jugs for most of the way.

| **⑨** | **Le Vivier***** | | ⚡ 4- |

30m | 4- | 3 | ○14○

A very good line. The crack at half height is magic.

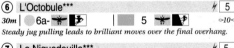

| **⑩** | **Super Mollasson*** | | ⚡ 3 |

28m | 3- | 3 | ○12○

Ignore the belay at half height, which is purely for teaching.

| **⑪** | **Les Mollasons** | | ⚡ 2 |

10m | 3- | 3 | ○3○

Why bother!

LE MARTINE 7a-, Combe Obscure; Jim Bacon

La ville de Bédoin est une ville provençale typique avec des rues étroites et une histoire qui remonte à plus de 1000 ans. Tout d'abord les Romains l'envahirent puis les Moors et c'est maintenant le tour des Mercédes des riches européens. Cette invasion moderne trouble la tranquilité du village qui est cependant en plein épanouissement grâce à l'augmentation du commerce touristique. En été les cafés et les restaurants sont remplis de monde. Il y a de nombreux campings certains avec des piscines, d'autres offrant un charme pittoresque. Par manque d'indication, il est difficile de trouver la route qui mène depuis le village jusqu'à Malaucène en passant par le Col de la Madeleine. Cependant vous serez si vous allez dans la bonne direction si le Mont Ventoux se trouve à votre droite.

Les falaises de Combe Obscure portent bien leur nom, elles sont en effet situées dans une petite vallée cachée par les collines en face d'elle. Il y a quelques falaises sur les pentes les plus basses du Mont Ventoux qui sont visibles depuis la route cependant très peu d'entre elles offrent de bonnes voies ou sont suffisamment hautes pour valoir une visite. Juste au-dessus de la vallée se trouve un petit secteur qui a été équipé. Sur ce secteur, la roche s'effrite facilement. La roche est de bien meilleure qualité sur les falaises principales. Il faut suivre un petit sentier caillouteux pour accéder, après 15 minutes d'une marche bien agréable, aux falaises. Elles apparaissent soudainement, pas très immenses mais superbes et parfaites, avec un calcaire qui ressemble à celui du Verdon. Le plus de cette falaise c'est son orientation sud-est qui est absolument parfaite. Vous profitez de la chaleur du soleil d'une part le matin et d'autre part lors de journées fraiches lorsque le Mistral souffle. Il y a deux chênes en bas de la falaise qui vous permettent, si vous le souhaitez, d'assurer à l'ombre. Il y a également des rochers plats pour s'asseoir et pique-niquer. La majorité de la falaise reste fraîche puisqu'elle est à l'ombre à partir de 14h. La plupart des voies ont d'excellentes prises mais elles restent tout de même assez abruptes pour la majorité des grimpeurs. A la fin de votre visite vous réaliserez que c'est une falaise où les voies ne sont en général pas très difficiles mais où il vous faut être au top de votre forme!

The town of Bédoin sounds of eastern origin, and it certainly fulfils expectations as a typical provencal hill town with narrow streets, and history going back over a thousand years. First the Romans invaded, then it was the turn of the Moors, and so now it's the turn of the rich northern Mercedes driving Europeans to invade. It's a bilateral invasion of a sort, because this time the local inhabitants get a choice to accept the terms of dollops of dosh, rather than the ancient obligatory axe in the head. I am sure there is local disquiet to this modern invasion, but the town certainly seems to be thriving because of increased trade. In summer, the cafés and restaurants seem to be doing roaring business that they couldn't have dreamt of 15 years ago. There is no shortage of campsites in the area too, some with swimming pools, and others with their own particular quaint charm. Finding the road out of the village centre towards Malaucène via the Col de la Madeleine, is not that easy with a certain lack of signposts. You know if you are going in the right direction if Mont Ventoux is up to your right. The cliffs of Combe Obscure live up to their name, it is indeed a small Combe that is obscured by the hills in front of it. The lower slopes of Mont Ventoux have quite a few cliffs that you can see from the road up to the Col, but few of which offer good climbing or are high enough to warrant a visit. Just above the actual Combe is a small sector that has been equipped. The rock here is slightly brittle and not indicative to the better rock on the twin main cliffs themselves. To approach the cliffs, you need to take a stony footpath up a dry river valley bed. This 15min walk can be enjoyably flat if trail bikers haven't ripped it up to a stony mess. The rock in this valley is appalling, and after 14 mins of drudging in hot sun, you definitely think that going to this cliff might be a bad idea. Suddenly the cliff is there, nothing gigantic, but a superb sweep of perfect, Verdon style limestone. The gem for this cliff is its orientation, south-east, which is the perfect direction for this type of crag. You get lovely warming sunshine on the rock in the cool mornings after a star studded night time sky, and sunshine to take the chill off the coldest of Mistral blowing days. There are lovely separated oak trees at the bottom so you can belay either in the sun or the shade. There are some lovely flat stones to sit on and enjoy a really leisurely picnic. Most of the cliff critically goes into shade at 2pm, which is before the rock heats up too much and acts as a giant radiator. The rock stays cool, and an afternoon breeze flows through the mini gorge that is formed by a hillock opposite. Most of the climbs have excellent holds and are giantly exhilarating, but can just a bit too steep for the majority of mid grade climbers. After your visit - you realise that it's a cliff where the routes generally aren't that hard; it's just that - you're not that fit!

Malaucène - Bédoin

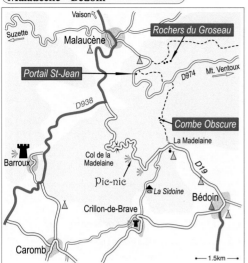

🛍 Bar: Malaucène, Caromb, Crillon-la-Brave. Bédoin
Shop: Malaucène, Caromb, Bédoin
Petrol Station: Malaucène, Caromb, Bédoin
Restaurant: Malaucène, Caromb, Crillon-la-Brave. Bédoin
Supermarket: Malaucène, Bédoin
Market day: Malaucène Wed-am; Bédoin Mon am
Tourist Bureau: Malaucène, Bédoin

⚠ Camping La Pinède 🏠
Bédoin
(W side of village - 7 mins walk into town)
Tel: 04 90 65 61 03
Notes: Big site with swimming pool next door.
Open: (13-03/31-10)
121 places

⚠ Camping La Garenne
Bédoin (300m from the village)
Tel: 04 90 65 63 05
Notes: Site with swimming pool.
Open: (1-04/31-10)
80 places

⚠ Camping Le Ménèque
Bédoin
Tel: 04 90 65 93 50
Notes: Site with swimming pool.
Open: (1-04/31-09)
100 places

⚠ Camping Pastory
Bédoin
Tel: 04 90 12 85 83
Notes: 1km out of town on Malaucene road
Open: (1-04/31-09)
100 places

⚠ Aire Naturelle Les Oliviers
Madeline, Bédoin
Tel: 04 90 65 68 89
Notes: 3km out of town on Malaucene road
Open: (1-04/31-09)
25 places

Combe Obscure

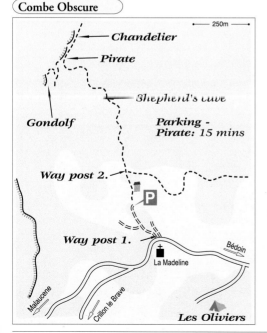

The meadow before way post 2.

Way post 1. - Take the track on the left here.

Street markets in this part of France are still very popular, and vary from traditional food buying, to anything up to beds, mattresses etc. All major villages and towns will have a designated day of the week as market day, and this is very much the social day of the week. Buying food can be fun – (as long as you have all morning), since there is a fabulous variety of food on offer. Many cheese makers come down from the alpine regions, so look out for Beaufort, which is a really creamy tasting hard cheese; it has a younger mate 'Comté' which is similar to taste but doesn't have the intense creamyness. You will often find a good Reblechon too

Buis les Baronnie

– yummy scrumptious and beyond old socks. Sauccison is very popular, with many additives such as olives and noix (hazelnuts), which you don't generally get in supermarkets. The ardèche is not far too, so you can get some mushrooms and cépes that are giant, well tasty and look from another planet. Towns such as Bédoin have very large markets that cater for tourists with pottery and gift items. It's generally a very good day to plan as a rest day, take your time, chill out and have a few beers, and watch the world go by. With markets on every day, you can actually avoid climbing all week if you want to – lardies. (Top tip - go early to avoid queues, & wrap up, as it is pretty cool first thing.)

Top of Mont Ventoux

Monday: Bédoin, Mazan, Saint-Didier
Tues: Beaumes-de-Venise, Vaison-la-Romaine, Caromb,
Wed: Buis-les-Baronnies, Malaucène, Sault,
(Wed: Nov-Mar Valréas-Truffle market)
Thur: Nyons, Orange
Fri: Carpentras
Sat: Aubignan, Pernes-les-Fontaines, Buis-l-B(mini veg)
Sun: Monteux, Sarrians

Malaucène

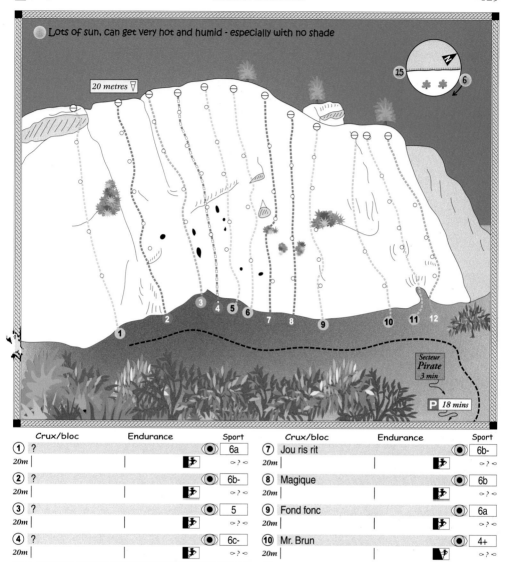

Lots of sun, can get very hot and humid - especially with no shade

20 metres

15   6

Secteur
Pirate
3 min

P 18 mins

BLANCHARD · ARCHÉO · CORNEIRETTE · QUINSAN · VENASQUE · ST.PIERRE · COLOMBIER · CLAPIS · GLISSE · TYROLIENNE · CASCADE-HAUT · CHRISTOPHE · A.LAGARDE · GRAND TRAV · COMBE OBS. · GROSEAU

	Crux/bloc	Endurance	Sport		Crux/bloc	Endurance	Sport
①	?		6a	⑦	Jou ris rit		6b-
20m			⇀?⇀	20m			⇀?⇀
②	?		6b-	⑧	Magique		6b
20m			⇀?⇀	20m			⇀?⇀
③	?		5	⑨	Fond fonc		6a
20m			⇀?⇀	20m			⇀?⇀
④	?		6c-	⑩	Mr. Brun		4+
20m			⇀?⇀	20m			⇀?⇀
⑤	?		6a-	⑪	Tartone coquine		6a-
20m			⇀?⇀	20m			⇀?⇀
⑥	?		6a-	⑫	Tête de Gondolf		5
20m			⇀?⇀	20m			⇀?⇀

Résumé. *A small sector that is high above the main cliff and up a steep slope to the left. Only 20m high, and the top is quite easy angled. The rock here is quite brittle and sounds hollow in many places. The routes are bloc in style and give single hard moves, and after you have sorted them out, do not present too much difficulty. The hard moves are on vertical rock, but you can usually get good rests in between. Not a very popular area and bushes tend to grow, so bring something to cut back the plants when you come here. The view is lovely and sunny, and out of the Mistral wind mostly. Not good on very hot days. The view however is very good, and also from the nice picnic plateau below. We didn't get a chance to recently check these routes, bloc grades could be interesting.*

Gondolf

Pirate - Solitaire - Joe le Maxi - Chandelier - Brisse

Left margin tabs (top to bottom):
BLANCHARD · ARCHÉO · CORNIERETTE · QUINSAN · VENASQUE · ST.PIERRE · COLOMBIER · CLAPIS · GLISSE · TIROLIENNE · CASCADE-HAUT · CHRISTOPHE · A.LAGARDE · GRAND TRAV · COMBE OBS. · GROSEAU

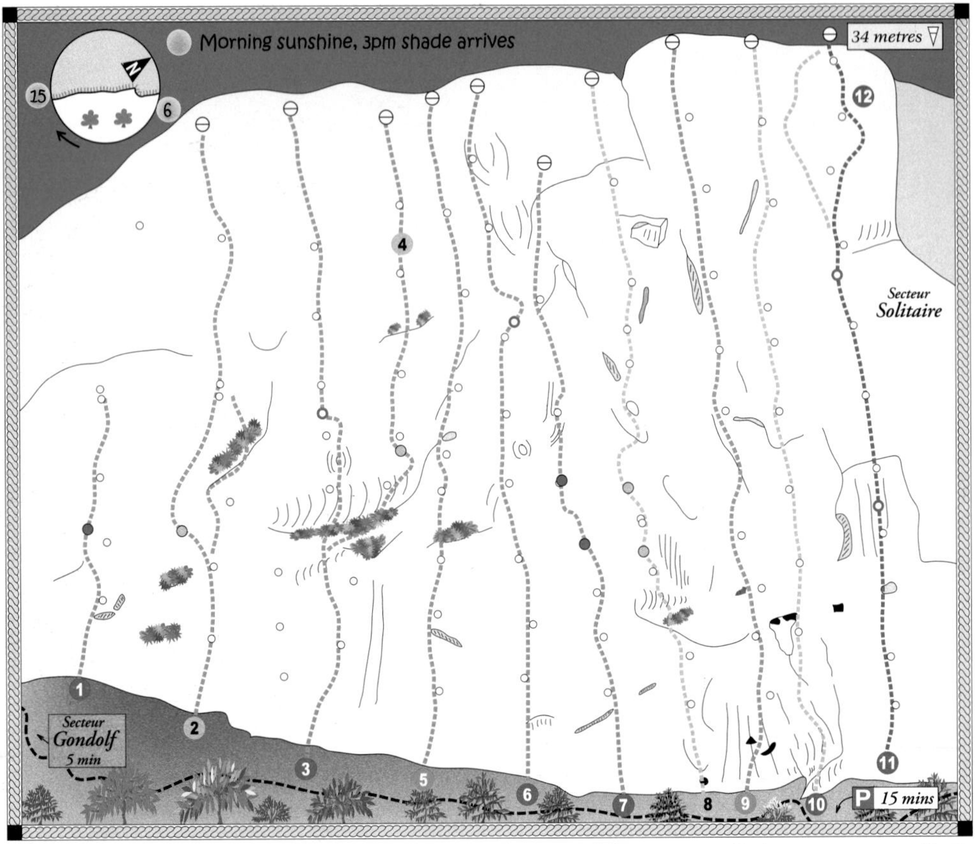

Morning sunshine, 3pm shade arrives

34 metres

Secteur **Solitaire**

Secteur **Gondolf** 5 min

Secteur Gondolf 5 min

P 15 mins

	Crux/bloc	Endurance	Sport

① Percussion 6b-
10m | 6b- Flexi | 5 | ⊶3⊷

A simple but fun little climb, very much a one move wonder. Bolts go all the way to the top of the crag - but with lots of vegetation.

② Jardin Secret 6a-
20m | 6a- | 5 | ⊶4⊷

Not very well bolted at present. Taking the left hand option is by far the best way. A bit green but should clear up with traffic.

③ Pirate* 6c-
29m | 6c- Flexi | 5 Bloc | ⊶7⊷

Not one for the morning hangover. A real stopper move to give a really bad start to the day. Easier for shorties or gorillas.

④ De la fuite dans les ideés* 6a-
29m | 6a- Bloc | 5+ Yum | ⊶7⊷

A lovely route with lots of holds and no brains needed. Crux is a good move. A very good route for a warm up.

⑤ 3000 F le kilo** 5+
29m | 5 Cool | 5+ Pump | ⊶8⊷

A friction warm up, a steep wall with good holds all the way.

⑥ La Domy* 6c-
31m | 6c- 747 CRIMP | 5+ Cool | ⊶9⊷

A route with a good bloc crux on a few polished holds. Short climbers will prefer quickdraws in place as 7th bolt will be out of reach. Can be made harder by going very direct.

⑦ Ralépas grimpe* 6b-
29m | 6b- CRIMP | 5+ 747 Pump | ⊶7⊷

A nice climb with a crimpy crux that is easy to fluf (4th bolt). At 5th go directly up. Top wall looks outrageous but superb holds.

⑧ Froggy one* 6a
31m | 6a- Cool | 6a Pump | ⊶8⊷

A very good climb with two testing moves. You get a good rest to plan around the lack of footholds, reach can be useful!

⑨ Vision** 5
34m | 5- | 4+ 747 Cool | ⊶9⊷

A superb classic with only on hard move, but quite a hard one that can't be frigged! Top wall is out there on jugs.

⑩ Ziziben** 6a+
32m | 6b- 747 | 6a+ 747 Pump | ⊶7⊷

A handful for an unfit mid grade climber! Running out of stamina will result in huge flyers! Solid climbing all the way.

⑪ La Martine* 6c-
34m | 6c- 747 | 6b 747 | ⊶9⊷

*Not that pleasant onsight lead at all, quite a lot of crimping on polished holds. Top section is run out but fantastic****

⑫ La Martine direct* 7a-
34m | 7a- 747 | 6c 747 Trick | ⊶10⊷

A full on stonker of a top section, bizarrely rebolted!! Top overhang is quite straightforward for thugs, footwork proooooving crucial.

Gondolf	**Résumé.** A superb Verdon style wall, good holds and not too steep - but interesting crux's.
	Pirate - Solitaire - Joe le Maxi - Chandelier - Brisse

Secteur Pirate, Combe Obscure; Jim Bacon

LES AILES BRISEES 7b- bloc, Combe Obscure; Carrie Atchison-Jones

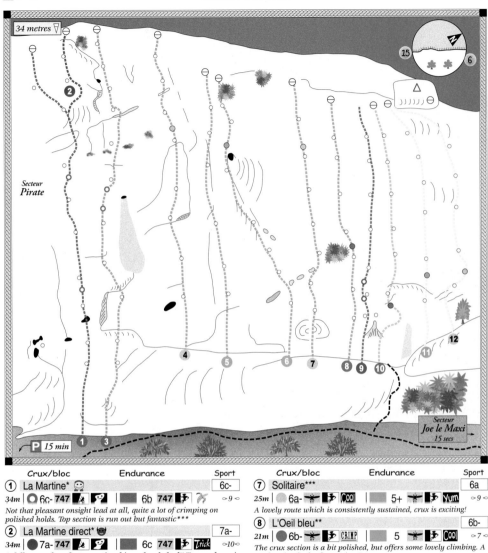

34 metres

Secteur Pirate

P 15 min

Secteur Joe le Maxi 15 secs

BLANCHARD · ARCHÉO · CORNEIRETTE · QUINSAN · VENASQUE · ST.PIERRE · COLOMBIER · CLAPIS · GLISSE · TYROLIENNE · CASCADE-HAUT · CHRISTOPHE · A.LAGARDE · GRAND TRAV · COMBE OBS. · GROSEAU

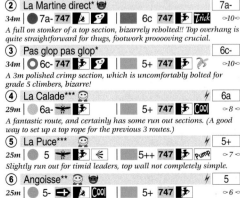

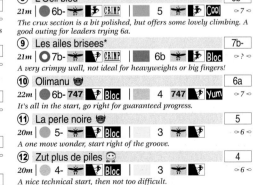

	Crux/bloc	Endurance	Sport

(1) La Martine* 😊 — **6c-**
34m | 6c- 747 | 6b 747 | ⊳9⊲
Not that pleasant onsight lead at all, quite a lot of crimping on polished holds. Top section is run out but fantastic***

(2) La Martine direct* 😊 — **7a-**
34m | 7a- 747 | 6c 747 Trick | ⊳10⊲
A full on stonker of a top section, bizarrely rebolted!! Top overhang is quite straightforward for thugs, footwork prooooving crucial.

(3) Pas glop pas glop* — **6c-**
34m | 6c- 747 | 5+ 747 | ⊳10⊲
A 3m polished crimp section, which is uncomfortably bolted for grade 5 climbers, bizarre!

(4) La Calade*** 😊 — **6a**
29m | 6a- | 5+ 747 Cool | ⊳8⊲
A fantastic route, and certainly has some run out sections. (A good way to set up a top rope for the previous 3 routes.)

(5) La Puce*** 😊 — **5+**
25m | 5 | 5++ 747 Pump | ⊳7⊲
Slightly run out for timid leaders, top wall not completely simple.

(6) Angoisse** 😊 😊 — **5**
25m | 5- Cool | 5+ 747 | ⊳6⊲
Best climbed as an eliminate, directly up the slab on small holds to the cave. O'hang has good holds, but a fall could put you in plaster.

(7) Solitaire*** — **6a**
25m | 6a- Cool | 5+ Yum | ⊳9⊲
A lovely route which is consistently sustained, crux is exciting!

(8) L'Oeil bleu** — **6b-**
21m | 6b- CRIMP | 5 Cool | ⊳7⊲
The crux section is a bit polished, but offers some lovely climbing. A good outing for leaders trying 6a.

(9) Les ailes brisees* — **7b-**
21m | 7b- CRIMP | 6b Bloc | ⊳?⊲
A very crimpy wall, not ideal for heavyweights or big fingers!

(10) Olimanu 😊 — **6a**
22m | 6b- 747 Bloc | 4 747 Yum | ⊳7⊲
It's all in the start, go right for guaranteed progress.

(11) La perle noire 😊 — **5**
20m | 5- Bloc | 3 | ⊳6⊲
A one move wonder, start right of the groove.

(12) Zut plus de piles 😊 — **4**
20m | 4- | ⊳6⊲
A nice technical start, then not too difficult.

Résumé. *A superb piece of rock, with usually good holds where you want them. Not much belay shade.*

Gondolf - Pirate - Solitaire - Joe le Maxi - Chandelier - Brisse

View from centre of cliff, out towards Carpentras

Combe Obscure, hidden in its own little valley

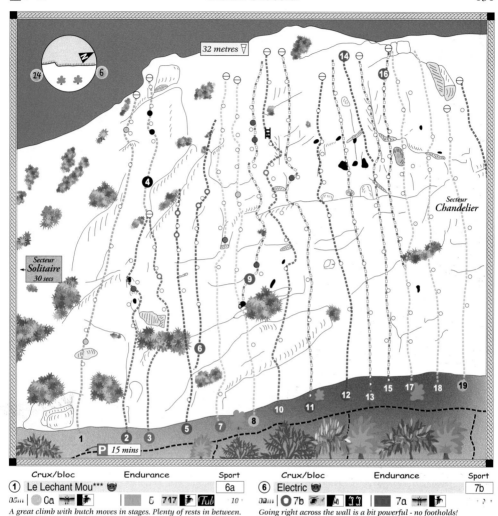

Secteur **Chandelier**

Secteur **Solitaire** 30 secs

32 metres

P 15 mins

Crux/bloc	Endurance	Sport

1 Le Lechant Mou*** 🔘 — **6a**

05m | Ca — 717 Tub — 10

A great climb with butch moves in stages. Plenty of rests in between. A perfect route for strong, unfit lardies.

2 La derniere minute* 🔘 — **6c**

21m | 7a- Trick | 6b — ∽5

A real move for a boulderer on a greasy undercut from hell. Short, sharp and abrupt, good footwork essential for grade.

3 Hard Pepper — **6c-**

21m | 6c- CRIMP | 6b Bloc ∽4

Not a good route to wake up on. A very dodgy block marks the start of the difficulty, crimps are the key to the onsight, low merit.

4 ? - (La dalle dans le ciel)* 🙂 — **7c-**

14m | 7c- CRIMP | 5 ∽5

A font 6b slab in the sky. Reading glasses not required, there ain't any holds to look for. A 3 metre crimpers dream.

5 Ushuaia — **7b**

? m | 7b- Bloc | 7a

A steep nasty wall, ouch.

Résumé. *Some very good routes on the left side of this steep wall. Good holds and good rests on these routes; good belay shade too*

6 Electric 🔘 — **7b**

03m | 7b ♫♫ | 7a

Going right across the wall is a bit powerful - no footholds!

7 Picon fatal** 🔘 — **6b-**

32m | 6b- Trick | 6a Yum ∽9

A superb route with mostly jugs all the way. Care with the loose flake under the big central pillar; a nice crux that feels very airy.

8 Soleil levant*** 🔘 — ⚡ **6a+**

31m | 6a- Cool | 6a+ 747 Pump ∽9

A big undertaking for a low grade climber. Lots of easier sections with big run outs. Requires a steady head.

9 Fou du pont** 🙂 — **7a**

31m | 7a- CRIMP | 7a Pump ∽9

Crimp city down below and up above, ideal for lightweights. For the rest of us, take the pain and just keep hanging in there.

10 Joe le Maxi** — **6c-**

31m | 6c- CRIMP | 6b Bloc ∽10

A very good climb up improbable rock with a reasonable grade; be prepared to crank for a move though, at least a good jug to clip after c.

11 La Biboufafait** — **7a-**

31m | 7a- Bloc | 6c ∽10

A very nice climb - except for the crux! Full on power where a long reach comes in very handy, nice jug to clip after crux.

Gondolf — Pirate - Solitaire - Joe le Maxi - Chandelier - Brisse

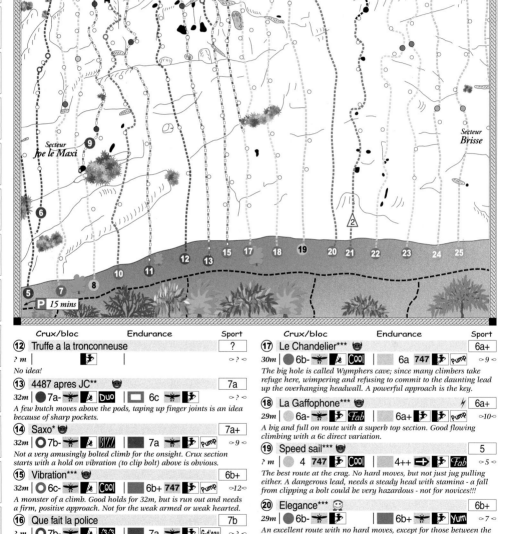

32 metres

Secteur
Joe le Maxi

Secteur
Brisse

P 15 mins

Crux/bloc	Endurance	Sport

12 Truffe a la tronconneuse   ?

? m ⋰?⋰

No idea!

13 4487 apres JC**   7a

32m 7a- Duo 6c ⋰?⋰

A few butch moves above the pods, taping up finger joints is an idea because of sharp pockets.

14 Saxo*   7a+

32m 7b- BIZ 7a Pump ⋰9⋰

Not a very amusingly bolted climb for the onsight. Crux section starts with a hold on vibration (to clip bolt) above is obvious.

15 Vibration**   6b+

32m 6c- Cool 6b+ 747 Pump ⋰12⋰

A monster of a climb. Good holds for 32m, but is run out and needs a firm, positive approach. Not for the weak armed or weak hearted.

16 Que fait la police   7b

? m 7b- 7a G-d'eau ⋰?⋰

A weird wall with a few tough moves. Long reach for a dyno is a distinct advantage as footholds are non existant. An easy tick for a fat, strong bastard.

Résumé. A fabulous and steep section. Gets the shade 2pm onwards and cools quickly, shady trees for hammocks below.

Crux/bloc	Endurance	Sport

17 Le Chandelier**   6a+

30m 6b- Cool 6a 747 Pump ⋰9⋰

The big hole is called Wymphers cave; since many climbers take refuge here, wimpering and refusing to commit to the daunting lead up the overhanging headwall. A powerful approach is the key.

18 La Gaffophone**   6a+

29m 6a- Fab 6a+ Pump ⋰10⋰

A big and full on route with a superb top section. Good flowing climbing with a 6c direct variation.

19 Speed sail**   5

? m 4 747 Cool 4++ Fab ⋰5⋰

The best route at the crag. No hard moves, but not just jug pulling either. A dangerous lead, needs a steady head with stamina - a fall from clipping a bolt could be very hazardous - not for novices!!!

20 Elegance**   6b+

29m 6b- 6b+ Yum ⋰7⋰

An excellent route with no hard moves, except for those between the 1st and 7th bolts. A sustained adventure.

21 Mariotte [A0-2]*   7a-

27m 6b- 6b+ Pump ⋰10⋰

A lovely 6b route, but with a font 6c top wall (crimp). Best frig - climb all the way until you are standing fully in control at the 4th bolt. Two pulls on quickdraws make getting to the belay easy.

Gondolf

Pirate - Solitaire - Joe le Maxi - Chandelier - Brisse

CHANDELIER 6b-, Combe Obscure; Hervé Pichon

LE BRISE DE LA PASTILLE 6b-, Combe Obscure; Hervé Pichon

27 metres

Secteur
Chandelier

P 15 mins

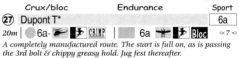
	Crux/bloc	Endurance	Sport

22 La brise de la pastille* 😃 | 6b

26m | 6b- | 6a+ **747** Cool | ◦8◦

A very intimidating climb with widely spaced bolts, may get a few knees trembling. The crux when it comes is quite pleasant, well protected and straightforward.

23 The Blue Breaker* 😃 | 6a+

25m | 6b- CRIMP | 6a+ | ◦7◦

A superb climb with a very good crux. Lovely fingertip wall climbing leads to obvious moves with obvious difficulty & obvious airtime.

24 Et moi alors* 😃 | 5-

27m | 5- Bloc | 4+ | ◦6◦

A run out lead in places, but good holds when you need them. A magnificent position for the grade. Short climbers may have stress.

25 Les soupirs* 😃 | 5-

26m | 5- Bloc | 4+ Yum | ◦7◦

A good warm up and jug fest. The crux needs attention, but the rest is like wallowing in Emmenthal fromagio juggerouni.

26 Aymondoï* 😃 | 5-

25m | 6a- mono | 4+ Bloc | ◦7◦

A one move wonder route. The rest is fun on Verdon style flutings.

27 Dupont T* | 6a

20m | 6a- CRIMP | 6a Bloc | ◦7◦

A completely manufactured route. The start is full on, as is passing the 3rd bolt & chippy greasy hold. Jug fest thereafter.

28 Les Broques* [A0] 😃 | ⚡ 6b

20m | 6b- Fun | 6b | ◦6◦

A nice route & low in the grade. Making the move off the mono is best done using the bolt.

29 Dupont D* 😃 | 6a

18m | 6a- | 6a | ◦5◦

A nice route despite the bad equipping, best done on a top rope.

30 Naissance* | 5-

16m | 5- CRIMP | 4 | ◦5◦

A very good short route that uses tiny holds; not steep enough to cause much trouble. (Holds to 1st clip are good; double krab it.)

31 Bons baisers de kincon* 😃 | 6b

13m | 6c- Flexi | 6a- | ◦6◦

A short route but excellent. Not easy to onsight. You need confidence in footwork on sloping holds - no crimps for once.

Résumé. This end gives easier climbing but still a lot of fun with some better protected routes. Good belay shade.

BLANCHARD | ARCHÉO | CORNEIRETTE | QUINSAN | VENASQUE | ST.PIERRE | COLOMBIER | CLAPIS | GLISSE | TYROLIENNE | CASCADE-HAUT | CHRISTOPHE | A.LAGARDE | GRAND TRAV | COMBE OBS. | GROSEAU

POTIRON, CITROUILLE & CIE 6c, Rochers du Groseau; Ollie Ryall

Si le Tour de France n'était pas passé par Malaucène, nous n'aurions peut-être jamais entendu parler de cette ville. C'est une ville ancienne sympathique située dans un joli cadre aux pieds des pentes du Mont Ventoux, et dont nous recommandons la visite. Il y a de nombreux bars et cafés dans le centre-ville, des magasins et un marché chaque mercredi matin. Il y a des panneaux d'indication depuis le centre-ville pour la source d'Groseau qui vous permetttront de la trouver facilement sans l'aide d'une carte. A l'opposé des falaises et des sources d'eau fraîche, il y a un bar qui rendra votre décision de grimper difficile lors des chaudes journées d'été. Nous espérons que les photos de ce guide vous motiveront pour grimper quelques voies avant de vous désaltérer.

Il y a plusieurs falaises autour des sources qui sont parfaites comme terrain de jeu pour les enfants. La zone d'escalade se trouve dans les bois à seulement quelques minutes de marche. Il y a 3 sections d'escalade sur cette falaise. La première est petite et rappelle le Frankenjura avec un calcaire pure, propre, d'excellente qualité et de bonnes prises. Au-dessus de cette zone sur la gauche, se trouve la deuxième section qui est bien plus intimidante avec des voies excellentes qui varient de difficile à très difficile et très très difficile. Nous avons dessiné des cartes pour cette section mais n'avons pu grimper que quelques voies. Vous aurez donc le plaisir de grimper à vu. Au-dessus de cette section et sur la gauche se trouve le troisième niveau qui forme une baie à angle droit (idéale pour pique-niquer). Il y a une large sélection de voies qui varient de courtes et faciles à difficiles et longues. Le calcaire de ces falaises est en général de très bonne qualité et offre d'immenses prises qui permettent de se relaxer. L'escalade est soutenue mais en général pas trop difficile si vous vous rappelez d'utiliser convenablement les larges prises pour vos pieds. La zone reste à l'ombre jusque vers la fin de l'après-midi. C'est donc un endroit parfait pour les jours chauds surtout si vous grimpez le matin. Attention le mistral y souffle très fort!

If it wasn't for the cycling challenge of the Tour de France, the world might never have heard of Malaucène. Then again, outside the world of cycling, who has heard of Malaucène – not many people. This is unfair of course; because it is a lovely old town, and set in a lovely and convenient spot on the lower slopes of Mont Ventoux, and is an excellent place to visit and stroll around in its own right. It has a busy centre with no shortage of popular cafés and bars that get the midday sunshine, plus ample shops and a thriving street market on Wednesday mornings. Many a time I have sat in a bar here drinking Pelforth brune (nearest thing that you get to English beer here), observing the steady stream of cyclists going through the town. Cycling up Mont Ventoux is an easy challenge to a climber, but to wear bright orange lycra all day - wow, now that is a hideous challenge! Signposts to the source d'Groseau from the town centre, will enable those with inept map reading inability to find this lovely beauty spot only 2km away. The attractive bar opposite the picturesque cliffs and spring water, makes a decision to climb on a hot day even harder. At least the photos in this book should keep you on the straight and narrow for a few hours, before you succumb to the dreaded drinking demon.

There are quite a few cliffs in the area around the actual spring waters, but these form a tourist style arena and are best left as a playground for kids etc. Taking a nature trail up through the woods, you find after a few minutes the lowest of the 3 tiers of cliffs that comprise of this climbing area. The first is small and highly reminiscent of Frankenjura – Maximillianswand style; pure, clean and high quality limestone with small and sharp pockets. Above this small area to the left is the second section that is far more daunting, and has a fair selection of excellent climbs that rate from hard, to very hard, to really hard. We drew diagrams to these but only got a chance to climb a few, so enjoy a good onsight challenge with these. Above this and again to the left, is the top tier that forms a right-angled bay (fine pic-nic spot). Here there is a very good selection of climbs that range from short and easy - to steep, hard, long and sustained. The general consistency of rock at the cliffs is good, but there are a few large, hollow lumps! The limestone in this area seems to have oversize pockets everywhere that give excellent rests, provided that you are fit enough to hang on in a vertical environment. The style of the climbing is sustained, but generally not too hard if you remember to use all of the hand pockets as footholds; its when you get a section without the big pockets that you hit the sudden crux's; dyno's etc. can be the answer. The whole area is somewhat of a recently developed area, and stays in the shade until early to late afternoon. A great spot on those hot days if you can be bothered to climb in the morning. Mistral, er – yes, gets it big time!

BLANCHARD | ARCHÉO | CORNEIRETTE | QUINSAN | VENASQUE | ST.PIERRE | COLOMBIER | CLAPIS | GLISSE | TYROLIENNE | CASCADE-HAUT | CHRISTOPHE | A.LA.GARDE | GRAND TRAV | COMBE OBS. | GROSEAU

Malaucène - Bédoin

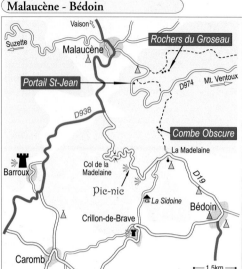

Bar: Malaucène, Caromb, Crillon-la-Brave. Bédoin
Shop: Malaucène, Caromb, Bédoin
Petrol Station: Malaucène, Caromb, Bédoin
Restaurant: Malaucène, Caromb, Crillon-la-Brave. Bédoin
Supermarket: Malaucène, Bédoin
Market day: Malaucène Wed-am; Bédoin Mon am
Tourist Bureau: Malaucène, Bédoin

Sector Womad getting the only sunshine it ever gets - very late in a summers evening. Very Frankenjura style of small pockets for both hands and feet, and hidden away in the trees.

Rochers du Groseau

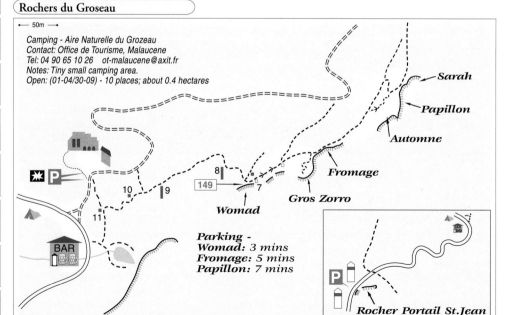

Camping - Aire Naturelle du Grozeau
Contact: Office de Tourisme, Malaucene
Tel: 04 90 65 10 26   ot-malaucene@axit.fr
Notes: Tiny small camping area.
Open: (01-04/30-09) - 10 places; about 0.4 hectares

Sarah
Papillon
Automne
Fromage
Gros Zorro

8
149
7
10
9
Womad
11

Parking -
Womad: *3 mins*
Fromage: *5 mins*
Papillon: *7 mins*

BAR

Rocher Portail St.Jean

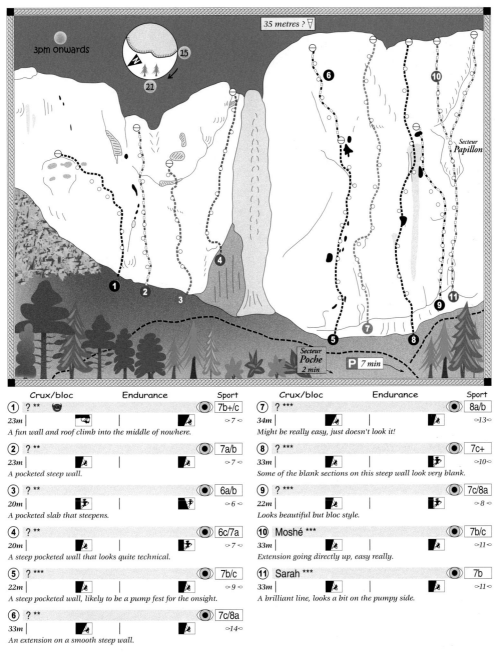

35 metres ?

3pm onwards

Secteur
Papillon

Secteur
Poche
2 min

P 7 min

	Crux/bloc	Endurance	Sport		
(1) ? **				7b+/c	23m — A fun wall and roof climb into the middle of nowhere. ∞7∞
(2) ? **				7a/b	23m — A pocketed steep wall. ∞7∞
(3) ? **				6a/b	20m — A pocketed slab that steepens. ∞6∞
(4) ? **				6c/7a	20m — A steep pocketed wall that looks quite technical. ∞7∞
(5) ? ***				7b/c	22m — A steep pocketed wall, likely to be a pump fest for the onsight. ∞9∞
(6) ? **				7c/8a	33m — An extension on a smooth steep wall. ∞14∞
(7) ? ***				8a/b	34m — Might be really easy, just doesn't look it! ∞13∞
(8) ? ***				7c+	33m — Some of the blank sections on this steep wall look very blank. ∞10∞
(9) ? ***				7c/8a	22m — Looks beautiful but bloc style. ∞8∞
(10) Moshé ***				7b/c	33m — Extension going directly up, easy really. ∞11∞
(11) Sarah ***				7b	33m — A brilliant line, looks a bit on the pumpy side. ∞11∞

Résumé. This is the farthest sector on the high cliff, and hides around the corner to keep in the shade to mid afternoon. Mixed routes of different difficulty. Un-checked routes, so you can have some really good on-sight climbing here. Rock has good pockets, but is steep and will test your stamina well. (A 60m rope, may be long enough!)

Sarah - Papillon - Automne   Fromage - Gros Zorro   Womad

BLANCHARD · ARCHÉO · CORNERETTE · QUINSAN · VENASQUE · ST.PIERRE · COLOMBIER · CLAPIS · GLISSE · TYROLIENNE · CASCADE-HAUT · CHRISTOPHE · ALAGARDE · GRAND TRAV · COMBE OBS. · GROSEAU

VOIE No.8   7c+, Rochers du Groseau; Michel Gouze

Be prepared

Don't waste your trip by not training first!

TOUCHE PAS À LA BELLE MÈRE 6b-, Rochers du Groseau; Steve Glennie

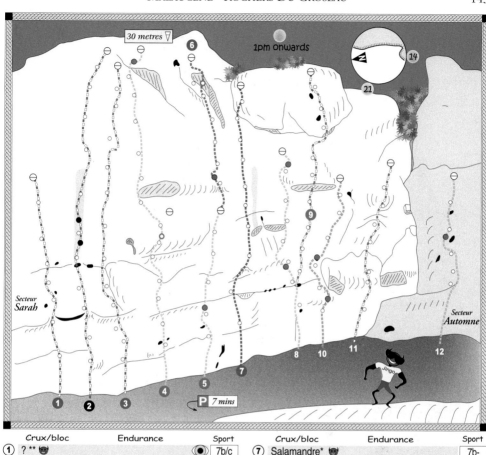

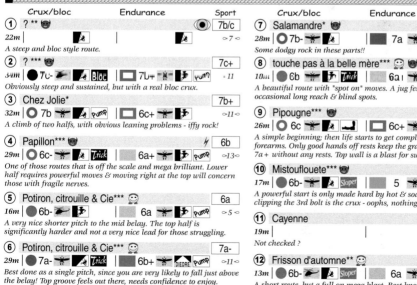

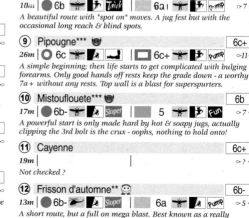

	Crux/bloc	Endurance	Sport
① ? **			**7b/c** ⌐7⌐

22m — A steep and bloc style route.

| **②** ? *** | 7c- | 7b+ | **7c+** ⌐11 |

34m — Obviously steep and sustained, but with a real bloc crux.

| **③** Chez Jolie* | 7b | 6c+ | **7b+** ⌐11⌐ |

32m — A climb of two halves, with obvious leaning problems - iffy rock!

| **④** Papillon*** | 6c- | 6a+ | **6b** ⌐13⌐ |

29m — One of those routes that is off the scale and mega brilliant. Lower half requires powerful moves & moving right at the top will concern those with fragile nerves.

| **⑤** Potiron, citrouille & Cie*** | 6b- | 6a | **6a** ⌐5⌐ |

16m — A very nice shorter pitch to the mid belay. The top half is significantly harder and not a very nice lead for those struggling.

| **⑥** Potiron, citrouille & Cie*** | 7a- | 6b+ | **7a-** ⌐11⌐ |

29m — Best done as a single pitch, since you are very likely to fall just above the belay! Top groove feels out there, needs confidence to enjoy.
Résumé. A very impressive sector with a lovely sunny picnic platform below. No belay shade & bad in the mistral wind.

	Crux/bloc	Endurance	Sport
⑦ Salamandre*	7b-	7a Pump	**7b-** ⌐10⌐

28m — Some dodgy rock in these parts!!

| **⑧** touche pas à la belle mère*** | 6b | 6a Pump | **6b** ⌐7⌐ |

10m — A beautiful route with "spot on" moves. A jug fest but with the occasional long reach & blind spots.

| **⑨** Pipougne*** | 6c | 6c+ Pump | **6c+** ⌐11⌐ |

26m — A simple beginning; then life starts to get complicated with bulging forearms. Only good hands off rests keep the grade down - a worthy 7a+ without any rests. Top wall is a blast for superspurters.

| **⑩** Mistouflouete*** | 6b- Sloper | 5 Fun | **6b** ⌐7⌐ |

17m — A powerful start is only made hard by hot & soapy jugs, actually clipping the 3rd bolt is the crux - oophs, nothing to hold onto!

| **⑪** Cayenne | | | **6c+** ⌐?⌐ |

19m — Not checked ?

| **⑫** Frisson d'automne** | 6b- Sloper | 6a Pump | **6b-** ⌐5⌐ |

13m — A short route, but a full on mega blast. Best known as a really awkward nastie, and exhausting to onsight - watch others first!!

| Sarah | - | Papillon | - | Automne | | Fromage | - | Gros Zorro | | Womad |

BLANCHARD · ARCHÉO · CORNEIRETTE · QUINSAN · VENASQUE · ST.PIERRE · COLOMBIER · CLAPIS · GLISSE · TYROLIENNE · CASCADE-HAUT · CHRISTOPHE · A.LAGARDE · GRAND TRAV · COMBE OBS. · GROSEAU

GROS COMME UNE MAISON 5+, Rochers du Groseau; Mark Glennie

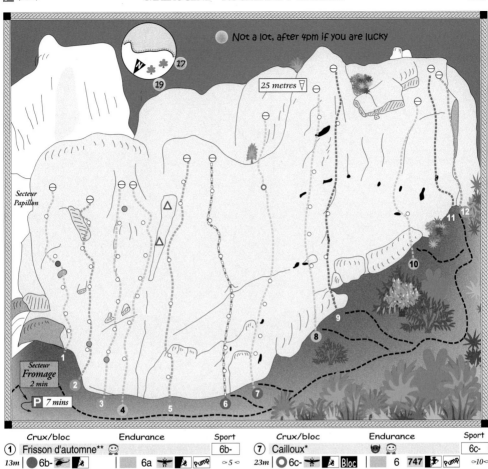

Not a lot, after 4pm if you are lucky

25 metres

Secteur Papillon

Secteur Fromage 2 min

P 7 mins

	Crux/bloc	Endurance	Sport
① Frisson d'automne** ☺			6b-
13m ⬤ 6b-	6a	Pump	◦5◦

A short route but a full on mega blast for any low grade climber. Most 6a climbers refer to this as a real awkward bugger of a nastie.

② Marque de tendresse*** ☺			5
14m ⬤ 5-	5	Pump	◦7◦

A lovely climb with a second half that needs a steady approach. Go left at the top to get to the belay & an extra good move.

③ Espèce protégée*** ☻ ☺			5-
15m ⬤ 5-	4+	Fun	◦7◦

A hard start followed by a succession of pockets designed by a genius.

④ Entreprise de travaux publics** ☺ △			4
15m ⬤ 4-	4+	Fun	◦6◦

An easy looking line that is a full on pump fest for a grade 4 climber. Tough for the grade but giant holds.   Loose pillar on the right.

⑤ Gros comme une maison*** ☺			5+
? m ⬤ 5-	5+	Pump	◦?◦

A really nice route.

⑥ La voie lactée			6c
? m			◦?◦

	Crux/bloc	Endurance	Sport
⑦ Cailloux* ☻ ☺			6c-
23m ◯ 6c- Bloc	6 747 Pump		◦10◦

Do one of the other routes in this area that are really good.

⑧ Vas-y-mulet		◉	6a+
? m			໐?໐

⑨ Mal aux seins		◉	6b
? m			◦?◦

⑩ Polarisant		◉	6a
? m			◦?◦

⑪ Time Code		◉	6b-
? m			◦?◦

⑫ Preview		◉	5+
? m			◦?◦

Résumé. A good small area running up the side of a hill and that gets excellent shade almost all day long. Belay positions up on the right are a bit awkward. Good choice for a hot morning. Stays damp after rain in the colder months.

BLANCHARD | ARCHÉO | CORNERETTE | QUINSAN | VENASQUE | ST.PIERRE | COLOMBIER | CLAPIS | GLISSE | TYROLIENNE | CASCADE-HAUT | CHRISTOPHE | A.LAGARDE | GRAND TRAV | COMBE OBS. | GROSEAU

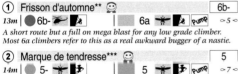

Sarah   -   Papillon   -   Automne

Fromage   -   Gros Zorro

Womad

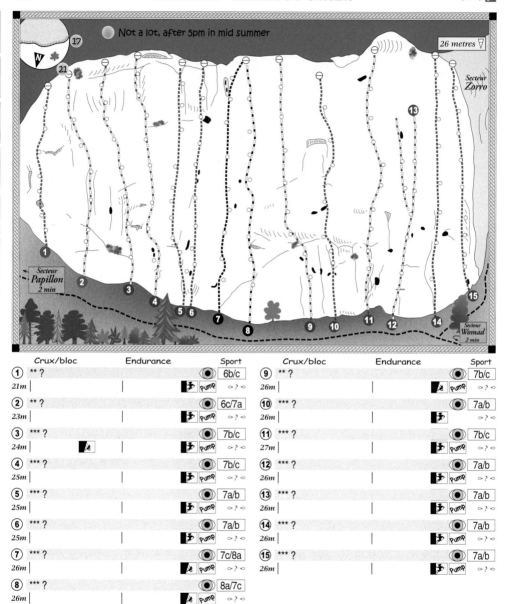

Not a lot, after 5pm in mid summer

26 metres

Secteur Zorro

Secteur Papillon 2 min

Secteur Womad 2 min

	Crux/bloc	Endurance	Sport
(1) ** ? 21m			6b/c
(2) ** ? 23m			6c/7a
(3) *** ? 24m			7b/c
(4) *** ? 25m			7b/c
(5) *** ? 25m			7a/b
(6) *** ? 25m			7a/b
(7) *** ? 26m			7c/8a
(8) *** ? 26m			8a/7c

	Crux/bloc	Endurance	Sport
(9) ** ? 26m			7b/c
(10) *** ? 26m			7a/b
(11) *** ? 27m			7b/c
(12) *** ? 26m			7a/b
(13) *** ? 26m			7a/b
(14) *** ? 26m			7a/b
(15) *** ? 26m			7a/b

Résumé. *This is a superb sector of smooth rock, covered in pockets just like cheese, hence our name for the sector. Most of the routes are not very steep, simply only vertical! The moves between the pockets are easy when they are close together, and the crux's tend to be bloc style power moves when the pockets don't run in comfortable sequences. Not a place to come if your finger tendons are iffy. Pointy shoes that work well in pockets are very useful here.*

Eyeball grade. *This is a new experiment for those climbers who really want to enjoy on-sight climbing. We give the length of the climb, angle and style - but only a grade to what it looks like - could be accurate or a complete sandbag! Now you can really climb on-sight. Should be fun for those who like climbing 7a and upwards, and don't mind having a hard time occasionally.*

Side tabs: BLANCHARD | ARCHÉO | CORNIRETTE | QUINSAN | VENASQUE | ST.PIERRE | COLOMBIER | CLAPIS | GLISSE | TYROLIENNE | CASCADE-HAUT | CHRISTOPHE | A.LAGARDE | GRAND TRAV | COMBE OBS. | GROSEAU

Sarah - Papillon - Automne   Fromage - Gros Zorro   Womad

Secteur Fromage, Rochers du Groseau; Frédéri Marcy

VOIE DE TROUS (No 2) 6c++, Rochers du Groseau; Ollie Ryall

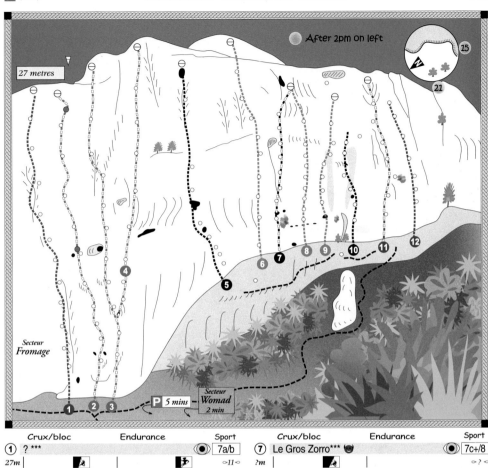

After 2pm on left

27 metres

Secteur
Fromage

P 5 mins

Secteur
Womad
2 min

	Crux/bloc	Endurance	Sport
① ? ***			7a/b
27m			○11○

A very clean and excellent looking route.

② ? ***			6c++
00m	O 0c ⬤ Duo ☐ 0c+ ✕ 🚶 PunK		○10○

A climb with superb moves, and a complete pocket jug fest. Not that easy to onsight, and with a real sting in the tail. Highly sustained.

③ ? ***			6c ?
27m			○ ? ○

An obvious easy looking route.

④ ? ***			6c ?
27m			○ ? ○

An obvious easy looking route.

⑤ Deux kilo six			7c ?
?m			○ ? ○

Bolts so close together - is a clue that this isn't a walk in the park.

⑥ ?			8a/b
?m			○ ? ○

Looks brutal.

⑦ Le Gros Zorro***			7c+/8
?m			○ ? ○

Nice line, nasty angle; looks the best warm up around here.

⑧ Pietra gala***			8a/b
?m			○ ? ○

Might feel easy for some!

⑨ ? ***			8a/b
?m			○ ? ○

Neck ache for the belayer.

⑩ ?			?
?m			○ ? ○

Bolts, but no obvious finishes?

⑪ ?			7b?
?m			○ ? ○

Poor quality rock in this area, with caution.

⑫ ?			7a/b
?m			○ ? ○

A line here somewhere.

Résumé. *Left side is a continuation of the Fromage wall in a similar style. Upper tier is hard - rock ard, and steep.*

Sarah	-	Papillon	-	Automne		Fromage	-	Gros Zorro		Womad

Source d'Groseau: A lovely spring of crystal clear water, opposite a very enticing ice cream café.

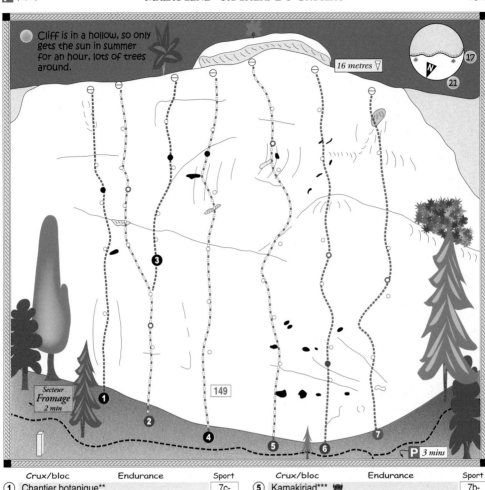

Cliff is in a hollow, so only gets the sun in summer for an hour, lots of trees around.

16 metres

Secteur **Fromage** 2 min

149

P 3 mins

BLANCHARD | ARCHÉO | CORNERETTE | QUINSAN | VENASQUE | ST.PIERRE | COLOMBIER | CLAPIS | GLISSE | TYROLIENNE | CASCADE-HAUT | CHRISTOPHE | A.LAGARDE | GRAND TRAV | COMBE OBS. | GROSEAU

	Crux/bloc	Endurance	Sport
①	Chantier botanique**		7c-

17m | 7c- | Bloc | 7a-

A hard bloc move - ouch.

| ② | Les années folles** | | 7b- |

17m | 7b- | CRIMP | 6c

Two moves, two chances to blow the onsight. Hard and uncompromising for the fingertips.

| ③ | Science fiction** | | 7c- |

17m | 7c- | Bloc | 6c

Steep and bloc style.

| ④ | La 149* | | 7c- |

17m | 7c- | Bloc | 6c | CRIMP

Nasty on the skin, crux hold is not on the large side.

| ⑤ | Kamakiriad*** | | 7b- |

10m | 7b | CRIMP | Co

A very good outing with sustained difficulty, and a crux that isn't hard for the grade we give it.

| ⑥ | Feeling*** | | 7a- |

15m | 7a- | Trick | 6b | CRIMP

A very annoying early move to catch out those who haven't woken up yet. Sustained but also with very good rests.

| ⑦ | Womad** | | 6c- |

14m | 6c- | Bloc | 6b-

Excellent holds until the 2nd bolt, where the difficulty is somewhat concentrated, and difficult.

Résumé. A small cliff that would be very at home in the Frankenjura. Just steeper than vertical, crimpy and demands very good footwork. Most routes only having one hard move, and a hard move at that (our twin grading system warns you of the moves). Ideal for lightweights.

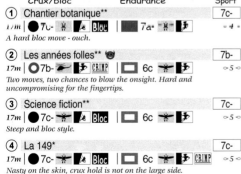

Sarah - Papillon - Automne

Fromage - Gros Zorro

Womad

Equip

Rocher du Portail Saint Jean - small, but still offers good fun.

28 metres

Nice afternoon sunshine

ST JEAN · VAISON · 3 RIVIÈRES · SAINT LÉGER · VIC · BRUNOTS · ST JULIEN · QUEBEC · LOU PASSO · UBRIEUX · M-ROUSSE · BOURDONS · AIGUIER · MIEYES · MÉVOUILLON · TOPOS

P 15 secs

	Crux/bloc	Endurance	Sport
(1)	Convexe** 😊		● 6c/7a
27m	DIEDRE	✴ 🧗 Pump	∞8∞

A very fine looking groove away from the crowds.

	Crux/bloc	Endurance	Sport
(2)	? ** 😊		⚡ 6b
24m	● 6b- ✴ 🧗 Pump	6a+ 747 🧗 ⚡	∞7∞

An awkward crux above the 2nd bolt. Not a route for timid or inexperienced leaders. Very technical but not fingery. Climbing gets easier as the runouts get longer; benefits from a positive approach.

	Crux/bloc	Endurance	Sport
(3)	? ** 😊		7a
28m	● 7a- ✴ 🧗 COOL	☐ 6c+ 747 🧗	∞7∞

A route that is best off on your list of routes to 'top rope!!!' A combination of flakey rock, really awkward clips, and giant falls - gives this climb a less than appetising zing. Full on 28m of 6c, and has two independent lines, to the left or right of the bolts; many variations, many panics.

	Crux/bloc	Endurance	Sport
(4)	?		● 7a/b
24m		🧗	∞?∞

Rock does look a bit on the dodgy side.

Résumé. *We just managed to visit here on the last day of the research for the book. As you approach from the left, there is a very nice area that is well laid out for novice climbers. The rock is suspect in parts, but the equipment looks plentiful and the angle is very reasonable. The harder routes over to the left provide engaging entertainment - that might not be everyones cup of tea. Good challenging routes with absolutely no polish! The general instability of the rock on the cliff is the biggest disappointment, since it is a very nice venue.*

Access: *Carry on up the road past Source d'Groseau dir-Mont Ventoux (D975). After 500m the GR91 footpath crosses the road. Another 100m there is a small cliff by the road, with red and white bollards on the opposite side. Here some small steps lead up to the larger part of the crag in 30 metres.*

	Crux/bloc	Endurance	Sport
(5)	? *		● 5 ?
8m		🧗	∞?∞
(6)	? *		● 4+ ?
9m		🧗	∞?∞
(7)	? *		● 3 ?
8m		🧗	∞?∞
(8)	? *		● 5 ?
12m		🧗	∞?∞
(9)	? '		● 5 ?
12m		🧗	∞?∞
(10)	? *		● 4 ?
20m		🧗	∞?∞
(11)	? *		● 4 ?
18m		🧗	∞?∞
(12)	? *		● 4 ?
20m		🧗	∞?∞
(13)	? *		● 3 ?
20m		🧗	∞?∞
(14)	? *		● 3 ?
21m		🧗	∞?∞

Equip ⚊O

Crillon-le-Brave

Crillon-le-Brave, view toward Dentelles de Montmirail

Crillon-le-Brave

This area is peppered with tranquil and peaceful hill top villages. Venasque is simply a classic, and Crillon-le-Brave has some of the finest views in the whole southern area, alongside a fine café and posh hotel. Caromb, Le Barroux, and Bédoin are a must. Sablet and Séguret are worth a wander, as is Faucon, La Roche-sur-Buis & Entrechaux. If its a swealtering day, you will at least find cool passage ways to flop along, from one bar to the next.

Pierrelongue

ST. JEAN

VAISON

3 RIVIÈRES

SAINT LÉGER

VIC

BRUNOTS

ST. JULIEN

QUEBEC

LOU PASSO

UBRIEUX

EM-ROUSSE

BOURDONS

AIGUIER

MIEYES

MÉYOUILLON

TOPOS

vaison-la-Romaine – Château bloc secteur

The major town to the North of Mont Ventoux is Vaison-la-Romaine. As the name would suggest, it has a strong history of Roman connections and there has been a lot of preservation work carried out here. The town is somewhat of a festive nature and really does organise a lot of events through the year: In June you often get a short Jazz festival, then there is an antique theatre which has celebrated a dance festival, established now over 70 years and occupies the best part of latter July. August sees the arrival of 'big choir' and general screeching escapades lasting the best part of the month. In autumn the concentration turns to food, with a soup festival held in October and then a five day gourmet festival in November, followed by a wine celebration from the new harvest. They certainly know how to have a good time here. If you do find yourself needing to work out from this giddy entertainment, then a few hours traversing and bouldering can be found on the south side of hill beneath the old Château. There were a few routes here once, but the rock is soft and bouldering seems by far the best use and safe entertainment.

C'est une de ces petites falaises qui perdit la côte lorsque Baume Rousse et Saint Léger devinrent très populaires. Les falaises sont sur terrain privé, donc pas de groupes, ni de clubs s'il vous plait et respectez la nature et les environs. Bien qu'il y ait suffisamment à faire sur les autres sites, Trois Rivières fait partie intégrante de l'escalade de cette région et offrent des voies d'un style différent. Située au milieu d'arbres très denses, c'est un lieu assez sinistre et après la pluie il rappelle le Venezuela. La falaise est orientée au nord et seulement quelques parties reçoivent les rayons du soleil en fin de journée. Elle reste donc fraîche même lorsqu'il fait très chaud. Cependant étant sous les arbres et dans une vallée non loin d'une rivière, le taux d'humidité y est assez important et si vous grimpez en cotation élevée vos doigts risquent de souffrir. La qualité des mouvements est exceptionnelle et il vous faut penser prudemment à votre voie avant même de quitter le sol.

La roche calcaire contient beaucoup de sable et fait parfois penser à du grès. Les secteurs sont variés et sont tous de style différent. Il y a en général peu de prises et puissance et dynamisme sont donc très utiles. Du fait du manque de prises, il est nécessaire d'avoir une bonne technique et un bon mental pour pouvoir grimper à vu avec succès. L'équipement est très spécifique et a été mis en place par des grimpeurs qui connaissent bien les voies. Les goujons sont toujours très bien placés, près des mouvements difficiles. Par contre sur les voies les plus courtes il vous faut parfois compter sur un seul goujon. Ainsi je vous recommande d'apporter un manche (clip stick) pour mettre vos dégaines. Certaines des voies les plus difficiles sont diaboliques mais également merveilleuses. En résumé, sur ce site, vous aurez toujours l'impression d'être mentalement épuisé!

This is one of those old fashioned, small cliffs that went out of fashion with the coming online of Baume Rousse and the extensive Saint Léger. The cliff is on private land and keeping a low profile is the order of the day, so please no groups or clubs, and be highly respectful of the nature and locality. For most climbers there is no reason to come here since there is ample to climb at other locations, however, Trois Rivières does form an essential part to the climbing heritage of this area, and offers climbing of a different style, and that is rare in the south of France. Its location in dense trees is somewhat spooky at the best of times, and after rain is more reminiscent of Venezuela, and not without the odd mosquito or two. The whole cliff faces north, with only a few bits getting the sun in late evening, hence the crag remains relatively cool – even in a very hot summer. However, its location set in the trees and on a bend in a river valley, means that you generally get relatively high humidity, and pushing your cranking grade is likely to start ripping the skin on your fingertips, (another reason why it is unpopular with those pushing their grade). The quality of the climbing moves however is exceptional, and you have to engage brain as soon, if not before you even leave the ground.

The rock is limestone with a generally high content of sand, that in some parts becomes genuine sandstone. One minute you are pocket pulling, then have to change to slippery slopers, then back again to crimping. There are many different sectors to climb here and all have their own character. In general though, there are less holds, rather than more holds, so power or dynamism to climb between holds is handy. With less holds, there is often demand for good technique and cerebral thinking to onsight successfully. It is very rewarding therefore to tick routes here onsight. The bolting of the routes is very specific and has been done by climbers of high ability who really know the routes. The good side is that you do nearly always get bolts where there is a hard move, but you often have to rely upon just a single bolt for safety on many of the shorter routes. Because of this, I would definitely recommend bringing a clip stick here, remember – karabiners although highly reliable, have been known to break! Some of the harder routes are fiendish, but wonderful at the same time. To sum up, it doesn't look steep and isn't steep, but you always seem to get pumped out of your brains here, weird, maybe too much plonk the night before.

Entrechaux - Mollons-sur-Ouvèze

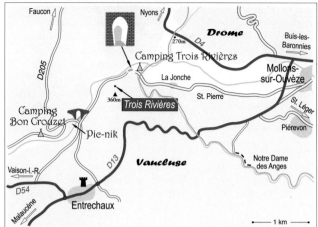

Camping Trois Rivières* 🚐 🏠
Quartier sea Jonches, Entrechaux 84340
(2km-NNE Entrechaux)
Tel: 04 90 46 01 72
www.camping-les3rivieres.com
Notes: General busy site by river.
Open: (01-04/30-09)
88 places; about 6 hectares

Camping Bon Crouzet*
Route de St. Marcellin, Entrechaux 84340
(1km-NNW Entrechaux)
Tel: 04 90 46 01 62
du.bon.crouzet.free.fr
Notes: General site by river.
Open: (01-04/30-10)
45 places; about 1.2 hectares

Bars: Mollons; nice position over river
Entrechaux, on main road
Shop: Mollons, Entrechaux
Petrol Station: Malaucène, Vaison-L-R.
Restaurant: Entrechaux (St. Herbert)
Supermarket: Malaucène, Vaison-L-R.
Market day: Malaucène Wed-am;
Tourist Bureau: Malaucène, Vaison-L-R.

Trois Rivières

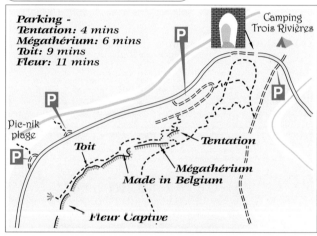

Parking -
Tentation: 4 mins
Mégathérium: 6 mins
Toit: 9 mins
Fleur: 11 mins

Access: Most people park before
the approach track at the bottom
of the cliff. Here you can park
completely off the road. If you
park opposite the Trois Rivières
campsite, be careful to get your
car close to the trees since the
track is used by other cars. The
walk up from here is slightly
longer but at a nice and even
angle all the way.

**Private land access: This cliff
is on private land. Most private
land owners want their land to
be quiet and have no
problems. If you visit this cliff,
please remember this. Only
climb here in small numbers,
be discreet, park considerately,
leave no litter. No club meets.**

Mollons; Just over bridge, a lovely bar with outside terrace - on right.

Side tabs: ST. JEAN · VAISON · 3 RIVIÈRES · SAINT LÉGER · VIC · BRUNOTS · ST.JULIEN · QUEBEC · LOU PASSO · UBRIEUX · B.L-ROUSSE · BOURDONS · AIGUIER · MIEYES · MÉVOUILLON · TOPOS

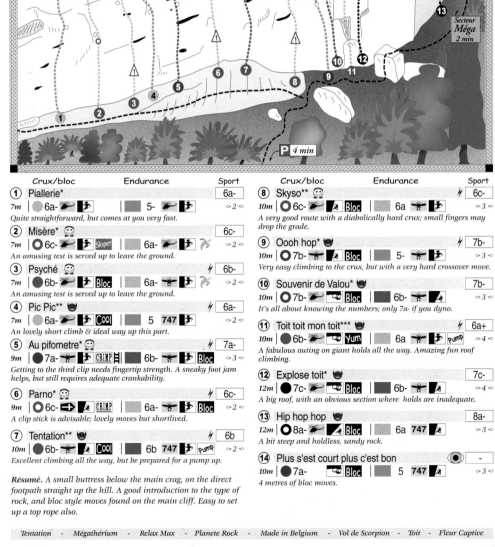

Late sum after 4pm, on top centre of buttress

10 metres

Secteur
Méga
2 min

P 4 min

Secteur Méga 2 min

	Crux/bloc	Endurance	Sport

(1) Piallerie*   6a-
7m | 6a- | 5- | ⌐2⌐
Quite straightforward, but comes at you very fast.

(2) Misère*   6c-
7m | 6c- Sloper | 6a- | ⌐2⌐
An amusing test is served up to leave the ground.

(3) Psyché   6b-
7m | 6b- Bloc | 6a- | ⌐2⌐
An amusing test is served up to leave the ground.

(4) Pic Pic*   6a-
7m | 6a- Cool | 5 747 | ⌐2⌐
An lovely short climb & ideal way up this part.

(5) Au pifometre*   7a-
9m | 7a- CRIMP | 6b- Bloc | ⌐3⌐
Getting to the third clip needs fingertip strength. A sneaky foot jam helps, but still requires adequate crankability.

(6) Parno*   6c-
9m | 6c- CRIMP | 6a- Bloc | ⌐2⌐
A clip stick is advisable; lovely moves but shortlived.

(7) Tentation*   6b
10m | 6b- Cool | 6b 747 Pump | ⌐2⌐
Excellent climbing all the way, but be prepared for a pump up.

(8) Skyso**   6c-
10m | 6c- Bloc | 6a | ⌐3⌐
A very good route with a diabolically hard crux; small fingers may drop the grade.

(9) Oooh hop*   7b-
10m | 7b- Bloc | 5- | ⌐3⌐
Very easy climbing to the crux, but with a very hard crossover move.

(10) Souvenir de Valou*   7b-
10m | 7b- Bloc | 6b- | ⌐3⌐
It's all about knowing the numbers; only 7a- if you dyno.

(11) Toit toit mon toit***   6a+
10m | 6b- Yum | 6a Pump | ⌐4⌐
A fabulous outing on giant holds all the way. Amazing fun roof climbing.

(12) Explose toit*   7c-
12m | 7c- Bloc | 6b- | ⌐4⌐
A big roof, with an obvious section where holds are inadequate.

(13) Hip hop hop   8a-
12m | 8a- Bloc | 6a 747 | ⌐3⌐
A bit steep and holdless, sandy rock.

(14) Plus s'est court plus c'est bon   -
10m | 7a- | 5 747 | ⌐3⌐
4 metres of bloc moves.

Résumé. *A small buttress below the main crag, on the direct footpath straight up the hill. A good introduction to the type of rock, and bloc style moves found on the main cliff. Easy to set up a top rope also.*

Tentation - Mégathérium - Relax Max - Planete Rock - Made in Belgium - Vol de Scorpion - Toit - Fleur Captive

ST. JEAN · VAISON · 3 RIVIÈRES · SAINT LÉGER · VIC · BRUNOTS · ST. JULIEN · QUEBEC · LOU PASSO · UBRIEUX · BM-ROUSSE · BOURDONS · AIGUIER · MIEVES · MÉVOUILLON · TOPOS

TOIT TOIT MON TOIT 6a+, Trois Rivières; Birgit Wrobel

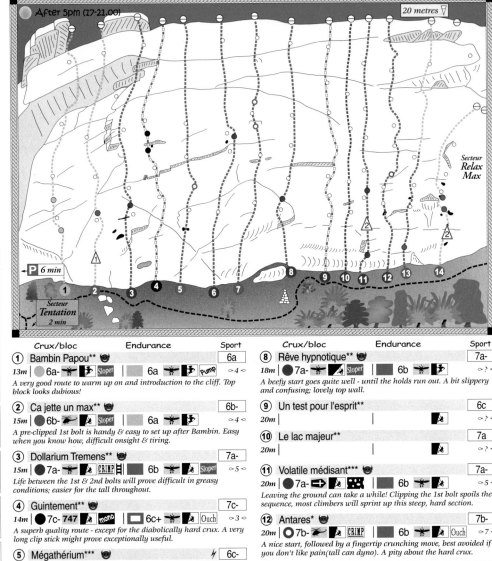

After 5pm (17-21.00)

20 metres

Secteur Relax Max

P 6 min

Secteur Tentation 2 min

Left column tabs: ST. JEAN · VAISON · 3 RIVIÈRES · SAINT LÉGER · VIC · BRUNOTS · ST JULIEN · QUEBEC · LOU PASSO · UBRIEUX · BM-ROUSSE · BOURDONS · AIGUIER · MIEYES · MÉVOUILLON · TOPOS

	Crux/bloc	Endurance	Sport

① Bambin Papou* 🖐
13m | 6a- ☀ 🏃 Sloper | 6a ☀ 🏃 Pump | ∞4∞ | **6a**
A very good route to warm up on and introduction to the cliff. Top block looks dubious!

② Ca jette un max* 🖐
15m | 6b- 🐦 🏃 Sloper | 6a ☀ 🏃 | ∞4∞ | **6b-**
A pre-clipped 1st bolt is handy & easy to set up after Bambin. Easy when you know how, difficult onsight & tiring.

③ Dollarium Tremens* 🖐
15m | 7a- ☀ 🏃 CRIMP | 6b 🏃 Sloper | ∞5∞ | **7a-**
Life between the 1st & 2nd bolts will prove difficult in greasy conditions; easier for the tall throughout.

④ Guintement* 🖐
14m | 7c- 747 🏃 mono | 6c+ ☀ 🏃 Ouch | ∞3∞ | **7c-**
A superb quality route - except for the diabolically hard crux. A very long clip stick might prove exceptionally useful.

⑤ Mégathérium* 🖐
17m | 6c- ☀ 🏃 | 6b 747 🏃 Pump | ∞4∞ | ⚡ **6c-**
Great climbing on very sharp! pockets. A climb with a definite crux, but should go onsight - top is awkward but not hard.

⑥ Fleur d'agonie* 🖐
18m | 7a- 🐦 Trick | 6b 747 🏃 | ∞4∞ | **7a-**
Nice flowing comes to an abrupt end at the 3rd clip. A pure sequence with hidden footholds unlocks this to a reasonable grade.

⑦ Nébulophobe* 🖐
18m | 6c- ☀ 🏃 Bloc | 6b ☀ 🏃 Pump | ∞4∞ | ⚡ **6c-**
A good rest at halfway is welcomed, and very useful. Top section has less footholds than you require, good edges prove useful.

⑧ Rêve hypnotique* 🖐
18m | 7a- ☀ 🏃 Sloper | 6b ☀ 🏃 | ∞?∞ | **7a-**
A beefy start goes quite well - until the holds run out. A bit slippery and confusing; lovely top wall.

⑨ Un test pour l'esprit* 🖐
20m | | 🏃 | ∞?∞ | **6c**

⑩ Le lac majeur* 🖐
20m | | 🏃 | ∞?∞ | **7a**

⑪ Volatile médisant** 🖐
20m | 7a- ➡ 🏃 | 6b ☀ 🏃 | ∞5∞ | **7a-**
Leaving the ground can take a while! Clipping the 1st bolt spoils the sequence, most climbers will sprint up this steep, hard section.

⑫ Antares* 🖐
20m | 7b- 🐦 🏃 CRIMP | 6b ☀ 🏃 Ouch | ∞7∞ | **7b-**
A nice start, followed by a fingertip crunching move, best avoided if you don't like pain(tall can dyno). A pity about the hard crux.

⑬ Le clochard analphabète** 🖐
20m | 6b ☀ 🏃 | 6a ☀ 🏃 | ∞5∞ | **6b**
A 7m sprint section of solid 6b gives you the key to this route, nice and technical thereafter, may cause problems for short but nice clips.

⑭ Fauve d'amazone* 🖐
20m | 6b- ➡ 🏃 | 6a- ☀ 🏃 Ouch | ∞7∞ | **7b-**
You certainly need a lot of power with all the hard climbing before the 1st clip, and you need to work out a good sequence. Very broken thereafter & best to lower from the ring at 16m.

Equip ⌒

Résumé. *A sector that looks vertical, but is actually quite overhanging. A clip stick is very useful for a lot of the 1st clips. Good stamina pays dividends as you are often working out crux moves - quite high above the bolt and you don't always get a good hold to clip from. Very Frankenjura style, gives pain to the fingertips by the end of the day. Not recommended 2 days in a row.*

Tentation - Mégathérium - Relax Max - Planete Rock - Made in Belgium - Vol de Scorpion - Toit - Fleur Captive

NÉBULOPHOBE 6c-, Trois Rivières; Martin Blumenstock

Secteur Fleur Captive, Trois Rivières

Bridge 1km downriver from Trois Rivières

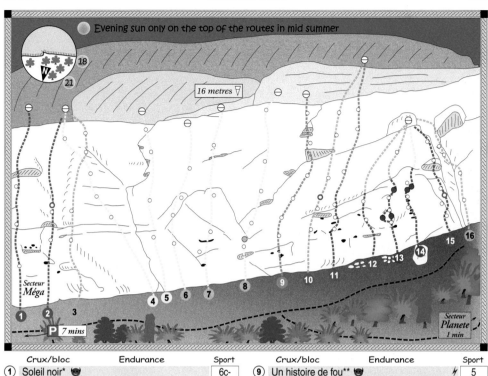

Evening sun only on the top of the routes in mid summer

18
21
N

16 metres

15 16

12 13 14

9 10 11

Secteur
Méga

4 5 6 7 8

1 2 3

P 7 mins

Secteur
Planete
1 min

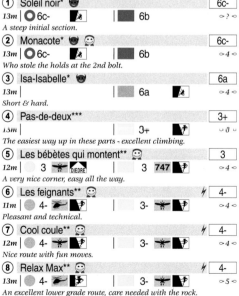

	Crux/bloc	Endurance	Sport

(1) Soleil noir* — 6c-
13m | 6c- | 6b | ○ ? ○
A steep initial section.

(2) Monacote* — 6c-
13m | 6c- | 6b | ○ 4 ○
Who stole the holds at the 2nd bolt.

(3) Isa-Isabelle* — 6a
13m | | 6a | ○ 4 ○
Short & hard.

(4) Pas-de-deux*** — 3+
13m | | 3+ | ○ 0 ○
The easiest way up in these parts - excellent climbing.

(5) Les bébètes qui montent** — 3
12m | 3 DIEDRE | 3 747 | ○ 4 ○
A very nice corner, easy all the way.

(6) Les feignants** — 4-
11m | 4- | 3- | ○ 4 ○
Pleasant and technical.

(7) Cool coule** — 4-
12m | 4- | 3- | ○ 4 ○
Nice route with fun moves.

(8) Relax Max** — 4-
13m | 4- | 3- | ○ 5 ○
An excellent lower grade route, care needed with the rock.

Résumé. A very useful area that combines very easy routes, with a few short and sharp hard problems. Doesn't get the sun late in the afternoon because of the trees.

(9) Un histoire de fou** — 5
13m | 5- Sloper | 5 | ○ 6 ○
A very hard start, followed by very nice slab moves, fun top wall.

(10) Inverse surprise* — 6c-
15m | 6c- Trick | 4 747 | ○ 4 ○
Good hard pulls lead up to the overhang, climbed with a few tiny holds and tricky.

(11) ? * — 6b-
15m | 6b- Pump | 6a | ○ 5 ○
A line of good holds, very pumpy onsight but fun though.

(12) ? * — 6c-
13m | 6c- Bloc | | ○ 4 ○
Big moves on big holds, tricky top (rotten rock).

(13) ? * — 7a-
13m | 7a- Sloper | 4 Bloc | ○ 5 ○
Short but hard, power dyno direct or crimp left. Top is very tricky with intelligent footwork needed.

(14) ? * — 7a-
13m | 7a- mono | 3 | ○ 3 ○
A dyno off a mono sorts out the crux.

(15) ? * — 6c-
13m | 6c- | 6b- | ○ 5 ○
Technical but good if climbed as an arête and using the right wall - awkward on-sight; direct up the left wall is a lot harder.

(16) ? * — 4
? m | DIEDRE | | ○ ? ○
A recently equipped corner.

Equip

Side tabs: ST. JEAN | VAISON | 3 RIVIÈRES | SAINT LÉGER | VIC | BRUNOTS | ST. JULIEN | QUEBEC | LOU PASSO | UBRIEUX | M-ROUSSE | BOURDONS | AIGUIER | MIEVES | MÉVOUILLON | TOPOS

LE FIL DU RASOIR 7b-, Trois Rivières; Mark Glennie

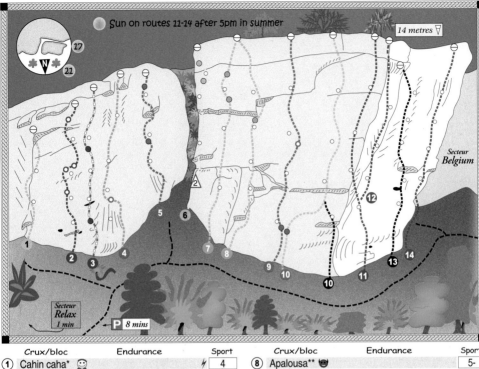

Sun on routes 11-14 after 5pm in summer

14 metres

Secteur Belgium

Secteur Relax 1 min

P 8 mins

Crux/bloc	Endurance	Sport

① Cahin caha* 🙂   **4**

8m | 4 ✳ DIEDRE | ∞ 2 ∞

A very short corner but still with interest.

② Planète rock** 🙂   **7b-**

10m | ⭕ 7b- ✳ 🏃 Sloper | 7a- ✳ 🏃 Trick | ∞ 4 ∞

A nice and technical slabby wall that has a confusing amount of non-existent holds. Technical at the 3rd bolt.

③ Chaud devant** 🙂   **7a-**

11m | ● 7a- ➰ 🏃 Bloc | ☐ 6c- ✳ 🏃 | ∞ 3 ∞

A powerful start leads to pleasant rambling until the 2nd bolt, where a problem ensues.

④ Disciple de Bacchus* 🙂   **6c-**

11m | ⭕ 6c- ➰ 🏃 Bloc | 5 ✳ 🏃 | ∞ 4 ∞

A bloc start will act as a delightful good morning to those still asleep! A lovely arête thereafter.

⑤ Mégallo phallo* 🙂   **6b-**

9m | ● 6b- ➰ 🏃 CRIMP | 6b- ➰ 🏃 Pump | ∞ 3 ∞

A bloc start will act as a delightful good morning to those still asleep! A lovely arête thereafter.

⑥ Tiens la bien* 🙂   **4-**

11m | ◐ 4- ✳ 🏃 COOL | 3 ➰ 🏃 | ∞ 3 ∞

A lovely route up a small arête, requires a steady head to the 1st bolt, then surprisingly interesting thereafter.

⑦ Est-se que tu la sens ?* 🙂   **5-**

12m | ● 5- ➰ 🏃 Sloper | 4- ✳ 🏃 COOL | ∞ 3 ∞

A very pleasant warm up outing that has some thoughtful moves.

Crux/bloc	Endurance	Sport

⑧ Apalousa** 🐚   **5-**

12m | ● 5- ✳ 🏃 ⛓ | 4- ✳ 🏃 COOL | ∞ 4 ∞

A very pleasant excursion following big holds at large distances apart.

⑨ Méfiate** 🙂   **6c-**

13m | ⭕ 6c- ✳ 🏃 Sloper | 6b ✳ 🏃 | ∞ 4 ∞

Moving between the 2nd and 3rd bolt seems impossible until you know how, flexibility helps - stamina is required to make the top.

⑩ Occupe toi d'Amélie** 🐚 🙂   **6b-**

13m | ● 6b- ➰ 🏃 🎲 | 6a- ✳ 🏃 | ∞ 4 ∞

A nice easier way of climbing this wall without the diabolical hard direct start. (Pre-clipping runner after Méfiate is useful)

⑪ Lactique attaque   **7a**

13m | 🏃 | 🏃 Pump | ∞ ? ∞

⑫ Attention titani   **7a+**

13m | 🏃 | 🏃 Pump | ∞ ? ∞

⑬ Hercule c'est dur   **7c**

13m | 🏃 | 🏃 | ∞ ? ∞

⑭ Coco Paradise   **7a**

13m | 🏃 | 🏃 | ∞ ? ∞

Résumé. *A weird area. The slab on the left is fun and technically very entertaining without mind blowing run outs. The right side is a complete cube that is detached from the cliff. Access can be made up the back in a grim gully to the top if you need to set up a top rope. Routes are generally physical and harder than they look - be prepared to be surprised.*

Equip ⌒

Facing north and only gets late afternoon sun in summer on routes 11-15 plus 22 & 23

Secteur *Scorpion*
Fissure Classique

22 metres

Secteur *Relax* 1 min — P 8 min

	Crux/bloc	Endurance	Sport
1	**Cahin caha*** 😊		⚡ 4
8m		4 — DIEDRE	∽2∽

A very short corner but still with interest.

2	**Planète rock**** 😊		7b-
10m	⬤7b- — Sloper	7a- — Trick	∽4∽

A nice and technical slabby wall that has a confusing amount of non-existent holds. Technical at the 3rd bolt.

3	**Chaud devant**** 😊		7a-
11m	⬤7a- — Bloc	▭ 6c-	∽3∽

A powerful start leads to pleasant rambling until the 2nd bolt, where a problem ensues.

4	**Disciple de Bacchus*** 😊		6c-
11m	⬤6c- — Bloc	5	∽4∽

A bloc start will act as a delightful good morning to those still asleep! A lovely arête thereafter.

5	**Mégallo phallo*** 😊		6b-
9m	⬤6b- — CRIMP	6b- — Pump	∽3∽

A bloc start will act as a delightful good morning to those still asleep! A lovely arête thereafter.

6	**Tiens la bien*** 😊		4-
11m	4- — Cool	3	∽3∽

A lovely route up a small arête, requires a steady head to the 1st bolt, then surprisingly interesting thereafter.

7	**Est-se que tu la sens ?*** 😊		5-
12m	5- — Sloper	4- — Cool	∽3∽

A very pleasant warm up outing that has some thoughtful moves.

8	**Apalousa**** 😊		5-
12m	5- —	4- — Cool	∽4∽

A pleasant excursion following big holds at large distances apart.

9	**Méfiate**** 😊		6c-
13m	⬤6c- — Sloper	6b	∽4∽

Moving between the 2nd and 3rd bolt seems impossible until you know how, flexibility helps - stamina is required to make the top.

10	**Occupe toi d'Amélie**** 😊😊		6b-
13m	⬤7c- —	6a-	∽4∽

The start only needs a lock off. (Pre-clipping runner after Méfiate is useful)

11	**Lactique attaque**		7a
13m		Pump	∽?∽

12	**Attention titani**		7a+
13m		Pump	∽?∽

13	**Hercule c'est dur**		7c
13m			∽?∽

14	**Coco Paradise**		7a
13m			∽?∽

15	**Le fil du rasoir**		7b-
13m		Pump	∽?∽

16	**Gadget du bras***		7a
12m	Bloc		∽?∽

17	**Deux doigts coupent tin**		6c
11m			∽?∽

18	**Exalte***		7a
18m	CRIMP		∽?∽

19	**Made in Belgium****		7a-
19m	Pump	Pump	∽?∽

20	**Que fait grand couillou**		7a-
? m		DIEDRE	∽?∽

21	**La tête en bas**		7c
? m			∽?∽

22	**Pour toit gris**		7b+
? m			∽?∽

23	**Dors tranquille Emile****		7a-
? m		Pump	∽?∽

Résumé. *The giant detactched bloc looks like the front of a ship, with very steep routes up it. The inside walls stay cool and in the shade, giving very bloc style routes. The quality of the rock to the right of Exalte is slightly questionable - sandy.*

Equip ⌒

Tentation - Mégathérium - Relax Max - Planete Rock - Made in Belgium - Vol de Scorpion - Toit - Fleur Captive

Side tabs: ST. JEAN | VAISON | 3 RIVIÈRES | SAINT LÉGER | VIC | BRUNOTS | ST JULIEN | QUÉBEC | LOU PASSO | UBRIEUX | BM-ROUSSE | BOURDONS | AIGUIER | MIÈTES | MÉVOUILLON | TOPOS

MADE IN BELGIUM 7a-, Trois Rivières; Steve Glennie

Left side tabs: ST. JEAN · VAISON · 3 RIVIÈRES · SAINT LÉGER · VIC · BRUNOTS · ST JULIEN · QUEBEC · LOU PASSO · UBRIEUX · BM-ROUSSE · BOURDONS · AIGUIER · MIÈTES · MÉVOUILLON · TOPOS

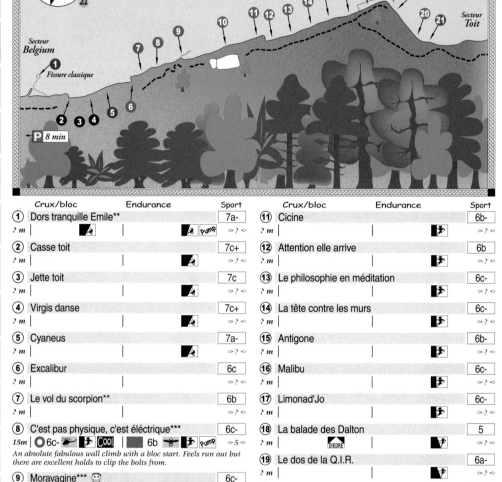

Facing north west and gets late afternoon sun - very good belay shade

15 metres

Secteur Belgium

Fissure classique

P 8 min

Secteur Toit

	Crux/bloc	Endurance	Sport
① Dors tranquille Emile**			7a-
? m		Pump	
② Casse toit			7c+
? m			
③ Jette toit			7c
? m			
④ Virgis danse			7c+
? m			
⑤ Cyaneus			7a-
? m			
⑥ Excalibur			6c
? m			
⑦ Le vol du scorpion**			6b
? m			
⑧ C'est pas physique, c'est éléctrique***			6c-
15m ⬤ 6c-	6b Pump		

An absolute fabulous wall climb with a bloc start. Feels run out but there are excellent holds to clip the bolts from.

⑨ Moravagine*** 😊			6c-
16m ⬤ 6b-	6a Pump		

This is a lot harder than it looks; top is a real sting in the tail - no clues but it isn't too hard.

⑩ Anaclosis**			6c-
16m ⬤ 6c- Bloc	6b Cool		

Very fine climbing with a stiff start for the short. Plenty of rests; top crux is problematic but very low in the grade - when you know how!

	Crux/bloc	Endurance	Sport
⑪ Cicine			6b-
? m			
⑫ Attention elle arrive			6b
? m			
⑬ Le philosophie en méditation			6c-
? m			
⑭ La tête contre les murs			6c-
? m			
⑮ Antigone			6b-
? m			
⑯ Malibu			6c-
? m			
⑰ Limonad'Jo			6c-
? m			
⑱ La balade des Dalton			5
? m	DIEDRE		
⑲ Le dos de la Q.I.R.			6a-
? m			
⑳ Jeu de vilain			6c-
? m			
㉑ Frime et châtiment			7a+
? m			

Notes. *The corner and last few routes have overgrown recently, but are there to be rediscovered for those with a strong soul.*

Résumé. *A mixed sector. Starting on the left are some big overhanging walls with sandy rock. Routes 6-17 are very good, mid grade, vertical routes. All tend to be quite hard with some very good technical moves. The views from the top part of these routes are superb and feel very airy. Keeps good shade during the day and gets any breeze that is going.*

Equip

Secteur Toit, Trois Rivières

No sun at all really, overhanging with edges in trees, sun on top part of 16 - late pm

Secteur *Fleur* 1 min

P 9 min

Secteur *Scorpion* 30 secs

	Crux/bloc	Endurance	Sport			Crux/bloc	Endurance	Sport
①				○	Pur et dur			7b
②				○	Le jeté d'Eole			7a & 8a
③				○	Le jeté d'Eole direct			7b
④				○	Défonce toit			7b+
⑤				○	Oeuvre postume			7b & 8a
⑥				○	Oeuvre postume direct			7c+ & 8a
⑦				○	La Variante			7b+
⑧				○	Viande au plafond			7a & 8a
⑨				○	?			7a+ & 8a
⑩				○	Juste une illusion			6b+ & 7c
⑪				○	Itinéraire au bis			6c & 7a
⑫				○	Les Valseuses			6c & 7a
⑬				○	Anti G			7b
⑭				○	Force G			7b
⑮				○	Hyper Hard			7a+
⑯								

Résumé. *This is a very exciting and impressive cave. Most of the first clips are high, but that doesn't matter - since you need to be as strong as an ox anyway to make this area worth a visit. Lower part has mostly good holds, upper part is obviously harder and its best to be a lightweight. I've been on most of the routes here over the past 14 years, but have never known which name goes with which route! The route grades are very subjective - simply; if you are light - you don't get very tired; and if you can Egyptian easily and lock off with one arm, then they are all easy. Lower wall is around 6c-7b, upper wall is 7b-8a. We found a list of names and grades - but could not make them fit. Any clues will be greatly received and updated on our website.*

Equip

Tentation - Mégathérium - Relax Max - Planete Rock - Made in Belgium - Vol de Scorpion - Toit - Fleur Captive

Side tabs: ST. JEAN | VAISON | 3 RIVIÈRES | SAINT LÉGER | VIC | BRUNOTS | ST. JULIEN | QUEBEC | LOU PASSO | UBRIEUX | BM-ROUSSE | BOURDONS | AIGUIER | MIÈVES | MÉVOUILLON | TOPOS

Facing north, late afternoon sun in summer

18
21

Secteur
Toit

30 metres

7 **8** **9**

P 10 min

4 **5** **6**

1 **2** **3**

ST. JEAN

VAISON

3 RIVIÈRES

SAINT LÉGER

VIC

BRUNOIS

ST.JULIEN

QUEBEC

LOU PASSO

UBRIEUX

BM-ROUSSE

BOURDONS

AIGUIER

MIEYES

MÉVOUILLON

TOPOS

Crux/bloc	Endurance	Sport		Crux/bloc	Endurance	Sport
① La nuit des Walpurgis		7a		**⑦** Spleen et idéale		6c+
28m		∾?∾		30m		∾?∾
② Salaire de la peur		7a+		**⑧** Fleur captive		6b+
28m		∾?∾		30m		∾?∾
③ Délire		7b+		**⑨** Lee miroir du temps		7b
28m		∾?∾		30m		∾?∾
④ Dérision à tous les étages		7a+				
28m		∾?∾				
⑤ La voie du seigneur		7a				
28m		∾?∾				
⑥ Sixe symbole		6b				
28m		∾?∾				

*Résumé. This is the far end that nobody ever goes to, so the
routes are not polished or worn. Very quiet and tranquil with a
lovely viewpoint overlooking the last 3 routes.*

La rivière Toulourenc prend sa source à l'opposé des falaises de Mévouillon puis se faufile à travers les collines et au milieu de gorges spectaculaires. La roche de ces gorges est impressionnante mais ressemble à du fromage. C'est l'endroit parfait pour un pique-nique mais pas pour l'escalade. La rivière part ensuite vers l'ouest en passant par le Mont Ventoux et le village de Brantes puis le hameau de St. Léger. Sur son passage la rivière a créé quelques petites falaises, Vic étant la plus remarquable, offrant des voies courtes très dispersées. Cette vallée est magnifique, calme et complètement dominée par le Mont Ventoux. Les sapins lui donnent un air alpin et le soleil la réchauffe de ses rayons durant toute l'année. Après le village de St. Léger, la vallée se prolonge sur une gorge de calcaire. Ce site secret isolé devint très populaire avec la visite durant le week-end d'une centaine de grimpeurs venus de toute l'Europe. Ils se rendirent compte très rapidement de la trop haute difficulté des voies. C'est cependant un endroit magnifique qui offre de nombreuses possibilitées de randonnée et nous vous conseillons entre autres celle qui vous emmène à Notre Dame des Angles.

Les gorges offrent un magnifique site d'escalade surtout si vous grimpez en 7c. Si non nous vous recommandons de visiter d'autres sites qui offrent des voies plus faciles et surtout plus intéressantes. Si vous êtes fort et léger alors ce site sera pour vous une véritable Mecque. Les falaises ont le soleil toute la journée mais si vous étudiez convenablement leur exposition vous arriverez à trouver des voies idéalement situées quelques soient les conditions atmosphériques. En hiver, et après une longue période de pluie, les voies en dévers suintent horriblement. En résumé, vous pouvez en principe grimper toute l'année mais soyez prêt à accepter les conditions que ce soit suintement ou soleil brûlant. Les voies ont toutes été equipées de différente manière par de nombreux grimpeurs. Soyez donc très prudent car il est possible que certaines voies aient été equipées par des grimpeurs qui se sentent à l'aise en 7c et qui ne s'inquiètent pas de chute dans les sections les plus faciles. Nous avons donné peu d'information sur ces voies puisque les grimpeurs en 7c-8a préfèrent en général grimper à vu. Vérifiez s'il a des panneaux indiquant si l'escalade y est interdite.

Toulourenc valley with the cliffs of Saint Léger

The river Toulourenc starts high up in the almost alpine meadows just opposite the remote cliffs of Mévouillon, it then cuts through the hills to form a dramatic gorge on the way to Montbrun-les-Bains. The rock in this gorge is spectacular, but is that of a deep yellow ochre, better known to climbers as soft cheese. A perfect spot for a two hour picnic, then leave. This river is forced to head west by Mont Ventoux and down past the village of Brantes and onto the hamlet of Saint Léger. It has kindly cut away a few small cliffs on the way, Vic being the most notable and providing a handful of short, but scattered routes. This long valley is simply beautiful, quiet, and totally dominated by the giant Mont Ventoux. Even though the fir trees give it a highly alpine feel outside the summer months, the steep angle of the surrounding hills is not too steep, and allows sunshine into the valley bottom for all of the year, unlike many typical alpine valleys. After the village of Saint Léger, the lavender fields and lush meadows come to an end with the closing of the valley into a long gorge of limestone cliffs. This remote secret location in the 1990's, became France's best known 'secret' location. By 2000, it was known as Europe's 'best known secret' climbing location, with only a few hundred cars every weekend stopping by! In actuality, it became Europe's biggest climbing spectator event, since everyone wanted to go and see this 'secret' location, only to find out that the routes were ridiculously hard and leaving the ground was reserved for anorexics. But as a sunny spot in a beautiful location, it was always going to be a winner. As a walking location it is very good, and the walk all the way down to Notre Dame des Angles is superb, with many parts of the gorge being a wet experience - but hardly canyoning.

The gorge is a tremendous climbing venue if you are a confident and strong 7c climber. If you are not, then I would hardly recommend a climbing visit here. There are a selection of easy routes to keep belay bunnies from complaining too much, but are naff compared with other mid grade routes in the region - so, get a life. If you are strong and light, then of course this is mecca. The predominant cliffs get the sun every day and classify as hot fryers. The gorge does twist and turn however, so if you plan your climbing well, you can pick ideal conditions that you like. Unfortunately, after a week of rain, the steeper routes do seep badly and in winter, an entire trip can be wasted for 8b-c tickers. You can climb here all year round, but be prepared to accept what is in condition, given seepage or roasting sunshine. The equipping of the routes here has been very sporadic, with each route often having a different equipper, many of which are purely climbers and not industrial bolt engineers. Consequently, be especially careful in what you do or don't trust. Many routes are often equipped by 7c climbers for their ability, and who are never going to fall off in the easier sections. There are a few routes with extra bolts in, and ideal for leading by belay bunnies of lower ability, but these are generally polished, and few in number. We don't give too much info for the routes here, 7c-8a climbers prefer a more onsight approach. Note: There is lot more of the gorge below our topos; check to see if there are signs which do not allow climbing in this area, there may be a biotope restriction.

Malaucène - Mollans - Buis - Montbrun

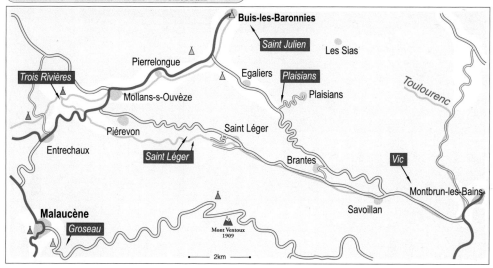

Bar: Brantes, Mollons-sur-Ouvèze
Shop: Mollons-sur-Ouvèze
Petrol Station: Entrechaux, Malaucène, Buis, Montbrun-les-Bains
Restaurant: Brantes, Entrechaux, Plaisians, Pierrelongue
Supermarket: Vaison-la-Romaine
Market day: Malaucène Wed-am
Tourist Bureau: Malaucène, Buis-les-Baronnies

Saint Léger

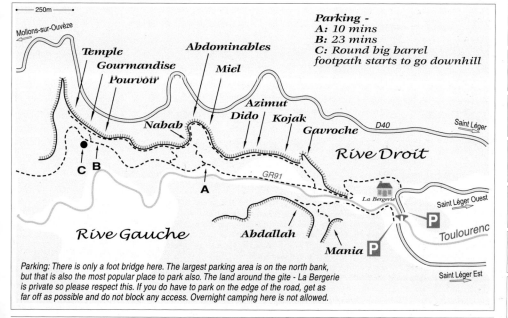

Parking: There is only a foot bridge here. The largest parking area is on the north bank,
but that is also the most popular place to park also. The land around the gite - La Bergerie
is private so please respect this. If you do have to park on the edge of the road, get as
far off as possible and do not block any access. Overnight camping here is not allowed.

ST.JEAN · VAISON · 3 RIVIÈRES · SAINT LÉGER · VIC · BRUNOTS · ST.JULIEN · QUEBEC · LOU PASSO · UBRIEUX · EM-ROUSSE · BOURDONS · AIGUIER · MIEYES · MÉVOUILLON · TOPOS

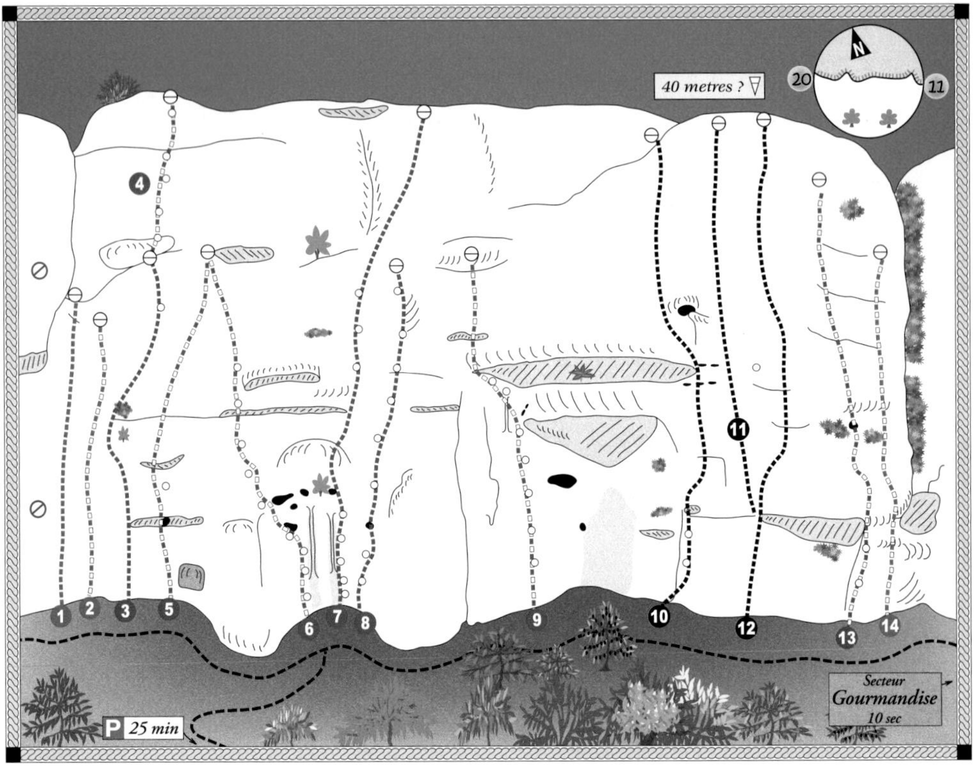

Sidebar tabs (left margin): ST. JEAN · VAISON · 3 RIVIÈRES · **SAINT LÉGER** · VIC · BRUNOTS · ST. JULIEN · QUÉBEC · LOU PASSO · UBRIEUX · BM-ROUSSE · BOURDONS · AIGUIER · MIEYES · MÉVOUILLON · TOPOS

40 metres ?

Secteur Gourmandise 10 sec

🅿 *25 min*

	Crux/bloc	Endurance	Sport		Crux/bloc	Endurance	Sport
①	Vivre libre		6b+	⑧	Cresecendo		7a+
	? m				*? m*		
②	?		6c+	⑨	Le temple de la méduse		7b
	? m				*? m*		*9*
③	Ouest	◉	6c/7a	⑩	Iaso		6c,7c
	? m				*40m*		
④	Ouest extra	◉	7b/c	⑪	Fi, Flo, Floty		7c+
	? m				*40m*		
⑤	Joe's Balade	◉	7b/c	⑫	Arqué pied tendre	**747**	7c
	? m				*40m*		
⑥	?	◉	7a/b	⑬	C'est comme un rêve		7b
	? m				*? m*		
⑦	La porte de Champs Elysées		7a+	⑭	Et derrière coule une rivière		6c
	38m				*? m*		

Résumé. A quiet sector a long way into the gorge. Steep and long. The Temple roof is very impressive, and there's no shortage of full length 40m routes here. There are more routes beyond this sector, but the rock does deteriorate before it turns, and you enter the Drome département. The area beyond may also be restricted as a nature reserve, so enquire before climbing any further into the gorge. There are some trees for belay shade, but in general it is a very hot sector. Not good after lots of rain - lots of drainage lines.
Note: There is no footpath above, but there is parking about 70 metres away and directly above. If anyone took a walk, they might knock stones off the top of the cliff.
 ⊘ *Sectors Left/Gauche: This area has been designated in the past as a bio-wildlife reserve, only climb beyond this point if you have up to date information that allows access.*

Temple - Gourmandise - Pouvoir - Praninia - Nabab - Piedre - Abdominables - Miel - Didoudidouda - Azimut - Baleine - Kojak - Gavroche
Mania   -   Abdallah   -   Billy de clown

MANO NÉGRA CLANDESTINA 7a+, Secteur Gourmandise; Steve Glennie

UN TRUC DE PASSAGE 6c+, Secteur Gourmandise; Steve Glennie

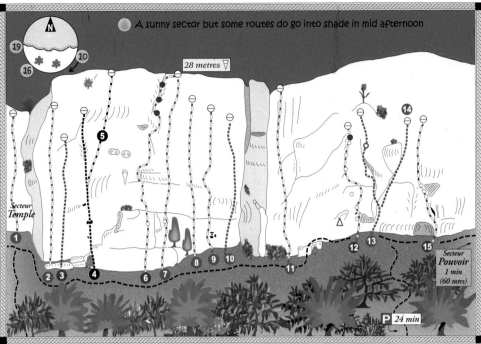

A sunny sector but some routes do go into shade in mid afternoon

28 metres

Secteur Temple

Secteur Pouvoir 1 min (60 mtrs)

P 24 min

		Crux/bloc	Endurance	Sport
1	Et derrière coule une rivière***			6c
	? m			◦ ? ◦
2	Je ne fais que passer ma route***			6c
	? m			◦ ? ◦
3	Passer entre les gouttes***			7a+
	? m			◦ ? ◦
4	Moby Dick			7c
	? m			◦ ? ◦
5	Al Andaluzo***			8a+
	? m			◦ ? ◦
6	Mano négra clandestina*** 😊			7a+
	28m	● 7a ✴ DIEDRE Pump	▢ 6c+ ✴ 🧗	◦12◦

A very good outing with an excellent first half to warm up before the fireworks begin. A test of acumen and stamina for the onsight.

		Crux/bloc	Endurance	Sport
7	La gourmandises***			6c
	27m			◦ ? ◦

Résumé. *A quiet area that offers some very good routes in the middle 6c-7a grades. Some of the easier routes have been undergraded in the past (they're not hard - but they're not easy either). Some of the rock in the first third of the cliff is suspect and un-nerving. However, when you get above 7 metres, the rock tends to be fantastic and of very high quality. Some trees offer a choice of belay shade or frost melting alcoves.*

		Crux/bloc	Endurance	Sport
8	Maître vautour			6b+ ?
	? m			◦ ? ◦
9	Les deux beaufs en vacances			6b/c
	? m			◦ ? ◦
10	Le maître et son disciple			6b
	? m			◦ ? ◦
11	Le vautour est là			6c
	? m			◦ ? ◦
12	Un truc de passage*** 😊			6c+
	16m	● 7a- 🐟 🦶 CRIMP	▢ 6c- ✴ 🦶 Ouch	◦7◦

Start best made easy by going right from 2nd bolt. Top wall gets you tired before whamming in a good crux.

		Crux/bloc	Endurance	Sport
13	Pensée Afghane*** 😊			6c-
	18m	○ 6c- ✴ 🦶 COOL	■ 6b- ✴ 🦶 Pump	◦7◦

A very good short route with a very pleasant first section. One of those awkward routes to lead with some hollow sounding rock.

		Crux/bloc	Endurance	Sport
14	Trafic de bouses ches les vautours			6b+ ?
	? m			◦ ? ◦
15	Sécheresse intellectuelle		◉	7a/b
	? m	🧗	🧗	◦ ? ◦

Equip

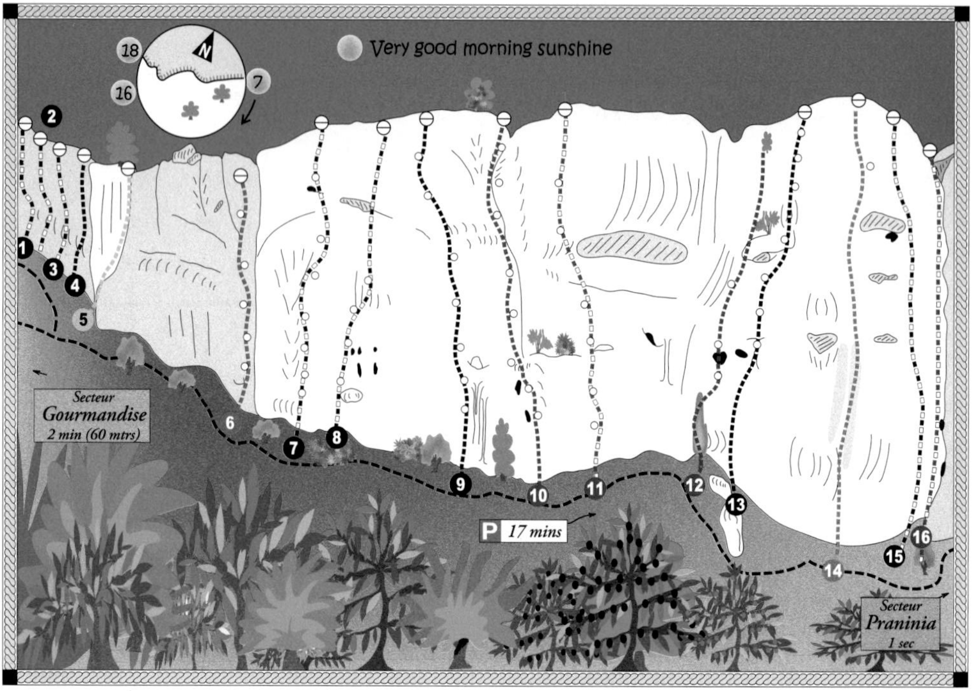

Very good morning sunshine

Secteur
Gourmandise
2 min (60 mtrs)

P 17 mins

Secteur
Prainia
1 sec

	Crux/bloc	Endurance	Sport
①	?		8a+
18m			
②	?		8a+
18m			
③	?		8a
18m			
④	Kiwasi ou la maison qui chante		7c
18m			
⑤	?		6a ?
? m		DIEDRE	
⑥	?		6b+ ?
15m			∞ 5 ∞
⑦	A doigts raccourcix		8a+
? m			
⑧	La thérapie du mal par le mâle		8a
? m			

	Crux/bloc	Endurance	Sport
⑨	?		7b/c
? m		Bloc	
⑩	Le pouvoir destructeur des		7a+
24m			
⑪	Le pouvoir constitutif de		7b
? m			
⑫	Victime d'un non noeud		7a+
? m			
⑬	La démocratie du plus fort		7c+
? m			
⑭	La tournée du patron		?
? m			
⑮	L'homme en bleu		8a
? m			
⑯	Crunch		6c & 7b
? m		DIEDRE	

Résumé. *A short sector with steep, and boulder style routes. The rock
curves up like a wave at the bottom, and the holds tend to be on the
small and sharp side - no tufas here. A lovely orange colour to the rock,
and some nice views to be had over the gorge. Generally a very quiet
sector. Best approached for the first time from Nabab sector and walking
along. Good on a very frosty cold winters morning with the sun to warm
the rock.*

Equip

Temple - Gourmandise - Pouvoir - Prainia - Nabab - Piedre - Abdominables - Miel - Didoudidouda - Azimut - Baleine - Kojak - Gavroche
     Mania   -   Abdallah   -   Billy de clown

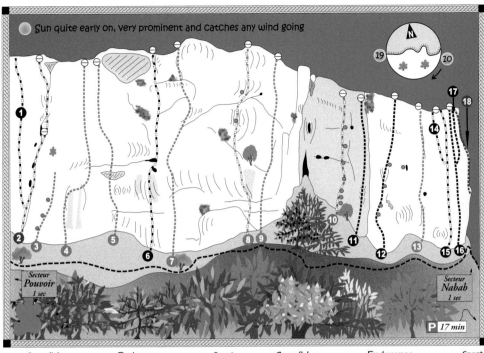

Sun quite early on, very prominent and catches any wind going

Secteur **Pouvoir** 1 sec

Secteur **Nabab** 1 sec

P 17 min

	Crux/bloc	Endurance	Sport
①	L'homme en bleu		8a
? m			
②	Crunch	DIEDRE	6c & 7b
? m			
③	?		?
? m			
④	En verve et contre tous		8b
34m			
⑤	Praninia		8b*
34m			
⑥	Mélodie pour un ami ardéchois		8a+
? m			
⑦	Project		8a/b
? m			
⑧	En attendant Ernest		8b/c
? m			
⑨	Project		8a/b
? m			

	Crux/bloc	Endurance	Sport
⑩	Mythoplastique 😊		6c+
23m			
⑪	Franco de porc		7c
? m			
⑫	Princessa		7c+
? m			
⑬	Project		?
? m			
⑭	Craokinotto		?
? m			
⑮	Sault qui peut		8a
25m			
⑯	Le petit chefs du néant		7c+
? m			
⑰	?		7c ?
? m			
⑱	?		7a
? m			

Résumé. *For the majority of climbers, when you reach this sector, either sunbathe or keep on walking. The rock is steeper than it looks and the holds tend to be on the smaller and more awkward side. A superb position and lovely place to climb if you have little weight and lots of strength.*

Temple - Gourmandise - Pouvoir - Praninia - Nabab - Piedre - Abdominables - Miel - Didoudidouda - Azimut - Baleine - Kojak - Gavroche
Mania - Abdallah - Billy de clown

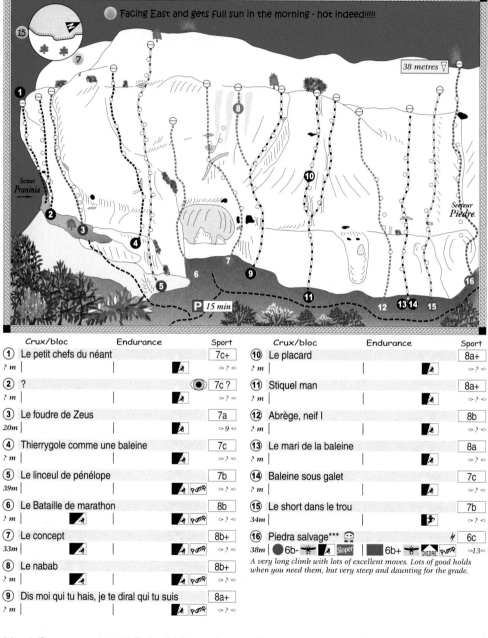

Facing East and gets full sun in the morning - hot indeed!!!!!

38 metres

Secteur Praninia

Secteur Piedre

P 15 min

	Crux/bloc	Endurance	Sport
①	Le petit chefs du néant		7c+
? m			∘ ? ∘
②	?	◉	7c ?
? m			∘ ? ∘
③	Le foudre de Zeus		7a
20m			∘ 9 ∘
④	Thierrygole comme une baleine		7c
? m			∘ ? ∘
⑤	Le linceul de pénélope	Pump	7b
39m			∘ ? ∘
⑥	Le Bataille de marathon	Pump	8b
? m			∘ ? ∘
⑦	Le concept		8b+
33m			∘ ? ∘
⑧	Le nabab	Pump	8b+
? m			∘ ? ∘
⑨	Dis moi qui tu hais, je te diral qui tu suis	Pump	8a+
? m			

	Crux/bloc	Endurance	Sport
⑩	Le placard		8a+
? m			∘ ? ∘
⑪	Stiquel man		8a+
? m			∘ ? ∘
⑫	Abrège, neif l		8b
? m			∘ ? ∘
⑬	Le mari de la baleine		8a
? m			∘ ? ∘
⑭	Baleine sous galet		7c
? m			∘ ? ∘
⑮	Le short dans le trou		7b
34m			
⑯	Piedra salvage*** 😊	⚡	6c
38m	6b- ❋ Sloper 6b+ ❋ DIEDRE Pump		∘13∘

A very long climb with lots of excellent moves. Lots of good holds when you need them, but very steep and daunting for the grade.

Résumé. *If you are competent at 8a/b, then this is a superb venue to have an easy work out. Full length routes that are steep, but with holds on. Even if you are a belay bunnie, the view is great and you can relax to take in the rays. A few easier routes, but they are pretty hard for the grade.*

Temple - Gourmandise - Pouvoir - Praninia - Nabab - Piedre - Abdominables - Miel - Didoudidouda - Azimut - Baleine - Kojak - Gavroche
Mania   -   Abdallah   -   Billy de clown

ST.JEAN | VAISON | 3 RIVIERES | SAINT LÉGER | VIC | BRUNOTS | ST.JULIEN | QUEBEC | LOU PASSO | UBRIEUX | BM-ROUSSE | BOURDONS | AIGUIER | MIÈYES | MÉVOUILLON | TOPOS

Secteur Nabab, Saint Léger

View from secteur Nabab, Saint Léger

Early morning sunshine, sheltered (some belay shade)

Secteur Abdom

Secteur Nabab

P 16 min

	Crux/bloc	Endurance	Sport
(1) Piedra salvage* 😊 ⚡	6c
38m	● 6b- ☀ 🐾 Sloper	▨ 6b++ ☀ DIEDRE Pump	∽13∽

A very long climb with lots of excellent moves. Lots of good holds when you need them, but very steep and daunting for the grade.

(2) 75 D, la totale			6c+
37m			∽ ? ∽

(3) ? * 😊			6c
34m	● 7a- 🐟 🐾 CRIMP	▢ 6c- 747 🧗 🌀	∽9∽

A funny sort of route with a tree stump to impale yourself on. Finding the holds is more difficult than doing the moves.

(4) Un treuil pour JB			7a+
32m			🐾	∽ ? ∽

A very impressive headwall in a fine position

	Crux/bloc	Endurance	Sport
(5) ?			?
? m			∽ ? ∽

(6) ?			?
? m			∽ ? ∽

(7) B.C. l'écornifleur* 👹 😊 ⚡	6b+
30m	○ 6c- 🐟 🛡 🐦	▨ 6b+ 747 🐾 Pump	∽8∽

Good moves that seem easy when you climb 8a and use this as a warm up. A bit full on for lower grade climbers.

(8) ? 👹			6c
? m			🐾 Pump	∽ ? ∽

(9) Tchatchounette 👹			7a-
? m			🐾 🚀 Pump	∽ ? ∽

Résumé. *This is one of the few areas in the gorge with lower grade routes. A nice position in a sheltered bay that keeps out of the mistral wind and catches the morning sun. Confusing to pick up beta; many use this sector to warm up, but you won't see anyone struggling on the hard bits since they are likely to crank high grades! Very good climbing with sustained sections. Routes don't look steep from below - believe me, they are; it's just that everything else around here is really, really steep.*

Getting the moves clear in the head prior to the flash

QI CUIT 7b, Secteur Abdominables; Steve Glennie

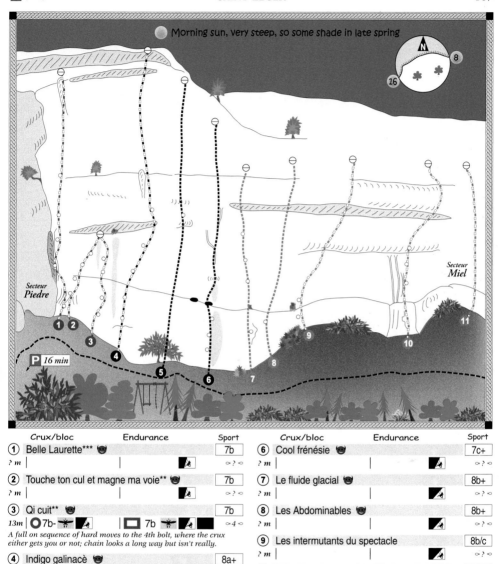

Morning sun, very steep, so some shade in late spring

Secteur Piedre

Secteur Miel

P 16 min

ST. JEAN
VAISON
3 RIVIÈRES
SAINT LÉGER
VIC
BRUNOTS
ST. JULIEN
QUEBEC
LOU PASSO
UBRIEUX
BM-ROUSSE
BOURDONS
AIGUIER
MIEYES
MÉVOUILLON
TOPOS

	Crux/bloc	Endurance	Sport
1	Belle Laurette***		7b
? m			◇ ? ◇
2	Touche ton cul et magne ma voie**		7b
? m			◇ ? ◇
3	Qi cuit**		
13m	● 7b-	☐ 7b	◇ 4 ◇

A full on sequence of hard moves to the 4th bolt, where the crux either gets you or not; chain looks a long way but isn't really.

	Crux/bloc	Endurance	Sport
4	Indigo galinacè		8a+
? m			◇ ? ◇
5	FFM meuh!...		7c+
? m			◇ ? ◇

	Crux/bloc	Endurance	Sport
6	Cool frénésie		7c+
? m			◇ ? ◇
7	Le fluide glacial		8b+
? m			◇ ? ◇
8	Les Abdominables		8b+
? m			◇ ? ◇
9	Les intermutants du spectacle		8b/c
? m			◇ ? ◇
10	En dépit du bon sens		8c ?
? m			◇ ? ◇
11	L'idéal chimérique		8c ?
? m			◇ ? ◇

Résumé. *This semi-circular cave area is somewhat overhanging & very suitable for lightweights. Very impressive and is a mid morning sun trap. Lots of drainage streaks and sopping wet after heavy rain. It overhangs a lot so you need a low angled winter sun to dry out the routes on the right. For most climbers, an excellent place to shelter when its raining.*

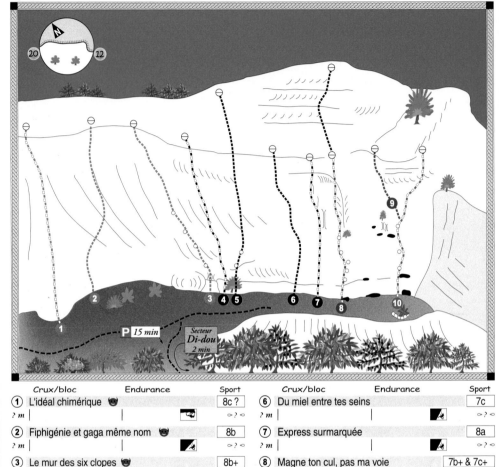

	Crux/bloc	Endurance	Sport
1	L'idéal chimérique 🌀		8c ?
	? m		◦ ? ◦
2	Fiphigénie et gaga même nom 😈		8b
	? m		◦ ? ◦
3	Le mur des six clopes 🌀		8b+
	? m		◦11◦
4	Les épinards aux violettes 🌀		8a
	? m		◦ ? ◦
5	Le mythomane 🌀		7c+
	? m		◦ ? ◦

	Crux/bloc	Endurance	Sport
6	Du miel entre tes seins		7c
	? m		◦ ? ◦
7	Express surmarquée		8a
	? m		◦ ? ◦
8	Magne ton cul, pas ma voie		7b+ & 7c+
	? m		◦14◦
9	Clément comme il respire		7a+
	? m		◦ ? ◦
10	Le torcheur d'éléphants		6c+
	? m		◦ ? ◦

Résumé. *To the right of the main overhanging area is a very good sector of steep climbs. Not so steep, but still with reasonable difficulty. To the right of the terrace are lots of project routs - but the rock looks very poor and broken! Has the merit of staying in shade until mid-day.*

Temple - Gourmandise - Pouvoir - Praninia - Nabab - Piedre - Abdominables - Miel - Didoudidouda - Azimut - Baleine - Kojak - Gavroche
Mania   -   Abdallah   -   Billy de clown

Secteur Praninia

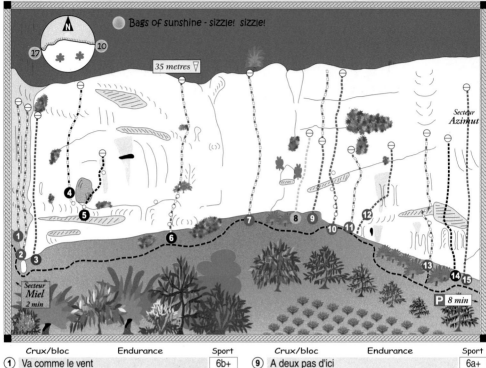

Bags of sunshine - sizzle! sizzle!

35 metres

Secteur Azimut

Secteur Miel 2 min

P 8 min

	Crux/bloc	Endurance	Sport
1	Va comme le vent		6b+
32m		
2	Qui court dans le prairie		6c
32m		
3	?		6c/7a
33m		
4	?		7c/8a
?m		
5	Lou Ravi		7c
?m		
6	?		7b
35m		
7	La violence éternelle		6c
30m		Pump
8	?		6a ?
? m		

	Crux/bloc	Endurance	Sport
9	A deux pas d'ici		6a+
? m		
10	Mélancolique et désabusé**		6b+
? m		
11	Didoudi douda de dadi de doudada		6c+
? m		
12	?		7a
? m		
13	Esthète éthique et toc**		7b
17m	7b-	7a	∞6∞

Not much of a warm up here, straight into thuggy pulling on jugs. Slopers then confuse matters, not that easy onsight for simple 7b.

14	Matie quiche, matie pizza**		7c+
17m	8a-	Bloc	7a	747	∞6∞

Yes, the steep wall does provide a few problems. A lot more beefier than its sister. Top wall is slopers and a bit nervy - escaping to the right onto 'Bamboo' is a common excursion.

15	Du vent dans des les coffres en bambou***		7a+
? m			∞13∞

A long but pleasant excursion.

Résumé. *This is quite a long section with quite a mixed variety of routes. The walls on the far left are very steep and are set in an incredible position with fine view. The centre part has dubious rock in parts, but is not that steep for a change. The routes on the right get progressively harder as the cliff steepens. There is good belay shade for most of the routes in this sector. A lot of the easier routes stay wet for a while after very heavy rain.*

Access. *It is best to get to this sector by turning right off the main path early on and following the cliff along and slowly uphill. There is also a path back to this sector from the Miel sector.*

MATIE QUICHE, MATIE PIZZA 7c+, Secteur Didoididouda; Ollie Ryall

SALE FEE MAL BROSSÉE 7b, Secteur Azimut; Arthur Guinet

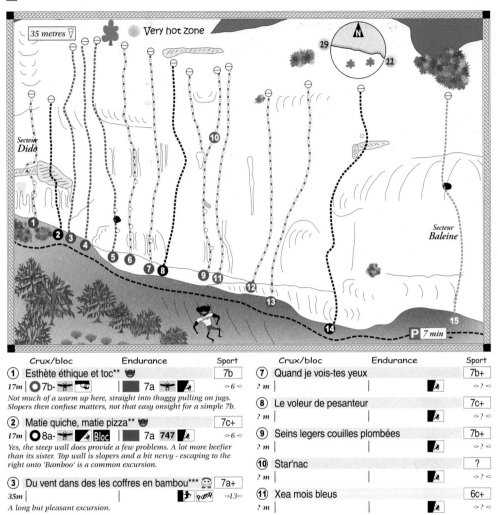

35 metres

Very hot zone

Secteur Dido

Secteur Baleine

P 7 min

ST. JEAN · VAISON · 3 RIVIÈRES · SAINT LÉGER · VIC · BRUNOTS · ST.JULIEN · QUEBEC · LOU PASSO · UBRIEUX · BM-ROUSSE · BOURDONS · AIGUIER · MIEYES · MÉYOUILLON · TOPOS

	Crux/bloc	Endurance	Sport
1	**Esthète éthique et toc****		7b

17m ⬤ 7b- ☀ | 7a ☀ ⌐6⌐

Not much of a warm up here, straight into thuggy pulling on jugs. Slopers then confuse matters, not that easy onsight for a simple 7b.

2	**Matie quiche, matie pizza****		7c+

17m ⬤ 8a- ☀ Bloc | 7a **747** ⌐6⌐

Yes, the steep wall does provide a few problems. A lot more beefier than its sister. Top wall is slopers and a bit nervy - escaping to the right onto 'Bamboo' is a common excursion.

3	**Du vent dans des les coffres en bambou*****		7a+

35m | Pump ⌐13⌐

A long but pleasant excursion.

4	**La levrotte***** **(equipment !)**		7a

35m | Pump ⌐?⌐

5	**Un monde à refaire****		7a+

35m | Pump ⌐?⌐

6	**Sale fee mal brossée**		7b

35m | Pump ⌐?⌐

	Crux/bloc	Endurance	Sport
7	Quand je vois-tes yeux		7b+

? m | ⌐?⌐

8	Le voleur de pesanteur		7c+

? m | ⌐?⌐

9	Seins legers couilles plombées		7b+

? m | ⌐?⌐

10	Star'nac		?

? m | ⌐?⌐

11	Xea mois bleus		6c+

? m | ⌐?⌐

12	Ah! tu verras, tu verras		7b+

? m | ⌐?⌐

13	Azimut		7b+

? m | ⌐?⌐

14	Oussama l'air explosif		7c

? m | ⌐?⌐

15	Project		?

? m | ⌐?⌐

Résumé. *This section of the main cliff at Saint Léger is classic style tufa wall climbing; long and sustained with plenty of agony for the forearms. You certainly want a 70 metre rope here. Very hot and with a sunny terrace at the bottom, ideal for very cold but sunny winter days. Bolts are spaced in parts which will make the routes somewhat fruity as they get more polished! From across the valley this cliff looks quite small and insignificant - half way up, you are likely to re-appraise!*

Temple - Gourmandise - Pouvoir - Praninia - Nabab - Piedre - Abdominables - Miel - Didoudidouda - Azimut - Baleine - Kojak - Gavroche
Mania   -   Abdallah   -   Billy de clown

ST JEAN
VAISON
3 RIVIÈRES
SAINT LÉGER
VIC
BRUNOTS
ST JULIEN
QUÉBEC
LOU PASSO
URRIEUX
BM-ROUSSE
BOURDONS
AIGUIER
MIÈTES
MÉVOUILLON
TOPOS

Mega heat zone - mega crank zone

Secteur Azimut

Secteur Kojak

P 7 min

	Crux/bloc	Endurance	Sport
1	Foetus trou du cus		8b+
	? m		
2	Chipolatas & Jakusi		?
3	Le diagonale Duboc		8b
	35m		
4	C'est clair et Nief		?
5	La farce tranquille		8a+
	35m		
6	Baribulle		8a
7	?		7c+
	35m		
8	T'as pas pissé là		8a
9	En voie dure Simone		8b+
	35m		
10	La réserve		8b
	35m		
11	Légitime démence		8a+
	35m		
12	Cétacé		8b
	35m		

	Crux/bloc	Endurance	Sport
13	Ousama		8b+
	? m		
14	La hyène		8c ?
15	J'sais pas		8a+
16	A.O.C. La Baleine		8b+
17	Project		?
18	Le prince du lactique		8a+
19	Slip Bouse		8a+
20	Spit Bull		8a+
21	?		8a
22	Hilti blues		8a
23	L'oeil du Cyclope		8a

Résumé. *This part of Saint Léger catches your eye straight away - with the giant pillar in the middle giving a few nice and easy ways up. Not a lot of use to most climbers apart from sheltering from the rain, which it doesn't do that much around here. Even though this part is steep and long, you still get a lot of drainage after heavy rain - at any time of the year. Impressive and superb climbing - if you can.*

Temple - Gourmandise - Pouvoir - Praninia - Nabab - Piedre - Abdominables - Miel - Didoudidouda - Azimut - Baleine - Kojak - Gavroche
Mania   -   Abdallah   -   Billy de clown

HILTI BLUES 8a, Secteur Baleine; Nicolas Campistron

ST. JEAN

VAISON

3 RIVIÈRES

SAINT LÉGER

VIC

BRUNOTS

ST. JULIEN

QUÉBEC

LOU PASSO

UBRIEUX

BM-ROUSSE

BOURDONS

AIGUIER

MIEYES

MÉVOUILLON

TOPOS

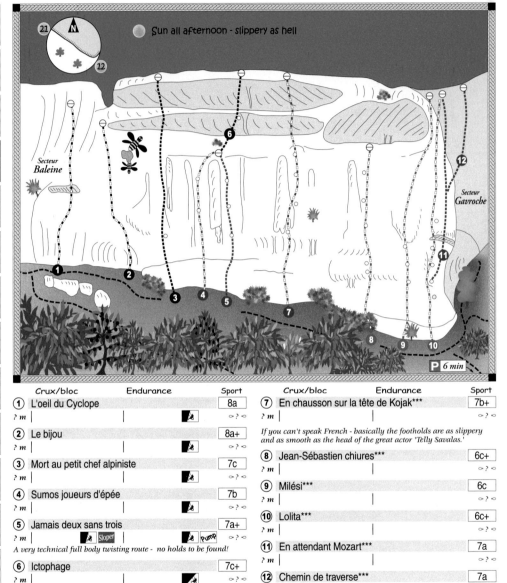

21

12

Sun all afternoon - slippery as hell

Secteur
Baleine

Secteur
Gavroche

1

2

3

4

5

6

7

8

9

10

11

12

P 6 min

	Crux/bloc	Endurance	Sport
①	L'oeil du Cyclope		8a
	? m		
②	Le bijou		8a+
	? m		
③	Mort au petit chef alpiniste		7c
	? m		
④	Sumos joueurs d'épée		7b
	? m		
⑤	Jamais deux sans trois		7a+
	? m	Sloper	Pump

A very technical full body twisting route - no holds to be found!

	Crux/bloc	Endurance	Sport
⑥	Ictophage		7c+
	? m		

	Crux/bloc	Endurance	Sport
⑦	En chausson sur la tête de Kojak***		7b+

If you can't speak French - basically the footholds are as slippery and as smooth as the head of the great actor 'Telly Savalas.'

	Crux/bloc	Endurance	Sport
⑧	Jean-Sébastien chiures***		6c+
	? m		
⑨	Milési***		6c
	? m		
⑩	Lolita***		6c+
	? m		
⑪	En attendant Mozart***		7a
	? m		
⑫	Chemin de traverse***		7a
	? m		

Résumé. *Giant tufa pillars to wrap your body around. When the light catches this sector it looks unreal - and like something from the planet alien. These superb forms of limestone have little to hold onto and you are forced to rely on all of your technique and friction skills. Useful sector that keeps a bit of shade till mid-day. You want it to be cool when you try these buggers. Easy walk in and a popular area. Note: watch out for the bees-hornets (Frelons) nest, avoid when buzzing is happening.*

BOREAL

Temple - Gourmandise - Pouvoir - Praninia - Nabab - Piedre - Abdominables - Miel - Didoudidouda - Azimut - Baleine - Kojak - Gavroche
Mania   -   Abdallah   -   Billy de clown

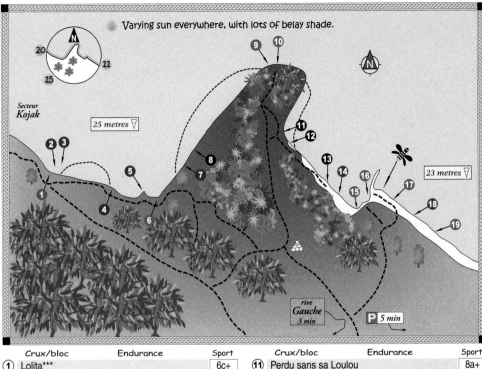

Varying sun everywhere, with lots of belay shade.

Secteur Kojak

25 metres

23 metres

rive Gauche 3 min

P 5 min

	Crux/bloc	Endurance	Sport
1	Lolita***		6c+
2	En attendant Mozart***		7a
3	Chemin de traverse***		7a
4	Laissez passer les rêves		7b
5	Gavroche et Mimi Pinson		7a
6	Des titis des grisettes		6b+
7	?		7a+
8	?		8a
9	Baisers volés		6b+
10	T'as le look coco		6b

	Crux/bloc	Endurance	Sport
11	Perdu sans sa Loulou		8a+
12	Supernova		7c+
13	Navigue sur la Flo		7c
14	Calm'ta joie		7b+
15	Entre chien et loups		6c+
16	Couenne fraîche		6c+
17	?**	23m 7a- Bloc 6b+ 747 Cool	6c

Excellent climbing moves, but invariably bolts are in the wrong places, not a recommendation for a grade 6 climber. (Bees nest left)

| 18 | ? | 23m 7b- Bloc 6c Pump | 7a |

A mother of undercuts begins this amusing day out. Easy for a 7b climber - impossible for a 6c climber.

| 19 | Cochon rose* | 23m 7a- Bloc 6c Cool | 6c |

More bolts just where you don't want em. A difficult and quite unpleasant trip onsight - a great shame.

Résumé. A very mixed sector with a good selection of mid level routes. They may seem easy compared to the rest of the routes in the area - but still have significant bloc hard moves. Some tree cover to give a few shaded routes, especially in the early morning when the big cliff on the left bank (rive gauche) is in the sun.

Le Toulourenc - between rive gauche & droit, ideal for a picnic

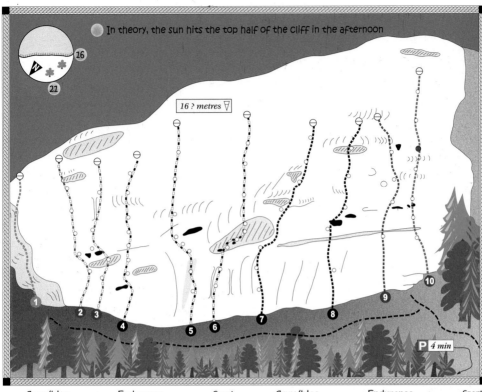

In theory, the sun hits the top half of the cliff in the afternoon

16 ? metres

P 4 min

	Crux/bloc	Endurance	Sport
①	Project		?
? m			⊸?⊸
②	Saint Léger Mania**		7b+
? m			⊸?⊸
③	Grimpe avec les loups		7b
? m			⊸?⊸
④	Le syndrome du Briançonnais		8a+
? m			⊸?⊸
⑤	Le Tacomaltéque		8a
14m			⊸8⊸
⑥	Massive attack		8a
14m			⊸10⊸

	Crux/bloc	Endurance	Sport
⑦	Le charme discret de la bourinette		7c+
? m			⊸7⊸
⑧	Brigades anti-bousses		7c/8a
? m			⊸5⊸
⑨	Congestion ariel		7a
? m			⊸4⊸
⑩	Moule mimette		7a-
? m		Bloc	⊸6⊸

Résumé. A newly developed sector that is short, very steep and demands very powerful climbing - bloc style moves. Very similar to UK-Cheedale and Frankenjura-Zwergenschloß. Ideal for those with strong fingertips who enjoy the odd Egyptian or two. Lots of trees around and keeps good shade until mid afternoon. The rock is shattered so holds may come and go - hence grades may change.

ST. JEAN · VAISON · 3 RIVIÈRES · SAINT LÉGER · VIC · BRUNOTS · ST.JULIEN · QUEBEC · LOU PASSO · UBRIEUX · BM-ROUSSE · BOURDONS · AIGUIER · MIÉVES · MÉVOUILLON · TOPOS

Temple - Gourmandise - Pouvoir - Praninia - Nabab - Piedre - Abdominables - Miel - Didoudidouda - Azimut - Baleine - Kojak - Gavroche
Mania - *Abdallah* - *Billy de clown*

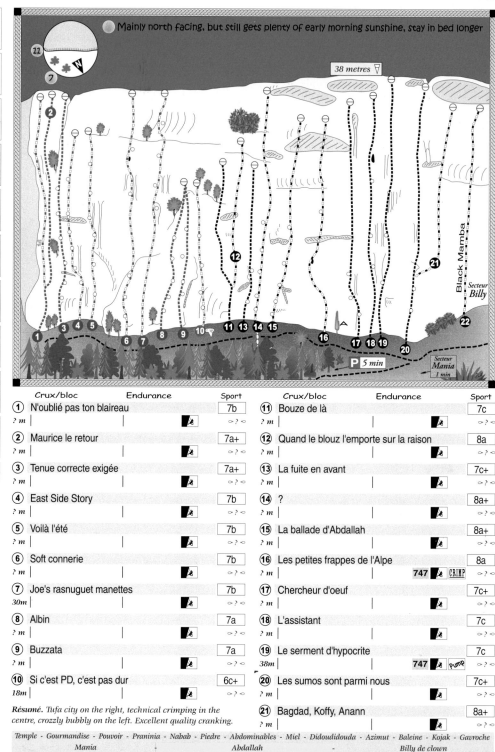

Mainly north facing, but still gets plenty of early morning sunshine, stay in bed longer

38 metres

Black Mamba

Secteur Billy

Secteur Mania 1 min

P 5 min

	Crux/bloc	Endurance	Sport
①	N'oublié pas ton blaireau		7b
	? m		
②	Maurice le retour		7a+
	? m		
③	Tenue correcte exigée		7a+
	? m		
④	East Side Story		7b
	? m		
⑤	Voilà l'été		7b
	? m		
⑥	Soft connerie		7b
	? m		
⑦	Joe's rasnuguet manettes		7b
	30m		
⑧	Albin		7a
	? m		
⑨	Buzzata		7a
	? m		
⑩	Si c'est PD, c'est pas dur		6c+
	18m		

	Crux/bloc	Endurance	Sport
⑪	Bouze de là		7c
	? m		
⑫	Quand le blouz l'emporte sur la raison		8a
	? m		
⑬	La fuite en avant		7c+
	? m		
⑭	?		8a+
	? m		
⑮	La ballade d'Abdallah		8a+
	? m		
⑯	Les petites frappes de l'Alpe	747 CRIMP	8a
	? m		
⑰	Chercheur d'oeuf		7c+
	? m		
⑱	L'assistant		7c
	? m		
⑲	Le serment d'hypocrite	747 Pump	7c
	38m		
⑳	Les sumos sont parmi nous		7c+
	? m		
㉑	Bagdad, Koffy, Anann		8a+
	? m		

Résumé. *Tufa city on the right, technical crimping in the centre, crozzly bubbly on the left. Excellent quality cranking.*

Temple - Gourmandise - Pouvoir - Praninia - Nabab - Piedre - Abdominables - Miel - Didoudidouda - Azimut - Baleine - Kojak - Gavroche
Mania   Abdallah   -   Billy de clown

ST. JEAN · VAISON · 3 RIVIÈRES · SAINT LÉGER · VIC · BRUNOTS · ST JULIEN · QUEBEC · LOU PASSO · UBRIEUX · BM-ROUSSE · BOURDONS · AIGUIER · MIEVES · MÉVOUILLON · TOPOS

LE PETITES FRAPPES DE L'ALPE 8a; Michel Gouze

Secteur Billy de Clown, Saint Léger

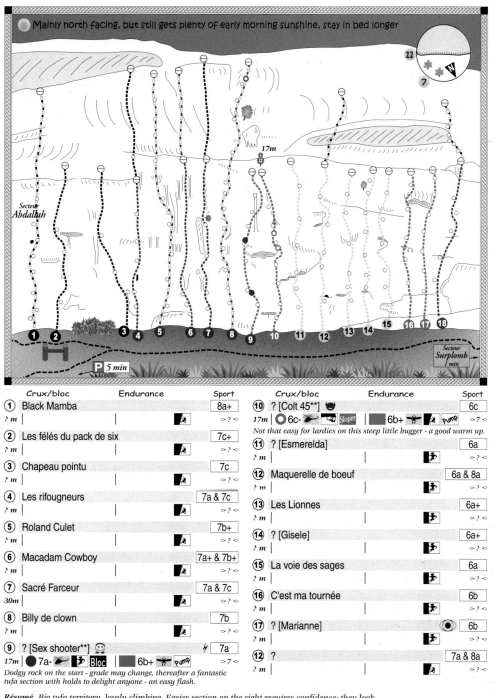

Mainly north facing, but still gets plenty of early morning sunshine, stay in bed longer

11
7

17m

Secteur
Abdallah

1 2 3 4 5 6 7 8 9 10 11 12 13 14 15 16 17 18

P 5 min

Secteur
Surplomb
1 min

ST. JEAN · VAISON · 3 RIVIÈRES · SAINT LÉGER · VIC · BRUNOTS · ST. JULIEN · QUEBEC · LOU PASSO · UBRIEUX · BA-ROUSSE · BOURDONS · AIGUIER · MIEYES · MÉVOUILLON · TOPOS

	Crux/bloc	Endurance	Sport
①	Black Mamba		8a+
	? m		∾ ? ∾
②	Les félés du pack de six		7c+
	? m		∾ ? ∾
③	Chapeau pointu		7c
	? m		∾ ? ∾
④	Les rifougneurs		7a & 7c
	? m		∾ ? ∾
⑤	Roland Culet		7b+
	? m		∾ ? ∾
⑥	Macadam Cowboy		7a+ & 7b+
	? m		∾ ? ∾
⑦	Sacré Farceur		7a & 7c
	30m		∾ ? ∾
⑧	Billy de clown		7b
	? m		∾ ? ∾
⑨	? [Sex shooter**] 😊	⚡	7a
	17m ● 7a- 🐟 Bloc	6b+ ✳ Pump	∾ 7 ∾

Dodgy rock on the start - grade may change, thereafter a fantastic tufa section with holds to delight anyone - an easy flash.

	Crux/bloc	Endurance	Sport
⑩	? [Colt 45**] ●		6c
	17m ○ 6c- 🐟 Sloper	6b+ ✳ 🦎 Pump	∾ 7 ∾

Not that easy for lardies on this steep little bugger - a good warm up.

	Crux/bloc	Endurance	Sport
⑪	? [Esmerelda]		6a
	? m		∾ ? ∾
⑫	Maquerelle de boeuf		6a & 8a
	? m		∾ ? ∾
⑬	Les Lionnes		6a+
	? m		∾ ? ∾
⑭	? [Gisele]		6a+
	? m		∾ ? ∾
⑮	La voie des sages		6a
	? m		∾ ? ∾
⑯	C'est ma tournée		6b
	? m		∾ ? ∾
⑰	? [Marianne]	●	6b
	? m		∾ ? ∾
⑫	?		7a & 8a
	? m		∾ ? ∾

Résumé. *Big tufa territory, lovely climbing. Easier section on the right requires confidence; they look like slab climbs, but are surprisingly steep. Many names here on the right are unknown - so we have given then [temporary names] in brackets.*

Temple - Gourmandise - Pouvoir - Praninia - Nabab - Piedre - Abdominables - Miel - Didoudidouda - Azimut - Baleine - Kojak - Gavroche
Mania   -   Abdallah   -   Billy de clown

Briançon - Vic

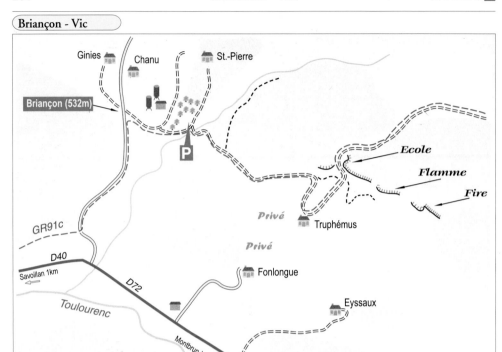

Parking: This is a very quiet area, so please park with respect and look for any notices that may direct parking. The house at Trumphémus is in a quiet location - and this should be respected. By parking where possible - before the small bridge at the Parking P on the map, you can simply walk along the GR91c footpath, which leads along a track to the base and start of the cliff. It is a quiet location and many routes will have the odd plant or two. This said, the rock is good, and the climbing is worthwhile.

Vic from the approach walk

Looking across the VOLVIC wall, Vic; towards Mont Ventoux

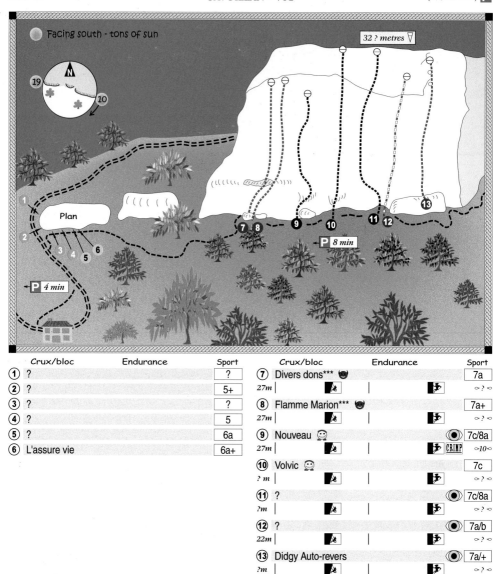

Facing south - tons of sun

32 ? metres

19

10

N

1
Plan
2
3 4 5 6

P 4 min

7 8

9

10

11 12

13

P 8 min

	Crux/bloc	Endurance	Sport
1	?		?
2	?		5+
3	?		?
4	?		5
5	?		6a
6	L'assure vie		6a+

	Crux/bloc	Endurance	Sport
7	Divers dons***		7a
	27m		⊶?⊶
8	Flamme Marion***		7a+
	27m		⊶?⊶
9	Nouveau	◉	7c/8a
	27m	CRIMP	⊶10⊶
10	Volvic		7c
	? m		⊶?⊶
11	?	◉	7c/8a
	?m		⊶?⊶
12	?	◉	7a/b
	22m		⊶?⊶
13	Didgy Auto-revers	◉	7a/+
	?m		⊶?⊶

Résumé. *There are 4 sections of cliffs in this first part. A small sector to the right of the main GR track on the left - with no routes on the broken cliff at the bottom of the river. There are about 6 routes on the first buttress just above the track. The 3rd sector is set back and up the hill, which is broken and of little interest. The 4th and main sector is a 4 min walk up the hill. To get to the 4th sector, take a zig zag path up the hill to prevent erosion. The two big blocks which you will find at the bottom are easily recognisable. This sector is a lovely wall with fabulous face routes on, not overhanging but very steep. Expect the rock to be sharp and damaging to the fingertips. The next sector has a nice picnic space, but is very awkward to get to across a diabolical gully.*

Side tabs: ST. JEAN · VAISON · 3 RIVIÈRES · SAINT LÉGER · VIC · BRUNOTS · ST. JULIEN · QUÉBEC · LOU PASSO · UBRIEUX · BM-ROUSSE · BOURDONS · AIGUIER · MIÈVES · MÉVOUILLON · TOPOS

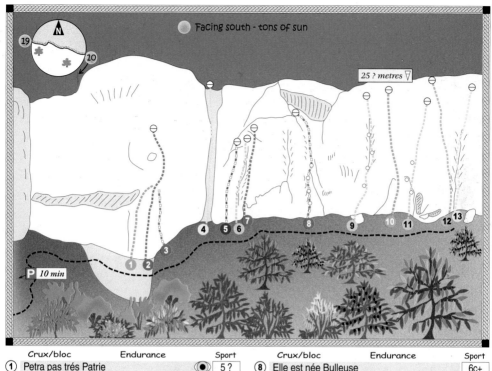

Facing south - tons of sun

25 ? metres

P 10 min

ST. JEAN

VAISON

3 RIVIÈRES

SAINT LÉGER

VIC

BRUNOTS

ST. JULIEN

QUEBEC

LOU PASSO

UBRIEUX

BM.-OUSSE

BOURDONS

AIGUIER

MIEYES

MÉVOUILLON

TOPOS

	Crux/bloc	Endurance	Sport
1	Petra pas trés Patrie		5 ?
? m			�50 ? �50
2	?		6b- ?
22m			�50 ? �50
3	?		?
? m			�50 ? �50
4	Oh le gars l'y fait		3 ?
? m		DIEDRE	�50 ? �50
5	Mas sacré		7b
? m			�50 ? �50
6	Fire crack		6a
? m		DIEDRE	�50 ? �50
7	Créme de salade		6b+
? m			�50 ? �50

	Crux/bloc	Endurance	Sport
8	Elle est née Bulleuse		6c+
? m			�50 ? �50
9	Mielésime		6a
? m			�50 ? �50
10	Crimimiel		5+
? m			�50 ? �50
11	Le Pilier mi-aile		6a+
? m			�50 ? �50
12	?		4+
? m			�50 ? �50
13	?		3+
? m			�50 ? �50

Résumé. *A more broken sector with scattered routes. Some impressive clean pieces of rock, but not with much in the way of routes or holds. Very quiet and ideal for something completely different - not to everybody's taste. The route names and grade information that we got for this area is a bit sketchy - so beware!*

The small village of Montbrun-les-Bains is about as remote as you get for a village in this area. If you want a nice day off, and like to amble around quiet streets with a damm good view, then this should just fit the ticket. The village itself has not fallen foul of tourism, but does sport a few small shops with excellent arrays of lavender, pottery, bits and bobs. The village itself became famous for the natural spring water that rises up to the top of the hill. There is a nice signposted walk that takes you on a rambling visit around the many separate fountains. The town is set up at 600m and has a very dry climate, making the surrounding area one of the best spots for lavender growing. The evocative aroma that you smell from these fields, will always remind you of this lovely spot at the very base of the Drome department.

Mont Ventoux as you can see from the photos, is hardly a mountaineering challenge. It is an uncanny mountain, since it doesn't look very high at all from the lower slopes. Yet from the top, the views are completely stunning and you soon realise that there is nothing remotely as high in the nearby area. To cycle up Mont Ventoux is one of those things you just have to do. There are 3 ways up of different flavour. The road from Sault is the nicest, especially bearing in mind that you start at 800m anyway, and have a lovely 20km of amble before the final 6km of daunting steepness across the white limestone desert. The road up from Malucène is another gentle way up, and seems a cool ride. The Tour de France naturally comes straight up the south side and does not come under great recommendation unless you seek an apocalyptic heart attack. The top can be a jamboree of market stalls, or a snowy blizzard - top tip, pick a nice day cos its brass monkeys on top.

Buis-les Baronnies ou Buis est un village ancien très tranquille et une Mecque de l'escalade. Situé à 380 mètres de haut c'est l'endroit parfait pour grimper avec un peu de fraîcheur durant l'été et pour savourer une bière fraîche sous les arbres et les tonnelles. Il y a suffisamment de monde, de magasins et de cafés pour faire de Buis une ville mais elle donne la sensation d'être dans un village. Il y a 3 campings tous faciles d'accès depuis le centre-ville. La diversité de l'escalade est excellente avec 7 falaises locales et une autre qui va bientôt être equipée de nouvelles voies. La plus grande et la plus splendide des falaises est celle de St. Julien, une fine tranche de calcaire, en position dominante au-dessus du village. La face exposée au sud a environ 80 voies, la plupart ayant 2 ou 3 longueures. Cette falaise est protégée en partie du Mistral mais lors des grandes chaleurs vous l'apprécierez car il vous rafraîchira. Cette face est également assez haute et ensoleillée assez tard en soirée permettant d'y grimper toute l'année. C'est une falaise avec des voies qui sont équipées pour vous faire bien travailler et ce n'est donc pas un site approprié pour l'apprentissage de l'escalade ou pour faire des voies en moulinette. Les longueures sont pour la plupart très longues – jusqu'à 50 mètres – et si vous ne connaissez pas très bien la falaise, les guides locaux recommandent des cordes doubles permettant une descente en rappel de 50 mètres. Cependant et personnellement je pense qu'une simple corde de 80 mètres permet de naviguer autour de la falaise plus aisément. Nous avons seulement detaillé une sélection de voies pour St. Julien puisque vous pouvez trouver toute l'information mise à jour pour ce site dans le topo en vente au syndicat d'initiative de Buis. Cette apport financier aidera le club d'escalade local pour la production du topo. Au nord de la ville, il y a la petite gorge d'Hannibal où le vent peut souffler fort et où le soleil ne se montre

jamais en hiver. En été, c'est un véritable sauna avec toutefois quelques journées qui sont parfaites pour grimper. La partie gauche est au-dessus de l'eau et y accéder est donc un gros problème. Je trouve plus facile de faire une voie puis de redescendre pour faire les autres voies en moulinette. Attention, votre partenaire risque de ne pas vous entendre avec les bruits de l'eau et de la circulation. Nous vous conseillons donc de faire un noeud au bout de votre corde pour éviter tout accident. En face il y a la falaise d'Ubrieux qui demande toujours un peu plus de développement. La falaise est proche de la route et est idéale pour les groupes. Plus vous montez la colline et plus la qualité des voies s'améliore. Après cette gorge se trouve Baume Rousse. Cette falaise complètement enfouie dans la verdure fut nettoyée et equipée dans les années 90 pour une compétition d'escalade. Elle offre

une grande variété de voies avec ou sans soleil. Les falaises éloignées de cette zone sont beaucoup plus petites, mais offrent de jolies vues. Le rocher Québec est un bloc de 20 mètres de haut, idéal pour les grimpeurs moins confiants. Rocher Brunots a de jolies dalles, quelques-unes assez horribles. Le parking est limité et il est préférable que les groupes l'évite. La falaise de Plaisians ne parait pas très stable. C'est un lieu d'escalade que j'éviterai certainement. (guides locaux – voir page 21).

A quiet ancient village, or an old railway town, or a laid back café culture hub, or a climbing mecca. Yes, Buis-les-Baronnies or Buis as it is known, is all of these, and superbly so. Its elevation of 380 meteres, makes it just a fraction cooler in the hot summer months, and an ideal location to enjoy many cool beers under a canopy of plane trees and high flying vines. There are enough people, shops and cafés to make it a town, but it actually feels like a village, and it doesn't take long to get to know people and feel the local flavour. There are three campsites, all within walking distance

of Buis centre, which makes it an ideal base for anyone planning to spend a week or longer in the area. The variety of climbing is excellent, with 7 local cliffs, and another one soon to be equipped with new routes. The biggest and most splendiferous cliff is that of Saint Julien, a precariously thin slice of limestone, up-ended and taking a commanding view over the town. It's south facing dominant face, gives around 80 routes, most of which are 2-3 pitches. This cliff is protected to an extent from the Mistral wind, but on a scorching day, you will want some wind to cool you down here. This south face also sticks up high and gets sun till late in the evening, making it an all year round venue. It's not a top roping or learning playground, but a full on adventure cliff with routes that equipped for an 'adventurous experience!' Many of the pitches are long – up to 50m, and if you don't know the cliff, twin ropes giving you a 50m abseil are recommended by the local climbing guides. However, I find that with the modern climbing style of single 80m ropes, navigating around the cliff is straightforward and easier, plus less rope to get in a tangle with the shorter 40m abseils. We only give you a selection of introductory routes on Saint Julien in this book, since you can generally pick up a very up to date topo from the tourist office in Buis, and this helps the local climbing club to keep their local topo in production. There is the small gorge of Hannibal just north of the town, where the wind can howl through and the sun doesn't get to in the winter. In summer though, it's a sauna. However, on some days the temperature to climb is just right. The left side overhangs the water and access is a problem. I find it best to do a route, then lower down to top rope the other climbs – beware, your belayer will find it difficult to hear

you with water and traffic noise, so put a knot in the rope to stop you going into the drink. The opposite cliff of Ubrieux is the beginning of a huge cliff that goes on and on, and is still waiting to be fully developed. It is a roadside cliff and makes an ideal group teaching venue. The further you go up the hill from the road, the less polished the routes get, plus there are more routes not in this book. Beyond this gorge and set high up on the hill, is Baume Rousse. This cliff was completely jungleified, but then cleared and equipped for a French junior climbing competition in the 1990's. It simply has everything, and is so multi-faceted, that you can find routes in or out of the sun at almost any time. The outlying cliffs of the area are much smaller, lack punch, but have great views. Rocher Québec is a small 20m block, ideal for timid climbers in the lower grades. Rocher Brunots has nice slabs, a few steep nasties to keep you awake. It has restricted parking and it is asked that groups avoid this cliff. The local cliff of Plaisians has questionable stability, I certainly avoid this one. (local guidebook also – see page 21)

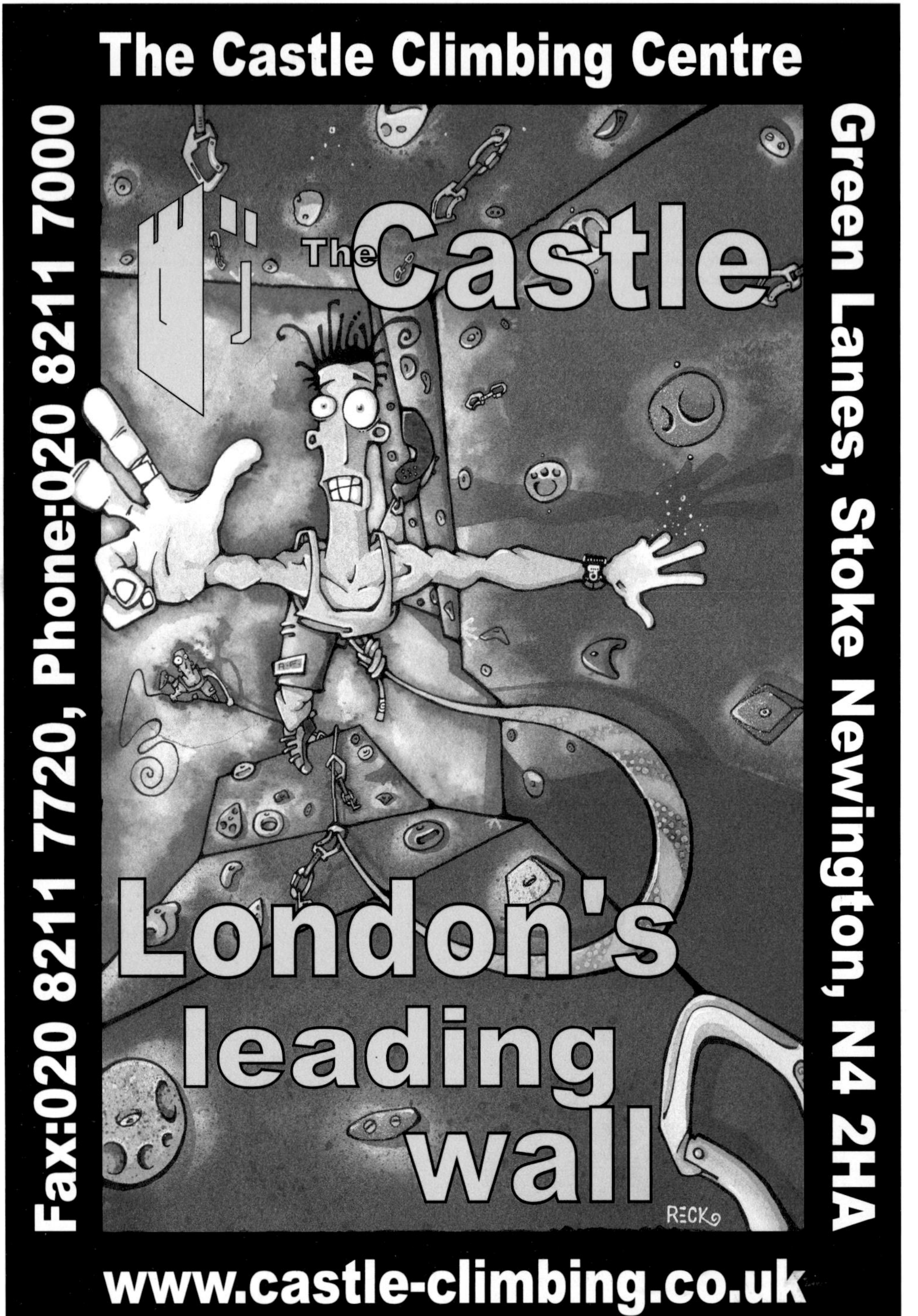
The Castle Climbing Centre
Fax:020 8211 7720, Phone:020 8211 7000
Green Lanes, Stoke Newington, N4 2HA
The Castle
London's leading wall
RECK
www.castle-climbing.co.uk

Buis-les-Baronnies

Sainte-Jalle
St.Saveur G.
Rocher Brunots
1034m
Col d'Ey
Baume Rousse
D546
Lou Passo
Les Brunots
Ubrieux
Sederon
Les Jonchiers
Buis-les-Baronnies
Québec
La Roche-sur-le-Buis
D147
D159
768m
Pierrelongue
& Mollons-sur-l'Ouvèze
Saint Julien

Baume Rousse

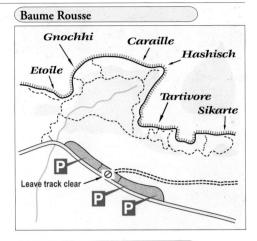

Gnochhi
Caraille
Hashisch
Etoile
Tartivore
Sikarte
Leave track clear

Lou Passo - Ubrieux

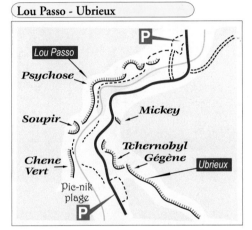

Lou Passo
Psychose
Mickey
Soupir
Tchernobyl
Gégène
Ubrieux
Chene Vert
pic-nik plage

Rocher Quebec

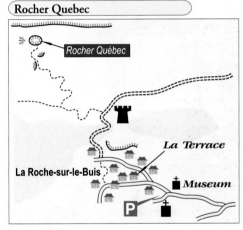

Rocher Québec
La Terrace
La Roche-sur-le-Buis
Museum

Rocher Brunots - Beauvoisin

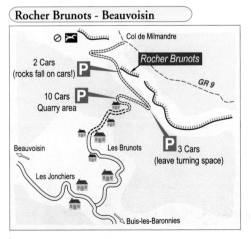

Col de Milmandre
2 Cars
(rocks fall on cars!)
Rocher Brunots
GR 9
10 Cars
Quarry area
Beauvoisin
Les Brunots
3 Cars
(leave turning space)
Les Jonchiers
Buis-les-Baronnies

Saint Julien

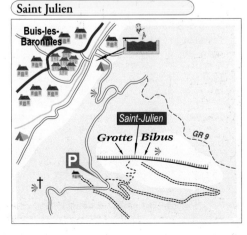

Buis-les-Baronnies
Saint-Julien
Grotte | *Bibus*
GR 9

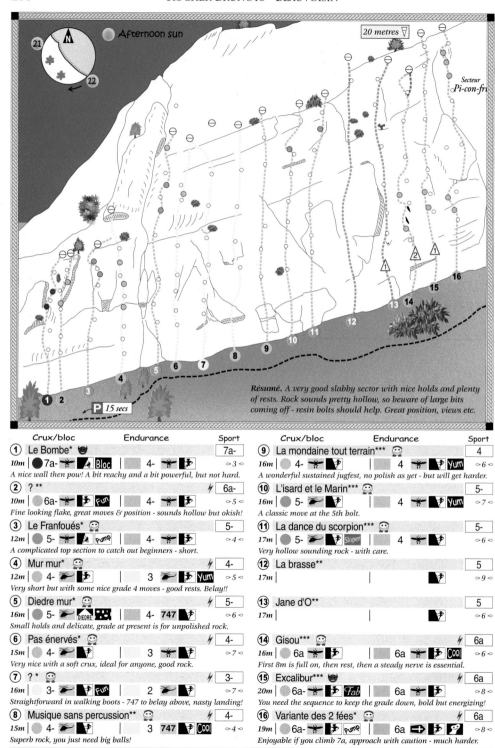

Afternoon sun

20 metres

Secteur
Pi-con-fri

Résumé. A very good slabby sector with nice holds and plenty of rests. Rock sounds pretty hollow, so beware of large bits coming off - resin bolts should help. Great position, views etc.

P 15 secs

	Crux/bloc	Endurance	Sport
① Le Bombe*			7a-
10m	7a- Bloc	4-	⌐3

A nice wall then pow! A bit reachy and a bit powerful, but not hard.

| **② ?**** | | | 6a- |
| 10m | 6a- Fun | 4- | ⌐5 |

Fine looking flake, great moves & position - sounds hollow but okish!

| **③ Le Franfoués*** | | | 5- |
| 12m | 5- Pump | 4- | ⌐4 |

A complicated top section to catch out beginners - short.

| **④ Mur mur*** | | | 4- |
| 12m | 4- | 3 Yum | ⌐5 |

Very short but with some nice grade 4 moves - good rests. Belay!!

| **⑤ Diedre mur*** | | | 5- |
| 16m | 5- DIEDRE | 4- 747 | ⌐6 |

Small holds and delicate, grade at present is for unpolished rock.

| **⑥ Pas énervés*** | | | 4- |
| 15m | 4- | 3 | ⌐7 |

Very nice with a soft crux, ideal for anyone, good rock.

| **⑦ ?*** | | | 3- |
| 16m | 3- Fun | 2 | ⌐7 |

Straightforward in walking boots - 747 to belay above, nasty landing!

| **⑧ Musique sans percussion**** | | | 4- |
| 15m | 4- | 3 747 COOl | ⌐4 |

Superb rock, you just need big balls!

	Crux/bloc	Endurance	Sport
⑨ La mondaine tout terrain***			4
16m	4-	4 Yum	⌐6

A wonderful sustained jugfest, no polish as yet - but will get harder.

| **⑩ L'isard et le Marin***** | | | 5- |
| 16m | 5- | 4 Yum | ⌐7 |

A classic move at the 5th bolt.

| **⑪ La dance du scorpion***** | | | 5- |
| 17m | 5- Sloper | 4 | ⌐6 |

Very hollow sounding rock - with care.

| **⑫ La brasse**** | | | 5 |
| 17m | | | ⌐9 |

| **⑬ Jane d'O**** | | | 5 |
| 17m | | | ⌐6 |

| **⑭ Gisou***** | | | 6a |
| 16m | 6a | 6a COOl | ⌐6 |

First 8m is full on, then rest, then a steady nerve is essential.

| **⑮ Excalibur***** | | | 6a |
| 20m | 6a- Fab | 6a | ⌐8 |

You need the sequence to keep the grade down, bold but energizing!

| **⑯ Variante des 2 fées*** | | | 6a |
| 19m | 6a- Pump | 6a | ⌐8 |

Enjoyable if you climb 7a, approach with caution - much harder.

Marin — Pi-con-fri

Rocher Brunots - secteur Marin (Cliff of Baume Noire is in the distance-bird restriction, no climbing please)

	Crux/bloc	Endurance	Sport

① Highlander — 5+
23m — ○7○

② Accroche-toi au balais — 6c
23m ● 7a-   6b   ○10○
A very bouldery style route with a distinct crux sction.

③ Bibendum — 7a
25m ○ 7b- CRIMP 6b ○11○
A nice first half, but then somwhat gnarls at you on the top headwall, crimp city.

④ Eh Jo ** 😊 — 6c+
? m ● 7a CRIMP 6b ○?○
A very straightforward first half, followed by crimp city above with technicality. Watch out for bees nest at mid break, maybe avoid

⑤ Pi-con-fri *** 😎 — ⚡ 5
33m ● 5- CRIMP 4++ 747 Pump ○11○
A fantastic long pitch. Very spaced bolts but at least come to hand near any hard moves. Top wall feels really out there - Verdon style.

⑥ Perf-O-romance ** — 7a-
25m ● 7a- CRIMP 6c- Pump ○7○
A tricky little bastard. Clipping 2nd bolt calms the nerves, but makes the onsight well more difficult if not clipped early. Nasty high move.

⑦ Les voisins déménagement * 😎 — ⚡ 6a
20m ● 6a- Pump 5 ○5○
A steep and intimidating short climb, with a few loose blocks at the top. Plenty of stamina helps the nerves.

⑧ Les voisins continuée *** 😊 — 6c+
40m ○ 6c- 747 Trick 6b+ 747 ○14○
Best done as an extension. Fiendish to read, dire to lead, mentally exhausting..... but brilliant climbing. Weave around to find easy line.

⑨ Clairette de Die 😎 — ⚡ 6b-
21m ● 6b- 5 ○5○
Only 5 metres of climbing, but a loose block worries the nerves. Grade may change.

⑩ Attention elle arrive.... 😎 — ⚡ 7a-
21m ● 7a- Cool 6c- Pump ○5○
A single hard move that should succumb onsight, steeper than it looks and low in the grade.

⑪ Peut-être ? 😊 — 7b-
? m CRIMP ○10○
A pretty flat wall gives difficulty - may have a continuation added?

⑫ **? — 7b-
? m ○10○
Fingery climbing leads to the overhang with a bloc move, better than it looks.

Résumé. *The cliff gets steeper and bigger to the right - hence the routes get more difficult. A lot of the climbing is surprisingly technical and absorbing! The exposure at the top sections of the climbs is all powerful. Some of the bolting is a bit bizzare. Watch out for loose stones being knocked down at the midway terrace.*

Marin   -   *Pi-con-fri*

ST. JEAN | VAISON | 3 RIVIÈRES | SAINT LÉGER | VIC | BRUNOTS | ST. JULIEN | QUEBEC | LOU PASSO | URRIEUX | BM-ROUSSE | BOURDONS | AIGUIER | MIEYES | MÉVOUILLON | TOPOS

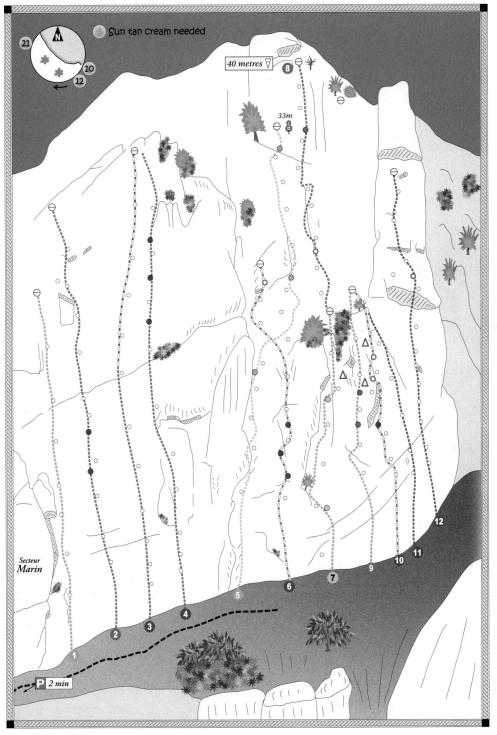

Sun tan cream needed

40 metres

33m

Secteur *Marin*

P 2 min

Marin - *Pi-con-fri*

ST. JEAN · VAISON · 3 RIVIÈRES · SAINT LÉGER · VIC · BRUNOTS · ST. JULIEN · QUEBEC · LOU PASSO · UBRIEUX · BM-ROUSSE · BOURDONS · AIGUIER · MIEYES · MÉVOUILLON · TOPOS

EUROPE - SPORT VERTICAL
A guidebook to the best rock climbing sites in Europe
How to plan your perfect climbing trip

If you get more than one weeks climbing holiday a year, you most probably browse the web, looking for ideas. Now you can have the whole of Europe at your fingertips in an instant, all with superb quality information and details that you can trust. It is the classic Jingo Wobbly size, so you can carry it with you to the Alps or anywhere, fits into the top of your rucksack or the car glove compartment. It works in 7 languages using special climbing icons. You will never want to leave home again - without it.

EUROPE SPORT VERTICAL 384 pages, colour, Flexibound, 210mm x 151mm (A5)

£ 19.95 - 32.50 Euros
ISBN: 1-873-665-21-0

Le Rocher de Saint-Julien

ST.JEAN
VAISON
3 RIVIÈRES
SAINT LÉGER
VIC
BRUNOTS
ST.JULIEN
QUÉBEC
LOU PASSO
UBRIEUX
BM-ROUSSE
BOURDONS
AIGUIER
MIÈYES
MÉVOUILLON
TOPOS

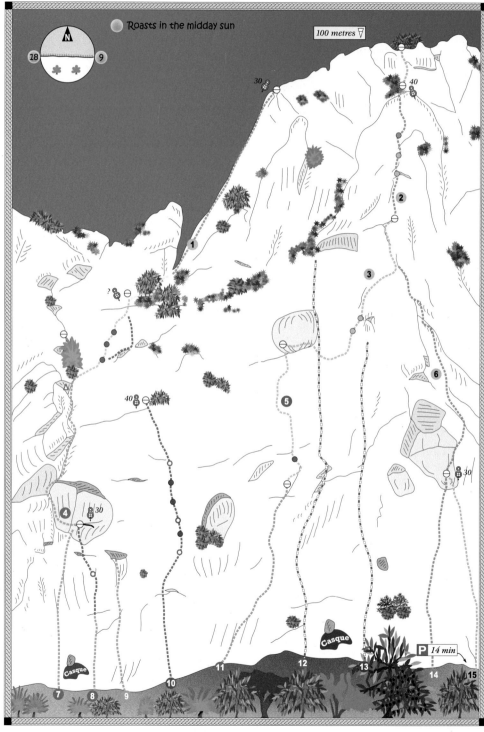

Roasts in the midday sun

100 metres

Raoul - Grotte - Aéroplane - Shanti - Bibus - Rampe - Mésange - Trous - l'éperon - Tranquille

Crux/bloc	Endurance	Sport
① La Grotte**		5+
30m	🐸	🐸 _Fab_ ◦?◦

A very out there pitch in the sky; not recommended when a big mistral is blowing. Stunning views.

Crux/bloc	Endurance	Sport
② L'Espadon***		5+
22m ● 6a- ✳ 🪨 Pump	5 ✳ COOL	◦5◦

A nice technical pitch in an amazing position. Looks amazing but has good chunky holds.

Crux/bloc	Endurance	Sport
③ L'Espadon**		5
29m ● 6a- ✳ CRIMP Flexi	4+ 747 Pump 🐸	◦7◦

Only a few hard moves but long runout sections. A positive approach helps

Crux/bloc	Endurance	Historique
④ La Grotte*** ⬤		6b
38m ● 6b- ✳ 🐸 Pump	6a+ 747 🐸 COOL	◦12◦

Joining two old pitches together makes this a fab outing of perfect length, a stunning pitch. Excellent holds in the groove. △ Loose block at the top - beware. Go right 3m before the old belay and take the rising traverse right. Looks terrifying but actually has great holds.

Crux/bloc	Endurance	Historique
⑤ L'Espadon** ⬤		6a
20m ● 6b- ✳ 🐸 CRIMP	6a ✳ 🐸	◦4◦

Yes the crux involves a tiny foothold, long may it live. Hits you hard straight after leaving the belay, not for the unconfident.

Crux/bloc	Endurance	Sport
⑥ Le Gastronome***		5+
? m		◦?◦

A very good long pitch that takes you into a superb and exposed position. Definitely worth belaying, run top two pitches together.

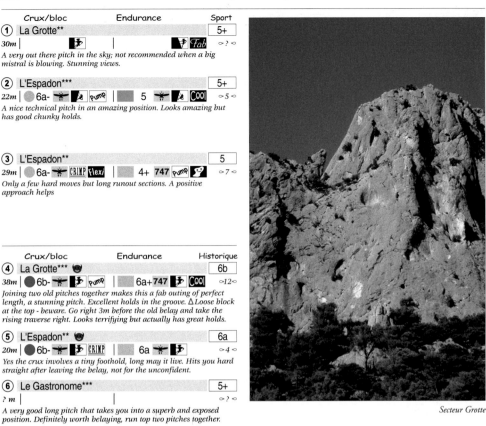

Secteur Grotte

Crux/bloc	Endurance	Historique
⑦ La plante à scion		5 ?
31m	🐸	◦?◦

?

Crux/bloc	Endurance	Historique
⑧ Trop de vin rouge*		6b
31m ○ 6c- ✳ 🐸 CRIMP	6b- ✳ 🐸 🐸	◦8◦

An excellent climb on a top rope. Rebolting has left a really awkward, silly and unpleasant clip. Sharp teeth to pull on - technical.

Crux/bloc	Endurance	Sport
⑨ La Grotte*** 😊		5
31m ● 6c- ✳ 🐸	6b 747 🐸 COOL	◦?◦

A very nice wall climb with holds! Then pass through the hole with amusement - and substantial polish.

Crux/bloc	Endurance	Sport
⑩ Love on the bite*		6c+
42m ○ 7b- 747 🐸 CRIMP	6b 747 🐸 🐸	◦?◦

A very straightforward first part, leads to a rather blank looking wall - looks don't deceive. Leaving the bolt, requires ability & not luck!

Crux/bloc	Endurance	Sport
⑪ L'Espadon 😊		5+
37m ● 5 ✳ 🐸 CRIMP	5+ 747 🐸 🐸	◦9◦

Not a very attractive pitch for grade 5 climbers, sustained and very poorly protected. Rock sounds pretty hollow, suggesting iffyness.

Crux/bloc	Endurance	Historique
⑫ Equinoxe		6c ?
? m		◦?◦

Blank wall climbing, technical

Crux/bloc	Endurance	Historique
⑬ Electrochoc***		6c ?
? m	747 🐸 COOL	◦?◦

A substantial face climb requiring good stamina and technical expertise.

Crux/bloc	Endurance	Historique
⑭ Le Gastronome		5 ?
? m	🐸	◦?◦

Crux/bloc	Endurance	Historique
⑮ Le Gastronome de Gris		6a ?
? m	🐸	◦?◦

Résumé. A very good sector to this giant cliff. A good place to start, by locating the obvious large grotto to the left of the approach footpath. 3 pitches to the top and great views of Buis. main face is often sheltered from Mistral.

ST. JEAN · VAISON · 3 RIVIÈRES · SAINT LÉGER · VIC · BRUNOTS · ST.JULIEN · QUEBEC · LOU PASSO · UBRIEUX · BM-ROUSSE · BOURDONS · AIGUIER · MIEVES · MÉVOUILLON · TOPOS

BIBUS 6b-, Secteur Bibus, Saint Julien; Carrie Atchison-Jones

LES LAMES 6b-, Secteur Bibus, Saint Julien; Mark Glennie

Sweltering in a heatwave, yummy on sunny cold days

100 metres

ST. JEAN · VAISON · 3 RIVIÈRES · SAINT LÉGER · VIC · BRUNOTS · STJULIEN · QUEBEC · LOU PASSO · UBRIEUX · BM-ROUSSE · BOURDONS · AIGUIER · MIÉYES · MÉVOUILLON · TOPOS

Casque

Casque

P 14 min

Raoul - Grotte - Aéroplane - Shanti - Bibus - Rampe - Mésange - Trous - l'éperon - Tranquille

Crux/bloc	Endurance	Sport
① Bibus*		6a
10m	6a DIEDRE	⌐?⌐

It's not over yet, short but worth keeping the rope on for.

Crux/bloc	Endurance	Sport
② La directissime		6b-
25m		⌐?⌐

A superb top pitch, light relief with only one chunky move.

Crux/bloc	Endurance	Sport
⑤ Bibus***		6a+
32m	6b- COOl 6a+ Pump	⌐11⌐

A superb finale, excitement high in the sky. Very well equipped when you need it. Requires a very positive approach for the flash. (Belay ❋)

Crux/bloc	Endurance	Sport
⑥ Les Lames***		6b
46m	6b- COOl 6b	⌐14⌐

A really good pitch, nothing too hard. Suspect rock in places, but generally very sound - exhilarating. (Belay shade ❋)

Crux/bloc	Endurance	Sport
⑦ La directissime		6b
35m		⌐?⌐

Easier than the first pitch, generally committing wall climbing.

Crux/bloc	Endurance	Sport
⑩ Bibus***		6b-
35m	6b- Bloc 6a+ Pump	⌐12⌐

A very exposed move left on shinny holds begins this crux pitch. Sustained moves to a horribly polished foot pocket. Not too hard - but not too easy.

Crux/bloc	Endurance	Sport
⑪ Ubick*		7b-
15m	7b- Bloc 7a	⌐?⌐

The obvious difficulty in leaving the cave straight up, and continuing with difficulty.

Crux/bloc	Endurance	Sport
⑫ Bibus directe		6b
30m		⌐?⌐

Crux/bloc	Endurance	Sport
⑬ Ubick		7a
30m		⌐?⌐

Technical wall climbing - sustained

Crux/bloc	Endurance	Sport
⑭ Bibus**		6c-
32m	6c- Bloc 6a COOl	⌐12⌐

A very reachy move at 10 metres, certainly gets you thinking. 6c bloc for the short. Lovely flowing wall moves thereafter - enjoyable.

Crux/bloc	Endurance	Sport
⑮ Désir		6c+
45m		⌐?⌐

Wall climbing

Crux/bloc	Endurance	Sport
⑯ Les Lames***		6a+
43m	6b- 6a+ 747 Pump	⌐?⌐

Very nice wall climbing, nothing too hard, but you are very likely to get pumped solid.

Crux/bloc	Endurance	Sport
⑰ La directissime		6c
45m		⌐?⌐

Highly sustained

Historique. Only the classic routes are shown here - for a full topo to this giant cliff, there should be a local topo available.

Crux/bloc	Endurance	Sport
③ Le Parat-Paris**		6b-
40m		⌐?⌐

A bit straightforward if you did the lower part. Good new routes to left and right of lower pitches.

Crux/bloc	Endurance	Sport
④ La rampe***		6a-
30m	6a- 5+ Pump	⌐14⌐

The best pitch of the climb. Much easier than the lower half and with no moves to make you think. Bridging in the top groove is spectacular. Don't forget to go to the top for the fab views. (Belay ❋)

Crux/bloc	Endurance	Sport
⑧ Le Parat-Paris**		7a
30m		⌐?⌐

Flat featureless rock, amusingly technical, of appeal to some!

Crux/bloc	Endurance	Sport
⑨ La rampe***		6b
30m	6b- COOl 6a Pump	⌐14⌐

Old peg scars and polished hand holds make this a sweaty and uncomfortable pitch to start with. Happily it gets better and better, and the holds get bigger and bigger. Stick in and you will be rewarded. (Belay shade ❋)

Saint Julien

Crux/bloc	Endurance	Sport
⑱ Le Parat-Paris		6c-
30m		⌐?⌐

An interesting adventure?

Crux/bloc	Endurance	Sport
⑲ La rampe***		6b-
30m	6b- Trick 6a 747 COOl	⌐?⌐

A very good warm up! Excellent climbing with a marvellous crux, one of those moves that is really exasperating - until you do it!

Crux/bloc	Endurance	Sport
⑳ Osiris***		6c
50m	6c 6c 747 COOl	⌐?⌐

A fantastic climb, simply wonderfully sustained. Bolts are well spaced but it seems to suit the climbing style, cool but not scary.

Résumé. This sector is the middle of the largest wall of the crag, and gives the 3 classic routes of Bibus, Les Lames and La Rampe. All are quite polished, but that doesn't detract from the position and superb climbing on them. All the routes have been historically undergraded, so we have re-graded them to keep in line with the other cliffs in the book. The routes seem easier when you get to know them, but it is the sort of cliff that has so much climbing, there never seems time to go back to the same routes. A steady head and strong nerve is an asset for this sector.

Raoul - Grotte - Aéroplane - Shanti - Bibus - Rampe - Mésange - Trous - l'éperon - Tranquille

ST JEAN · VAISON · 3 RIVIÈRES · SAINT LÉGER · VIC · BRUNOTS · ST JULIEN · QUEBEC · LOU PASSO · UBRIEUX · BM-ROUSSE · BOURDONS · AIGUIER · MIEVES · MÉVOUILLON · TOPOS

La Roche-sur-le-Buis is one of those tiny villages that perches on the side of a hill, and has fantastic views for just about everyone living there. There is a very well recommended restaurant La Terrace, just the ticket on a balmy summers evening. There is also a fascinating small museum on local old industries, inside a small chapel at the entry to the village, not always open but worth a look in for sure. Please consider local residents when parking.

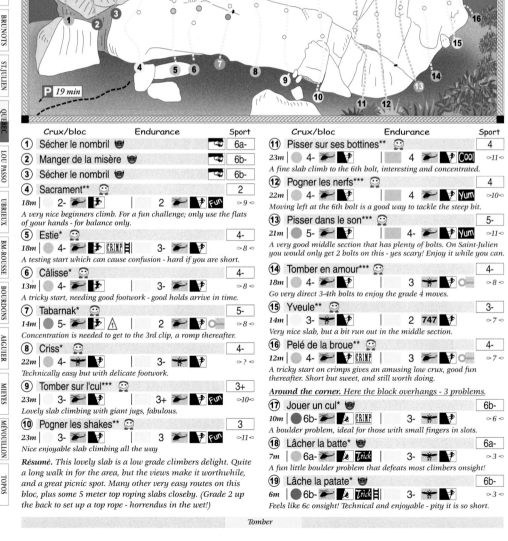

Highly sunny with no shade at all.

23 metres

P 19 min

	Crux/bloc	Endurance	Sport
1	Sécher le nombril		6a-
2	Manger de la misère		6b-
3	Sécher le nombril		6b-
4	Sacrament**		2

18m | 2- | 2 Fun | ⊸9

A very nice beginners climb. For a fun challenge; only use the flats of your hands - for balance only.

5	Estie*		4-

18m | 4- CRIMP | 3- | ⊸8

A testing start which can cause confusion - hard if you are short.

6	Câlisse*		4-

13m | 4- | 3- | ⊸8

A tricky start, needing good footwork - good holds arrive in time.

7	Tabarnak*		5-

14m | 5- | 2 | ⊸8

Concentration is needed to get to the 3rd clip, a romp thereafter.

8	Criss*		4-

22m | 4- | 3- | ⊸?

Technically easy but with delicate footwork.

9	Tomber sur l'cul***		3+

23m | 4- | 3+ Fun | ⊸10

Lovely slab climbing with giant jugs, fabulous.

10	Pogner les shakes**		3

23m | 3- | 3 Fun | ⊸11

Nice enjoyable slab climbing all the way

Résumé. *This lovely slab is a low grade climbers delight. Quite a long walk in for the area, but the views make it worthwhile, and a great picnic spot. Many other very easy routes on this bloc, plus some 5 meter top roping slabs closeby. (Grade 2 up the back to set up a top rope - horrendus in the wet!)*

	Crux/bloc	Endurance	Sport
11	Pisser sur ses bottines**		4

23m | 4- | 4 Cool | ⊸11

A fine slab climb to the 6th bolt, interesting and concentrated.

12	Pogner les nerfs***		4

22m | 4- | 4 Yum | ⊸10

Moving left at the 6th bolt is a good way to tackle the steep bit.

13	Pisser dans le son***		5-

21m | 5- | Yum | ⊸11

A very good middle section that has plenty of bolts. On Saint-Julien you would only get 2 bolts on this - yes scary! Enjoy it while you can.

14	Tomber en amour***		4-

18m | 4- | 3 | ⊸8

Go very direct 3-4th bolts to enjoy the grade 4 moves.

15	Yveule**		3-

14m | 3- | 2 747 | ⊸7

Very nice slab, but a bit run out in the middle section.

16	Pelé de la broue**		4-

12m | 4- CRIMP | 3 | ⊸7

A tricky start on crimps gives an amusing low crux, good fun thereafter. Short but sweet, and still worth doing.

Around the corner. *Here the block overhangs - 3 problems.*

17	Jouer un cul*		6b-

10m | 6b- CRIMP | 3- | ⊸6

A boulder problem, ideal for those with small fingers in slots.

18	Lâcher la batte*		6a-

7m | 6a- Trick | 3- | ⊸3

A fun little boulder problem that defeats most climbers onsight!

19	Lâche la patate*		6b-

6m | 6b- Trick | 3- | ⊸3

Feels like 6c onsight! Technical and enjoyable - pity it is so short.

TOMBER EN AMOUR 4-, Rocher Québec; Mira Irion

POGNER LES SHAKES 3, Rocher Québec; Sybille Imhof

TOPO GUIDEBOOKS THAT ARE DESIGNED FOR HOLIDAYS

PORTUGAL: A country that has sea cliffs, inland limestone, and granite bouldering.
BOURGOGNE: Central France, sleepy canals, very high quality single pitch limestone.
FONTAINEBLEAU: A bouldering book for any mid grade 5-7a climber, magical circuits.
SANDSTONE: South of London, quiet technical soft sandstone problems, laidback.
AVIGON: Sunny days in the south of France with tremendous climbing variety.
WATCH THIS SPACE: www.jingowobbly.com for new ideas and more titles in future.

The Atchison-Jones
CLIMBERS
POCKET BOOK

This is an essential yearly book
for every climber. Based on a
week to view diary, with a week
to view climbing log, crag and
topo of the week, indoor wall
of the week, plus fully up to
date maps and data of all UK
climbing walls and shops

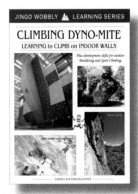

CLIMBING DYNOMITE: The essential
book for bouldering & sport climbing

All on sale at good climbing shops in the UK - Au Vieux Campeur, across France

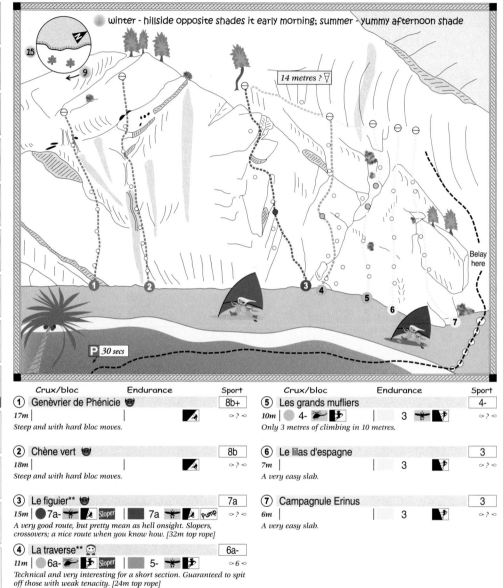

winter - hillside opposite shades it early morning; summer - yummy afternoon shade

15

9

14 metres ?

Belay here

P 30 secs

1 2 3 4 5 6 7

	Crux/bloc	Endurance	Sport
(1) Genèvrier de Phénicie			8b+
17m			

Steep and with hard bloc moves.

	Crux/bloc	Endurance	Sport
(2) Chêne vert			8b
18m			

Steep and with hard bloc moves.

	Crux/bloc	Endurance	Sport
(3) Le figuier**			7a
15m	7a-	7a Pump	

A very good route, but pretty mean as hell onsight. Slopers, crossovers; a nice route when you know how. [32m top rope]

	Crux/bloc	Endurance	Sport
(4) La traverse**			6a-
11m	6a- Sloper	5-	6

Technical and very interesting for a short section. Guaranteed to spit off those with weak tenacity. [24m top rope]

	Crux/bloc	Endurance	Sport
(5) Les grands mufliers			4-
10m	4-	3	

Only 3 metres of climbing in 10 metres.

	Crux/bloc	Endurance	Sport
(6) Le lilas d'espagne			3
7m		3	

A very easy slab.

	Crux/bloc	Endurance	Sport
(7) Campagnule Erinus			3
6m		3	

A very easy slab.

Résumé. *A very impressive looking cliff that overhangs the river, but offers very little. A lovely spot to hang out at, and take a dip in the river. The deep river and very smooth start makes the grade 8 climbs very problematic. The others on the right can easily be top roped and lowered into. The easy routes are not brilliant (understatement).*

BOREAL

Secteur Chêne Vert, Lou Passo

Secteur Soupir, Lou Passo

Windy gorge which makes it a chilly place; morning sun is a blessing

N

9

15

Secteur
Aqualand

Secteur
Chène
20 secs

5

8 Cabin Caha

6

4

3

7

1

2

P 1 min

Crux/bloc	Endurance	Sport

(1) Le Dièdre du délire* ☺ ⚡ 5**

28m | 6a- 🪨 CRIMP | 4+ 🔺 DIÈDRE Yum | ∘12∘

A superb corner with giant jugs, followed by a lovely delicate finish. Foot placements essential. Sustained at the grade but not pumpy.

(2) Soupir* ☺ ⚡ 5**

28m | 6a- | 4+ 🔺 Cool | ∘11∘

A fun start, easy middle, and one more move than the dièdre. Only technique required - not strength.

Top rope. *Very wet at the start - top rope lower Soupir [27m]*

(3) Ça Mouille ☺ 6b**

16m | 6b- Sloper | 6a | ∘6∘

Short but nice, with a couple of very good moves - tricky onsight.

(4) La Calanca* 6c-**

16m | 6c- CRIMP | 6b- | ∘6∘

A good 6b start, but with a good move later on - easy redpoint.

(5) Piana Piano ☺ 6c-**

16m | 6c- CRIMP | 6a | ∘6∘

A nice short wall with a good rest at halfway, easy red point.

(6) Le Pilier de la rampe* ☺ 6a**

20m | | | ∘?∘

Interesting approach to the start, but lovely position.

(7) De l'Ouvèze au Ciel* 7a

20m | | | ∘?∘

Résumé. *A fun section of two pillers with water below. Both the routes Dièdre and Soupir could be 5 or 6a. Access to the routes on the right is impossible with the water below. Good idea is to lower onto the routes from Soupir; a 50m rope works well but 52m is perfect - and not too long to allow your belayer to lower you into the water. Road and river noise make communication difficult. The climbing on this sector is very good indeed, and worth the fun adventure with rope tricks.*

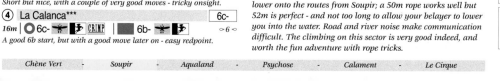

Chène Vert - Soupir - Aqualand - Psychose - Calament - Le Cirque

PSYCHOSE 7b, Lou Passo, Steve Glennie (sector Aqualand behind)

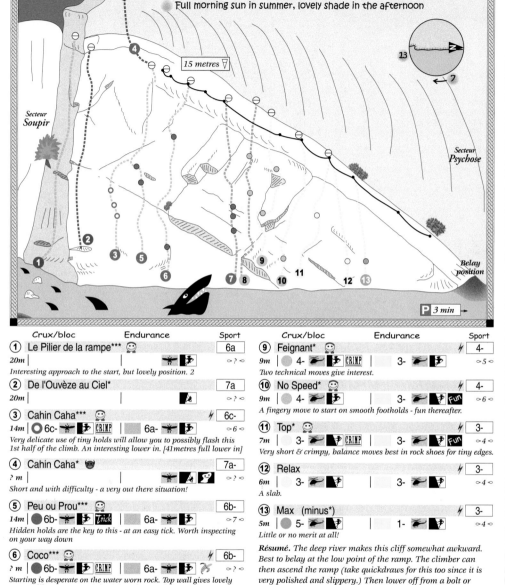

Full morning sun in summer, lovely shade in the afternoon

15 metres

Secteur *Soupir*

Secteur *Psychose*

Belay position

P 3 min →

	Crux/bloc	Endurance	Sport
①	Le Pilier de la rampe*** ☺		6a

20m | | ∘?∘
Interesting approach to the start, but lovely position. 2

| ② | De l'Ouvèze au Ciel* | | 7a |

20m | | ∘?∘
...

| ③ | Cahin Caha*** ☺ | | 6c- |

14m | ○ 6c- | 6a- | ∘6∘
Very delicate use of tiny holds will allow you to possibly flash this 1st half of the climb. An interesting lower in. [41metres full lower in]

| ④ | Cahin Caha* | | 7a- |

? m | | ∘?∘
Short and with difficulty - a very out there situation!

| ⑤ | Peu ou Prou*** | | 6b- |

14m | ● 6b- *Trick* | 6a- | ∘7∘
Hidden holds are the key to this - at an easy tick. Worth inspecting on your way down

| ⑥ | Coco*** ☺ | | 6b- |

? m | ● 6b- CRIMP | 6a- | ∘?∘
Starting is desperate on the water worn rock. Top wall gives lovely moves - like a very easy Saint-Léger, sharp rock.

| ⑦ | Aqualand** | | 6b- |

? m | ● 6b- CRIMP | 5- Pump | ∘?∘
A really hard start to onsight - excellent work out for fingertips.

| ⑧ | Dakin** ☺ | | 6a- |

? m | ● 6a- CRIMP | 5- Pump | ∘?∘
A very good short route indeed. Feels like 6b, when done for the first time. Sharp crimps.

	Crux/bloc	Endurance	Sport
⑨	Feignant* ☺		4-

9m | ● 4- CRIMP | 3- | ∘5∘
Two technical moves give interest.

| ⑩ | No Speed* ☺ | | 4- |

9m | ● 4- | 3- Fun | ∘6∘
A fingery move to start on smooth footholds - fun thereafter.

| ⑪ | Top* ☺ | | 3- |

7m | ● 3- CRIMP | 3- Fun | ∘4∘
Very short & crimpy, balance moves best in rock shoes for tiny edges.

| ⑫ | Relax | | 3- |

6m | ● 3- | 3- | ∘4∘
A slab.

| ⑬ | Max (minus*) | | 3- |

5m | ● 5- | 1- | ∘4∘
Little or no merit at all!

Résumé. *The deep river makes this cliff somewhat awkward. Best to belay at the low point of the ramp. The climber can then ascend the ramp (take quickdraws for this too since it is very polished and slippery.) Then lower off from a bolt or chain (use your own screwgate karabiner so that you do not wear any insitu metal). Best to use a quickdraw with 2 screwgates that doesn't cause a twist in your rope to form. Max lower off is Cahn at 41 metres. The routes on the right are nice and easy, but the routes to the left side are particularly difficult onsight. Water has worn the base of the routes to glass, so placing a long sling on the penultimate bolt maybe handy in case you get stuck at the bottom, and would have to swim out! Most routes on the left are not done much, and the rock is still spectacularly sharp. You can actually climb the routes on the pillar, then place quickdraws and get back without wetting the rope.*

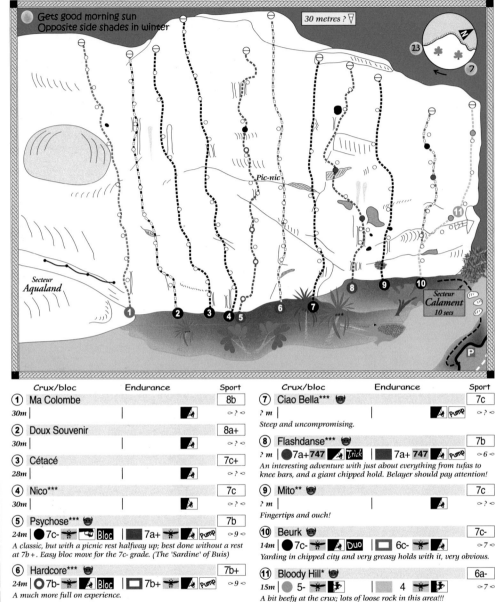

Gets good morning sun
Opposite side shades in winter

30 metres ?

13
7

Pic-nic

Secteur
Aqualand

Secteur
Calament
10 secs

1   2   3   4   5   6   7   8   9   10   11

	Crux/bloc	Endurance	Sport
(1) Ma Colombe			8b
30m			◦?◦

	Crux/bloc	Endurance	Sport
(2) Doux Souvenir			8a+
30m			◦?◦

	Crux/bloc	Endurance	Sport
(3) Cétacé			7c+
28m			◦?◦

	Crux/bloc	Endurance	Sport
(4) Nico***			7c
30m			◦?◦

	Crux/bloc	Endurance	Sport
(5) Psychose***	7c- Bloc	7a+ Pump	7b
24m			◦9◦

*A classic, but with a picnic rest halfway up; best done without a rest
at 7b +. Easy bloc move for the 7c- grade. (The 'Sardine' of Buis)*

	Crux/bloc	Endurance	Sport
(6) Hardcore***	7b- Bloc	7b+ Pump	7b+
24m			◦9◦

A much more full on experience.

Résumé. *This overhanging bay catches your eye from the road
immediately, and with the golden morning sun on the yellow
rock - looks fabulous. A nasty inferno in mid summer - and
doesn't really cool down in July, very sweaty. At most other
times of the year, the wind rushes through this gorge and keeps
the temperature cool, and the humidity low. Full on hard
routes, that will suit any lightweight climber with stamina.*

	Crux/bloc	Endurance	Sport
(7) Ciao Bella***		Pump	7c
? m			◦?◦

Steep and uncompromising.

	Crux/bloc	Endurance	Sport
(8) Flashdanse***	7a+ 747 Trick	7a+ 747 Pump	7b
? m			◦6◦

*An interesting adventure with just about everything from tufas to
knee bars, and a giant chipped hold. Belayer should pay attention!*

	Crux/bloc	Endurance	Sport
(9) Mito**			7c
? m			◦?◦

Fingertips and ouch!

	Crux/bloc	Endurance	Sport
(10) Beurk	7c- Duo	6c-	7c-
14m			◦7◦

Yarding in chipped city and very greasy holds with it, very obvious.

	Crux/bloc	Endurance	Sport
(11) Bloody Hill*	5-	4	6a-
15m			◦7◦

A bit beefy at the crux; lots of loose rock in this area!!!

BOREAL

Vertical tab labels (left margin):
ST. JEAN · VAISON · 3 RIVIÈRES · SAINT LÉGER · VIC · BRUNOTS · ST. JULIEN · QUEBEC · LOU PASSO · UBRIEUX · BM-ROUSSE · BOURDONS · AIGUIER · MIEVES · MÉVOUILLON · TOPOS

PSYCHOSE 7b, Lou Passo; Nicolas Labedan

ECLIPSE 6b-, Lou Passo; Birgit Wrobel

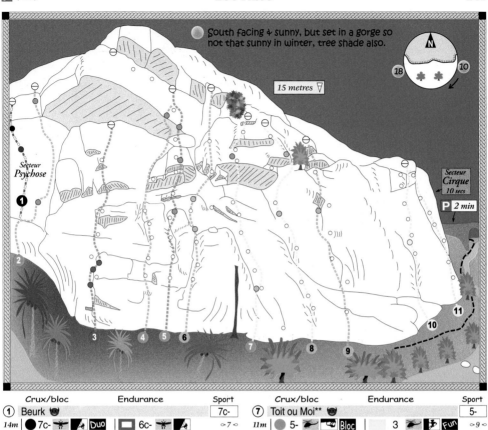

South facing & sunny, but set in a gorge so not that sunny in winter, tree shade also.

15 metres

18   10

Secteur *Psychose*

Secteur *Cirque* 10 secs

P 2 min

1

2

3   4   5   6   7   8   9   10   11

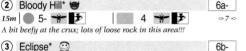

	Crux/bloc	Endurance	Sport
(1) Beurk	7c-	6c-	7c-

14m | 7c- Duo | 6c- | ◌7◌

Yarding in chipped city and very greasy holds with it, very obvious.

(2) Bloody Hill* | 6a-

15m | 5- | 4 | ◌7◌

A bit beefy at the crux; lots of loose rock in this area!!!

(3) Eclipse* | 6b-

11m | 6b- | 5- | ◌5◌

Highly technical at the 2nd clip, and very slippery. Being tall is a huge advantage (6c- shorties), nice thereafter with interest.

(4) Cana* | 5-

13m | 5- | 4 | ◌9◌

Start with a very nice easy section, then one hard pull taking the overhang on the right.

(5) Fonctionnaire* | 5

13m | 5- | 5 | ◌9◌

Polished to hell, but a lot of fun on giant holds. All thrust and no brain - quite sustained.

(6) Calament* | 4

13m | 4- | 4 | ◌8◌

Mostly easy climbing, but with polished holds & a steep angle. You still have to crank pretty hard.

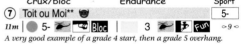

	Crux/bloc	Endurance	Sport
(7) Toit ou Moi*	5-	3	5-

11m | 5- Bloc | 3 Fun | ◌9◌

A very good example of a grade 4 start, then a grade 5 overhang.

(8) Cro Magnon* | 4-

11m | 4- | 3- DIEDRE | ◌8◌

An easy groove leads to an overhang, climbed in adventurous fashion; steep but good holds.

(9) La Voie Souple* | 6a-

11m | 6a- CRIMP | 4 | ◌6◌

A nice technical wall is climbed on the left of the bolts with the use of tiny foot edges.

(10) 20 Cents | 3-

12m | 3- | 1 | ◌6◌

Only one move but good fun scrambling.

(11) Poussin | 1

12m | 1 | 1 | ◌?◌

Of little interest.

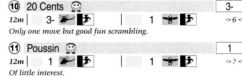

Résumé. *This sector is mainly hidden from the road by trees and can easily go unnoticed. Very popular with beginners and hence the routes are polished, however this doesn't make much difference since the handholds are good enough in most parts. Belay shade and by the river for a picnic.*

Note: Be careful when lowering climbers off routes 7 & 8, when you descend over the top overhang, you swing in and can easily hit your face on the lip of the overhang - be aware of this.

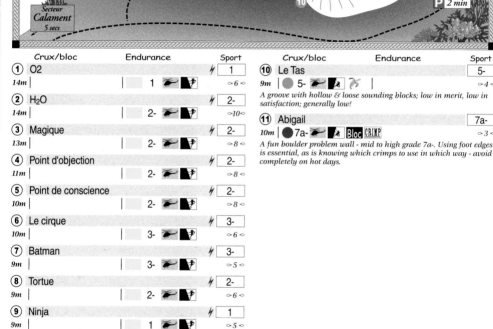

14 metres

Morning sunshine big time - hot & sunny

N

8

16

1 2 3 4 5 6 7 8 9

11

10

Secteur
Calament
5 secs

P 2 min

	Crux/bloc	Endurance	Sport
1	O2		1
14m		1	∽6∽
2	H$_2$O		2-
14m		2-	∽10∽
3	Magique		2-
13m		2-	∽8∽
4	Point d'objection		2-
11m		2-	∽8∽
5	Point de conscience		2-
10m		2-	∽8∽
6	Le cirque		3-
10m		3-	∽6∽
7	Batman		3-
9m		3-	∽5∽
8	Tortue		2-
9m		2-	∽6∽
9	Ninja		1
9m		1	∽5∽

	Crux/bloc	Endurance	Sport
10	Le Tas		5-
9m	5-		∽4∽

A groove with hollow & loose sounding blocks; low in merit, low in satisfaction; generally low!

	Crux/bloc	Endurance	Sport
11	Abigail		7a-
10m	7a- Bloc CRIMP		∽3∽

A fun boulder problem wall - mid to high grade 7a-. Using foot edges is essential, as is knowing which crimps to use in which way - avoid completely on hot days.

Résumé. *Two very small sectors, but very useful for small kids having a go at leading outside. A very easy angled cove on the left with 9 very easy climbs. They seem easy, but you certainly wouldn't like to descend this area if it was wet! Be careful, you could seriously hurt yourself falling down the slab; it is more dangerous than it looks. The routes on the right are on very poor rock, so the grades could easily change.*

Equip **O**

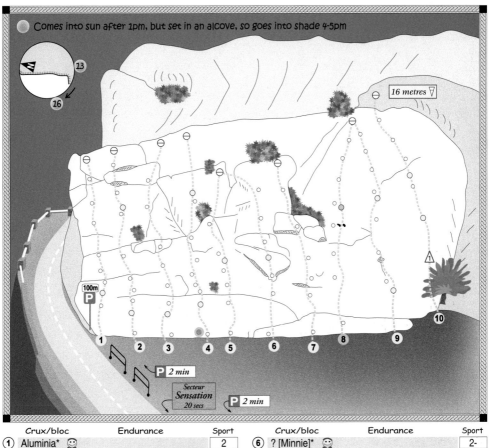

Comes into sun after 1pm, but set in an alcove, so goes into shade 4-5pm

16 metres ▽

100m P

Secteur *Sensation* 20 secs

P 2 min

P 2 min

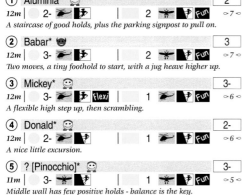
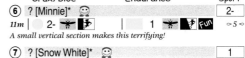

	Crux/bloc	Endurance	Sport

① Aluminia* ☺ — 2
12m | 2- | 2 Fun | 7
A staircase of good holds, plus the parking signpost to pull on.

② Babar* — 3
12m | 3- | 2 Fun | 7
Two moves, a tiny foothold to start, with a jug heave higher up.

③ Mickey* ☺ — 3-
12m | 3- Flexi | 1 Fun | 6
A flexible high step up, then scrambling.

④ Donald* ☺ — 2-
12m | 2- | 1 Fun | 6
A nice little excursion.

⑤ ? [Pinocchio]* ☺ — 3-
11m | 3- | 1 Fun | 5
Middle wall has few positive holds - balance is the key.

⑥ ? [Minnie]* ☺ — 2-
11m | 2- | 1 Fun | 5
A small vertical section makes this terrifying!

⑦ ? [Snow White]* ☺ — 1
11m | 1 | 1 Fun | 5
'Sains mains' keep your hands off Snow White. A lovely climb with feet only and using elbows to balance; strictly - no hands allowed.

⑧ ? [Tenggren]* — 4-
11m | 4- Bloc | 2 Fun | 7
One very good hard move, best attempted on a top rope - and keeping right of the bolts of course.

⑨ ? [Albert]* — 3-
11m | 3- | 2- Fun | 7
A tricky start; middle section involves a long reach for kids.

⑩ ? [Pluto]* — 3-
16m | 3- ⚠ | 2- Fun | 4
A good lower wall. High first clip, easy 8 metres thereafter.

Résumé. *A nice small wall right by the road, ideal for intro sessions for kids or adults just starting. Nothing scary remotely. Useful morning and late afternoon shade, plus the wind tends to naturally blow in here on hot summer afternoons. (Some names to these routes have been lost - so we have included [temporary names in the same style])*

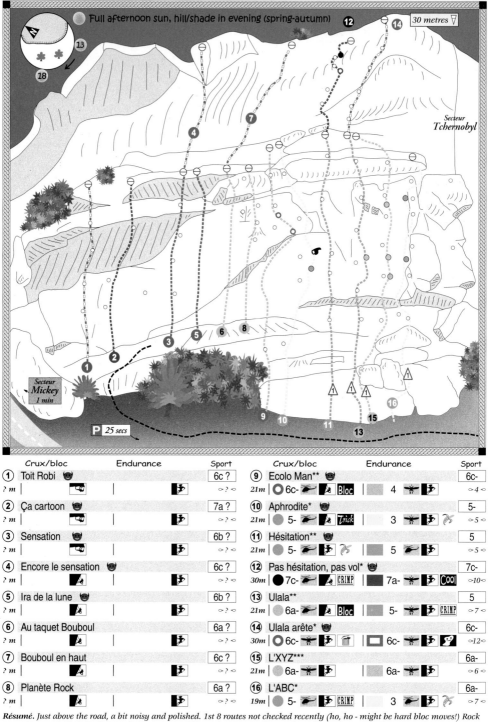

Full afternoon sun, hill/shade in evening (spring-autumn)

30 metres

Secteur
Tchernobyl

Secteur
Mickey
1 min

P 25 secs

Left margin tabs (top to bottom): ST. JEAN · VAISON · 3 RIVIÈRES · SAINT LÉGER · VIC · BRUNOTS · ST. JULIEN · QUEBEC · LOU PASSO · **UBRIEUX** · BM-ROUSSE · BOURDONS · AIGUIER · MIEVES · MÉVOUILLON · TOPOS

	Crux/bloc	Endurance	Sport
1	Toit Robi		6c ?
2	Ça cartoon		7a ?
3	Sensation		6b ?
4	Encore le sensation		6c ?
5	Ira de la lune		6b ?
6	Au taquet Bouboul		6a ?
7	Bouboul en haut		6c ?
8	Planète Rock		6a ?

	Crux/bloc	Endurance	Sport
9	Ecolo Man**	21m · 6c- · Bloc · 4	6c-
10	Aphrodite*	21m · 5- · Trick · 3	5-
11	Hésitation**	21m · 5- · 5	5
12	Pas hésitation, pas vol*	30m · 7c- · CRIMP · 7a- · COOL	7c-
13	Ulala**	21m · 6a- · Bloc · 5- · CRIMP	5
14	Ulala arête*	30m · 6c- · 6c-	6c-
15	L'XYZ***	21m · 6a- · 6a-	6a-
16	L'ABC*	19m · 5- · CRIMP · 3	6a-

Résumé. Just above the road, a bit noisy and polished. 1st 8 routes not checked recently (ho, ho - might be hard bloc moves!) Rock on main prow is diabolical, & top finishes are very bloc style. Deservedly popular with grade 5-6a climbers on easier routes.

Mickey - Sensation - Tchernobyl - Beaux Parleurs - Gégène - Symphonie - Bébé - Ripoux

TCHERNOBYL 7b- bloc, Ubrieux; Urs Wildeisen

ST. JEAN | VAISON | 3 RIVIÈRES | SAINT LÉGER | VIC | BRUNOTS | ST.JULIEN | QUEBEC | LOU PASSO | UBRIEUX | BM-ROUSSE | BOURDONS | AIGUIER | MIEYES | MÉVOUILLON | TOPOS

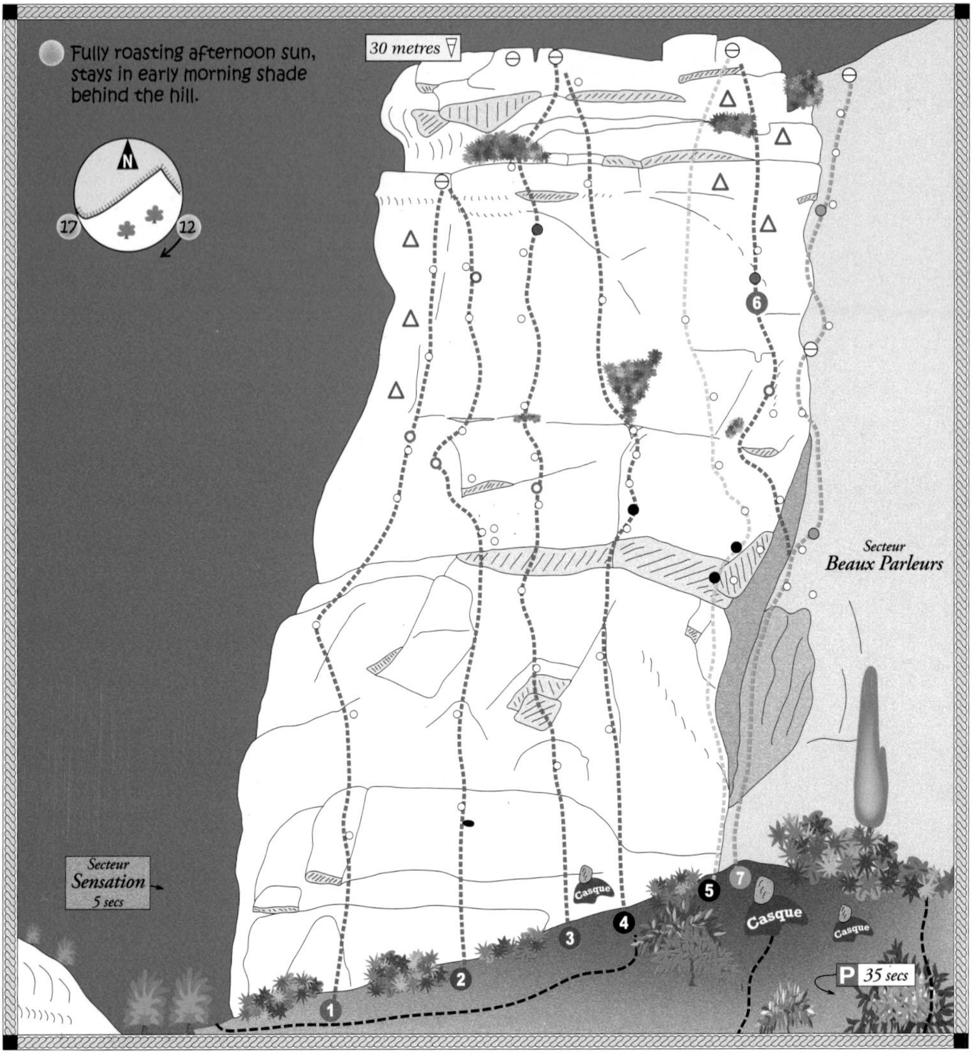
Fully roasting afternoon sun, stays in early morning shade behind the hill.
30 metres
N
17
12
Secteur Beaux Parleurs
Secteur Sensation 5 secs
Casque
Casque
Casque
P 35 secs
1
2
3
4
5
6
7

Crux/bloc — Endurance — Sport

1 La Casse dalle △ — 6c-
28m | ○ 6c- CRIMP | 6b | ~7~
A run out climb that if things go wrong you could seriously end up worse off! Loose rock in the top section.

2 Tchernobyl — 7b-
28m | ○ 7b- CRIMP | 6b 747 | ~7~
Technical top wall, otherwise scary and about as unattractively bolted as they come.

3 Le grand chaos* — 7a-
28m | ● 7a- CRIMP | 6b 747 Cool | ~10~
An interesting first half with a fun and interesting overhang. Top wall is sustained and is not with large ledges.

4 Oraison funèbre* — 7c-
28m | ● 7c- Bloc | 6b 747 Cool | ~8~
A highly powerful lock off at the top of the overhang - or a dyno. Of very little merit - but a fabulous position.

5 Passeport pour l'enfer — 7c-
30m | ● 7c- Bloc | 6a 747 Cool | ~10~
A couple of boulder moves on slopers, not ideal in summer. Of very limited interest.

6 Dernier soupir — 6b
30m | ○ 6c- | 6b △ | ~10~
A long reach is helpful. Very poor rock in the top half, belayers watch out!

7 Mammouth Cave — 5+
28m | ● 5 DIEDRE | 5+ DIEDRE | ~7~
Polish actually doesn't spoil this route at all, the climbing is very good. Ridiculous run outs - not for beginners remotely!

Résumé. *This buttress certainly looks the part, but has poor sections of rock, and very hard bloc moves to make the routes disjointed. Routes to tick when you are feeling strong, and you need to be near the car in case it rains.*

LE GRAND CHAOS 7a- bloc, Ubrieux; Dave Potts

LE PARADIS 6b+, Ubrieux; David Atchison-Jones (photo Dave Potts)

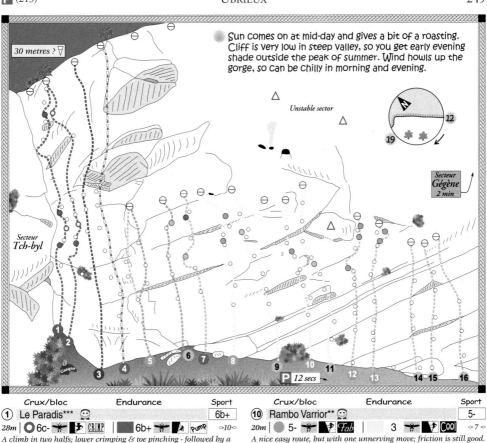

30 metres ?

Sun comes on at mid-day and gives a bit of a roasting. Cliff is very low in steep valley, so you get early evening shade outside the peak of summer. Wind howls up the gorge, so can be chilly in morning and evening.

Unstable sector

Secteur Gégène 2 min

Secteur Tch-byl

Casque

P 12 secs

Sidebar (right margin): ST JEAN · VAISON · 3 RIVIÈRES · SAINT LÉGER · VIC · BRUNOTS · ST JULIEN · QUEBEC · LOU PASSO · UBRIEUX · BM-ROUSSE · BOURDONS · AIGUIER · MIEYES · MÉVOUILLON · TOPOS

	Crux/bloc	Endurance	Sport
1	Le Paradis*** ☺		6b+
28m	○ 6c- CRIMP	6b+ Pump	∞10∞

A climb in two halfs; lower crimping & toe pinching - followed by a sustained top wall where finding the good holds quickly is crucial.

2	Le Mythe*** ☺		6c
28m	○ 6c CRIMP	6b+	

Two very good 6c moves. Lower wall is more fun if 1st 2 bolts are pre clipped. Keep right at the top to make a harder and sustained finish.

3	Le K d'Annibal***		7a- ?
30m	CRIMP	Pump	∞ ? ∞

4	Nuage***		6c- ?
30m	CRIMP	Pump	∞ ? ∞

5	Le clou foireux**		5
15m			∞ ? ∞

6	Samiby** ☺		6a-
16m	6a- CRIMP	5- Flexi	∞4∞

Very polished, so take your time; if you're not flexible 6b i'm afraid.

7	Andropose** ●		6b-
16m	6b- CRIMP	4 747	∞4∞

A very hard fingery pull at the top - not enjoyable for novices.

8	Maybe** ☺		5-
16m	5-	3	∞6∞

Only marginally harder than Mikado - slightly smaller holds.

9	Mikado** ●		4-
16m	4-	3	∞7∞

A hard move for a 4, but good holds & not sustained - ideal.

	Crux/bloc	Endurance	Sport
10	Rambo Varrior** ☺		5-
20m	5- Fab	3 Cool	∞7∞

A nice easy route, but with one unnerving move; friction is still good.

11	Beaux Parleurs*** ●		4-
21m	4-	3 Fun	∞8∞

Massive holds all the way, but it ain't no helicopter ride. Good and proper leading without panic attacks.

12	Mercure*** ☺		5-
19m	5-	4 Fun	∞9∞

A classic style move for the 1st crux; typical Saint-Julien concentration required for the top section.

13	Jupiter*** ●		5-
19m	5-	4 Cool	∞9∞

A superb top wall gives the fine entertainment. Going right is handy grade 5, direct is still comfortable at 6a - both are fab.

14	Kipertou		4

15	Splach		4

16	Perfo / Clero		4

Résumé. This is a slabbly area opposite the car park - say no more, it is often busy with groups and most of the routes have some polish. The lower slab is a real sun trap and is a silly place to visit on hot afternoons. There are a few picnic tables nearby, and the river opposite. A very handy venue and also popular with those tending kiddywinks.

Mickey - Sensation - Tchernobyl - Beaux Parleurs - Gégène - Symphonie - Bébé - Ripoux

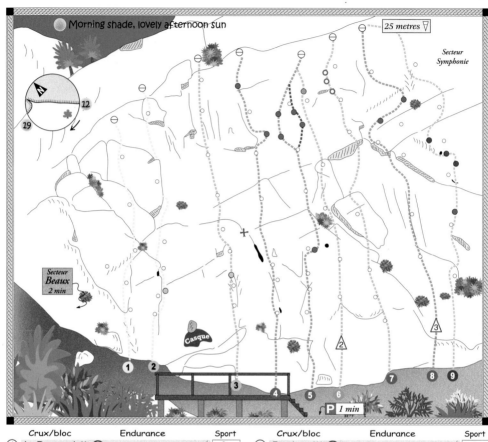

Morning shade, lovely afternoon sun

25 metres

Secteur
Symphonie

Secteur
Beaux
2 min

Casque

P 1 min

	Crux/bloc	Endurance	Sport

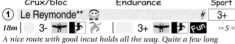

① Le Reymonde** 😊   3+

18m | 3- | 3+ Fun | ~5~

A nice route with good incut holds all the way. Quite a few long reaches.

② Le grand Jo**   4-

22m | 4- Bloc | 3+ 747 | ~5~

Good climbing, but the lower crack is polished, making it a very tough grade 4 move. Long reaches throughout.

③ Le Gégène***   4+

23m | 4 | 4+ | ~8~

A fab climb with superb holds all the way; only the steepness and sustained nature will get you.

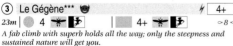

④ Post natal** 😊   6b-

22m | 6b- Bloc | 5- 747 G-d'eau | ~6~

A classic route with a classic crux; suited to flexible people with good balance.

⑤ L'enface de l'art** 😊   6b-

23m | 6b- Bloc | 5 | ~7~

A bit of a horror this little bastard. Bottom wall will stump the first group of candidates. Top wall is alarmingly steep, tricky and damm difficult. An excellent challenge/sandbag. Very difficult to onsight - go either left or right below the bolt.

	Crux/bloc	Endurance	Sport

⑥ Psychose*** 😊   5-

26m | 5- CRIMP | 4+ | ~5~

Best to start up l'enface (5m clip stick). Lower wall is fun, but top wall is fantastic with crux well bolted. Feels hard for a 5.

⑦ Déséquuilibre* 😊   6c-

28m | 6c- CRIMP | 4 747 | ~?~

Just the sort of route you don't like, 1st time round. Knowing the holds to go for is essential - best top roped.

⑧ Subtilité tactile*** 😊   6b-

30m | 6b- | 5 747 Pump | ~7~

An excellent route, highly sustained. High 1st clip seems adequate, thereafter lots of brilliant moves using good route finding (low in 6b)

⑨ Faille qui maille** 😊   7a-

32m | 7a- CRIMP | 6a Trick | ~8~

Small nasty holds, & hands on footholds, make this a right bugger onsight; 3-4 fiendish moves in a row - top is delightfully easy.

Résumé. *This sector is easily recognised with the Passerelle at the bottom (wooden gantry). This also makes it a very popular hang out and where groups tend to congregate. If busy, head right to the other very good sectors. Certainly loose stones on the left hand side of the cliff, so groups should think of wearing helmets. A real dolly mixture bag of tricks here, easy to hard routes, and a lot with good beefy crux's. An enjoyable sector.*

L'ENFACE DE L'ART 6b- bloc, Ubrieux; Mira Irion

Secteur Symphonie, Ubrieux (Bloc move city)

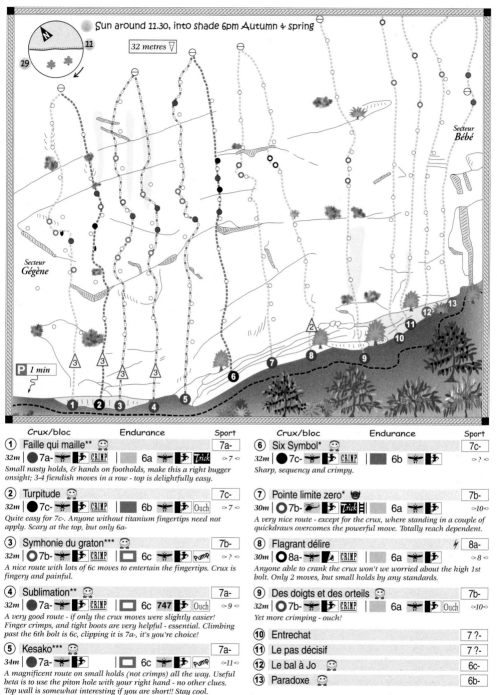

Sun around 11.30, into shade 6pm Autumn & spring

32 metres

Secteur **Bébé**

Secteur **Gégène**

P *1 min*

	Crux/bloc	Endurance	Sport
①	Faille qui maille** ☺		7a-

32m ● 7a- 🔆 🔧 CRIMP | 6a 🔆 🏃 Trick ∽7∽

Small nasty holds, & hands on footholds, make this a right bugger onsight; 3-4 fiendish moves in a row - top is delightfully easy.

| ② | Turpitude ☺ | | 7c- |

32m ● 7c- 🔆 🔧 CRIMP | 6b 🔆 🏃 Ouch ∽7∽

Quite easy for 7c-. Anyone without titanium fingertips need not apply. Scary at the top, but only 6a

| ③ | Symhonie du graton*** ☺ | | 7b- |

32m ○ 7b- 🔆 🔧 CRIMP | 6c 🔆 🏃 Pump ∽?∽

A nice route with lots of 6c moves to entertain the fingertips. Crux is fingery and painful.

| ④ | Sublimation** ☺ | | 7a- |

32m ● 7a- 🔆 🔧 CRIMP | 6c **747** 🏃 Ouch ∽9∽

A very good route - if only the crux moves were slightly easier! Finger crimps, and tight boots are very helpful - essential. Climbing past the 6th bolt is 6c, clipping it is 7a-, it's you're choice!

| ⑤ | Kesako*** ☺ | | 7a- |

34m ● 7a- 🔆 🏃 | 6c 🏃 Pump ∽11∽

A magnificent route on small holds (not crimps) all the way. Useful beta is to use the piton hole with your right hand - no other clues. Top wall is somewhat interesting if you are short!! Stay cool.

	Crux/bloc	Endurance	Sport
⑥	Six Symbol* ☺		7c-

32m ● 7c- 🔆 🔧 CRIMP | 6b 🔆 🏃 ∽?∽

Sharp, sequency and crimpy.

| ⑦ | Pointe limite zero* ☻ | | 7b- |

30m ● 7b- 🐟 🏃 Trick II | 6a 🔆 🏃 ∽10∽

A very nice route - except for the crux, where standing in a couple of quickdraws overcomes the powerful move. Totally reach dependent.

| ⑧ | Flagrant délire | ⚡ | 8a- |

30m ○ 8a- 🔆 🪨 CRIMP | 6a 🔆 🏃 ∽8∽

Anyone able to crank the crux won't we worried about the high 1st bolt. Only 2 moves, but small holds by any standards.

| ⑨ | Des doigts et des orteils ☺ | | 7b- |

32m ○ 7b- 🔆 🏃 CRIMP | 6a 🔆 🏃 Ouch ∽10∽

Yet more crimping - ouch!

⑩	Entrechat		7 ?-
⑪	Le pas décisif		7 ?-
⑫	Le bal à Jo ☺		6c-
⑬	Paradoxe ☺		6b-

Résumé. *Taking a dose of painkillers for your fingertips is advisable before climbing in this sector. Routes in general are very unbalanced with ludicrously easy top and bottom sections. [The old local grades 6a-b, for this sector were some of the best sandbags in history - unless old 6a-b meant font 6a-b. Unless you are a Fontainebleau crimp expert, give this sector a miss.]*

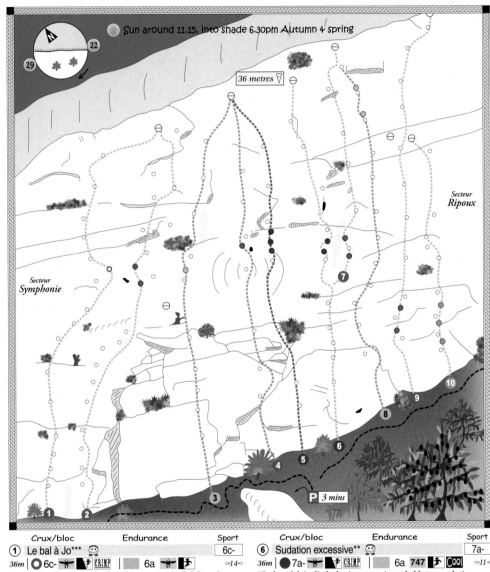

Sun around 11.15, into shade 6.30pm Autumn & spring

11

19

36 metres

Secteur
Ripoux

Secteur
Symphonie

7

10

9

8

6

5

4

3

P 3 mins

2

1

	Crux/bloc	Endurance	Sport
①	**Le bal à Jo*** 😊		6c-

36m ⚪ 6c- 🔅 🧗 CRIMP | 6a 🔅 🧗 | ∽14∽

A surprising first section leads to the crux - moving left from the shared pocket, will get harder with use. Top wall is excellent 6a.

② **Paradoxe*** 😊 | | 6b-

36m ⚫ 6b- 🔅 🧗 CRIMP | 6a- 🧗 | ∽12∽

Avoid the mid pitch belay; take top wall 1m right of bolts for 6a.

③ **Le repos du grimpeur*** 😊 | | 6a-

36m ⚫ 6a- 🔅 🧗 CRIMP | 5- 🧗 | ∽12∽

A lovely long route with grade 4 most of the way - grade may change.

④ **Dévers-gondage*** 😊 | | 6a-

34m ⚫ 6b- 🔅 🏃 ▓▓ | 5- 🧗 | ∽8∽

A lovely long route with grade 4 most of the way - grade may change.

⑤ **H.S.*** 😊 | | 6a-

33m ⚫ 7a- 🔅 🦶 Bloc | 6b- 🧗 CRIMP | ∽10∽

Miniscule edges for both hands and feet.

	Crux/bloc	Endurance	Sport
⑥	**Sudation excessive** 😊		7a-

36m ⚫ 7a- 🔅 🧗 CRIMP | 6a 747 🧗 COOl | ∽11∽

The low slab is climbed using non existant holds to a pocket!

⑦ **Bébé s'amuse*** 😊 | | 6b-

36m ⚫ 6b- 🔅 🧗 CRIMP | 6a+ 747 🧗 | ∽11∽

A complete and superb route, combining slab and wall moves & view

⑧ **Symphonie inachevée*** 😊 | | 6a

35m ⚪ 6a 🔅 🧗 | 5 747 🧗 COOl | ∽11∽

A very fine route, easy low down and delicate upper section.

⑨ **Éléphant Girl *** 😃 | | 6b-

36m ⚫ 6b- 🔅 🧗 Bloc | 6a+ 🔅 🧗 COOl | ∽13∽

Two good hard moves low down, great position.

⑩ **Ciao l'enfoiré !*** 😃 | | 5-

28m ⚪ 5- 🔅 🧗 Bloc | 4+ 🔅 🧗 ✂ | ∽15∽

A very polished start with good hard climbing to the mid belay. Top half is very soft 6a, but well run out, ideal for a cool leader.

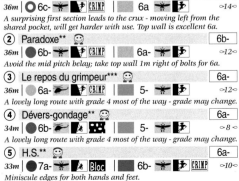

Mickey - Sensation - Tchernobyl - Beaux Parleurs - Gégène - Symphonie - Bébé - Ripoux

Side tabs (left margin): ST. JEAN · VAISON · 3 RIVIÈRES · SAINT LÉGER · VIC · BRUNOTS · ST JULIEN · QUEBEC · LOU PASSO · UBRIEUX · BM-ROUSSE · BOURDONS · AIGUIER · MIEVES · MÉVOUILLON · TOPOS

SUDATION EXCESSIVE 7a- bloc, Ubrieux; Nathalie Welch

EMBRACE-TOI 6c- bloc, Ubrieux, Dave Potts

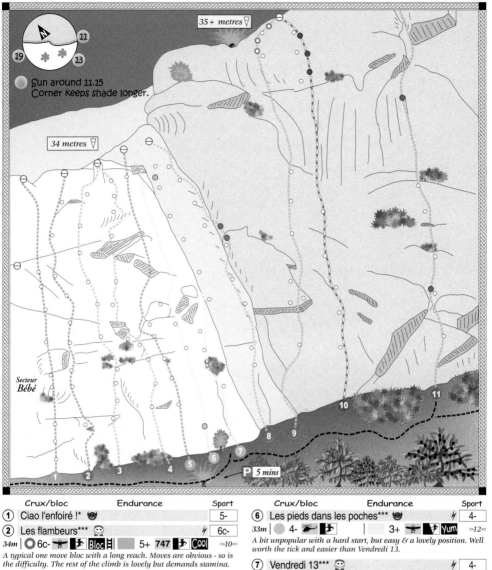

35 + metres

Sun around 11.15
Corner keeps shade longer.

34 metres

Secteur
Bébé

P 5 mins

Secteur side tabs: ST. JEAN · VAISON · 3 RIVIÈRES · SAINT LÉGER · VIC · BRUNOTS · ST JULIEN · QUEBEC · LOU PASSO · UBRIEUX · BM-ROUSSE · BOURDONS · AIGUIER · MIEYES · MÉVOUILLON · TOPOS

	Crux/bloc	Endurance	Sport

1 Ciao l'enfoiré !* 😊 — 5-

2 Les flambeurs*** 🙂 — ⚡ 6c-
34m | ⬤ 6c- ✳ 🏃 Bloc ▦ | 5+ 747 🏃 Cool | ∽10∽
A typical one move bloc with a long reach. Moves are obvious - so is the difficulty. The rest of the climb is lovely but demands stamina.

3 Cupidos*** 🙂 — ⚡ 6b-
34m | ⬤ 6b- ✳ 🏃 G-d'eau | 6a+ 747 🏃 Pump | ∽10∽
A fantastic route with lovely sustained moves of 6a on fingertips. Nothing hard at all - an amazing mono pull in the middle.

4 Embrace-toi*** 🙂 — ⚡ 6c-
32m | ⬤ 6c- ✳ 🏃 | 6a+ ✳ 🏃 | ∽11∽
A very fine route with lots of excellent climbing. Top pillar is fiendishly confusing with a fingertip swap - feet are critical. By going right at the top you get a better and more balanced 6a+ route.

5 Ripoux*** 🙂 — ⚡ 5
33m | ⬤ 5- ✳ 🏃 ✂ | 5 ✳ 🏃 Cool | ∽12∽
A superb route & polish does not detract or limit enjoyment. A concentrated first half is followed by giant jugs.

	Crux/bloc	Endurance	Sport

6 Les pieds dans les poches*** 😊 — ⚡ 4-
33m | ⬤ 4- ✳ 🏃 | 3+ ✳ 🏃 Yum | ∽12∽
A bit unpopular with a hard start, but easy & a lovely position. Well worth the tick and easier than Vendredi 13.

7 Vendredi 13*** 🙂 — ⚡ 4-
32m | ⬤ 4- ✳ 🏃 Bloc | 3+ ✳ 🏃 Fab | ∽10∽
An ideal easy climb; highly sustained grade 3 climbing with the crux at the very end - excellent.

8 Le diagonale du fou* — 6b-
29m | ⬤ 6b- ✳ 🪨 Cool | 6a ✳ DIEDRE 🎨 | ∽9∽
One of those classic corners with few holds where you want them. Awkward and not easy to read, unavoidably unfriendly - low merit.

9 Désir*** — 6c
? m | ⬤ 6c ✳ 🏃 Cool | 6a ✳ DIEDRE | ∽?∽
Sustained climbing on the top headwall.

10 Surprise sur prise*** — 7a

11 Caresse-la*** — 6b

Résumé. *A quieter sector, and with more routes beyond.*

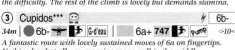

Mickey   -   Sensation   -   Tchernobyl   -   Beaux Parleurs   -   Gégène   -   Symphonie   -   Bébé   -   Ripoux

Baume Rousse, not too difficult walk in.

Saint-Julien in the near distance. Mont Ventoux behind.

Rahan, fils de Crao 7b+. Baume Rouse-Sec Haschisch; Eric Biancarelli

Tres dur - nasty bugger to start; 2002 l'Epicier de "Espace 7a- bloc

LES RAVIOLIS DE L'ENFER 7b- Baume Rousse; Patrick Barone

ST JEAN · VAISON · 3 RIVIÈRES · SAINT LÉGER · VIC · BRUNOTS · ST JULIEN · QUÉBEC · LOU PASSO · URRIEUX · BM-ROUSSE · BOURDONS · AIGUIER · MIEYES · MÉVOUILLON · TOPOS

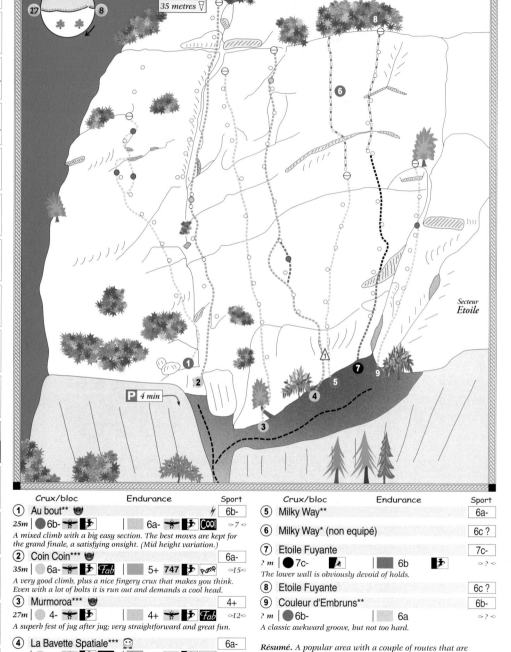

Bags of sun, slap on the sun tan lotion, bring out the lager

35 metres

Secteur
Etoile

P 4 min

	Crux/bloc	Endurance	Sport
(1)	**Au bout****		6b-

25m | 6b- ☀ ↯ | 6a- ☀ ↯ Cool | ○7○

A mixed climb with a big easy section. The best moves are kept for the grand finale, a satisfying onsight. (Mid height variation.)

(2)	**Coin Coin*****		6a-

35m | 6a- ☀ ↯ Fab | 5+ **747** ↯ Pump | ○15○

A very good climb, plus a nice fingery crux that makes you think. Even with a lot of bolts it is run out and demands a cool head.

(3)	**Murmoroa*****		4+

27m | 4- ☀ ↯ | 4+ ☀ ↯ Fab | ○12○

A superb fest of jug after jug; very straightforward and great fun.

(4)	**La Bavette Spatiale***** 😄		6a-

29m | 6a- ↯ Fab | 5+ ↯ Pump | ○10○

A very sustained and excellent route - crux is climbing to the 1st clip. Going left to avoid a nasty move - makes life very enjoyable.

	Crux/bloc	Endurance	Sport
(5)	**Milky Way****		6a-
(6)	**Milky Way*** (non equipé)		6c ?
(7)	**Etoile Fuyante**		7c-

? m | 7c- ↯ | 6b ↯ | ○?○

The lower wall is obviously devoid of holds.

(8)	**Etoile Fuyante**		6c ?
(9)	**Couleur d'Embruns****		6b-

? m | 6b- | 6a | ○?○

A classic awkward groove, but not too hard.

Résumé. *A popular area with a couple of routes that are absolute classics. Great views and plenty of sunshine.*

Murmoroa - Etoile - Gnocchi - Caraille - Haschisch - Tartivore - L'Eperon - Sikarate

AU BOUT 6b- Baume Rousse; Mark Glennie

L'EMILE ET UNE NUIT 4, Baume Rousse; Vicky Hardy

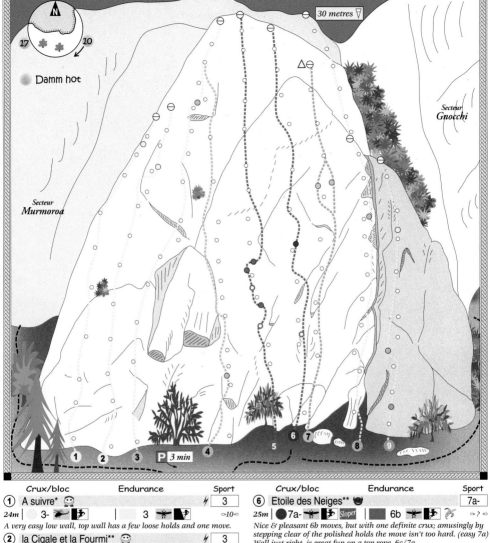

N

17   10

Damm hot

Secteur
Murmoroa

30 metres

Secteur
Gnocchi

P 3 min

1   2   3   4   5   6   7   8   9

Crux/bloc	Endurance	Sport

(1) A suivre*
24m   3-   3   **3**   ○10○
A very easy low wall, top wall has a few loose holds and one move.

(2) la Cigale et la Fourmi**
23m   3-   3   **3**   ○11○
Easiest line here, jugs all the way and well equipped.

(3) Concombre Masqué**
25m   4-   2   **4-**   ○14○
An easy first half, then a really beautiful move stepping onto the top slab. OK, but requires footwork.

(4) L'Emile et Une Nuit**
25m   4-   4   **4**   ○15○
A tricky start, then climb the corner on the left - top wall, rock is !

(5) Soleil Levant**
25m   6c-   CRIMP   6b   Pump   **6c-**   ○14○
A very difficult onsight; solid 6b moves with a soft 6c crux. Knowing the sequence lowers the grade dramatically. A lot of climbing on polished holds in a short space of time.

(6) Etoile des Neiges**
25m   ●7a-   Sloper   6b   **7a-**   ○ ? ○
Nice & pleasant 6b moves, but with one definite crux; amusingly by stepping clear of the polished holds the move isn't too hard. (easy 7a) Wall just right, is great fun on a top rope. 6c/7a

(7) Pleine Lune**
30m   6a-   Trick   5   **6a-**   ○12○
Lovely climbing with a fun crux. Belay at 25m in dodgy rock!

(8) Le Dièdre**
20m   4-   3   DIEDRE Fun   **6a-**   ○11○
Very simple climbing on giant holds, but one move to make you think. Continuation is grade 2, 10 metres and 6 extra draws.

(9) Le Pillier**
20m   5-   3   **5-**   ○11○
A fine position. Low moves with polish make life difficult.

Résumé. *The first obvious buttress that everyone goes to. An ideal spot for beginners, with a few big trees to make a shady picnic. Great views and surprisingly difficult climbing on the flatter sections that have become a bit polished.*

ST JEAN

VAISON

3 RIVIÈRES

SAINT LÉGER

VIC

BRUNOTS

ST JULIEN

QUÉBEC

LOU PASSO

UBRIEUX

BM-ROUSSE

BOURDONS

AIGUIER

MIÈTES

MÉVOUILLON

TOPOS

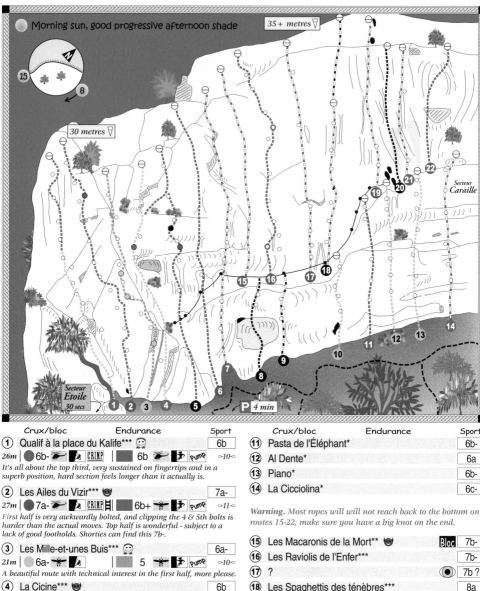

Morning sun, good progressive afternoon shade

35 + metres

30 metres

Secteur Caraille

Secteur Etoile 30 secs

P 4 min

	Crux/bloc	Endurance	Sport
①	Qualif à la place du Kalife***		6b

26m | 6b- | CRIMP | 6b | Pump | ∽10∽

It's all about the top third, very sustained on fingertips and in a superb position, hard section feels longer than it actually is.

②	Les Ailes du Vizir***		7a-

27m | 7a- | CRIMP | 6b+ | Pump | ∽11∽

First half is very awkwardly bolted, and clipping the 4 & 5th bolts is harder than the actual moves. Top half is wonderful - subject to a lack of good footholds. Shorties can find this 7b-.

③	Les Mille-et-unes Buis***		6a-

21m | 6a- | | 5 | Pump | ∽10∽

A beautiful route with technical interest in the first half, more please.

④	La Cicine***		6b

22m | 6b- | Bloc | 6a | Pump | ∽8∽

Very good & sustained to finish up the route to the right at 6b.

⑤	Les Bellecombaises**		7c-

25m | 7c- | Bloc | 6b | | ∽9∽

Even with nifty footwork, you have to crimp like a beaver on heat.

⑥	O.K.**	Bloc	7b-
⑦	Gnocchi on heaven's door***		6c
⑧	Clash*	Bloc	7c-
⑨	Le Mythe*	Bloc	8a-
⑩	Cheloup Plage**		6a

	Crux/bloc	Endurance	Sport
⑪	Pasta de l'Éléphant*		6b-
⑫	Al Dente*		6a
⑬	Piano*		6b-
⑭	La Cicciolina*		6c-

Warning. *Most ropes will will not reach back to the bottom on routes 15-22; make sure you have a big knot on the end.*

⑮	Les Macaronis de la Mort**	Bloc	7b-
⑯	Les Raviolis de l'Enfer***		7b-
⑰	?		7b ?
⑱	Les Spaghettis des ténèbres***		8a
⑲	Les Nouilles de l'Obscur**		7b+
⑳	Barilla Sound System		7c
㉑	Pasta à Shout		7b
㉒	La giclette du Graou		7a+

Résumé. *A sector in 3 parts with routes of different grades and styles to suit most levels of climber. Popular in the shade of afternoon. The big wall with the harder routes on has some superb tufas; the big wall is also grey with a lot of drainage streaks and is not the best choice after heavy rain. Semi sheltered from the mistral wind.*

LES RAVIOLIS DE L'ENFER 7b- (bloc) Baume Rousse; Patrick Barone

PIANO 6b-, Baume Rousse; Birgit Wrobel

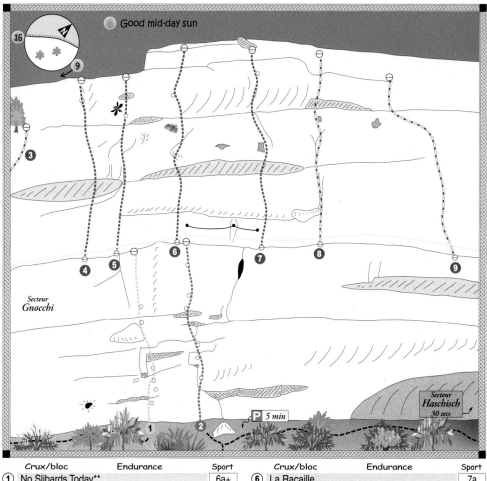

Good mid-day sun

Secteur **Gnocchi**

P 5 min

Secteur **Haschisch** 30 secs

Crux/bloc	Endurance	Sport
① No Slibards Today**		6a+
② La Caraille**		6b
③ Pasta à shout		7b
④ La giclette du Graou		7a+
⑤ Les Voie des Abeilles ✳		7a+

Crux/bloc	Endurance	Sport
⑥ La Racaille		7a
⑦ Alband Fils de Crapaud		7a+
⑧ Jimmy Petit Fils de Crao, Père de Rahan		7b+
⑨ Pipouze Line		7b

Warning. *Do not try to lower off from the routes on the terrace to the bottom of the cliff; make sure you have a big knot on the end in case your rope is shorter than you think, or either you or your belayer are dozy and fail to spot the obvious.*

Résumé. This centre section of the cove is a good sun trap and can be a good place to shelter from the wind. Although it faces south, it does get some shade in the morning and afternoon because of the high sides to the concave cove. Only a couple of routes low down - they look scrappy but are actually quite good. The routes higher up can be accessed by a wire gangway on the left. 7b climbers will easily climb this without ropes, but lesser climbers are not advised. Definitely not a sensible place for a non climbing belay bunny - plus you need to belay attached to the rock. The routes off the terrace are not that long - 25-30m, but are far too long to then lower off back to the very bottom. (Lots of belay shade at the bottom, none on the terrace ledge)

L'ECOLO NET 7a, Baume Rousse; Moniek Steenis

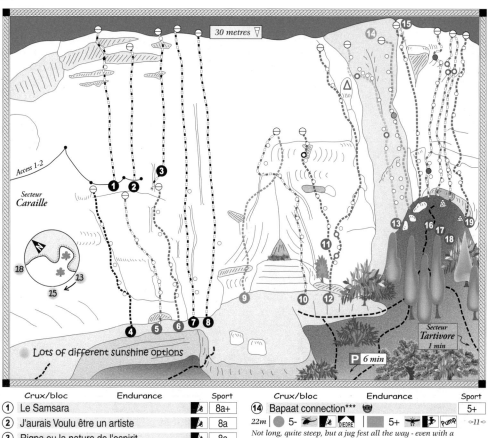

Access 1-2

Secteur Caraille

30 metres

Lots of different sunshine options

Secteur Tartivore 1 min

P 6 min

	Crux/bloc	Endurance	Sport
①	Le Samsara		8a+
②	J'aurais Voulu être un artiste		8a
③	Rigpa ou la nature de l'espirit		8a
④	6662* 😎		7c+
⑤	Tout Court Tout Dur**		7b
⑥	L'Ecolo net**	Bloc	7a
⑦	Rigpa ou la nature de l'esprit***	Pump	7c++
⑧	Les Secrets de Régine***	Pump	7c++
⑨	Saga Corsica	Bloc	8b-
⑩	Rahan, fils de Crao***	Pump	7b+
⑪	Si t'as rien d'autre à faire	Bloc	8a-

Résumé. *Now for something more amenable!*

⑫	Haschisch B*** 😎 😊	⚡	6c-
29m	○ 6c- ☀ 🔥 Sloper	6b ☀ 🔥 Pump	∞?∞

A full on 7 metre sprint gets you to the rest ledge. Very tentative middle section with the giant balanced bloc! Technical top section.

⑬	Rigni, Rignette et Rignoulou*** 😎		6c-
24m	○ 6c- ☀ 🔥 Bloc	6a+ ☀ 🔥 Pump	∞13∞

A wonderful climb in an exciting position. A lack of power in the centre will wean out the scrawnies; positive adventurous climbing will pay good rewards in the top half.

	Crux/bloc	Endurance	Sport
⑭	Bapaat connection*** 😎		5+
22m	● 5- ☀ 🔥 DIEDRE	5+ ☀ 🔥 Pump	∞11∞

Not long, quite steep, but a jug fest all the way - even with a blindfold you could still work this one out.

⑮	La Sirène en Pyjama*		6b
? m		☀ 🔥 DIEDRE 🌊	∞?∞

A dramatic corner with a few serious looking blocks!

⑯	Dévers et des Pas Mûrs*** 😎		7a-
28m	● 7a- ☀ 🔥 Bloc	6c ☀ 🔥 Pump	∞13∞

A full on fest of the beast from within you - or a 7c warm up! Start is no pushover, mid overhang needs commitment, top is a good fest.

⑰	Go up*** 😎		7b-
28m	○ 7b- ☀ 🔥 Bloc	6c ☀ 🔥 Pump	∞13∞

Power start - hard 7b bloc. Another 7b bloc move at the roof, but far easier - sensational position.

⑱	Vindiou*** 😎		7b-
28m	○ 7b- ☀ 🔥 Bloc	6c ☀ 🔥 Pump	∞?∞

Another silly hard start, plus problems at halfway.

⑲	2002 l'Epicier de l'Espace***		7a-
28m	● 7a- ☀ 🔥 Bloc	6b ☀ 🔥 Cool	

A monster roof to play on at the start; the rest is comfortable with jugs, and you don't see the bolts until you are level with them - requires positive attitude. (belay in hollow rock! - 2005)

Résumé. *This is the most impressive part to the whole of Baume Rousse, and has a concentrated cluster of hard routes that are of excellent quality. Tufa climbs are in abundance, plus a good selection of roof problems. The cove to the right looks a bit dank, but when you get halfway up, the position feels amazing. A real asset.*

Lovely sunny spot to be on a nice day.

30 metres

Secteur Hash 1 min

Secteur L'Eperon

Casque

P 7 min

Sidebar tabs: ST. JEAN · VAISON · 3 RIVIÈRES · SAINT LÉGER · VIC · BRUNOTS · ST. JULIEN · QUÉBEC · LOU PASSO · UBRIEUX · BM ROUSSE · BOURDONS · AIGUIER · MIÉVES · MÉVOUILLON · TOPOS

	Crux/bloc	Endurance	Sport

① La Reine des Bouses
- 18m | 2- | 2+ Fun | ○9○
- 31m | 3- | 3 Fun | ○19○

With 19 bolts, you have to be selective with your quick draws. Keeping to the right on the top section offers the best climbing.

② Tilt* — 3-
- 28m | | 2+ Pump | ○13○

A very nice route with a thumpy crux at the overhang - agile bridging.

③ Tartivore* — 3 & 5-
- ? m | 3 | 3 Fun | ○10○
- 19m | 5- Bloc | 2 | ○7○

A nice technical first pitch with bolts where you want them. Then a good o-hang to engage the arms, falling onto the belayer is common.

④ Fleur Bleue* — 4+
- 30m | 4- Cool | 4+ | ○13○

Some very good climbing, but very airy for a beginner. Good rests.

⑤ Handy-Cap Repos* — 3
- 28m | 3 | 3 Fun | ○10○

No shortage of juggy handholds, just keep looking for footholds.

⑥ Julie Quensand — 3
- 28m | 3- | 2 Fun | ○10○

Climbing to the 1st bolt is indeed the crux! A nice varied climb with lots of moves that require thought, but hardly represent problems.

⑦ Lolotte Glaciaire — 4 ?

⑧ Les Bandits — 4-
- 23m | 4- | 3+ 747 Fun | ○7○

Some nice moves in the 1st half, followed by easy slab above.

⑨ Pile Poil — 5 ?

⑩ Les Lézards — 4-
- 29m | 4- | 3 | ○10○

A good crackline to an energetic overlap on jugs. Beefy but simple. There is a pretty naff second pitch that also has a lot of loose stones, helmets for all in the area - best avoided.

⑪ Vielle Chenille* — 5-
- 29m | 5- Trick | 4 | ○12○

All the excitement is in the first half, plenty of technical moves on friction smears.

Résumé. A superb sector for lower grade climbers and anyone wanting a leisure days climbing. Most of the routes are very well equipped and sport fine incut holds. The polish on the rock is not too bad and doesn't affect the routes at all at present. A the top of the cliff is an easy angle so climbing the 2nd pitches is quite dull, and until there is a lot more traffic - is hazardous to those below from falling stones. Belay shade at the bottom of most routes.

LES BANDITS 4-, Baume Rousse; Yvorel Albane

L'EPERPON 1 6c-, Baume Rousse; Mark Glennie

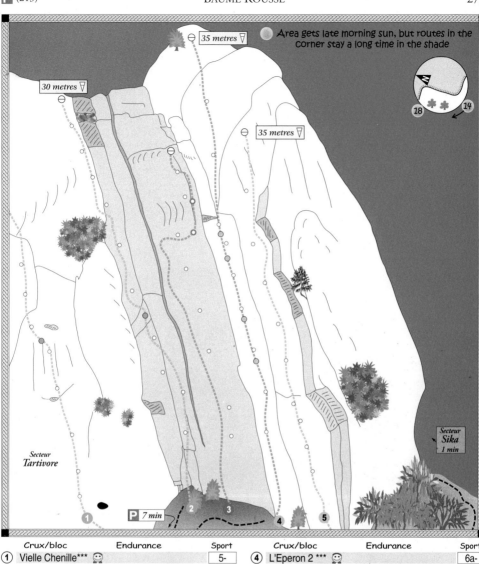

Area gets late morning sun, but routes in the corner stay a long time in the shade

35 metres

30 metres

35 metres

18 14

Secteur Sika 1 min

Secteur Tartivore

P 7 min

1 2 3 4 5

	Crux/bloc	Endurance	Sport

① Vielle Chenille* 😊   5-**

29m 5- Trick | 4 ⊘12

All the excitement is in the first half, plenty of technical moves on friction smears.

② Chou Roi pour Léa* 😊   5-**

30m 5- | 4+ DIEDRE Fab ⊘13

A very good route with only a single hard move, lovely all the way.

③ L'Eperon 1   6c-**

24m 6c- Bloc | 5 Cool ⊘9

A fiendish crux to read, making the onsight a real challenge; a route with a canny effect of getting the heart beating faster.

④ L'Eperon 2 * 😊   6a-**

35m 6a- | 5+ DIEDRE Pump ⊘11

An absolutely fab pitch. A few moves in the groove seem hard, but its just a matter of getting your balance sorted out. Final top slab still requires fingertip strength.

⑤ L'Eperon 3 * 😊   6a-**

35m 6a- | 6a DIEDRE ⊘? ⊘

No hard moves, but quite sustained. Only marginally harder than the groove - L'Eperon 2.

Résumé. A very good thin - but tall sector that keeps shade all morning. Lovely routes in a fantastic position that feel better than they look. Routes L'Eperon 2 and 3 are groove climbs, but you can have a lot of fun by top roping them, and climbing just as slabs - and is almost impossible in places.

L'EPERPON 2   6a-, Baume Rousse; Yvorel Albane

Full all day sun, starts to get shade on left after 4pm - very quick drying

35 metres ▽

Secteur
L'Eperon

Secteur
L'Eperon
1 min

P 8 min

	Crux/bloc	Endurance	Sport
①	**L'Eperon 3** *** ☺		⚡ 6a-
35m	6a- 💥	6a 💥 DIEDRE	○?○

No hard moves, but quite sustained. Only marginally harder than the groove - L'Eperon 2.

②	**Thorodin** ** ☺		⚡ 5-
35m	5- 💥	4+ **747** DIEDRE ←	○14○

A very good and striking corner, but then dubious hollow rock around the mid belay gives good moves, easy finish slab.

③	**Sikarate** *** ☺		⚡ 4+
31m	4- 🐟	4+ 💥 ←	○12○

A lovely slab climb with highly sustained grade 4 moves, very nicely bolted.

	Crux/bloc	Endurance	Sport
④	**Tyrex** *** ☺		⚡ 4
29m	4- **747** 👻	4 **747** COOl	○9○

A magnificent route with not many hard moves - but really spaced bolts. Definitely not for a novice who is unsteady.

⑤	**Douce Colère** *** ☺		⚡ 3
29m	3- COOl	3 💥	○14○

A lovely route with two definite crux's, you need good confidence and balance.

⑥	**Dou Dou** ** ☺		⚡ 4-
30m	4-	3-	○8○

A good start leads to very pleasant climbing in a lovely position.

Résumé. *This is the big slab round the corner. Very impressive and without too much hard climbing. It offers plenty of holds, but not everything, so it really does make a good challenge for a lot of low grade climbers. Nice views, good picnic area, just about ideal for a nice day out - very hot in summer!*

Murmoroa　-　Etoile　-　Gnocchi　-　Caraille　-　Haschisch　-　Tartivore　-　L'Eperon　-　Sikarate

SÉRIE NOIRE 7a- bloc, Les Bourdons; Carrie Atchison-Jones

The cliff of Les Bourdons, is not the largest cliff in the south of France - in fact, it's tiny. Yes, it's so small that you can hardly see it on the hillside above the town of Nyons. However, it is vertical and does have a nice selection of short routes in the lower grades. The position is pretty good for a semi urban crag, and the noise of Nyons below is more distant than invasive. The plus points are ease of access, only a couple of mins walk - and the bolting is very close together, making it an ideal spot for novices and less adventurous leaders. The climbs are short, and the limestone is of good granular texture with plenty of grip. This gives rise to very enjoyable climbing, both technically and mentally. The minus points are that it does attract local teaching groups, and with so little to go round, you might wish you chose somewhere else. Essentially, it is a crag that you want to know about, just for the single time when it will perfectly fit the bill. The town of Nyons looks of similar size to Vaison-la-Romaine on the map, but is a lot smaller and has a lot less restaurants and general shops. It still ia a fun place to visit however on a rest day, and it has a lovely old big square (set back to the east of the main roundabout), with cafés to hang out around and chill. You owe it to yourself to have a good time here. Access: Follow the map, but watch out for the one way roads. Road at the top is very steep.

Nyons - Les Bourdons

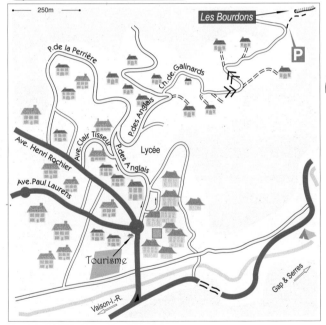

Camping Les Clos****
Route de Gap 84340
Tel: 04 75 26 29 90
www.campinglesclos.com
Open: (01-03/31-10)
115 places

Bars: Nyons in old town square
Shop: Nyons
Petrol Station: Nyons
Restaurant: Nyons
Supermarket: Nyons
Market day: Thurs-am;
Tourist Bureau: Centre roundabout

Notes: The tourist office here is
very good and publishes a good
brochure of what is on. The town
is famous for its olive oil, and
there are a couple of museums.
Also an archeological museum.

14 metres

	Crux/bloc	Endurance	Sport
(1)	?		6/7
4m			?

	Crux/bloc	Endurance	Sport
(2)	?		6/7
4m			?

| **(3)** | ? | | 6/7 |
| 5m | | | ? |

| **(4)** | ? | | 6/7 |
| 5m | | | ? |

| **(5)** Ganja* | | | 5- |
| 9m | 5- Bloc | 4 | 3 |

A steep start, and fun thereafter.

| **(6)** Bop* | | | 7a- |
| 4m | 7a- Sloper | | ? |

A fun boulder start before the bolt - best on a top rope - not hard.

	Crux/bloc	Endurance	Sport
(7) Xanadu*			6c-
10m	6c- Sloper	5-	4

A short and hard start, a real good tick onsight.

| **(8)** Tortilla*** | | | 6a- |
| 12m | 6a- | 5- | 4 |

Fun moves on big holds with a long reach in the middle.

| **(9)** Série Noire** | | | 7a- |
| 12m | 7a- CRIMP | 5- Cool | 4 |

Lovely small holds on the top wall, keeping the feet calm is essential.

| **(10)** Triomphe des bosses*** | | | 6c- |
| 13m | 6c- Bloc | 6b- G-d'eau | 3 |

A very good climb, easy to make the clips when you know the sequence, otherwise gets a bit gripping! Practise reduces grade a lot.

| **(11)** Fouchtri-Touchtra*** | | | 6b- |
| 13m | 6b- Bloc | 6a- | 4 |

Short, but lovely pockets all the way.

| **(12)** Extase*** | | | 6b- |
| 11m | 6b- Sloper | 6a- Pump | 4 |

Short, and lots of big pockets - except for one move.

Triomphe - Astra

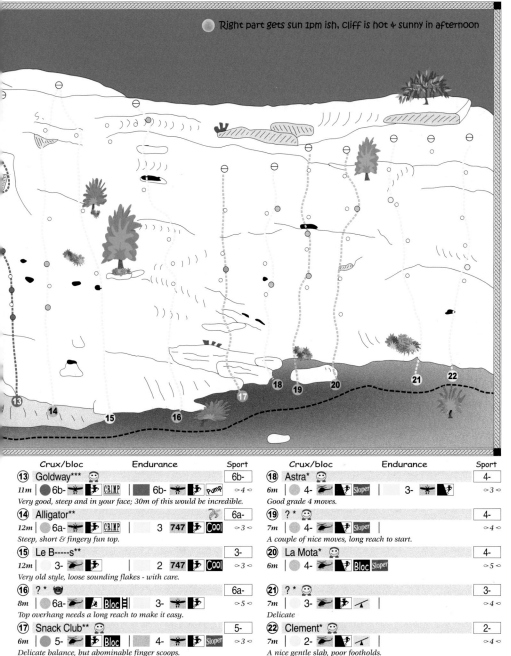

Right part gets sun 1pm ish, cliff is hot & sunny in afternoon

	Crux/bloc	Endurance	Sport
(13) Goldway* 😀			6b-
11m	6b- ☀ 🦎 CRIMP	6b- ☀ 🦎 Pump	◦4◦

Very good, steep and in your face; 30m of this would be incredible.

	Crux/bloc	Endurance	Sport
(14) Alligator*		🦎	6a-
12m	6a- ☀ 🦎 CRIMP	3 747 🦎 Cool	◦3◦

Steep, short & fingery fun top.

	Crux/bloc	Endurance	Sport
(15) Le B-----s*			3-
12m	3- 🦎 🦎	2 747 🦎 Cool	◦3◦

Very old style, loose sounding flakes - with care.

	Crux/bloc	Endurance	Sport
(16) ? * 😀			6a-
8m	6a- 🦎 🦎 Bloc	3- ☀ 🦎	◦5◦

Top overhang needs a long reach to make it easy.

	Crux/bloc	Endurance	Sport
(17) Snack Club* 😀			5-
6m	5- 🦎 🦎 Bloc	4- ☀ 🦎 Sloper	◦3◦

Delicate balance, but abominable finger scoops.

	Crux/bloc	Endurance	Sport
(18) Astra* 😀			4-
6m	4- 🦎 🦎 Sloper	3- 🦎	◦3◦

Good grade 4 moves.

	Crux/bloc	Endurance	Sport
(19) ? * 😀			4-
7m	4- 🦎 🦎 Sloper		◦4◦

A couple of nice moves, long reach to start.

	Crux/bloc	Endurance	Sport
(20) La Mota* 😀			4-
6m	4- 🦎 🦎 Bloc Sloper		◦5◦

	Crux/bloc	Endurance	Sport
(21) ? * 😀			3-
7m	3- 🦎 🦎 🪂		◦4◦

Delicate

	Crux/bloc	Endurance	Sport
(22) Clement* 😀			2-
7m	2- 🦎 🪂		◦4◦

A nice gentle slab, poor footholds.

Résumé. *One long sector with some very good climbing in the centre section. Plenty of room at the bottom to spread out and leave equipment. Some loose rock up high, but generally sound. Popular with groups.*

L'approche la plus sympathique pour cette zone est par la route qui mène au Col d'Ey en passant par Baume Rousse. Tout en haut de cette longue route sinueuse, il y a des tables de pique-nique offrant de jolies vues sur la vallée de l'Ennuye, la lavande et les abricotiers. Il faut bien fouiller l'horizon pour trouver les falaises, Aiguier reste cachée dans l'ombre matinale et Mieyes se cache juste sous la ligne d'horizon. Finalement, la falaise du rocher de l'Aiguier devient apparente juste derrière le hameau de Bellecombe Tarendol. Ce n'est pas une falaise qui convient aux groupes ou à une grande concentration de grimpeurs. Si quelqu'un grimpe sur la partie la plus haute, il est préférable de ne pas s'attarder en bas de la falaise du fait des chutes de pierres. Les voies sont soutenues et difficiles. Il est conseillé d'avoir un manche (clip stick) pour mettre les dégaines. La location est sensationnelle, les mouvements sont superbes mais il est difficile d'assurer confortablement. C'est une falaise facile d'accès avec en prime un joli bar avec terrasse situé tout près. Au contraire, Mieyes est loin de la route et nécessite de suivre un sentier pendant 3kms. La falaise est toute en dévers et de nombreux rochers sont prêts à tomber. Certaines sections sont superbes et d'excellente qualité et les vues et la location sont imprenables. Si vous vous sentez extrêmement fort, c'est l'endroit parfait pour grimper.

Bellecombe-Tarendol - Rocher de l'Aiguier

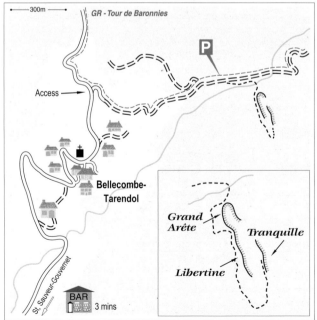

⌂ La Ferme des Argensolles
St. Sauveur-Gouvernet
Tel: 04 75 27 32 77
Notes: Very small farm site.
Open: (01-04/30-09)
14 places

⌂ Camping Municipal Les Cigales
Sainte Jalle
Tel: 04 75 27 34 88
Notes: Small quiet site in village
Open: (01-05/30-9)
33 places

Bars: St.Sauveur-G, Sainte Jalle
Shop: Sainte Jalle
Petrol Station: ?
Restaurant: Sainte Jalle
Supermarket: Nyons

Access: Make sure you take the 2nd track on the right after coming out of the village. This track is used by farmers tending vineyards regularly, so drive with care and expect a tractor round each bend. Park in the area where the hillside has been cut out. Path is obvious to river.

Rocher de L'Aiguier

A lovely way to approach this area is by taking the road up to Col d'Ey past Baume Rousse. At the top of this long and winding road, there are some nice picnic tables on the northern side of the col, and where you can look over the l'Ennuye valley, with its rich treasure of apricots and lavender. The village of Sainte Jalle is down to the left, and an ideal respite should you picnic hamper be a bit on the lightweight side. At most times of the year, you can smell the lavender fields as you drift along in your open top Alfa-spyder. You have to scour the horizon in search of any cliffs; clandestinely, Aiguier remains hidden in the shade of morning, and Mieyes hides just under the skyline up to the right. Eventually the cliff of Rocher de L'Aiguier becomes apparent behind the small hamlet of Bellecome Tarendol, a tiny village by any standards. After leaving the hamlet, take care to find the correct track, 2nd, and it leads to a small dug out area with limited parking just past the vineyards. It isn't a crag that suits many people climbing at the same time, and especially groups. If there are any climbers on the top tier, it is best to leave immediately since loose stones are very likely to come down and give you big grief. The walls look flat and highly sustained – they are! If you are bad at wall climbing, you might have a bad time here – you certainly will! Having a long clip stick could be a handy thing – yup! It is a sensational location, wonderful climbing position, fine moves; but the belaying is a pain, and it's a highly uncomfortable picnic spot – except the top tier. It is a handy crag to drive to, and has a lovely bar with terrace, only a short drive back down the road. Mieyes on the other hand, is a full bore - off road crag, some 3 km up a pretty gnarly dirt track. Its overhanging nature and climbing style has the subtlety of a tank pressing wild flowers, and has more than its fair share of brittle rock. Some sections are stunning and of high quality, and the views and location are admittedly - incredible. It's great when you are feeling humungously strong, a completely jingo style day out.

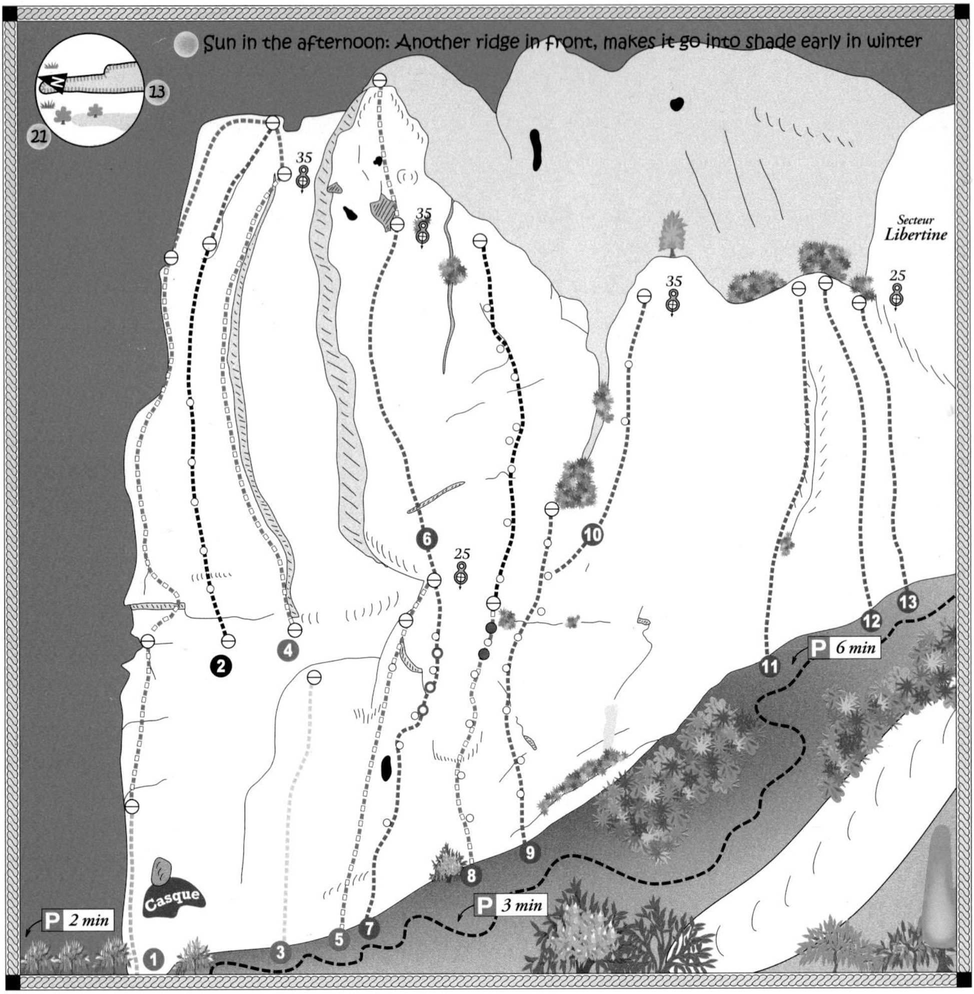

Sun in the afternoon: Another ridge in front, makes it go into shade early in winter

13

21

35

35

35

Secteur *Libertine*

25

6

25

10

12

13

11

P 6 min

2

4

9

8

P 3 min

1

Casque

3

5

7

P 2 min

	Crux/bloc	Endurance	Sport
(1)	Grande Arête*** 😊		6c-
? m		🏃 ☕ COOl	∞?∞

A highly stunning arête in an incredible position.

(2)	Maravilla		7c
(3)	Le Sas*		6a-
(4)	Dulf**	DIEDRE	6c
(5)	L'Eau de Là*		6c-
(6)	L'Haut de Là***		7b-
(7)	Ascensur pour le plasir***		7b

31m | ⭕ 7b ☀ 🏃 Pump | 🟥 7a ☀ 🏃 COOl | ∞6∞

Rather pleasant for a while, then excruciatingly fingery. The only thing obvious about the holds - is the lack of! - sequence.

	Crux/bloc	Endurance	Sport
(8)	Hard Saga*** 😊		7c
? m		COOl	∞?∞

Very well named; big saga, falling saga, retreating saga, scary saga - you get the gist don't you!

(9)	Mat**		7a
(10)	Petit Roque***		7a
(11)	Rêve de crémallière***	DIEDRE	7a
(12)	Ultime limite***		7a
(13)	Nouvelles données***		7a

Résumé. This part of the cliff has some of the best routes in the whole area, not for the faint hearted. Lower pitches are fun, whilst the top sections are completely out there in space. The arête is very out there and with some loose rock on - go carefully, not too hard but very committing and for cool heads only. Routes here feel hard for there grade.
(bottom of the face gets a lot of shade in winter - top is always sunny)

Tranquille

Grand Arête   -   Libertine

Secteur Grand Arête, Rocher de l'Aiguier

ELLE EST DOUCE 7a, Aiguier; Mark Glennie (photo Libertine, page 3)

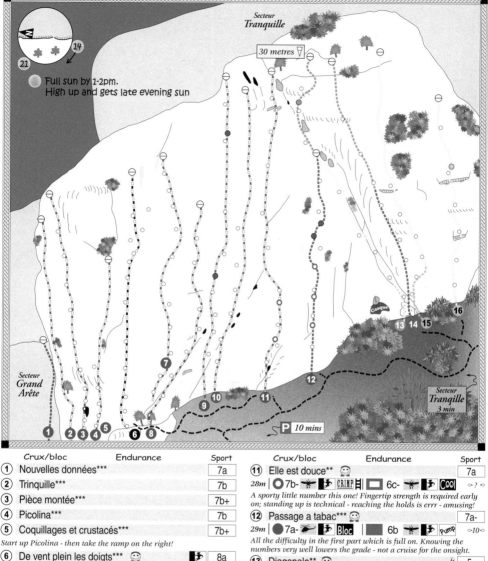

Secteur *Tranquille*

30 metres

Full sun by 1-2pm.
High up and gets late evening sun

Secteur *Grand Arête*

P 10 mins

Secteur *Tranquille* 3 min

	Crux/bloc	Endurance	Sport
1	Nouvelles données***		7a
2	Trinquille***		7b
3	Pièce montée***		7b+
4	Picolina***		7b
5	Coquillages et crustacés***		7b+

Start up Picolina - then take the ramp on the right!

	Crux/bloc	Endurance	Sport
6	De vent plein les doigts***		8a
7	Panettone***		7b+
8	Court message***		7b
9	Libertine***		6c++

? m | 7a- Pump | 6c++ Cool ∘9∘

A full on epic adventure. Two full on bloc 7a moves (not 7b), that come at you when you are completely pumped. Amazingly good holds in general though. One of the hardest 6c's in the area!

	Crux/bloc	Endurance	Sport
10	Passage aux aveux***		6c+

Résumé. *A very impressive sector with some tremendous vertical wall climbing. Tight fitting shoes are essential - plus very pump resistant forearms.*
Warning: Loose stones above - avoid if top tier is busy.

	Crux/bloc	Endurance	Sport
11	Elle est douce**		7a

28m | 7b- CRIMP | 6c- Cool ∘?∘

A sporty little number this one! Fingertip strength is required early on; standing up is technical - reaching the holds is err - amusing!

	Crux/bloc	Endurance	Sport
12	Passage a tabac***		7a-

29m | 7a- Bloc | 6b Pump ∘10∘

All the difficulty in the first part which is full on. Knowing the numbers very well lowers the grade - not a cruise for the onsight.

	Crux/bloc	Endurance	Sport
13	Diagonale**		5-

27m | 5- Yum | 3 DIEDRE Cool ∘8∘

A broken first half with loose stones. Stepping right onto the final headwall is superb and in a lovely position.

	Crux/bloc	Endurance	Sport
14	La buchrie*		6b

29m | 6b Pump | 5 ∘10∘

A short hard section that will test anyone lacking fitness.

	Crux/bloc	Endurance	Sport
15	Les trois sœurs***		5

? m | 6a- Bloc | 3+ 747 ∘?∘

It's all in the start, then a doddle.

	Crux/bloc	Endurance	Sport
16	Arostiche**		5

17m | 4- Bloc | 3+ 747 Pump ∘6∘

A lovely short route that should prove fun for anybody.

| Grand Arête | - | Libertine | | Tranquille |

ST. JEAN
VAISON
3 RIVIÈRES
SAINT LÉGER
VIC
BRUNOTS
ST JULIEN
QUEBEC
LOU PASSO
UBRIEUX
BM-ROUSSE
BOURDONS
AIGUIER
MIEVES
MÉVOUILLON
TOPOS

Full afternoon sun
Very high up and gets late evening sun

13

21

16 metres ▽

9
10
11

8

7

6

Secteur
Libertine
2 min

P 12 min

5

3
4

1
2

	Crux/bloc	Endurance	Sport

① Rataillon*** — 6b

② Quignan*** — 6a

③ Désaccord Mineur*** ☺ — 6c-

16m ○ 6c- ✺ 🐾 CRIMP | 6b- ✺ 🐾 Pump ∽5∽

A classic orange crimpy wall with poor footholds. Be aware of the birds nest at the top.

④ Sulmona*** ☺ — 6b-

15m ● 6b- ✺ 🐾 Pump | 6a ✺ 🐾 O— ∽6∽

This completely blank wall has an amazing amount of good foot holds. Feels a lot longer than 15m.

⑤ Des Bourgeons Plein les Poches*** ☺ ⚡ — 6b-

14m ● 6b- ✺ 🐾 Pump | 6a ✺ 🐾 Cool ∽5∽

A good route of 2 halves, comfortable to the 3rd bolt, thereafter the footholds become invisible, as the pumped forearms become distinctly visible.

⑥ Vol d'Autochtones*** ☺ ⚡ — 6a

15m ● 6a- ✺ 🐾 | 6a ✺ 🐾 Pump ∽5∽

A very sustained route that will pump solid most 6a leaders; bridging for the feet is essential.

⑦ Pas Si Tranquille*** ☺ — ⚡ 5

16m ● 5- ✺ 🐾 | 5 ✺ 🐾 Pump ∽6∽

A classic route of lovely holds in a fabulous position. Sustained with no hard moves.

⑧ L'Heure Folle** ☺ — 6b-

16m ● 6b- ✺ 🚀 ℤ | 5- 747 🐾 Cool ∽4∽

Good jugs take plenty of finding on this highly rivuleted rock. The crux is hard for the grade and demands a powerful approach. Shorties may have difficulty.

⑨ Relance et Croise** ☺ — 6c-

13m ○ 6c- ✺ 🚀 Bloc | 5- ✺ 🐾 Cool ∽4∽

A funny climb that involves a full on crux, then tactical left drifting ensures a succession of giant holds. Top run out is long but steady. (Crux is either crimps for the short, or a long reach - mid size climbers; er!! good luck!).

⑩ La Cerise — ?

Lovely looking rock, but the holds keep sending you left or right.

⑪ Local Roc*** ☺ — ⚡ 6a-

12m ● 6a- ✺ 🐾 🧗 | 3 747 🐾 Fun ∽3∽

The first short wall that you come to on the top tier, just left of the tiny corner. Climbing the wall without the corner is best and keeps the climb nice and interesting. Not strenuous.

Résumé. *A small but superb top tier of fantastic climbing. The views are worth the exhausting walk up here. Make sure you are attached to the rock at the base of the climbs! Definitely not the place for kids or anyone out of control! It's also a long hike down to the car, so bring the picnic up here with you.*
Warning: Climbers may be below so do not kick stones down.

Tranquille

Grand Arête   -   Libertine

SULMONA 6b-, Aiguier; Jim Bacon

Lavender fields of the l'Ennuye valley above Sainte-Jalle

Col de Bodon - Mieyes

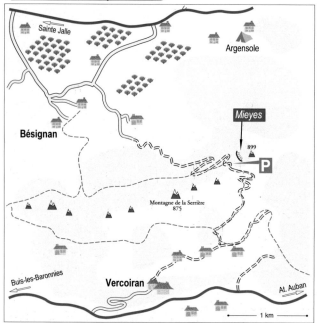

⛺ *La Ferme des Argensolles*
St. Sauveur-Gouvernet
Tel: 04 75 27 32 77
Notes: Very small farm site.
Open: (01-04/30-09)
14 places

⛺ *Camping Municipal Les Cigales*
Sainte Jalle
Tel: 04 75 27 34 88
Notes: Small quiet site in village
Open: (01-05/30-9)
33 places

💼 *Bars: St.Sauveur-G, Sainte Jalle*
Shop: Sainte Jalle
Petrol Station: ?
Restaurant: Sainte Jalle
Supermarket: Nyons

Access: Approach from the north for least car damage. Road is long but is at a reasonable angle and relatively flat - except for the top part which is interesting! Parking for a few cars at the col, then a path leads along the ridge, go left after 5 mins.

LARME DE TAILLE 7b-, Mieyes; Steve Glennie

LARME DE TAILLE 7b-, Mieyes; Mark Glennie

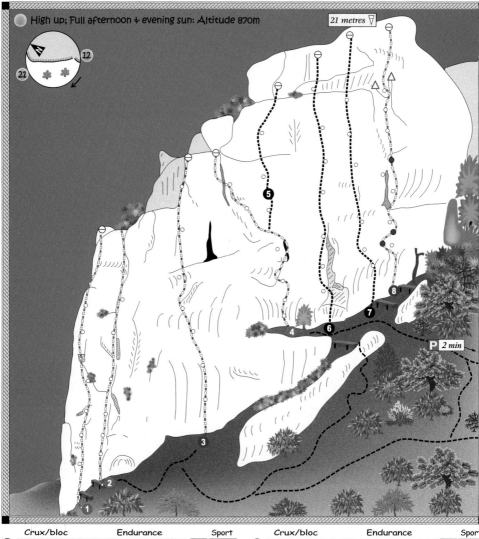

High up; Full afternoon & evening sun: Altitude 870m

21 metres

	Crux/bloc	Endurance	Sport
1	L'essence de l'avis**		6c+
2	L'eau racle**		6c
3	Bon aplati		7b+
4	Larme de taille**		7b-

15m | 7b- | 6c | ∞5∞

Short, sharp and full on for 6 moves. Footholds keep coming off so grade might even get a bit harder, already close to 7c-

	Crux/bloc	Endurance	Sport
5	Patchwork***		7c

19m | 7c- | 7b | ∞6∞

Ideal for those climbers falling asleep on the easy section of Larme.

	Crux/bloc	Endurance	Sport
6	Toucouleur***		7c+
7	Cicatrice**	CRIMP	7c
8	Rose de Thuringe*		7a-

21m | 7a- | 6c- | ∞7∞

Several big spans to link the first section. Middle is still hard but good. Top is abominable, loose and dangerous.

Résumé. *A very isolated crag in a very, very quiet position. The rock quality is not brilliant and you are likely to pull off a few holds, especially since you will need to be quite strong to operate here. Routes are not that long, but lowering off is amusing and safer with a 60m rope. Slope at the bottom makes belaying rather tiresome. Routes worth doing, but not repeating. Nearby parking is lovely for a picnic though.*

Toucouleur

ST. JEAN | VAISON | 3 RIVIÈRES | SAINT LÉGER | VIC | BRUNOTS | ST. JULIEN | QUEBEC | LOU PASSO | UBRIEUX | BM-ROUSSE | BOURDONS | AIGUIER | MIEYES | MÉVOUILLON | TOPOS

ARIELLE ET JOHANNA 6c+, Mévouillon Ouest; Steve Glennie

C'est l'une des falaises les plus isolées située à 1100m d'altitude. Depuis Buis-les-Baronnies, vous passez les oliviers, puis les chênes, les sapins et enfin arrivez à un plateau. Vous serez très impressionné lorsque vous verrez les falaises pour la première fois cependant si vous arrivez le matin de bonne heure dans les nuages, vous risquez de ne pas les voir. Même si vous ne souhaitez pas grimper, la route qui mène à la falaise est exceptionnelle et les randonnées sont merveilleuses, très isolées et donc très calmes. De là, vous pouvez toujours voir le Mont Ventoux. La colline de Mévouillon se dresse très fière au milieu du paysage et offre des voies sur ses deux versants. L'accès doit être bien respecté. Un accord a été signé par la FFME pour que l'escalade se développe peu. Rappelez-vous que les personnes qui vivent à cet endroit recherchent le calme et la solitude, donc venez en petit nombre (pas de groupes, ni de clubs), garez-vous avec considération et soyez discret. Le côté droit du versant est hors limite cependant il est impératif de ne grimper que sur les voies équipées. Le climat à cette altitude est très différent mais la face est en général protégée du Mistral et il est donc très agréable d'y grimper sous le soleil matinal. La face ouest est très abrupte et très froide, à tout moment de la journée sauf durant les après-midi ensoleillées. En tant que site d'escalade, il est idéal pour ceux qui aiment grimper dans une jolie location et pour ceux qui apprécient de faire une longue marche pour arriver à la falaise.

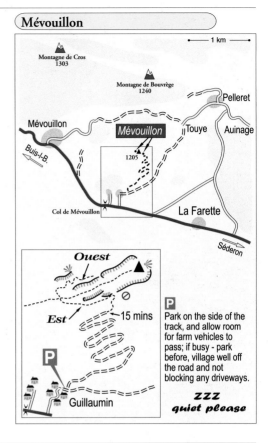

Mévouillon

← 1 km →

Montagne de Cros 1303

Montagne de Bouvrège 1240

Pelleret

Mévouillon

Mévouillon

Touye   Auinage

Buis-l-B.

1205

Col de Mévouillon

La Farette

Séderon

Ouest

Est ← 15 mins

P Park on the side of the track, and allow room for farm vehicles to pass; if busy - park before, village well off the road and not blocking any driveways.

zzz quiet please

P

Guillaumin

This is one of the most remote cliffs included in this book, and situated very high up at 1100m altitude. The drive up from Buis-les-Baronnies is uphill all the way and really feels it; the scenery changing from low scrub with olive trees, to oak trees, alpine gorges, then fir trees, and eventually up onto an open plateau. Seeing the cliffs for the first time will surely be an impressive experience, however, I have arrived up here in early morning cloud with no clue where the mountain was at all! I have also left the lower valleys in cloud on some occasions with big weather doubts, only to arrive up at Mévouillon on the edge of the weather front, and be in sunshine all day. Even if you don't fancy climbing, the drive up to this area is exceptional, and the walking is lovely in really remote and quiet countryside. You haven't gone far enough to escape the fine views of Mont Ventoux and still feel attached to the whole area, even though the climate/temperature is likely to be vastly different. The hill of Mévouillon stands proud of the landscape, and has climbing on both sides. Access here must be highly respected. An agreement has been made with the FFME to keep climbing here to a minimum. Please remember that anyone choosing to live here, does so because they want to live in peace, quiet and solitude; so please come in small numbers (no groups or clubs), park very considerately, and go about your day discretely, and leave no traces. The right hand side of the east face is clearly out of bounds, and please only climb on the equipped routes. The climate at this altitude is vastly different, but the east face is generally protected from the Mistral wind, and is delightful in early morning sunshine. The west face is alarmingly steep, and ice cold at any other time than a summers afternoon. As a climbing venue, it is small and suited for those who like a good situation with a long walk to the cliff, rather than flowing climbing moves.

PETER PAN 7b+, Mévouillon Ouest; Steve Glennie

Views of Mont Ventoux from the summit of Mévouillon

Mévouillon Ouest from the village of Mévouillon

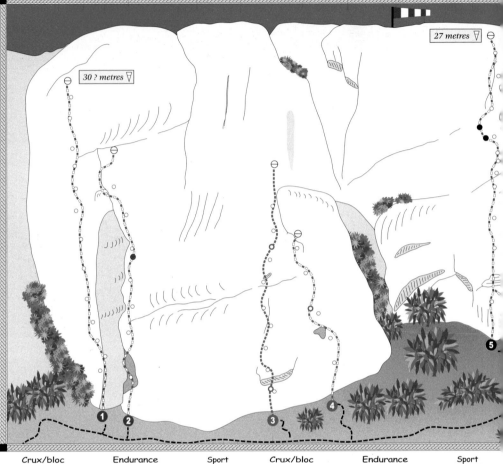

30 ? metres

27 metres

	Crux/bloc	Endurance	Sport
①	**Ou s'en vent***		7b+
②	**Arielle et Johanna***		6c+

21m 7a- | 6c+ DIEDRE Pump ⟜7⟜

A really imposing line in a fabulous position. Full on, all the way to the top - a classic.

Résumé. *The left side has climbing on the lower tier of this semi giant wall - the really giant wall to the far left has not been equipped yet but looks high grade 8 territory. This wall has some very good routes. The limestone is very coarse and feels just like sandstone. Good friction but holds might break. Steeper than it looks, and routes harder than they look. Views are incredible and gets nice warm afternoon sunshine.*

	Crux/bloc	Endurance	Sport
③	**Hyppolène***		6c-

20m 6c- Bloc 6b+ Pump ⟜8⟜

This is a route where 20 metres seems a very long way. A 6c start easily gets you to the overhang. The top crack past the 6th bolt feels like 7a if you are tired.

④	**Jaffar***		6c

12m 6c 6c Pump ⟜6⟜

Not a long route, but sustained and constantly brutal, plus awkward clips - not ideal for lower grade climbers.

⑤	**Peter Pan***		7b+

27m 7c- Bloc 7b Pump ⟜11⟜

A splendid route for those with a good long reach. Nice sustained climbing but with a definite crux - a clip stick can be useful.

Arielle - Pirate   Orphys - Puision

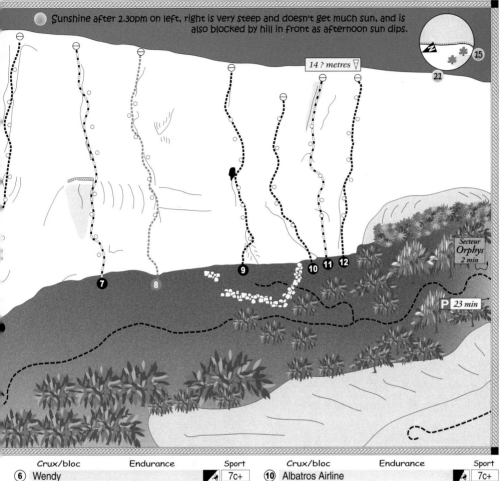

Sunshine after 2.30pm on left, right is very steep and doesn't get much sun, and is also blocked by hill in front as afternoon sun dips.

14 ? metres

15

21

Secteur Orphys 2 min

P 23 min

ST. JEAN
VAISON
3 RIVIÈRES
SAINT LÉGER
VIC
BRUNOTS
ST. JULIEN
QUEBEC
LOU PASSO
UBRIEUX
BM-ROUSSE
BOURDONS
AIGUIER
MIEYES
MÉVOUILLON
TOPOS

	Crux/bloc	Endurance		Sport
(6)	Wendy			7c+
(7)	La maison de Robinson			8a+
(8)	Le petit lutin larcineur	⊙		8b ?
(9)	Mickey Mür			8a+

	Crux/bloc	Endurance		Sport
(10)	Albatros Airline			7c+
(11)	Pirate			8a
(12)	Fantasia			7c

Résumé. *The right side of this section is very steep and devoid of normal - useful sized holds. Very bloc style involving power and egyptians. Stays pretty cool in the morning and looses sun quite early as it is enclosed in a small bay tucked into the top of the hill. (No nice views for the belayer, and is often cold, chilly and breezy - best not to volunteer unless its a heatwave)*

ST.JEAN · VAISON · 3 RIVIÈRES · SAINT LÉGER · VIC · BRUNOTS · ST.JULIEN · QUEBEC · LOU PASSO · UBRIEUX · BM-ROUSSE · BOURDONS · AIGUIER · MIEYES · MÉVOUILLON · TOPOS

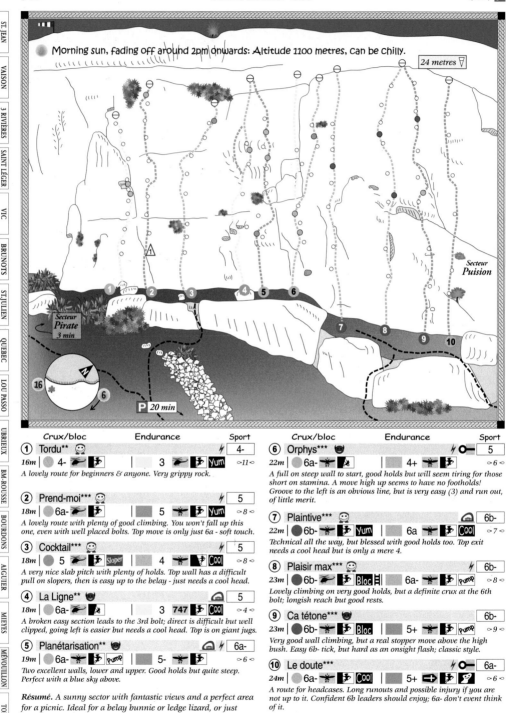

Morning sun, fading off around 2pm onwards: Altitude 1100 metres, can be chilly.

24 metres

Secteur Puision

Secteur Pirate 3 min

P 20 min

Crux/bloc — Endurance — Sport

① Tordu**   4-
16m | 4- | 3 | Yum | ◦11◦

A lovely route for beginners & anyone. Very grippy rock.

② Prend-moi***   5
18m | 6a- | 5 | Yum | ◦8◦

A lovely route with plenty of good climbing. You won't fall up this one, even with well placed bolts. Top move is only just 6a - soft touch.

③ Cocktail***   5
18m | 5 | Sloper | 4 | Cool | ◦8◦

A very nice slab pitch with plenty of holds. Top wall has a difficult pull on slopers, then easy up to the belay - just needs a cool head.

④ La Ligne**   5
18m | 6a- | 3 | 747 | Cool | ◦4◦

A broken easy section leads to the 3rd bolt; direct is difficult but well clipped, going left is easier but needs a cool head. Top is on giant jugs.

⑤ Planétarisation**   6a-
19m | 6a- | Pump | 5- | ◦6◦

Two excellent walls, lower and upper. Good holds but quite steep. Perfect with a blue sky above.

Résumé. A sunny sector with fantastic views and a perfect area for a picnic. Ideal for a belay bunnie or ledge lizard, or just reading a book. Climbing is good too. Molasses limestone with gritty texture, pocketed and pumpy.

Crux/bloc — Endurance — Sport

⑥ Orphys***   5
22m | 6a- | 4+ | ◦6◦

A full on steep wall to start, good holds but will seem tiring for those short on stamina. A move high up seems to have no footholds! Groove to the left is an obvious line, but is very easy (3) and run out, of little merit.

⑦ Plaintive***   6b-
22m | 6b- | Yum | 6a | Cool | ◦7◦

Technical all the way, but blessed with good holds too. Top exit needs a cool head but is only a mere 4.

⑧ Plaisir max***   6b-
23m | 6b- | Bloc | 6a- | Pump | ◦8◦

Lovely climbing on very good holds, but a definite crux at the 6th bolt; longish reach but good rests.

⑨ Ca tétone***   6b-
23m | 6b- | Bloc | 5+ | Pump | ◦9◦

Very good wall climbing, but a real stopper move above the high bush. Easy 6b- tick, but hard as an onsight flash; classic style.

⑩ Le doute***   6a-
24m | 6a- | Cool | 5+ | ◦6◦

A route for headcases. Long runouts and possible injury if you are not up to it. Confident 6b leaders should enjoy; 6a- don't event think of it.

Arielle - Pirate   Orphys - Puision

LA LIGNE 5, Mévouillon Est; Carrie Atchison-Jones

PAS NICK 6b-, Mévouillon Est; David Atchison-Jones

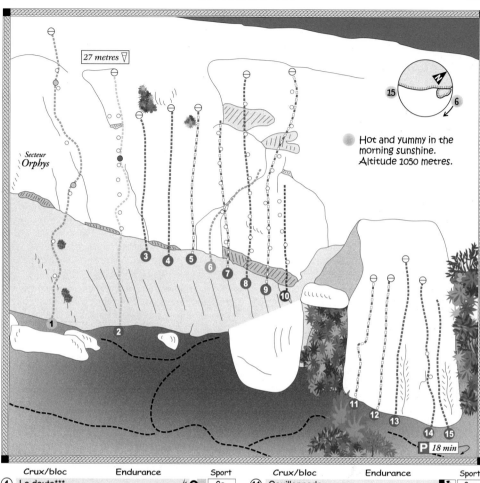

27 metres

Secteur Orphys

Hot and yummy in the morning sunshine. Altitude 1050 metres.

P 18 min

St Jean · Vaison · 3 Rivières · Saint Léger · Vic · Brunots · St Julien · Quebec · Lou Passo · Ubrieux · BM-Rousse · Bourdons · Aiguier · Mieyes · Mévouillon · Topos

		Crux/bloc	Endurance	Sport
①	Le doute***	⚡ ⊶		6a-

24m | 6a- 💀 🐾 COOL | 5+ ➡️ 🐾 ∽6 ∽

A route for headcases. Long runouts and possible injury if you are not up to it. Confident 6b leaders should enjoy; 6a- don't event think of it.

		Crux/bloc	Endurance	Sport
②	Pas Nick*** 🙂		⚡	6b-

27m | 6b- 🐾 Pump | 6a+ 💥 🔪 🏃 ∽8 ∽

A tremendous pitch that is full on all the way. Crux is very soft 6b, but feels desperate when you are pumped. Top wall is easy but airy!!

③	Douce extase		🐾	6b
④	Subliminal		🐾	6b+
⑤	Pulsation		🐾	6c
⑥	Dichotomique		🐾	5
⑦	Aérofrein		🐾	6c
⑧	Doux frisson		🐾	6b+
⑨	Puision		🐾	6c
⑩	?		🐾	7a

		Crux/bloc	Endurance	Sport
⑪	Couillonnade		🐾	6c+
⑫	Que de Trous		🐾	6c
⑬	Cartésienne		🐾	6b+
⑭	Cupuloman		🐾	6b+
⑮	Burlesque		🐾	6b

Résumé. Two very good sectors indeed. Steep and strenuous on the left, but reasonable for onsight climbing. The small buttress of Burlesque is very classic molasses limestone pockets in their thousands. Finding the correct pockets first time is almost impossible. Grades for this section only apply if you know the climbs like the back of your hand.

Both parts of this cliff are protected from the mistral wind and get lovely warm morning sunshine. In summer however, even the high altitude doesn't make much difference, it roasts - nice in the afternoon though.

There are 52 cliffs at present equipped in the Mont Ventoux region. We do not include 17 of these for a variety of reasons, but have included them here so you at least know generally what else is out there. There are also plenty of more cliffs in the Buis area that await development; such as the Renard overlooking Fontaine d'Annibal, the cliffs above La Roche-sur-le-Buis, the giant ridges also before Rocher Brunots and beyond Baume Rousse; and the massive continuation of Ubrieux. To the north west you also have the excellent new development of Pont-de-Baret, and on to Saou. There are also some esoteric cliffs to the north east & hidden in the forests of Rémuzat, plus plenty of scruffy rock on the way to Serres.

MALAVAL: See page 23 Gorges de la Nesque
BELVEDERE: See page 23 Gorges de la Nesque
VAULONGUE: This valley has plenty of tottering rock. A few sections (20-25m) on the side of the road have been recently equipped. The centre section of limestone is very good and offers 6c-7a bloc style moves that are difficult to read and onsight. The base is sloping and awkward, and the top third is really shattered. Setting lower offs much lower down might have been preferable. So much rock came down when we climbed there, that we were very lucky to escape without very serious injury!

GRAND MONTMIRAIL: An old sector of the Dentelles that faces North East, terrain adventure.
CLAPIS NORD: The north side of the Chaîne du Clapis does have some very good routes, but the rock is far smoother and offers very little to grip. Definitely worth investigating for something different if you climb 7a-b, confidently.
CLAPIS CENTRE: This is the big wave on the front of the cliff with 80 single pitch routes of 7a upwards. A magnificent climbing area and popular with the local hot shots. Like Céüse, but without the walk.
GRAND MURAILLE: This is the giant cliff to the right of the main Dentelles sector. There is a bird restriction for this cliff, but you can climb here 2nd September though till the end of February, which is when the weather is ideally temperate and warm. Lots of routes up to 3 pitches. Not really fully developed, demands good positive attitude.
CASCADE: A very impressive bay of rock up to 70m high. Suits three sorts of climber; the 7c addict who can really crank (20 routes), the mid grade climber who likes steep routes with pretty good holds (5 routes), and the beginner who likes very short diddy routes (10 routes).

Chaîne-du-Gigondas, gauche - secteur Pousterle

Saint Christophe

looks excellent; the climbing is on the large cliff to the side. The rock is very fractured and lumps have fallen off here big time. The top tower is ready to go at any time! The climbing is actually very good and all the moves tend to be excellent, especially on some 7a-b bloc style routes on the left. You certainly take a risk here. A few small routes low down to the right that are ideal for first time climbers. Very quick access and morning shade.

SAINT JULIEN: I only include a very small taster of this giant cliff. Over 200 pitches all over the place. There is also some climbing on the north face, but this is very steep and will take a while to develop as access is problematic.

PELLERET: A few lovely looking cliffs but we were short of time and did not know the correct access; didn't explore – just had a lovely picnic instead, very tranquil.

SAINT CHRISTOPHE: We only include the west face as a taster. The east face is 7a-b super climbing on 30m routes of fantastic quality. The NW face is being developed for the harder climber with stunning lines; and there is an easy area right up the top to the NW with 8 routes of negligible difficulty and non-negligible polish.

GIGONDAS FACE SUD: A couple of cliffs 25-35m high with around 30 routes, just through the gap at Aig.Lagarde. Nice and sunny, well suited to the mid grade climber.

GIGONDAS POUSTERLE: A huge sector of the north face of the Chaîne-du-Gigondas. A lot of adventure routes, and smooth rock to test any climber of the 7a and upwards category. A lot of old and slippery diedre's, plus some mentally testing lines – a fantastic area but not for the faint hearted.

LES FLORETS: Stacks more climbing, adventure style on rock with loosish attitude.

VAGUE D'ETRAVE: 30m cliff, south facing and popular with beginners.

ROCHER DU CAYRON: 30 routes around 7a in the steep and in your face category. Keeps warm and worth investigating.

MONTBRUN-LES-BAINS: A very small cliff that was equipped, but now has a roadworks yard up against the cliff. A lost cliff that was suited to kids for the first time out, and that's about it.

PLAISIANS: A small gorge of rock that the road goes through. The gorge itself has no climbing but the rock

Plaisians

SPORT 3- **UK·TECH·3**	FLYING BUTTRESS, top crux; Stanage (easy)	LITTLE CHAMONIX, Shepherds Crag (mid)
	ARROW ROUTE, Cioch, Skye (easy)	SMOOTH CHIMNEY, Harrisons (mid)
	FLYING BUTTRESS, top crack, Cromlech (mid)	ORANGE 54 CAROLINE, Dame Jouanne (hard)
SPORT 4- **UK·TECH·4a**	BLACK HAWK HELL CRACK, crux, Stanage	CRACK AND CAVE, groove; Harrisons
	CHRISTMAS CURRY, Tremadoc	TENNIS SHOE; Idwal slabs
	TOPHET WALL, overlap crux; Napes	ORANGE 2, highball, Potala
SPORT 5- **UK·TECH·4b**	HELL WALL, top crux; Harrison's Rocks (easy)	ROCKING CHAIR, Gribbin (mid)
	BLUE SKY, Saddle Head, Pembroke (easy)	ORANGE 39, groove, Canard-aux-Merciers
	HEATHER WALL, 1st two moves; Stanage	GREAT WESTERN, most moves (hard)
SPORT 6a- **UK·TECH·5a**	VALKRIE, top step up - going left; Froggatt (easy)	QUEERSVILLE 3 crux's - all 5a; Stanage (mid)
	MESHACH, wall peg move; Tremadoc (easy)	BLUE 43 Last prob, La Roche-aux-Sabots (mid)
	PIGS NOSE, top crux; Bowles Rocks	THE FANG, either crux, Tremadoc (hard)
SPORT 6b- **UK·TECH·5b**	LEFT UNCONQUERABLE, m-at 2/3rds ht; Stanage	STRAPIOMBANTE, top moves Froggatt (mid)
	DIADIC, top crux-vector; Tremadoc (easy)	ORANGE 26, highball; Apremont (hard)
	UNCLIMBED WALL, paw move; Harrisons	BROWNS ELIMINATE, Froggatt (hard)
SPORT 6c- **UK·TECH·5c**	VECTOR, slab move; Tremadoc (easy)	TIME FOR TEA, top wall; Millstone (mid)
	FERN HILL, 1st crux; Cratcliffe (easy-mid)	DEAD BANANA CRACK, Stoney Middleton (H)
	CENOTAPH CORNER, top crux; Cromlech	ECTOPLASME, classic wall at 95.2 (top end)
SPORT 7a- **UK·TECH·6a**	THE KNOCK, Burbage (easy)	CONSENTING ADULTS, any crux; Malham
	HATE, wall pull or shelf mantle; Bowles Rocks	OLD FRIENDS, either crux; Stanage
	BLUE 23 Last prob-mantle, Diplodocus	BLACK KABUL, mid crux, Stoney Middleton
SPORT 7b- **UK·TECH·6a+**	SOSSBLITZ, lower crux; Harrisons Rocks (easy)	SARDINE, mid crux; Ravens Tor (mid)
	DOWNHILL RACER, mid cruxs; Froggatt (easy)	DOMANITRIX, crux; Kilnsey
	OUR FATHER, start, Stoney Middleton (mid)	RED TOIT, classic roof at Cul de Chien (hard)
SPORT 7c- **UK·TECH·6b**	PROPHET OF DOOM, Curbar (easy)	NEW DAWN, each of low 3 cruxs; Malham
	WHITE WALL, Millstone (mid)	COMEDY, mid crux, Kilnsey
	WOOLY BEAR, mid crux; Harrisons Rocks	EL POUSSAH, Isatis (hard)
SPORT 8a- **UK·TECH·6c**	DELIVERANCE, Stanage (easy)	DANGEROUS BROS, going right, Rubicon
	MECCA, low crux; Ravens Tor (easy)	BERENZINA, Bas Cuvier (mid)
	WEST SIDE STORY, Curbar	BRAD PITT, Stanage (hard)
SPORT 8b- **UK·TECH·7a**	REVELATIONS, start, Ravens Tor (easy)	HIGH FIDELITY, Caley (mid)
	KARMA, Isatis (mid-hard)	DREAMTIME, Cresciano (mid)
	NORTHERN LIGHTS, start; Kilnsey	THE ACE, Stanage (hard)
SPORT 8c- **UK·TECH·7b/c**	7b-GOSSIP, Frankenjura (low end)	7c-MONKS LIFE, Kyloe in the Wood (easy)
	7b-HUBBLE, mid crux; Ravens Tor (mid))	7c-AT THE HEART OF IT ALL, Woodwell
	7b-KHÉOPS, Cuvier Rempart (mid)	7c-VIOLENT NEW BREED, Giggleswick (high)

This chart is only intended to represent the individual bloc moves found on the included routes. With nice thanks to messrs: Horscroft, Simmonite, Robertson, Gresham, Pretty, Dawes, Housey, Landman, Moon & Gaskins; who of course all agreed to dissagree, but gave positive help.

	Deutschland	Italia	English	Français	
(14)	Gesamter Parcours in diesem Kletterführer beschrieben	Circuiti completi inclusi in questa guida	Full circuit included in this guidebook	Circuit complet inclus dans ce guide	(14)
●	Kreis – im Waldgebiet ein weiterer offiziell markierter Parcours	Cerchio: circuito nel bosco marcato ufficialmente	Circle - Another circuit in the forest that is officially painted	Cercle - Un autre circuit dans la forêt bien balisage officiel	●
■	Viereck/Raute - unmarkierter Parcours	Quadrati-diamanti:circuiti non marcati	Square/diamond - Circuit that is not marked	Carré/diamant - Circuit non balisé	■
⚲	Pfeil, der den Startpunkt des Parcours angibt	freccia per mostrare inizio circuito	Arrow to illustrate the starting point of a circuit	Flèches pour indiquer le point de départ du circuit	⚲
TD+	Gesamtschwierigkeitsgrad des Parcours Erläuterung auf der Umschlaginnenseite	Graduatoria del circuito: guarda ultima pagina	Overall grade for a circuit - see inside back flap for explanation	Cotation générale du circuit - consultez le volet	TD+
3a-6b	Bandbreite der Schwierigkeitsgrade im Parcours	varietà dei gradi trovati entro i pericoli del circuito	Range of grades found within the problems on the circuit	Gamme de cotations des passages du circuit	3a-6b
	Üblicher Felswinkel im Gebiet/ Beispiel: Überhang	Angolatura di roccia in zona: problemi di tetto	General rock angle in the area / roof problems in this example	Angle des blocs sur un site / toits dans cet exemple	
Q-D	Schnell trocknend, meist ohne auf den Fels tropfende Bäume	Asciugamento veloce	Quick drying - generally with no trees above to drip on the rock	Séchage rapide - pas d'arbres au-dessus des blocs	Q-D
	Pinien, die den Fels im Sommer und Winter beschatten	Pinete che ombreggiano le rocce d'inverno e d'estate	Pine trees that shade the rock in winter and summer	Pins qui ombragent les blocs en hiver et en été	
	Laubbäume – guter Schatten im Sommer aber tropfnass nach Regen	Alberi decidui: tanta ombra in estate	Deciduous trees - heavy summer shade and drip after rain	Arbres à feuilles caduques, ombre l'été, humide après la pluie	
	Grün, schmierig und oft feucht – perfekt bei einer Hitzewelle	verde e scivoloso	Green, slimy and often wet - perfect in a heat wave	Rocher vert et souvent humide parfait pendant la canicule	
Yum	Gute Landung auf meist ebenem Grund	buoni arrivi su terreno generalmente piatto	Good landings on generally flat ground	Bonnes aires de réception sur terrain plat	Yum
CP	Ein Crashpad ist einer steinigen Landung vorzuziehen	Uso di crash pad preferibile con arrivo roccioso	Using a crash pad is preferable with rocky landings	Sols rocheux, crash pad recommandé	CP
S	Ein Spotter wäre sinnvoll, Rückwärtsfall ist wahrscheinlich	Utile avere un osservatore: probabile caduta all'indietro	Handy to have a spotter, falling back first is very likely	Une parade est nécessaire	S
Cool	Oben musst du dich gut konzentrieren, zitternde Knie sind nicht besonders nützlich	Nec. molta concentrazione, tremito di gambe pericoloso	You need good concentration high up, leg shake is not useful!	Concentration nécessaire, évitez de trembler !	Cool
HBall	Highball- hohes Problem bei dem die Landung gefährlich sein kann	Highball: alto problematica con arrivo difficile	Highball - high problem where landing can be hazardous	Un passage haut avec une mauvaise aire de réception	HBall
	Meist hohe moves, die einen fürchten Sturz zur Folge haben könnten	di solito mosse alte che includono una caduta difficile	Scary - usually high moves that would involve an awkward fall	Des mouvements qui peuvent entraîner une mauvaise chute	
DBall	Deathball- ein echt hoher Boulder- Todesgefahr beim Sturz!	problematica grave: potresti morire	Deathball - a significantly high problem, you could die!	Un passage très haut qui peut vous emmener au cimetière	DBall
D	Anfangspunkt des Parcours- im Buch nicht unbedingt die Nr. 1	Punto di partenza per un circ. sul libro: non sempre N. 1	Depart point for a circuit in the book, not always no.1	Point de départ du circuit, pas toujours le no.1	D
○	Farbe mit weißem Mittelpunkt: ein Problem im Parcours	Colore con centro bianco:un arrampica circuito	Colour with a white centre, a problem on the circuit	Blanc au centre de la couleur - un passage sur le circuit	○
•	Farbe im Mittelpunkt: spring von einem Boulder zum anderen – Spaß	col. al centro:salta da un boulder all'altro.divertente	Colour in the centre - jump from one boulder to another - fun	Couleur au centre - saut d'un bloc à un autre - divertissant	•
A	Endpunkt des Parcours- klopf dir selbst auf die Schulter	Punto di arrivo alla fine del circuito; complimenta	Arrival point at the end of the circuit - pat yourself on the back	Fin du circuit - félicitez-vous	A
☂	Regenschirm- Überhang als Unterstand bei Regenschauern	pensilina per ripararsi da un acquazzone	Rain umbrella - overhang to shelter in a heavy downpour	Surplomb pour s'abriter lors de fortes averses	☂
.M°	Magique- ein ganz besonderes Problem, das sich magisch anfühlt	un problematica speciale, un senso di magia	Magique - a special problem with a magical feel to it	Magique - un passage exceptionnel et plein de charme	.M°
	Jingo- Armkraft erforderlich, um einen power move durchzuführen	Jingo: movimento di forza, è necessaria forza di braccia	Jingo - to represent a power move, arm strength essential	Puissant - bras musclés nécessaires.	
	Wobbly- erfordert technische Fähigkeiten gepaart mit Intelligenz	Wobbly: si richiede capacità tecnica e intelligenza	Wobbly - technical skill required along with cerebral intelligence	Technique et intelligence nécessaires.	
Fun	Fun- Geniesserproblem ohne böse Konsequenzen- meistens!	Divertente: problema piacevole	Fun - enjoyable problem without nasty consequences - usually!	Passage sympathique sans conséquences désagréables	Fun
CRIMP	Kante- kleine Ecken für die Finger, meist schmerzhaft	piccoli spigoli per le dita, di solito dolorosi	Crimp - small edges for the fingers and usually painful	Petites réglettes, fines et douloureuses.	CRIMP
	Manteln- die Fontainebleau Spezialität. Achtung am Ausstieg	Ristabilimento. Specialità di Fontainebleau, atten. in alto	Mantelshelf - a Fontainebleau speciality, beware high up	Rétablissement - spécialité de Fontainebleau, att. aux sorties	
Sloper	ein glatter und schmieriger Griff, nicht einfach zu halten	Una presa liscia e in discesa difficile da afferrare e tenere	Sloper - a hold that is smooth and sloping, not easy to grip	Aplat - une prise ronde et inclinée, difficile à utiliser	Sloper
	Dynamo- dynamische Züge sind gefragt	Dovrai lanciarti per una presa dinamica	Dyno - you will need to lunge for a hold dynamically	Mouvement dynamique nécessaire pour atteindre la prise	
目	Zwergentot- wenn Ihr klein seid, erwartet euch eine harte Zeit	Scala per nani.se sei basso avrai difficoltà	Ladder for dwarfs - if you are short then expect a hard time	Si vous êtes petits ce passage est difficile	目
	Sup-Dyn. Sprung- Ihr müsst zum Start vom Boden aus springen	Salto superdinamico.Devi saltare dal suolo per iniziare	Super dyno/jump - You need to jump off the ground to start	Saut nécessaire pour commencer	
	Glitschig wie eine Ban-schale, oft durch Abrieb an einem oft genutzten Problem	Scivoloso come buccia di banana	Slippery as a banana skin, often by wear on a popular problem	Passage fréquent, glissant comme une peau de banane	
Flexi	Achtung: Gelenkigkeit ist gefragt, der Fuß muss weit nach oben	Attenzione, è necessario essere agile	You need to be flexible and get your foot very high up, beware!	Être flexible est essentiel pour placer votre pied très haut	Flexi
Pump	Hier gibt es dicke Arme	limite di resistenza/soglia della	A long problem that causes the forearms to pump - sustained	Un passage soutenu pour travailler les bras	Pump
	Pfeil, der die beste Richtung für das Problem angibt	Tenere la destra	Direction arrow which gives the best route for the problem	Une flèche pour indiquer le meilleur sens du passage	
Trick	Trick-ganz leicht, wenn man weiß wie	????????	Not straightforward - you may need to be shown how to do it	Astuce - Il y a une façon cachée de faire le passage	Trick
NAF	Ein unnötiges Problem, das man getrost auslassen kann	spazzatura/rifiuti	A problem that is basically terrible and not worth doing	Un passage horrible qui ne vaut pas la peine	NAF

	Check	Check	Relevant details
Tickets & credit card used to pay (E)			
Car hire details & agreement			
Driving licence			
Money - Euros for France			
Travellers Cheques			
Main Credit Card			
Reserve - Credit Card			
Passport - check expiry date			
European health insurance card			
Climbing health insurance policy			
phone numbers - stolen credit cards			
Mobile phone & charger (int.-roam)			
Camera & Charger (Europlug adaptor)			
Film & memory cards			
MP3 music system			
Rope - short (50-60m) & bag			
Rope (70-80m) - long			
Harness			
Quickdraws (15)			
Clip stick			
Gri Gri - belay device			
Rock shoes			
Chalk Bag & chalk supply			
Helmet for big crags			
Rucksack			
Tent			
Sleeping bag			
Sleeping mat & pillow			
Cooker (No fuel on aircraft)			
Pots			
Plates			
Cutlery			
Compass, torch & penknife			
[Sharp objects - in big luggage]			
Clothes			
Wash bag & beach towel			
Warm jacket - cold in evenings			
Sun tan lotion			
Shades, floppy sun hat			
Mosquito rep - only for 3 cliffs			
Internet details & email access code			
Travel guides and books - specs too			
Local language dictionary			
Emergency contact numbers			
Jingo Wobbly climbing pocket book			
This book !			

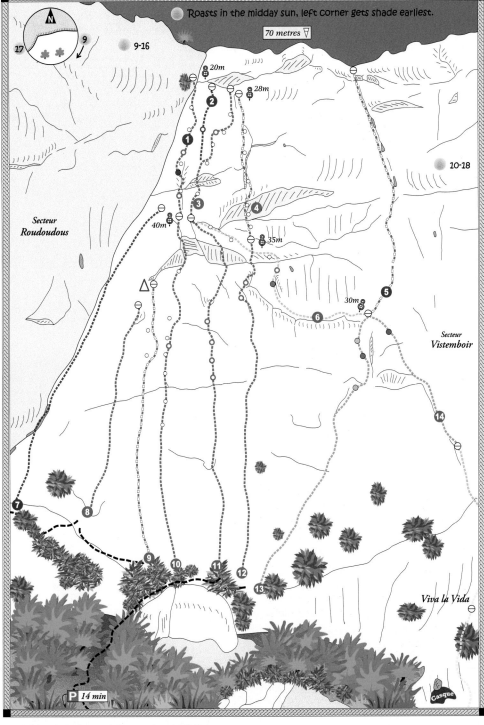

Roasts in the midday sun, left corner gets shade earliest.

70 metres

N

9-16

17 9

20m

28m

Secteur Roudoudous

40m

35m

30m

Secteur Vistemboir

10-18

14

Viva la Vida

Casque

P 14 min

ST. JEAN | VAISON | 3 RIVIÈRES | SAINT LÉGER | VIC | BRUNOTS | ST. JULIEN | QUEBEC | LOU PASSO | UBRIEUX | BM-ROUSSE | BOURDONS | AIGUIER | MIEYES | MÉVOUILLON | TOPOS

Crux/bloc   **Endurance**   **Sport**

① Vires rouges**
19m | ●7a- | Bloc | 6b | | 6c-

All the difficulty is in the first half - we give no clues, except that the second half is on excellent pockets and a fun technical teaser.

② Rapt à la tronçonneuse*   7a
20m | ●7b- 747 | CRIMP | 7a- 747 | Cool

You won't find people que-ing to lead this bundle of laughs! A nasty pitch onsight, but a very rewarding onsight. Moving left out of Le Ph. begins quite easily with tiny ripples and sharp edges providing inadequate support. Self levitation on imaginary holds is the key to success. Knowing where to grab the final ramp - is convenient!

③ Le philanthrope**   6c-
18m | ○6c- | B/N/H | 6b | Pump

A very difficult pitch to onsight. Challenging & steep moves lead up from the belay to the right. A silly long reach to a crimp, is the beginning of some moves that require flexibility and ingenuity. Highly sustained with poor rests.

Crux/bloc   **Endurance**   **Sport**

⑥ Vires rouges***
? m | ●6c- | Bloc | 6a | Cool

Not a pitch for incompetent wally's. A good traverse line is easy but still cock-up-able, with a second falling into space and unloverable! The crux headwall is possible due to the giant flake glued on, enough to unsettle nerves; finding holds at the top is problematic!!!

Crux/bloc   **Endurance**   **Sport**

⑦ Le philanthrope   7a
? m | | DIEDRE

A groove that looks a tremendous line, and doesn't look too easy either.

⑧ Andropète   6b
? m |

A climb that enjoys popularity, but not so many clean ascents.

⑨ Grotte à gâteau   6c-
30m | ●6c- 747 | CRIMP | 6b 747

Not an enjoyable lead at all. Very sustained crimping, and keep to the right of the last 3 bolts for the easiest way up. Calm nerves are essential, since a fall would be somewhat abrasively painful Agghh!

⑩ Rêve d'ô**   6c-
40m | ●6c- | CRIMP | 6b+ | Fab

A superb long pitch with 35 metres of solid climbing. A crimpy mid wall can catch you out, and is tiring onsight. The top overhang is a stroll, but short climbers have to maximise their technique. The final headwall on jugs proves exhilarating.

Crux/bloc   **Endurance**   **Sport**

④ New Baby**   6c
25m | ○6c- | CRIMP | 6c | Cool

Sufficient holds appear just when you need them. The steepness may appear daunting, but presents little difficulty. Stamina and crimping delicate brown cornflakes - requires coolness in the top part. Not a climb to take a struggling second on, as they will be faffing out in space and out of sight - drama or what!

⑤ Philippus**   6c
? m | | Pump

A superb line and up a very impressive headwall. Be alert for any birds nesting in the large pockets, maybe keep for autumn.

Crux/bloc   **Endurance**   **Sport**

⑪ Rapt à la tronçonneuse*   6c-
39m | ○6c 747 | CRIMP | 6b+ 747

Plenty of bolts low down on the easy section, then it all goes wrong and the climbing gets hard and run out - sustained fingertip crimping. Top overhang is a jugfest - whoopee!

⑫ New Baby**   6b+
35m | ○6c- | CRIMP | 6b+ | Pump

A fabulous pitch. The first half warms you up, but as the angle increases, so does the difficulty. Everything tends to go very pear shaped at the top of the ramp. Stamina is essential, as is luck in unlocking the sequence first time. You can power through at 7a/b easily, but you avoid the challenge. Seems longer than 35m.

⑬ Vires rouges**   6a
? m | ●6b- | CRIMP | 6a- | Cool

A good intro pitch, but hardly a warm up. The slab steepens with increased attitude, then a combination of moves near dodgy rock lead to the hanging belay - bottleneck.

⑭ Philippus*   6a
? m | |

Résumé. This is one of the great sectors in the Dentelles. A 70m rope is essential, and an 80m corde is even better (saves having to ab off New Baby all the time). A real mixed bag of equipping with some very challenging flat walls. When you know the routes and all the correct crimps are chalked up - it can seem a doddle. First time out it feels very lonely and you get very razzed fingertips. The top routes are very exposed and will test the nerves for those straight out of the climbing gym. Be very careful when lowering anyone down here, and have a spare rope if yours is not long enough.
There is a nice picnic terrace in front, and is clear of most stonefall, a lovely position.

Tear out topo - back of book

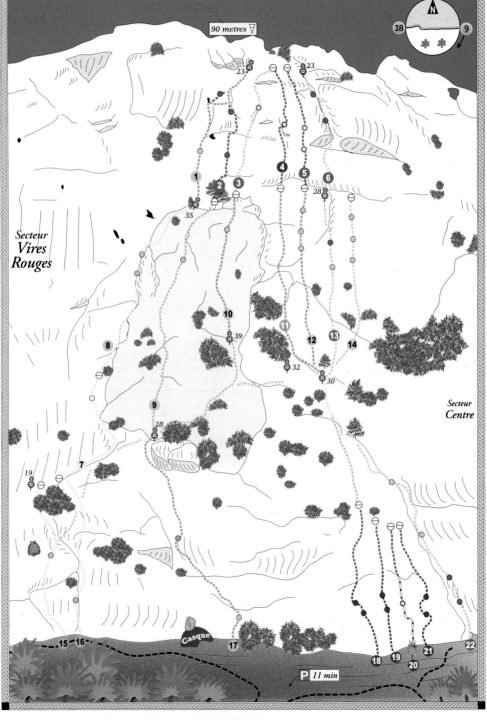

90 metres

Secteur
*Vires
Rouges*

Secteur
Centre

Casque

P 11 min

ST. JEAN | VAISON | 3 RIVIÈRES | SAINT LÉGER | VIC | BRUNOTS | ST JULIEN | QUEBEC | LOU PASSO | UBRIEUX | BM-ROUSSE | BOURDONS | AIGULER | MIEYES | MÉYOUILLON | TOPOS

Left margin tabs (top to bottom): ST JEAN, VAISON, 3 RIVIERES, SAINT LÉGER, VIC, BRUNOTS, ST JULIEN, QUEBEC, LOU PASSO, UBRIEUX, BM-ROUSSE, BOURDONS, AIGUIER, MIETES, MÉVOUILLON, TOPOS

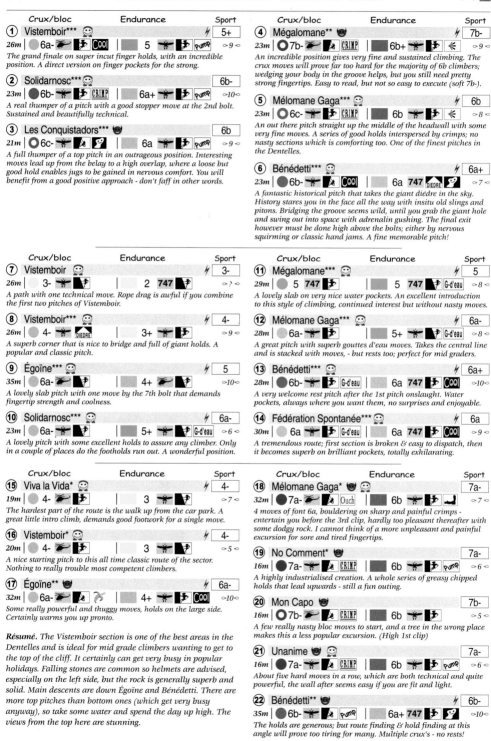

	Crux/bloc	Endurance	Sport
1	Vistemboir*** 😎		5+

26m | 6a- | 5 | ∞9∞

The grand finale on super incut finger holds, with an incredible position. A direct version on finger pockets for the strong.

| 2 | Solidarnosc*** 😎 | | 6b- |

23m | 6b- CRIMP | 6a+ PUMP | ∞10∞

A real thumper of a pitch with a good stopper move at the 2nd bolt. Sustained and beautifully technical.

| 3 | Les Conquistadors*** 😎 | | 6b |

21m | 6c- | 6a PUMP | ∞9∞

A full thumper of a top pitch in an outrageous position. Interesting moves lead up from the belay to a high overlap, where a loose but good hold enables jugs to be gained in nervous comfort. You will benefit from a good positive approach - don't faff in other words.

| 4 | Mégalomane** 😎 | | 7b- |

23m | 7b- CRIMP | 6b+ ← | ∞9∞

An incredible position gives very fine and sustained climbing. The crux moves will prove far too hard for the majority of 6b climbers; wedging your body in the groove helps, but you still need pretty strong fingertips. Easy to read, but not so easy to execute (soft 7b-).

| 5 | Mélomane Gaga*** 😎 | | 6b |

23m | 6c- CRIMP | 6b ← | ∞8∞

An out there pitch straight up the middle of the headwall with some very fine moves. A series of good holds interspersed by crimps; no nasty sections which is comforting too. One of the finest pitches in the Dentelles.

| 6 | Bénédetti*** 😎 | | 6a+ |

23m | 6b- COOL | 6a 747 DIEDRE | ∞7∞

A fantastic historical pitch that takes the giant diédre in the sky. History stares you in the face all the way with insitu old slings and pitons. Bridging the groove seems wild, until you grab the giant hole and swing out into space with adrenalin gushing. The final exit however must be done high above the bolts; either by nervous squirming or classic hand jams. A fine memorable pitch!

	Crux/bloc	Endurance	Sport
7	Vistemboir 😎		3-

26m | 3- | 2 747 | ∞?∞

A path with one technical move. Rope drag is awful if you combine the first two pitches of Vistemboir.

| 8 | Vistemboir*** 😎 | | 4- |

26m | 4- DIEDRE | 3+ | ∞9∞

A superb corner that is nice to bridge and full of giant holds. A popular and classic pitch.

| 9 | Égoïne*** 😎 | | 5 |

35m | 6a- | 4+ | ∞10∞

A lovely slab pitch with one move by the 7th bolt that demands fingertip strength and coolness.

| 10 | Solidarnosc*** 😎 | | 6a- |

23m | 6a- | 5+ G-d'eau | ∞6∞

A lovely pitch with some excellent holds to assure any climber. Only in a couple of places do the footholds run out. A wonderful position.

| 11 | Mégalomane*** 😎 | | 5 |

29m | 5 747 | 5 747 G-d'eau | ∞8∞

A lovely slab on very nice water pockets. An excellent introduction to this style of climbing, continued interest but without nasty moves.

| 12 | Mélomane Gaga*** 😎 | | 6a- |

28m | 6a- | 5+ G-d'eau | ∞8∞

A great pitch with superb gouttes d'eau moves. Takes the central line and is stacked with moves, - but rests too; perfect for mid graders.

| 13 | Bénédetti*** 😎 | | 6a+ |

28m | 6b- G-d'eau | 6a 747 COOL | ∞10∞

A very welcome rest pitch after the 1st pitch onslaught. Water pockets, always where you want them, no surprises and enjoyable.

| 14 | Fédération Spontanée*** 😎 | | 6a |

30m | 6a G-d'eau | 6a 747 COOL | ∞9∞

A tremendous route; first section is broken & easy to dispatch, then it becomes superb on brilliant pockets, totally exhilarating.

	Crux/bloc	Endurance	Sport
15	Viva la Vida* 😎		4-

19m | 4- | 3 | ∞7∞

The hardest part of the route is the walk up from the car park. A great little intro climb, demands good footwork for a single move.

| 16 | Vistemboir* 😎 | | 4- |

20m | 4- | 3 | ∞5∞

A nice starting pitch to this all time classic route of the sector. Nothing to really trouble most competent climbers.

| 17 | Égoïne** 😎 | | 6a- |

32m | 6a- | 4+ COOL | ∞10∞

Some really powerful and thuggy moves, holds on the large side. Certainly warms you up pronto.

Résumé. The Vistemboir section is one of the best areas in the Dentelles and is ideal for mid grade climbers wanting to get to the top of the cliff. It certainly can get very busy in popular holidays. Falling stones are common so helmets are advised, especially on the left side, but the rock is generally superb and solid. Main descents are down Égoïne and Bénédetti. There are more top pitches than bottom ones (which get very busy anyway), so take some water and spend the day up high. The views from the top here are stunning.

| 18 | Mélomane Gaga* 😎😎 | | 7a- |

32m | 7a- Ouch | 6b | ∞7∞

4 moves of font 6a, bouldering on sharp and painful crimps - entertain you before the 3rd clip, hardly too pleasant thereafter with some dodgy rock. I cannot think of a more unpleasant and painful excursion for sore and tired fingertips.

| 19 | No Comment* 😎 | | 7a- |

16m | 7a- CRIMP | 6b PUMP | ∞6∞

A highly industrialised creation. A whole series of greasy chipped holds that lead upwards - still a fun outing.

| 20 | Mon Capo 😎 | | 7b- |

16m | 7b- CRIMP | 6b | ∞5∞

A few really nasty bloc moves to start, and a tree in the wrong place makes this a less popular excursion. (High 1st clip)

| 21 | Unanime 😎😎 | | 7a- |

16m | 7a- CRIMP | 6b PUMP | ∞6∞

About five hard moves in a row, which are both technical and quite powerful, the wall after seems easy if you are fit and light.

| 22 | Bénédetti** 😎 | | 6b- |

35m | 6b- PUMP | 6a+ 747 | ∞10∞

The holds are generous; but route finding & hold finding at this angle will prove too tiring for many. Multiple crux's - no rests!

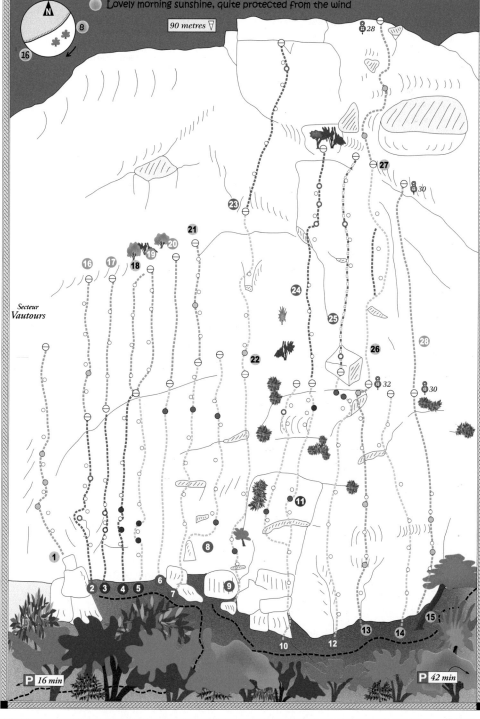

Lovely morning sunshine, quite protected from the wind

90 metres

Secteur *Vautours*

ST. JEAN
VAISON
3 RIVIÈRES
SAINT LÉGER
VIC
BRUNOTS
ST. JULIEN
QUEBEC
LOU PASSO
UBRIEUX
BM-ROUSSE
BOURDONS
AIGUIER
MIEYES
MÉVOUILLON
TOPOS

P 16 min

P 42 min

ST. JEAN · VAISON · 3 RIVIÈRES · SAINT LÉGER · VIC · BRUNOTS · ST JULIEN · QUÉBEC · LOU PASSO · UBRIEUX · BM-ROUSSE · BOURDONS · AIGUIER · MIÈVES · MÉVOUILLON · TOPOS

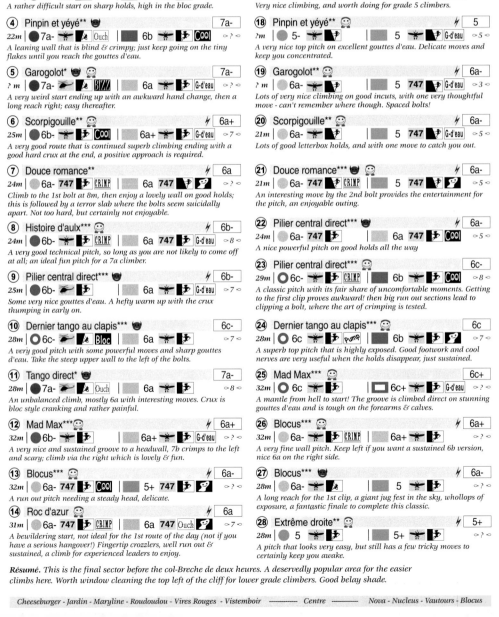

	Crux/bloc	Endurance	Sport
① Gueule de loup*			6a-
30m	6a-	5+ 747	⌐7⌐

Start from the top of the pinnacle on very hollow sounding flakes, go carefully. Top 20 metres is wonderful on lovely water pockets - bold.

② Italian shoes*			6c-
22m	6c- 747	6b 747 Cool	⌐5⌐

A butch start to a hollow flake, taken well on the left. Mid section is very fingery & run out - needs confidence & ability to enjoy.

③ Turbostyle			7b-
22m	7b-	6b	⌐?⌐

A rather difficult start on sharp holds, high in the bloc grade.

④ Pinpin et yéyé*			7a-
22m	7a- Ouch	6b Cool	⌐?⌐

A leaning wall that is blind & crimpy; just keep going on the tiny flakes until you reach the gouttes d'eau.

⑤ Garogolot*			7a-
? m	7a- BIZZ	6a G-d'eau	⌐?⌐

A very weird start leading up with an awkward hand change, then a long reach right; easy thereafter.

⑥ Scorpigouille*			6a+
25m	6b- Cool	6a+ G-d'eau	⌐7⌐

A very good route that is continued superb climbing ending with a good hard crux at the end, a positive approach is required.

⑦ Douce romance*			6a
24m	6a- 747 CRIMP	6a 747	⌐?⌐

Climb to the 1st bolt at 8m, then enjoy a lovely wall on good holds; this is followed by a terror slab where the bolts seem suicidally apart. Not too hard, but certainly not enjoyable.

⑧ Histoire d'aulx*			6b-
24m	6b- CRIMP	6a 747 G-d'eau	⌐8⌐

A very good technical pitch, so long as you are not likely to come off at all; an ideal fun pitch for a 7a climber.

⑨ Pilier central direct*			6b-
25m	6b-	6a G-d'eau	⌐7⌐

Some very nice gouttes d'eau. A hefty warm up with the crux thumping in early on.

⑩ Dernier tango au clapis*			6c-
28m	6c- Bloc	6a	⌐7⌐

A very good pitch with some powerful moves and sharp gouttes d'eau. Take the steep upper wall to the left of the bolts.

⑪ Tango direct*			7a-
28m	7a- Ouch	6a	⌐8⌐

An unbalanced climb, mostly 6a with interesting moves. Crux is bloc style cranking and rather painful.

⑫ Mad Max*			6a+
32m	6b-	6a+ G-d'eau	⌐?⌐

A very nice and sustained groove to a headwall, 7b crimps to the left and scary; climb via the right which is lovely & fun.

⑬ Blocus*			6a-
32m	6a- 747 Cool	5+ 747	⌐?⌐

A run out pitch needing a steady head, delicate.

⑭ Roc d'azur			6a
31m	6a- 747 CRIMP	6a 747 Ouch	⌐7⌐

A bewildering start, not ideal for the 1st route of the day (not if you have a serious hangover!) Fingertip crozzlers, well run out & sustained, a climb for experienced climbers to enjoy.

	Crux/bloc	Endurance	Sport
⑮ Extrême droite*			6a-
31m	6a-	5+	⌐?⌐

A well protected nice wall with good balance moves. Nothing too hard or complicated. (Pitches 1 & 2 together, rope drag is terrible)

⑯ Italian shoes*			6a-
23m	6a- CRIMP	5 Cool	⌐?⌐

A butch start to a hollow flake, taken well on the left. Mid section is very fingery & run out - needs confidence & ability to enjoy.

⑰ Turbostyle*			5
?m	5-	5 G-d'eau	⌐?⌐

Very nice climbing, and worth doing for grade 5 climbers.

⑱ Pinpin et yéyé*			5
?m	5-	5 G-d'eau	⌐5⌐

A very nice top pitch on excellent gouttes d'eau. Delicate moves and keep you concentrated.

⑲ Garogolot*			6a-
? m	6a-	747 G-d'eau	⌐3⌐

Lots of very nice climbing on good incuts, with one very thoughtful move - can't remember where though. Spaced bolts!

⑳ Scorpigouille*			6a-
21m	6a-	747 G-d'eau	⌐5⌐

Lots of good letterbox holds, and with one move to catch you out.

㉑ Douce romance*			6a-
21m	6a- 747 CRIMP	5 747	⌐5⌐

An interesting move by the 2nd bolt provides the entertainment for the pitch, an enjoyable outing.

㉒ Pilier central direct*			6a-
24m	6a- 747	6a 747 Cool	⌐5⌐

A nice powerful pitch on good holds all the way

㉓ Pilier central direct*			6c-
29m	6c- CRIMP	6b Cool	⌐8⌐

A classic pitch with its fair share of uncomfortable moments. Getting to the first clip proves awkward! then big run out sections lead to clipping a bolt, where the art of crimping is tested.

㉔ Dernier tango au clapis*			6c
28m	6c Pump	6b	⌐7⌐

A superb top pitch that is highly exposed. Good footwork and cool nerves are very useful when the holds disappear, just sustained.

㉕ Mad Max*			6c+
32m	6c	6c+ G-d'eau	⌐?⌐

A mantle from hell to start! The groove is climbed direct on stunning gouttes d'eau and is tough on the forearms & calves.

㉖ Blocus*			6a+
32m	6a- CRIMP	6a+	⌐?⌐

A very fine wall pitch. Keep left if you want a sustained 6b version, nice 6a on the right side.

㉗ Blocus*			6a-
28m	6a-	5	⌐?⌐

A long reach for the 1st clip, a giant jug fest in the sky, whollops of exposure, a fantastic finale to complete this classic.

㉘ Extrême droite*			5+
28m	5	5+	⌐?⌐

A pitch that looks very easy, but still has a few tricky moves to certainly keep you awake.

Résumé. This is the final sector before the col-Breche de deux heures. A deservedly popular area for the easier climbs here. Worth window cleaning the top left of the cliff for lower grade climbers. Good belay shade.

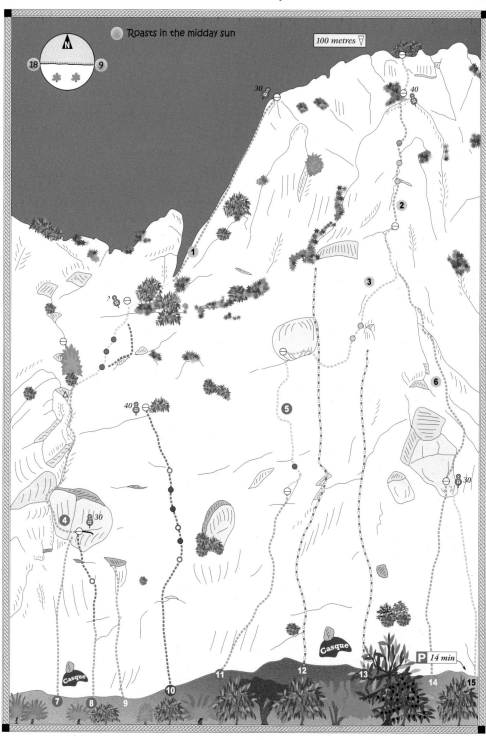

Roasts in the midday sun

100 metres

ST. JEAN
VAISON
3 RIVIÈRES
SAINT LÉGER
VIC
BRUNOTS
ST.JULIEN
QUEBEC
LOU PASSO
UBRIEUX
BM-ROUSSE
BOURDONS
AIGUIER
MIEYES
MÉVOUILLON
TOPOS

Casque

Casque

Casque

P 14 min

Raoul - Grotte - Aéroplane - Shanti - Bibus - Rampe - Mésange - Trous - l'éperon - Tranquille

ST. JEAN
VAISON
3 RIVIÈRES
SAINT LÉGER
VIC
BRUNOTS
ST. JULIEN
QUEBEC
LOU PASSO
UBRIEUX
BM. ROUSSE
BOURDONS
AIGUIER
MIÈVES
MÉVOUILLON
TOPOS

Crux/bloc	Endurance	Sport
①　La Grotte**		5+

30m | | | 🎿 *Fab* | ∘?∘

A very out there pitch in the sky; not recommended when a big mistral is blowing. Stunning views.

Crux/bloc	Endurance	Sport
②　L'Espadon***		5+

22m | 6a- ✳ 🪓 pump | 5 ✳ 🪓 Cool | ∘5∘

A nice technical pitch in an amazing position. Looks amazing but has good chunky holds.

Crux/bloc	Endurance	Sport
③　L'Espadon**		5

29m | 6a- ✳ CRIMP flexi | 4+ 747 pump 🎿 | ∘7∘

Only a few hard moves but long runout sections. A positive approach helps

Crux/bloc	Endurance	Historique
④　La Grotte*** 🌑		6b

38m | ● 6b- ✳ 🎿 pump | 6a+ 747 🎿 Cool | ∘12∘

Joining two old pitches together makes this a fab outing of perfect length, a stunning pitch. Excellent holds in the groove. △Loose block at the top - beware. Go right 3m before the old belay and take the rising traverse right. Looks terrifying but actually has great holds.

Crux/bloc	Endurance	Historique
⑤　L'Espadon** 🌑		6a

20m | ● 6b- ✳ 🎿 CRIMP | 6a ✳ 🎿 | ∘4∘

Yes the crux involves a tiny foothold, long may it live. Hits you hard straight after leaving the belay, not for the unconfident.

Crux/bloc	Endurance	Historique
⑥　Le Gastronome***		5+

? m | | | ∘?∘

A very good long pitch that takes you into a superb and exposed position. Definitely worth belaying, run top two pitches together.

Crux/bloc	Endurance	Historique
⑦　La plante à scion		5 ?

31m | | | 🎿 | ∘?∘

?

Crux/bloc	Endurance	Historique
⑧　Trop de vin rouge*		6b

31m | ○ 6c- ✳ 🎿 CRIMP | 6b- ✳ 🎿 🎿 | ∘8∘

An excellent climb on a top rope. Rebolting has left a really awkward, silly and unpleasant clip. Sharp teeth to pull on - technical.

Crux/bloc	Endurance	Historique
⑨　La Grotte*** 🙂		5

31m | ● 6c- ✳ 🎿 | 6b 747 🎿 Cool | ∘?∘

A very nice wall climb with holds! Then pass through the hole with amusement - and substantial polish.

Crux/bloc	Endurance	Historique
⑩　Love on the bite*		6c+

42m | ○ 7b- 747 🎿 CRIMP | 6b 747 🎿 🎿 | ∘?∘

A very straightforward first part, leads to a rather blank looking wall - looks don't deceive. Leaving the bolt, requires ability & not luck!

Crux/bloc	Endurance	Historique
⑪　L'Espadon 🙂		5+

37m | 5 ✳ 🎿 CRIMP | 5+ 747 🎿 🎿 | ∘9∘

Not a very attractive pitch for grade 5 climbers, sustained and very poorly protected. Rock sounds pretty hollow, suggesting iffyness.

Crux/bloc	Endurance	Historique
⑫　Equinoxe		6c ?

? m | | | ∘?∘

Blank wall climbing, technical

Crux/bloc	Endurance	Historique
⑬　Electrochoc***		6c ?

? m | | 747 🎿 Cool | ∘?∘

A substantial face climb requiring good stamina and technical expertise.

Crux/bloc	Endurance	Historique
⑭　Le Gastronome		5 ?

? m | | | 🎿 | ∘?∘

Crux/bloc	Endurance	Historique
⑮　Le Gastronome de Gris		6a ?

? m | | | 🎿 | ∘?∘

Résumé. *A very good sector to this giant cliff. A good place to start, by locating the obvious large grotto to the left of the approach footpath. 3 pitches to the top and great views of Buis. main face is often sheltered from Mistral.*

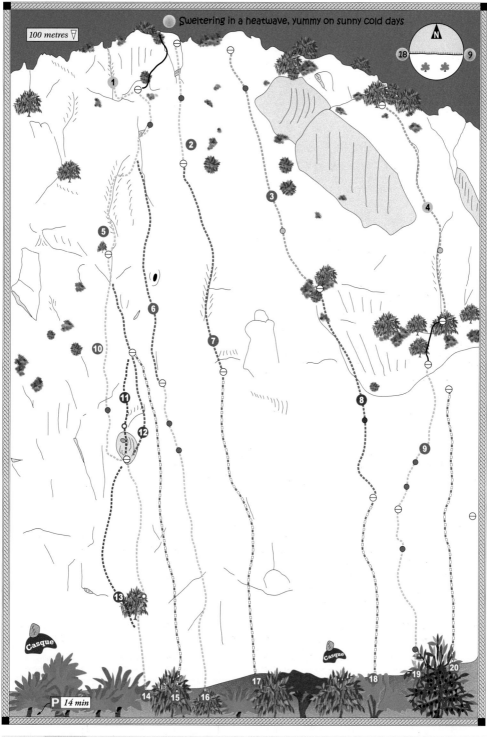

Sweltering in a heatwave, yummy on sunny cold days

100 metres

ST. JEAN · VAISON · 3 RIVIÈRES · SAINT LÉGER · VIC · BRUNOTS · ST.JULIEN · QUEBEC · LOU PASSO · UBRIEUX · BM-ROUSSE · BOURDONS · AIGUIER · MIEYES · MÉVOUILLON · TOPOS

P 14 min

ST. JEAN · VAISON · 3 RIVIÈRES · SAINT LÉGER · VIC · BRUNOTS · ST. JULIEN · QUEBEC · LOU PASSO · UBRIEUX · BM-ROUSSE · BOURDONS · AIGUIER · MIEYES · MÉVOUILLON · TOPOS

	Crux/bloc	Endurance	Sport
① Bibus*			6a
10m		6a	

It's not over yet, short but worth keeping the rope on for.

② La directissime			6b-
25m			

A superb top pitch, light relief with only one chunky move.

	Crux/bloc	Endurance	Sport
⑤ Bibus*	6b-	6a+	6a+
32m			‹11›

A superb finale, excitement high in the sky. Very well equipped when you need it. Requires a very positive approach for the flash. (Belay ☀)

⑥ Les Lames*	6b-	6b	6b
46m			‹14›

A really good pitch, nothing too hard. Suspect rock in places, but generally very sound - exhilarating. (Belay shade ☀)

⑦ La directissime			6b
35m			

Easier than the first pitch, generally committing wall climbing.

	Crux/bloc	Endurance	Sport
⑩ Bibus*	6b-	6a+	6b-
35m			‹12›

A very exposed move left on shinny holds begins this crux pitch. Sustained moves to a horribly polished foot pocket. Not too hard - but not too easy.

⑪ Ubick*	7b-	7a	7b-
15m	Bloc		‹?›

The obvious difficulty in leaving the cave straight up, and continuing with difficulty.

⑫ Bibus directe			6b
30m			

	Crux/bloc	Endurance	Sport
⑬ Ubick			7a
30m			

Technical wall climbing - sustained

⑭ Bibus	6c-	6a	6c-
32m	Bloc		‹12›

A very reachy move at 10 metres, certainly gets you thinking. 6c bloc for the short. Lovely flowing wall moves thereafter - enjoyable.

⑮ Désir			6c+
45m			

Wall climbing

⑯ Les Lames*	6b-	6a+ 747	6a+
43m			‹?›

Very nice wall climbing, nothing too hard, but you are very likely to get pumped solid.

⑰ La directissime			6c
45m			

Highly sustained

Historique. Only the classic routes are shown here - for a full topo to this giant cliff, there should be a local topo available.

	Crux/bloc	Endurance	Sport
③ Le Parat-Paris*			6b-
40m			‹?›

A bit straightforward if you did the lower part. Good new routes to left and right of lower pitches.

④ La rampe*	6a-	5+	6a-
30m			‹14›

The best pitch of the climb. Much easier than the lower half and with no moves to make you think. Bridging in the top groove is spectacular. Don't forget to go to the top for the fab views. (Belay ☀)

	Crux/bloc	Endurance	Sport
⑧ Le Parat-Paris*			7a
30m			‹?›

Flat featureless rock, amusingly technical, of appeal to some!

⑨ La rampe*	6b-	6a	6b
30m			‹14›

Old peg scars and polished hand holds make this a sweaty and uncomfortable pitch to start with. Happily it gets better and better, and the holds get bigger and bigger. Stick in and you will be rewarded. (Belay shade ☀)

	Crux/bloc	Endurance	Sport
⑱ Le Parat-Paris			6c-
30m			‹?›

An interesting adventure?

⑲ La rampe*	6b-	6a 747	6b-
30m	Trick		‹?›

A very good warm up! Excellent climbing with a marvellous crux, one of those moves that is really exasperating - until you do it!

⑳ Osiris*	6c	6c 747	⚡ 6c
50m			‹?›

A fantastic climb, simply wonderfully sustained. Bolts are well spaced but it seems to suit the climbing style, cool but not scary.

Résumé. This sector is the middle of the largest wall of the crag, and gives the 3 classic routes of Bibus, Les Lames and La Rampe. All are quite polished, but that doesn't detract from the position and superb climbing on them. All the routes have been historically undergraded, so we have re-graded them to keep in line with the other cliffs in the book. The routes seem easier when you get to know them, but it is the sort of cliff that has so much climbing, there never seems time to go back to the same routes. A steady head and strong nerve is an asset for this sector.

Aurel - A quiet hill town situated on a bend in the road, nice & quiet with a few bars.

Avignon - Lots of tourists. Very ancient walled city, park outside & wander around.

Le Barroux, p154 - Small old hill town village with superb views.

Le Beaucet, p 41 - Classic Provence hill town, 'hugging its rocky cradle,' apparently. (Boulangerie)

Beaumes-de-Venise, p73 - Lovely small village with an excellent Muscat sweet white wine

Bédoin, p124 - Thriving village with a superb market on Monday mornings, good restaurants too.

Brantes, p154 - Hillside village with great views of Mont Ventoux, lovely bar-restaurant nearby.

Buis-les-Baronnies, p210 - Main town with most shops, Jazz festival, good bars, lovely atmosphere.

Cairanne, p110 - Wine village with its own Côtes du Rhone appellation.

Caromb, p154 - Very old hill village, worth a casual stroll around, nice bar in the sunshine in centre.

Carpentras - Big town with medieval walls, lots of quaint shops inside, good bars, busy ring road.

Châteauneuf-du-Pape, p109 - Very famous wine village, expensive but good wines, few bargains.

Col de la Madeleine, p120 - Lovely quiet road with a very nice picnic plateau, giving fine views & shade.

Crillion-la-Brave, p154 - Hill top village with expensive restaurant, nice bar on top, superb views.

Entrechaux, p156 - Old castle and quiet town, good restaurant.

Faucon, p156 - Nice old hill village to wander around, expensive restaurant, nice views, bar down the road.

Fontaine-de-Vaucluse, p42 - Popular tourist town.

Gigondas, p110 - Wine village with its own Côtes du Rhone appellation.

Gorges de la Nesque, p22 - Stunning gorge to drive or cycle up, you can walk in it too, great day out.

Gringnan - A château to check out.

La-Roque-Alric - A tiny hamlet, nothing except quietness, a few gites to rent, great views.

Malaucène, p136 - Good market town, old but busy feeling, great square with cafés, easy parking.

Mazan, p124 - Old village, a few good and trendy bars, busy main road, good in most seasons.

Mollons-sur-l'Ouvéze, p124 - Quiet village with a shop and a couple of bars, one with a nice terrace.

Monieux, p22 - Really tiny village, but with a very good restaurant, don't miss a meal here.

Mont Ventoux, p209 - Cycle mountain, skiing in winter, your own rally drive up, burning rubber time.

Montbrun-les-Bains, p208 - Natural springs on a hill, very old and charming, great for a wander.

N.D. des Anges, p175 - A nice spot down by the river for splashing and walking up the gorge to cool off.

Nyons, p279 - Town with most shops, very old square with cafés, restaurants, old bits to walk around.

Orange - Closed on tuesdays! Big town, usual stuff, iffy roman amphitheatre, traffic nightmare.

Plaisians, p92 - Tiny hamlet with a very rustic restaurant, Fromage de la tête a speciality, veggies pass.

Pont l'Ouvèze, p157 - The narrowest bridge in France, good bathing in the river, relaxation spot.

Rasteau, p110 - Wine village with its own Côtes du Rhone appellation.

Rémuzat - Very quiet spot, good to explore quiet walks north of here.

Roaix, p110 - Wine village with its own Côtes du Rhone appellation.

La Roche-sur-le-Buis, p226 - Tiny hamlet but with a restaurant terrace to die for, not always open.

La Roque-sur-Pernes, p42 - Classic Provencal hill village with an old church etc.

Sablet, p110 - Wine village with its own Côtes du Rhone appellation.

Sainte-Jalle, p282 - Old village by a river, lovely cafés under vines, valley full of lavender & apricots.

Sarrians, p77 - Old village with bustle and bars, just down the road from Super Intermarché.

Sault, p23 - High village, quiet and the place to get away from it all.

Savoillans - Old and quiet village, sort of artists retreat.

Séderon - Never got there!

Séguret, p110 - Wine village with its own Côtes du Rhone appellation.

Source d'Groseau, p138 - Natural spring with wonderfully clear water, café opposite - great banana boats.

St.Auban-sur-l'Ouvèze - Really quiet village, little restaurant/auberge with terrace, fab views, rustic.

Vacqueyras, p110 - Wine village with its own Côtes du Rhone appellation, busy on main road, great wine.

Vaison-La-Romaine, p155 - Roman town, excellent Pizza restaurant in old hill part, and posh gourmet too.

Vallée Toulourenc, p204 - Upper valley is very picturesque, ideal for a picnic out of car rally season.

Valréas - A town.

Venasque, p42 - Very old village with great views, Les Ramparts Logis with a terrace, great views, hic, hic!

Villes-sur-Auzon - Quiet scenic village, rustic arts shops, not too touristy.